Buildings and Projects   Bauten und Projekte   Ackermann und Partner

Prestel   München · New York   Editor Ingeborg Flagge · Introduction Wolfgang Jean Stock
                                       Herausgeberin Ingeborg Flagge · Einführung Wolfgang Jean Stock

Buildings and Projects 1978–1998
Bauten und Projekte

Ackermann und Partner

Inhalt
Contents

Building Culture instead
of Building Art
The Architecture of
Kurt Ackermann
and Partners

Wolfgang Jean Stock

Logisch konstruiert wie
ein Zirkuszelt ist das
1983 fertiggestellte
Eislaufzelt im Münchner
Olympiagelände.

The ice-skating rink at
the Olympia Park in
Munich, completed in
1983, was logically
conceived to resemble
a circus tent.

"Why is German architecture of such subordinate
status?" Some years ago, Dieter Hoffmann-Axthelm
published an outline of West German construction since
the Second World War with this title. His intention was
to demonstrate the "mediocrity" of modern architecture
in that country.[1] He argued that the situation had been
brought about in the first instance by two key figures who
represented quite contrary positions: Günter Behnisch,
the "head of school and dogmatic authority", who was
responsible for the increasing desensualization of architecture; and Oswald Mathias Ungers, the "head of school
and dogmatic authority responsible for the rescue of
stone architecture – and thus of architecture per se".
In both positions, despite their differences, the author
identifies a joint weakness, namely "lack of expression".

Quite apart from the fact that this somewhat grandilo-
quent settling of accounts is based on superficial compar-
isons with foreign examples, the fixation on two "dogmatic" father figures, with whom succeeding generations
are also identified, narrows the field of view unnecessar-
ily. At least one major pillar of German architecture in the
20th century is overlooked in all this: the many representatives of modernism who have not made a name for
themselves with spectacular individual works, but have
created buildings that have to do with the ordinary,
everyday activities of working, learning and living. Even
if one compares these on an international level, they are
important buildings whose design quality in no way
reduces their functional value. What is more, their design
is not placed at the service of some ideology; on the contrary, it expresses a social sensibility that is lacking in
most "built visions".

As examples of a kind of manifesto architecture, such
visions – ranging from high-density, large-scale housing
developments to hospital complexes – have been largely
responsible for the fact that modern architecture lost
much of its renown within the space of a few decades. In
contrast, the architecture of "gentle modernism" cultivated abroad, particularly in Switzerland and Finland, has
enabled many people in those countries to accept the
building of their own times and to feel at home in it. In
such cases, modern architecture can provide users with
a sense of security or even "warmth" if they are not over-
taxed by design concepts.

This approach has a tradition that existed even in Germany after the 1920s. In the post-war period, it is Egon
Eiermann's name that initially comes to mind. His precise
steel structures, which exhibit a fine sense of scale, have
been a source of inspiration for many architects. The German Pavilion he designed jointly with Sep Ruf in 1958 for
the World Exposition in Brussels was regarded inter-
nationally as genuine proof of a new democratic beginning in the Federal Republic of Germany. In many German cities, buildings by architects such as Bernhard Pfau,
Ferdinand Kramer or Rudolf Schwarz helped modern
architecture to reassert itself with a new vigour. The work
of Ackermann and Partners represents a continuation of
this line of development.

In the early 1950s, when young Kurt Ackermann – without
school-leaving exams or an academic diploma, but qualified as a bricklayer and carpenter – opened his own architect's office, there was a mood of enterprise in society,
a feeling that one was setting out for new horizons. The
"neon-Biedermeier"[2] restoration that had manifested

»Warum ist die deutsche Architektur so subaltern?« Unter diesem Titel hat Dieter Hoffmann-Axthelm vor einigen Jahren eine Skizze des bundesdeutschen Bauens seit dem Zweiten Weltkrieg veröffentlicht, mit der Absicht, der zeitgenössischen Architektur in unseren Landen ihre »Mittelmäßigkeit« nachzuweisen.[1] Verantwortlich dafür seien in erster Linie zwei gegensätzliche Leitfiguren: Günter Behnisch als »das Schulhaupt und die dogmatische Instanz« für eine zunehmende Entsinnlichung von Architektur, Oswald Mathias Ungers hingegen als »Schulhaupt und dogmatische Instanz für die Rettung der steinernen Architektur, und damit der Architektur überhaupt«. Beiden Positionen bescheinigt der Autor eine trotz aller Unterschiede gemeinsame Schwäche: »Ausdrucksmangel«.

Ganz abgesehen davon, daß diese vollmundige Abrechnung auf oberflächlichen Vergleichen mit ausländischen Beispielen beruht, verengt die Fixierung auf zwei »dogmatische« Leitfiguren, denen die nachfolgenden Generationen dann schlicht zugeordnet werden, das Blickfeld. Übergangen wird eine entscheidende Säule der deutschen Architektur im 20. Jahrhundert: jene Moderne nämlich, die nicht durch spektakuläre Einzelleistungen hervorgetreten ist, sondern durch Bauten, die mit dem gemeinen Alltag von Arbeiten, Lernen und Wohnen verbunden sind. Es sind – auch im internationalen Vergleich – bedeutende Bauten, deren Gestaltqualität aber nicht den Gebrauchswert mindert, deren Entwurf keine Ideologie bedient, vielmehr eine soziale Sensibilität zum Ausdruck bringt, die den meisten ›gebauten Visionen‹ abgeht.

Als Manifest-Architekturen haben solche Visionen, von der verdichteten Großsiedlung bis zu den Krankenhaus-Aggregaten, viel dazu beigetragen, daß die Moderne binnen weniger Jahrzehnte weithin an Ansehen verlor. Die im europäischen Ausland – vor allem in der Schweiz und in Finnland – gepflegte Architektur der ›sanften Moderne‹ dagegen hat es vielen Menschen ermöglicht, Bauten ihrer eigenen Zeit anzunehmen, in ihnen heimisch zu werden. Moderne Architektur kann den Nutzern dann Geborgenheit oder gar ›Wärme‹ geben, wenn diese sich nicht von gestalterischen Konzepten überfordert fühlen.

Für diese Haltung gibt es auch in Deutschland seit den zwanziger Jahren eine Tradition. Aus der Nachkriegszeit wäre an erster Stelle Egon Eiermann zu nennen, dessen präzises, maßstäbliches Bauen mit Stahl viele Architekten begeistert hat. Sein zusammen mit Sep Ruf entworfener deutscher Pavillon auf der Weltausstellung 1958 in Brüssel wurde auch international als ein glaubwürdiges Zeugnis für den demokratischen Neubeginn in der Bundesrepublik betrachtet. In zahlreichen deutschen Städten zeigte sich die Moderne mit Bauten von Bernhard Pfau, Ferdinand Kramer oder Rudolf Schwarz in neuer Frische. In dieser Kontinuität steht das Werk von Ackermann und Partner.

In den frühen fünfziger Jahren, in eben jener Zeit, als der junge Kurt Ackermann – ohne Abitur und akademisches Diplom, aber geprüft als Maurer und Zimmermann – sein eigenes Architekturbüro eröffnete, herrschte Aufbruchstimmung. Die gesellschaftliche Restauration im Zeichen des »Neon-Biedermeier«[2] wurde als Herausforderung angenommen. Neben einigen älteren Architekten, die meist im Nazi-Deutschland ›überwintert‹ hatten, nahmen vor allem junge Kräfte das Heft in die Hand. Ihnen ging es nicht allein um Planen und Bauen, sondern fachübergreifend um eine gemeinsame kulturelle Aufgabe, um jene Lebensreform, für die der Werkbund schon um 1930 eingetreten war. Zum Zentrum der neuen Bestrebungen in Deutschland wurde die Ulmer Hochschule für Gestaltung (HfG), deren umfassendes Programm bereits in einem Vorentwurf aus dem Jahr 1949 formuliert worden war: »Das Ziel der Arbeit und Ausbildung an dieser Schule ist der politisch denkende und mit den modernen Methoden vertraute schöpferische Mensch, der mit sozialem Verantwortungsbewußtsein die Lebensform unseres technischen und industriellen Zeitalters gestaltet.«[3]

Wie zahlreiche Architekten seiner Generation, die in den zwanziger Jahren geboren wurden, fühlte sich Kurt Ackermann von diesem Programm angezogen. Er suchte die Verbindung und gewann Otl Aicher, den damaligen HfG-Rektor, Anfang der sechziger Jahre zum Freund.[4] Aus dieser Verbindung sind gemeinsame Projekte hervorgegangen, zum Beispiel die Struktur- und Gestaltplanung für ein neues Skidorf Sportgastein (1973–1975), die leider nicht ausgeführt wurde. Aicher gestaltete auch, als erstes von mehreren Büchern seines Freundes, die durchgehend bebilderte Übersicht der Bauten und Projekte von Kurt Ackermann und Partner aus den Jahren 1953 bis 1978.[5] Dieser von der Stiftung Buchkunst ausgezeichnete Band ist eine wichtige Ergänzung der vorliegenden Publikation und

Wolfgang Jean Stock

Baukultur statt Baukunst
Zur Architektur von Kurt Ackermann und Partner

emerges from among the forested hills, a kind of "second nature" in its design in our technically dominated modern environment. For exactly 40 years now, Kurt Ackermann has been working on the construction of this constantly expanding plant, the operations of which originally complied with the constraints of the old building fabric rather than following technical needs. Based on a long-term works plan, new building elements were realized, most of which were executed in exposed concrete left in its natural state. These range from the massive sculpture of the blending bed and the high towers of the homogenization plant with the bold ribs that serve as tensioning elements, to the group of clinker silos. The fact that, in his intense but not always untroubled collaboration with the client, Kurt Ackermann managed to convince a cement manufacturer to build the heat-exchange tower in steel reflects not only the open-mindedness of the client, but also his personal relations with the architect.[6]

Ackermann has long had the reputation of being an assiduous worker who does not let up until he has found the ideal solution. He is also credited with a great gift for implementing his projects. He succeeded, for example, in realizing the School for Air Force Officers in Fürstenfeldbruck (1974–77) as a generously landscaped campus and not in the form of a military barracks. Furthermore, the elegant lightness of the façades – the outcome of the open walkways round the outside – confirm Ackermann's remark that Egon Eiermann was a guiding example for him.[7]

This cultivated form of architectural expression is missing in some of the Munich office developments Ackermann designed at roughly the same time. An example of this is the VBB administration building (1977), where tight constraints imposed by the conservation authorities led to a number of unsatisfactory compromises. As in the work of all architects, not everything designed by Ackermann and Partners is immediately convincing. Nevertheless, the evidently weaker projects – to which the Directorate-General 2 of the European Patent Office in Munich (1988–93) could probably be reckoned, despite the high quality of its workplaces – can be counted on the fingers

of one hand. Universally acclaimed as a masterpiece is the Marienhof Estate Sewage Treatment Plant outside Munich (1984–88), which Gottfried Knapp regards as a milestone in building culture: "Nowhere was any attempt made to camouflage the industrial character of the plant

itself was accepted as a challenge. Alongside a number of older architects who had "hibernated" in Nazi Germany, it was primarily the younger generation that took things into their own hands. They were concerned not only with planning and building, but with universal cultural objectives, with the reform of all aspects of life – something the Werkbund had propagated around 1930. The Ulm School of Design (HfG) became the centre of these new endeavours in Germany. Its comprehensive programme had been drafted as early as 1949: "The work and training of this school is aimed at the politically thinking, creative person who is familiar with modern techniques, and who is designing the life forms of our technical and industrial age with a sense of social responsibility."[3]

Like many other architects of his generation who were born in the 1920s, Kurt Ackermann was attracted by this programme. He sought contacts with like-minded people and at the beginning of the 1960s made friends with Otl Aicher, who was rector of the HfG at that time.[4] This friendship led to a number of joint projects, such as the structural planning and design for a new skiing village, Sportgastein (1973–75), which was unfortunately never realized. Aicher also designed the richly illustrated review of the buildings and projects by Kurt Ackermann and Partners dating from the years 1953 to 1978[5] – the first of many books on which he collaborated with his friend. Awarded a prize by the Stiftung Buchkunst, this work forms an important complementary volume to the present publication and is an indispensable source of material for any assessment of Ackermann's complete oeuvre. One discovers in it, for example, that the first large commission came after a number of modest housing schemes. It was for the hop store *Hopfenhalle* in Mainburg, Lower Bavaria, which was completed in 1958. This first competition success points to an important aspect of Kurt Ackermann's later work: the industrial and functional buildings that were to become an important focus of the office's activities, without Ackermann and his later partners ever specializing in this area, however.

Clients with a Feeling for Quality

Even an industrial complex can be an architectural event. As one approaches the little Swabian town of Harburg along the gently curving federal highway from Donauwörth, a splendid, concisely drawn silhouette rises above the horizon. The Märker Cement Works gradually

Märker Zementwerk in
Harburg, seit 1958.
Linke Seite: Faultürme
des Klärwerks Gut
Marienhof bei München,
fertiggestellt 1988

The Märker Cement
Works in Harburg,
project since 1958.
On the left: sapropal
chambers of the Marien-
hof Estate Sewage
Treatment Plant, com-
pleted in 1988

sollte zur Bewertung des Gesamtwerks herangezogen werden. Ihm läßt sich entnehmen, daß nach mehreren, eher
bescheidenen Wohnhäusern schon bald der erste große
Auftrag einging, die 1958 fertiggestellte Hopfenhalle im
niederbayerischen Mainburg. Dieser erste Wettbewerbs-
erfolg weist auf eine Richtung in der künftigen Arbeit hin,
ohne daß sich Kurt Ackermann mit seinen späteren Partnern spezialisiert hätte: Der Industrie- und Zweckbau wurde zu einem Schwerpunkt in der Tätigkeit des Büros.

Bauherren mit Qualität

Auch eine Industrieanlage kann zum Ereignis werden. Eine
großartige, straff gezeichnete Silhouette wächst am Hori-
zont empor, wenn man sich von Donauwörth her auf den
sanften Kurven der Bundesstraße dem schwäbischen
Städtchen Harburg nähert. Inmitten bewaldeter Hügel tritt
allmählich – als eine Gestalt der ›zweiten Natur‹ unserer
technisch geprägten Umwelt – das Märker Zementwerk in
Erscheinung. Seit genau vierzig Jahren arbeitet Kurt Ackermann am Bau der stetig gewachsenen Werksanlage, deren
Betriebsablauf sich zuvor mehr nach der alten Bausubstanz
gerichtet hatte als nach technischen Erfordernissen. Auf
der Grundlage einer langfristigen Werksplanung entstanden dann die neuen Bauteile, überwiegend ausgeführt in
naturbelassenem Sichtbeton: von der mächtigen Skulptur
der Mischbettanlage über die hohen Türme der Homogeni-
sierungsanlage mit den markanten Rippen der Vorspan-
nung bis zur Gruppe der Klinkersilos. Daß Kurt Ackermann
während der intensiven, wenngleich nicht immer konflikt-
freien Zusammenarbeit mit dem Bauherrn ausgerechnet
einen Zementhersteller davon überzeugen konnte, den
Wärmetauscherturm als Stahlkonstruktion zu errichten,
hat mit der Aufgeschlossenheit des Bauherrn zu tun, in
gleicher Weise aber auch mit seinem persönlichen Verhältnis zum Architekten.[6]
    Daß er nicht nur ein konzentrierter Arbeiter sei, der
nicht ruhe, bis er die für ihn optimale Lösung gefunden
habe, sondern ebenso begabt bei der Durchsetzung seiner
Entwürfe, dieser Ruf geht Kurt Ackermann seit jeher voraus. So gelang es ihm, die Offiziersschule der Luftwaffe in
Fürstenfeldbruck (1974–1977) als einen großzügig durch-
grünten Campus anzulegen, und nicht als Kaserne. Hinzu
kommt die Eleganz der durch ihre offenen Umgänge sehr
leicht wirkenden Fassaden, die Ackermanns Äußerung,
Egon Eiermann zähle zu seinen Leitbildern[7], eindrucksvoll
belegt.

Technikgebäude der Ge-
samthochschule Kassel,
erbaut 1990 bis 1995

Building containing the
technical institutes of
the Comprehensive Uni-
versity, Kassel, built
between 1990 and 1995

with beguiling design expedients or to play down urban
waste disposal problems through rural masquerade."[8]
Here, too, the client demonstrated his feeling for quality.

Architecture as Urban Design

Solitary buildings set on the periphery of towns or on a
virgin site are able to define their own ambient. The situation is quite different where architecture is located in an
urban context. In this respect, the new Technology Centre
of the Comprehensive University of Kassel (1990–95), for
which a residual inner-city site was made available, represented a particularly difficult assignment for Ackermann
and Partners, who won first prize in the competition held
in 1985. Immediately adjoining the site was the newly
completed university complex by Horst Höfler and Lutz
Kandel, a brick development with a mansard roof. The
competition scheme had to take account of this complex.
Kurt Ackermann resolved the tangled urban situation with
a compact, but finely articulated, building that was
designed with a technical aesthetic matching its function:
a research institute for mechanical and building engineering. In this way, the existing small-scale, misjudged
university complex acquired an effective edge – at least
on its southern flank, facing the city. At the same time,
Ackermann's self-assured constructional aggregate is a

modern reminder of the former Henschel works, on the
site of which the university was erected.

This project provides a good example of the modern
contrast between building art and building culture. In
1913, in his famous essay on modern industrial architecture,[9] Walter Gropius could still write quite unabashedly
of "the art of building", as indeed many pioneers of the
Modern Movement were to do after him. Today, however, the expression is likely to elicit a smile. Wherever
emphasis is laid on the art of building, one should be on
one's guard. There is no lack of examples of "artistic"
creation, from Ungers's addiction to the square to Hans
Hollein's glittering Haas House in Vienna or Frank Gehry's
"dancing" corner building on the River Vltava in Prague.
Painfully trumped-up buildings of this kind are the true
"ugly boils" in the face of our cities – to quote Prince
Charles out of context.

At the beginning of the 1980s in Kassel, Höfler and
Kandel wanted to create a university that would be "like a
pyrotechnic display". All they achieved, however, was an
ill-judged assortment of buildings large and small that
Kurt Ackermann's new structure on one side of the main
square mercifully masks. Unlike the historical quotations,
the expressive excrescences or the deconstructivist
affronts of an architectural art of only vague content –
however celebrated it may be in the media – present-day
building culture asserts itself through its deliberate
restraint and cultivated simplicity. It is characterized by
the "timeless and enduring quality" that was attested to
the buildings of the Munich architects in the laudation
spoken on the award of the Heinrich Tessenow Medal to
Kurt Ackermann in 1994.[10]

Building is always a collective act. That is why architects should not misuse it for self-indulgent ends, as Kurt
Ackermann emphasizes. Ackermann sees himself "as a
technical craftsman, as a master builder in the traditional
sense of the term".[11] That may sound somewhat too
modest, but it is not. Kurt Ackermann and Partners have
demonstrated the exceptional quality of their design both
in assignments of a special nature and in demanding projects in an urban context, such as the head post office in
Regensburg (1988–91). Situated next to the railway, this
development brings a breath of fresh air to what is otherwise a humdrum location.

One of the finest works of the office, and indeed a rare
highlight in the Munich architectural landscape of the
recent past, is the tent roof structure over the ice-skating
rink in the Olympia Park. It was completed in 1983. With
a triangular arched truss spanning a length of roughly
100 metres and supporting the lightweight, large-area,
load-bearing membrane roof, the structure has the constructional logic of a circus tent and presents a fascinat-
ing view from the inside. The daylight entering this space
through the elliptical openings along the crest of the roof
seems to dissolve the boundaries between inside and
outside. Technical aesthetics help to create an enchanting
tent that comes close to an experience of classical beauty.

Standpoint instead of Style

In the words of a former assistant, the distinguishing
feature of the Ackermann office is its "inspiring atmosphere".[12] The fact that different talents and tempera-
ments are brought to bear in the design work is decisive
for a climate in which discussion is encouraged. Kurt
Ackermann himself, who still acts as a *primus inter pares*,

Spannung zwischen Alt
und Neu: Pfortenhof des
Benediktinerklosters
Andechs bei München,
fertiggestellt 1993

The tension between
old and new: The
entrance courtyard of
the Benedictine Mona-
stery of Andechs near
Munich, completed in
1993

Diese Kultiviertheit des architektonischen Ausdrucks vermißt man bei einigen, fast gleichzeitig entstandenen Münchener Bürohäusern, etwa beim Verwaltungsgebäude VBB
(1977), wo auch strenge Auflagen der Denkmalpflege zu
unbefriedigenden Kompromissen geführt haben. Wie im
Werk aller Architekten ist auch bei Ackermann und Partner
nicht alles gleich überzeugend. Die offenkundig schwäche-
ren Beispiele, zu denen wohl auch die Generaldirektion 2
des Europäischen Patentamts in München (1988–1993)
trotz hoher Arbeitsplatzqualität zu rechnen ist, lassen sich
freilich an einer Hand abzählen. Ein allseits anerkanntes
Meisterwerk bildet dagegen das Klärwerk Gut Marienhof
bei München (1984–1988). Gottfried Knapp sieht in ihm
einen Meilenstein der Baukultur: »Nirgends wurde versucht, den industriellen Charakter der Anlage durch anbie-
dernde Design-Gefälligkeiten zu überspielen oder das
großstädtische Entsorgungsproblem durch ländliche Mas-
keraden zu verniedlichen.«[8] Auch hier bewies ein Bauherr
Sinn für Qualität.

Architektur als Städtebau

Solitäre Bauten am Ortsrand oder auf der grünen Wiese
können ihr Umfeld selbst definieren. Anders verhält es sich
bei Architektur im städtischen Zusammenhang. Eine unter
diesem Gesichtspunkt besonders schwierige Aufgabe stellte für Ackermann und Partner das neue Technikgebäude
der Gesamthochschule Kassel dar (1990–1995), für das
eine innerstädtische Restfläche zur Verfügung stand. Als
unmittelbarer Nachbar war im Wettbewerb von 1985 das
gerade fertiggestellte Backstein- und Mansarddachgebirge
der Hochschulbauten von Horst Höfler und Lutz Kandel zu
berücksichtigen. Die insgesamt verfahrene städtebauliche
Situation klärte Kurt Ackermann durch einen kompakten,
gleichwohl gegliederten Baukörper, der entsprechend
seiner Funktion als Forschungsgebäude für Maschinen-
bauer und Bauingenieure eine durch technische Ästhetik
bestimmte Erscheinung erhielt. Auf diese Weise bekam
der kleinmaßstäblich mißratene Hochschulbereich zumin-
dest nach Süden, zur Stadt hin, eine wirkungsvolle Ge-
bäudekante. Zugleich bildet das selbstbewußte bauliche
Aggregat eine zeitgemäße Erinnerung an die früheren
Henschel-Werke, auf deren Gelände die Hochschule
errichtet wurde.

An diesem Projekt läßt sich beispielhaft der heutige
Gegensatz von Baukunst und Baukultur vorführen. Konnte
Walter Gropius 1913 in seinem berühmten Aufsatz über
moderne Industriearchitektur noch ganz unbefangen von
»Baukunst« sprechen[9], wie nach ihm viele Pioniere des
Neuen Bauens, so ist dieser Begriff heute zur Karikatur ver-
kommen. Wo immer betont von Baukunst die Rede ist,
sollte man auf der Hut sein. Beispiele für ›künstlerische‹
Schöpfungen gibt es zuhauf: angefangen bei Ungers' Sucht
nach dem Quadrat über Hans Holleins glitzerndes Wiener
Haas-Haus bis hin zu Frank Gehrys ›tanzendem‹ Eckgebäu-
de an der Moldau in Prag. Solche verquält auftrumpfenden
Bauten sind – um einmal Prinz Charles gegen den Strich zu
bürsten – die eigentlich »häßlichen Furunkel« im Gesicht
unserer Städte.

In Kassel wollten Höfler und Kandel Anfang der achtziger Jahre »eine Universität wie ein Feuerwerk« inszenie-
ren, doch entstanden ist lediglich eine verquere Ansamm-
lung von Häusern und Häuschen, die der Neubau von Kurt
Ackermann am Hauptplatz nun gnädig verdeckt. Gegen die
historischen Zitate, die expressiven Ausformungen oder
die dekonstruktivistischen Zumutungen eines inhaltlich
vagen, wenngleich in den Medien gefeierten Baukünstler-
tums behauptet sich die Baukultur der Gegenwart durch

Die im Herbst 1997
eröffnete Halle 13 ist
das bislang größte
Ausstellungsgebäude
auf dem Messegelände
in Hannover.

Hall 13, opened in the
autumn of 1997, is by far
the largest exhibition
building at the trade fair
complex in Hanover.

has stressed the importance of teamwork at numerous
prize-giving ceremonies. The influence of partners of
many years' standing on constructional and design solutions is evident in the striking differences that manifest
themselves in the work of the office. A clear "style",
frequently cultivated in other practices as a kind of trade
mark – in some cases, to the point of schematic repetition
(e.g. Richard Meier) – was neither desired nor possible.
Even in their use of materials, Ackermann and his
partners are not committed in advance. In addition to
exposed concrete and steel, which recur in their work,
they also use facing bricks, rendering, metal and glass.
One will look in vain, however, for a "stone fascia".

Nevertheless, the buildings and projects do have
something in common, namely, the standpoint from
which the architects approach their designs. Feeling
themselves borne out by their broad experience, especially in the design of industrial buildings, they are concerned in a quite "old-fashioned"[13] way with sensible
layouts, with structural honesty and a meaningful articulation of the various volumes of a scheme. In nearly every
case, one can see at a glance from their buildings that the
functional requirements of the brief formed the starting
point of the design. Without considering the question of
expression initially, Ackermann and his partners develop
their projects in three main steps: from the load-bearing
system as a static framework, via the subsystems of the
load-bearing components and elements – the assembly of
the parts to provide a structural solution – to the final
form of the load-bearing structure. The structure is usually enclosed in a protective skin that lends the building
architectural form. The guiding principle of the work of
the office might be summarized under the heading
"structural intelligence": achieving the highest quality
with the most economical means. As a practising and
influential architect and as a professor of many years'
standing at Stuttgart University, Kurt Ackermann has
been able to uphold his principle of not approaching a
task with preconceived ideas and certainly not in a dogmatic manner, thereby remaining open to ever new
challenges. The exhibition *Industriebau*, issued by his
institute in Stuttgart, has been particularly successful and
has toured through 25 university towns. The catalogue
has been reprinted several times.[14]

ihre bewußte Zurückhaltung und kultivierte Einfachheit – durch eine »zeitlose Dauerhaftigkeit«, wie sie den Bauten des Münchner Architekten 1994 bei der Verleihung der Heinrich-Tessenow-Medaille an Kurt Ackermann vom Laudator bescheinigt wurde.[10]

Bauen sei stets eine Gemeinschaftsaufgabe, deshalb dürfe es kein Schauplatz für die Selbstverwirklichung eines Architekten sein, betont Kurt Ackermann, der sich »als technischer Handwerker, als ein Baumeister im hergebrachten Sinn« versteht.[11] Das mag manchen allzu bescheiden klingen, ist es aber nicht. Sowohl bei anspruchsvollen Aufträgen im städtischen Kontext, zu denen das unmittelbar an der Bahn gelegene, den biederen Ort auffrischende Hauptpostamt in Regensburg zählt (1988–1991), als auch bei Sonderaufgaben haben Kurt Ackermann und Partner eine außergewöhnliche Qualität bewiesen. Ein Höhepunkt in ihrem Werk, zugleich ein seltenes Glanzlicht der neueren Münchner Architektur, ist das 1983 fertiggestellte Eislaufzelt im Olympiagelände. Durch den rund einhundert Meter überspannenden Dreigurtfachwerkbogen so logisch konstruiert wie ein Zirkuszelt, fasziniert das leichte Flächentragwerk auch von innen. Die Grenzen zwischen innen und außen scheinen aufgehoben, wenn das durch die ellipsenförmigen Öffnungen im Dach einfallende Licht während des Tages durch den Raum wandert. Technische Ästhetik verzaubert das Zelt in einer Weise, die dem Erlebnis klassischer Schönheit nahekommt.

Haltung statt Stil

Das Büro Ackermann habe sich durch eine »inspirierende Atmosphäre« ausgezeichnet, berichtet ein früherer Mitarbeiter.[12] Entscheidend für das diskussionsfreudige Klima sei gewesen, daß an den Entwürfen unterschiedliche Begabungen und verschiedene Temperamente mitgearbeitet hätten. Kurt Ackermann selbst, der bis heute die Rolle des Primus inter pares einnimmt, hat die Teamarbeit bei zahlreichen Preisverleihungen immer wieder betont. Die Einflüsse seiner langjährigen Partner auf konstruktive und gestalterische Lösungen sind denn auch angesichts markanter Unterschiede offensichtlich. Ein eindeutiger, häufig als Markenzeichen bewußt eingesetzter ›Stil‹, wie ihn andere Büros pflegen (bis hin zu schematischen Wiederho-

lungen, siehe Richard Meier), sollte und konnte nicht entstehen. Auch bei den Materialien legen sich Ackermann und Partner nicht von vornherein fest. Neben den bevorzugten Materialien Sichtbeton und Stahl wurden auch Putz, Sichtmauerwerk, Metall und Glas verwendet. Eine ›Stein-Tapete‹ wird man allerdings nicht finden.

Dennoch haben die Bauten und Projekte eine Gemeinsamkeit. Sie besteht in der Haltung, mit der die Architekten ihre Entwürfe angehen. Bestärkt durch ihre breiten Erfahrungen besonders im Industriebau, geht es ihnen ganz »altmodisch«[13] um eine vernünftige Disposition der Grundrisse, um konstruktive Ehrlichkeit und eine sinnfällige Gliederung der Volumina. Fast ohne Ausnahme läßt sich schon beim ersten Blick auf die Bauten nachvollziehen, daß jeweils die funktionalen Anforderungen einer Aufgabe den Ausgangspunkt gebildet haben. Ohne zunächst an den gestalterischen Ausdruck zu denken, entwickeln Ackermann und Partner ihre Projekte in einem Dreischritt: vom Tragsystem als statisches Gerüst über die Subsysteme der Tragwerksteile und Tragwerkselemente, der Fügungen als konstruktive Lösung, bis zur endgültigen Form des Tragwerks mit einer meist schützenden Hülle, wodurch das Bauwerk dann architektonisch in Erscheinung tritt. Ihr Leitbild lautet »konstruktive Intelligenz« – höchste Qualität soll mit sparsamsten Mitteln erreicht werden. Weil praktizierender Architekt und dadurch beispielgebend, konnte Kurt Ackermann seinen Grundsatz, nicht mit vorgefaßten Vorstellungen oder gar dogmatisch einer Aufgabe zu begegnen, sondern sich offenzuhalten für stets neue Herausforderungen, auch als langjähriger Stuttgarter Ordinarius mit Nachdruck vertreten. Besonders erfolgreich war die Ausstellung ›Industriebau‹ seines Instituts, die durch 25 Hochschulstädte ging. Das Katalogbuch wurde mehrfach nachgedruckt.[14]

Walter Gropius hatte in dem bereits erwähnten Aufsatz vehement den »Mummenschanz« im Industriebau angeprangert, das Verkleiden von Fabriken mit einer vorgeblich künstlerischen Formensprache.[15] Umgekehrt erinnert das Beharren von Kurt Ackermann auf funktionaler Gestalt, klarer Konstruktion und Materialgerechtheit an eine geradezu klassische Äußerung von Adolf Behne: »Das Zurückgehen auf den Zweck wirkt also immer wieder revolutionierend, wirft tyrannisch gewordene Formen ab, um aus der Besinnung auf die ursprüngliche Funktion aus einem möglichst neutralen Zustand eine verjüngte, lebendige, atmende Form zu schaffen.«[16]

In the essay mentioned above, Walter Gropius vehement-
ly attacked the "masquerade" that went on in the name
of industrial building: the use of an ostensibly artistic formal language as a means of disguise for factories.[15] In
contrast, Kurt Ackermann's insistence on functional form,
clear structures and appropriate materials recalls a truly
classical remark by Adolf Behne: "A return to function
always seems revolutionary – throwing off forms that
have become tyrannical in order to create, from as neu-
tral a state as possible, a rejuvenated, lively, breathing
form that does not lose sight of the original purpose."[16]

As architects, Ackermann and Partners have remained
true to the commitment they entered into decades ago to
continue the tradition of the Modern Movement without
resorting to fashionable trappings (low tech rather than
high tech). In doing so, they suffered losses in competitions during the heyday of Postmodernism and Decon-
structivism. In the long run, however, their "black-bread"
architecture has proved more palatable than the at times
much-vaunted cream puffs. Their most recent works,
including the largest hall to date on the Hanover trade
fair site and the newly completed pumping station in
Wilmersdorf, Berlin, disprove the popular belief that
"truth" in functional architecture today – in the aftermath
of Robert Venturi – can exist only in the form of "decorat-
ed sheds".[17]

Together with his partners, to whom his son Peter
Ackermann has belonged since 1993, and in close collaboration with dedicated specialist engineers who share his
attitude, Kurt Ackermann has developed well-functioning,
adaptable, environmentally sustainable architectural systems upon which future generations may build. Another
object lesson to be learned from his work is the need to
gain the support of specialists for structural engineering
and mechanical services as partners in the planning,
without the architect letting himself be relegated to the
role of a chief artistic manager. The profession still has a
future if the architect, as a custodian of building culture,
can succeed in reducing the demands of the specialist
engineers to a reasonable level in their work together.

Rational architecture and a personal living culture
need not be mutually exclusive. Many master builders
appreciate a good drop of wine and fine cuisine. Kurt
Ackermann also attaches importance to cultivating links
with modern painters and sculptors – links that go
beyond the obligatory programme of "art in building".
His contacts to the rebellious group of Munich artists
known as SPUR[18] in the 1960s earned him the name "Red
Kurt", which is not exactly an honorary title in Bavaria.
But in describing his standpoint, one might aptly cite the
old adage that only dead fish swim with the current.

Notes

[1] Dieter Hoffmann-Axthelm, "Warum ist die deutsche
Architektur so subaltern?", in ARCH+, No. 118, September
1993, p. 92 ff.

[2] See Christoph Hackelsberger, Die aufgeschobene
Moderne. Ein Versuch zur Einordnung der Architektur
der fünfziger Jahre, Munich 1985.

[3] Preliminary design for a prospectus for the Geschwister
Scholl Hochschule. Quoted from: Ulmer Museum,
HfG-Archiv (ed.), Hochschule für Gestaltung in Ulm – Die
frühen Jahre, exhibition catalogue, Ulm 1995, p. 20.

[4] Kurt Ackermann, "Brotzeit oder Picknick – auf die Qualität kam's an", in: Stiftung Hochschule für Gestaltung
Ulm (ed.), Freundschaft und Begegnung. Erinnerungen
an Otl Aicher, Ulm 1997, p. 45.

[5] Kurt Ackermann und Partner, Bauten und Projekte,
Stuttgart 1978.

[6] Kurt Ackermann in: Jochen Blumbach (ed.), Wolfgang
Märker – in unserer Mitte, private impression, Harburg
1995, p. 21 ff.

[7] Discussion between the author and Kurt Ackermann
in Munich on 13th January 1998.

[8] Gottfried Knapp, "Orte der Verdrängung. Was nicht
geliebt wird, muß auch nicht schön sein", in: Baumeister,
Zeitschrift für Architektur, 1998, No. 3, pp. 38–41.

[9] Walter Gropius, "Die Entwicklung moderner Industriebaukunst", in: Jahrbuch des Deutschen Werkbundes,
Jena 1913, p. 17 ff.

[10] Klaus Stiglat in: Alfred Toepfer Stiftung F.V.S., Fritz
Schumacher Stiftung 1994, (no place or date given)
(Hamburg 1995), p. 13.

[11] Discussion with Kurt Ackermann (see note 7).

[12] Discussion between the author and Patrick Deby in
Munich on 15th December 1997.

[13] Kurt Ackermann in: Alfred Toepfer Stiftung F.V.S.
(see note 10), p. 18.

[14] Kurt Ackermann, Universität Stuttgart, Institut für
Entwerfen und Konstruieren (ed.), Industriebau,
Stuttgart 1994.

[15] Walter Gropius, (see note 9), p. 19.

[16] Adolf Behne, Der moderne Zweckbau, reprint of
original edition of 1923, Bauwelt Fundamente, vol. 10,
Frankfurt/Main and Berlin 1964, p. 11.

[17] Martin Steinmann, "Gesicht und Maske", in "Zweckarchitektur", archithese, 1983, No. 3, p. 2.

[18] See Gruppe SPUR 1958–1965, Eine Dokumentation,
exhibition catalogue, Galerie van de Loo, Munich, 1979.

Ihrer vor Jahrzehnten eingangenen Selbstverpflichtung, die Tradition der Moderne ohne modische Anleihen fortzuführen (eher Low Tech statt High Tech), sind die Architekten Ackermann und Partner treu geblieben, auch wenn sie während der Blütezeiten von ›Postmoderne‹ und Dekonstruktivismus bei Wettbewerben Einbußen hinnehmen mußten. Über die Jahre hinweg hat sich ihr ›Schwarzbrot‹ im Vergleich zu den zeitweise hochgejubelten Sahnetorten als beständiger erwiesen. Ihre jüngsten Werke, darunter die bislang größte Halle auf dem Hannoveraner Messegelände und das soeben fertiggestellte Pumpwerk in Berlin-Wilmersdorf, widerlegen zugleich die gängige Auffassung, die »Wahrheit« von Zweckarchitektur könne heutzutage – in der Nachfolge von Robert Venturi – nur noch im »dekorierten Schuppen« bestehen.[17]

Zusammen mit seinen Partnern, zu denen seit 1993 auch sein Sohn Peter Ackermann gehört, und in enger Zusammenarbeit mit engagierten Fachingenieuren, die seine Haltung unterstützen, hat Kurt Ackermann gebrauchstüchtige, veränderbare, umweltverträgliche Systeme der Architektur entwickelt, auf denen kommende Generationen aufbauen können. Ein Vorbild sollte auch die Einsicht in die Notwendigkeit sein, Spezialisten für Tragwerk und Haustechnik als Planungspartner zu gewinnen, ohne daß sich der Architekt zum künstlerischen Oberleiter herabstufen läßt. Sein Beruf hat eine Zukunft, sofern es ihm als Treuhänder der Baukultur gelingt, die unterschiedlichen Ansprüche der Fachingenieure im Rahmen gemeinsamer Projekte auf ein vernünftiges Maß zurückzuschrauben.

Rationale Architektur und persönliche Lebenskultur müssen sich keineswegs ausschließen. Einen anständigen Wein und gutes Essen wissen viele Baumeister zu schätzen. Kurt Ackermann sind aber auch – über ›Kunst am Bau‹ hinaus – die Verbindungen zu zeitgenössischen Malern und Bildhauern wichtig. Wegen seiner Kontakte zur rebellischen Münchner Künstlergruppe SPUR[18] nannte man ihn während der sechziger Jahre sogar den »roten Kurt« – in Bayern nicht gerade ein Ehrentitel. Doch auch bei ihm trifft das Sprichwort zu: Nur tote Fische schwimmen mit dem Strom.

Anmerkungen

[1] Dieter Hoffmann-Axthelm, Warum ist die deutsche Architektur so subaltern?, in: ARCH+, Heft 118, September 1993, S. 92 ff.

[2] Siehe dazu Christoph Hackelsberger, Die aufgeschobene Moderne. Ein Versuch zur Einordnung der Architektur der fünfziger Jahre, München 1985.

[3] Vorentwurf zum Prospekt der Geschwister Scholl Hochschule. Zitiert nach: Ulmer Museum, HfG-Archiv (Hrsg.), Hochschule für Gestaltung in Ulm – Die frühen Jahre, Ausst. Kat. Ulm 1995, S. 20.

[4] Kurt Ackermann, Brotzeit oder Picknick – auf die Qualität kam's an, in: Stiftung Hochschule für Gestaltung Ulm (Hrsg.), Freundschaft und Begegnung. Erinnerungen an Otl Aicher, Ulm 1997, S. 45.

[5] Kurt Ackermann und Partner, Bauten und Projekte, Stuttgart 1978.

[6] Kurt Ackermann in: Jochen Blumbach (Red.), Wolfgang Märker – in unserer Mitte, Privatdruck, Harburg 1995, S. 21 ff.

[7] Gespräch des Autors mit Kurt Ackermann in München am 13. Januar 1998.

[8] Gottfried Knapp, Orte der Verdrängung. Was nicht geliebt wird, muß auch nicht schön sein, in: Baumeister, Zeitschrift für Architektur, 1998, Heft 3, S. 38–41.

[9] Walter Gropius, Die Entwicklung moderner Industriebaukunst, in: Jahrbuch des Deutschen Werkbundes, Jena 1913, S. 17 ff.

[10] Klaus Stiglat, in: Alfred Toepfer Stiftung F.V.S., Fritz Schumacher Stiftung 1994, o. O. o. J. (Hamburg 1995), S. 13.

[11] Gespräch mit Kurt Ackermann (Anm. 7).

[12] Gespräch des Autors mit Patrick Deby in München am 15. Dezember 1997.

[13] Kurt Ackermann in: Alfred Toepfer Stiftung F.V.S. (Anm. 10), S. 18.

[14] Kurt Ackermann, Universität Stuttgart, Institut für Entwerfen und Konstruieren (Hrsg.), Industriebau, Stuttgart ⁴1994.

[15] Walter Gropius (Anm. 9), S. 19.

[16] Adolf Behne, Der moderne Zweckbau, Nachdruck der Originalausgabe von 1923, Bauwelt Fundamente, Bd. 10, Frankfurt/Main und Berlin 1964, S. 11.

[17] Martin Steinmann, Gesicht und Maske, in: Zweckarchitektur, archithese, 1983, Heft 3, S. 2.

[18] Siehe dazu: Gruppe SPUR 1958–1965, Eine Dokumentation, Ausst. Kat. Galerie van de Loo, München 1979.

Bauten und Projekte 1978–1998
Buildings and Projects

Marienhof Estate
Sewage Treatment
Plant of the City of
Munich, Dietersheim

Commencement of
planning: 1975
Construction period:
1984 – 88

To relieve the load of the existing
sewage treatment plant in
Freimann, Munich, a second
plant was built to the north of the
city on land belonging to the
municipality of Eching. The location – in a suburban recreation
zone on the edge of a protected
landscape area in the meadows
along the River Isar – had a major
influence on the design of the
above-ground structures and
their integration into the meadow
landscape. The brief required as

high a degree of biological purification for sewage as possible,
with provision for the following
functional realms: sewage purification, sludge treatment, a
mechanical-technical tract and a
service block.

Work on this project extended
over a period of more than
13 years. Before it began, however, it was necessary to make a
close study of the location, the
contents of the brief and the
long-term developments that the

various functions were likely to
undergo. Priority was given to
ecological aspects and to the
integration of the complex into
the landscape. This implied a
carefully considered design of
all engineering structures, keep-
ing a close watch on scale, and
restraint in the selection of materials. The various studies and
the conditions imposed by the
respective authorities – which
contradicted each other in part –
had to be coordinated with each

Zur Entlastung des bestehenden Klärwerks München-Freimann sollte im Norden Münchens, auf dem Gebiet der Gemeinde Eching, ein zweites Klärwerk entstehen. Der Standort am Rand des Landschaftsschutzgebietes der Isarauen, einem Naherholungsgebiet, war bestimmend für die Gestaltung der Hochbauten und ihre Einfügung in die Auenlandschaft. Es waren eine weitestgehende biologische Abwasserreinigung mit den Funktionsbereichen Abwasserreinigung, Schlammbehandlung, maschinentechnischer Bereich und Betriebsgebäude gefordert.

Die Realisierung des Auftrags erstreckte sich über dreizehn Jahre und erforderte eine intensive und vorausschauende Auseinandersetzung mit dem Standort, den Inhalten der Bauaufgabe und der langfristigen Entwicklung der Nutzungen. Priorität hatten die ökologischen Komponenten und die Einfügung in die Landschaft. Das Einfügen als Planungsziel bedeutete eine sorgfältige Gestaltung aller Ingenieurbauteile bei strenger Beachtung der Maßstäblichkeit und die behutsame Wahl des Baumaterials. Die sich manchmal widersprechenden Gutachten und Auflagen der beteiligten Behörden mußten koordiniert werden. Es wurde ein durchgängiges Konzept für das architektonische Erscheinungsbild entwickelt. Kurzlebige Architekturmoden sollten vermieden werden. Qualitätvolle Vorbilder für bauliche Anlagen von Klärwerken lagen nicht vor. Dies kam der Entwurfsarbeit zugute. Sie wurde geprägt von der Überzeugung, eine rein durch Technik bestimmte Architektursprache für das Klärwerk verwenden zu wollen.

other. An overall planning concept was drawn up to determine the architectural appearance of the scheme, since there were no examples of a sewage treatment plant of any quality on which the present development might be based. Ultimately, however, this proved to be of advantage for the design, which sought an architectural language based entirely on the technology. Ephemeral architectural fashions were to be avoided.

Klärwerk Gut Marienhof
der Landeshauptstadt München, Dietersheim

Planungsbeginn: 1975
Bauzeit: 1984–1988

Abwassereinzugsgebiete
der Stadt München für
die beiden Klärwerke.
Links: Luftaufnahme von
Südwesten

Catchment area of
the two Munich sewage
treatment plants. Left:
aerial view of sewage
treatment plant from the
south-west

Werden und Vergehen
von Leben: ›Lebensbogen‹
von Hannsjörg Voth

Growth and decay in the
course of life: Hannsjörg
Voth's "Curve of Life"

The aim of the treatment process
is to remove from the sewage all
anorganic solids plus organic
matter in either a solid or dis-
solved state. The purification of
the waste matter occurs in a
number of stages.

In the mechanical part of this
process, solid matter is removed
from the sewage in the screening
chamber. Via a series of screw
pumps in the intake basin, the
foul water is then pumped to aer-
ated sand traps, where sand, fat
and oil are separated out. From
here it runs to the preliminary
settling tank, where heavy solids
are deposited.

In the most important biological section of the sewage treatment plant, a process of self-
purification takes place within a
very short time and within a very
small space. In the activating
sludge tank, bacteria and lower
forms of life are cultivated that,
with the input of large quantities
of air, feed on the undissolved
soil material. The flocculent
sludge formed as a result of this
process is sedimented out in the
intermediate settling and final
clarification tanks. This purification process takes place in two
stages, in which carbon compounds and then ammonium
compounds are broken down.

The bulk of the oxygen-con-
suming substances that are converted into solid matter during
the process of biological purification is sedimented out in the final
stage of clarification. A small
amount is left, however. The
waste water is, therefore, fed

through a filter, consisting of a
bed of fine sand 1. 50 m thick,
that removes the residue. The
treated water, now 99 per cent
pure, runs to the intake port
in the River Isar. The sludge
deposited during the various
stages of purification is consolidated and digested in three
sapropel or digestion chambers.
Further dehydration occurs in the
sludge consolidation tanks. The
digester gas given off in this
process is retained and used as
self-generated energy for a largely autonomous operation of the
plant. The energy-supply centre
is in the powerhouse, where the
air blowers and generators used
in the biological stage of the
process are operated by gas-
burning motors. The sludge is
stored in containers and pumped
via sewage treatment plant 1 to
the northern power station,
where it is burnt. The deposits
collected in the screening plant
and sand traps are also transported to the power station for
incineration.

The complex is based on a
simple, rational design principle.
The various functions are expressed in clear, memorable
geometric forms. Cubes, cones,
truncated cones and cylinders
are the principal elements. Their
construction and cladding are

Ziel des Klärprozesses ist es, dem Abwasser alle anorganischen Feststoffe sowie feste und gelöste organische Stoffe zu entziehen. Die Reinigung des Abwassers erfolgt in mehreren Stufen.

Im mechanischen Teil wird das Abwasser im Rechenhaus von groben Stoffen befreit und läuft über Schneckenpumpen im Einlaufhebewerk zu den belüfteten Sandfängen, wo Sand, Fette und Öle zurückgehalten werden; es fließt weiter zu den Vorklärbecken zum Absetzen der schweren festen Stoffe.

Im wichtigsten biologischen Teil der Kläranlage geschieht die Selbstreinigung in kürzester Zeit und auf engstem Raum. In den Belebungsbecken werden Bakterien und niedere Lebewesen gezüchtet, die sich von den ungelösten Schmutzstoffen unter hoher Luftzufuhr ernähren; die sich dabei bildenden Schlammflocken setzen sich in den Zwischen- und Nachklärbecken ab. Dieser Reinigungsprozeß geschieht in zwei Stufen: Abbau von Kohlenstoffverbindungen und Abbau von Ammoniumverbindungen.

Die nach der biologischen Reinigung in Feststoffe umgewandelten sauerstoffzehrenden Stoffe setzen sich zum größten Teil in der Nachklärung ab. Ein geringer Teil bleibt jedoch zurück. Darum wird das Abwasser durch eine Sandfilteranlage geleitet, deren 1,5 m dicke Sandschicht mit feiner Körnung diese Feststoffe abfiltert. Das Abwasser fließt zu 99 % gereinigt zum Einlaufbauwerk in der Isar. Der bei den Reinigungsvorgängen anfallende Klärschlamm wird eingedickt und in den drei Faulbehältern ausgefault. In Nacheindickern erfolgt eine weitere Entwässerung. Bei dem Faulprozeß entsteht Klärgas, das im Gasbehälter gespeichert wird und eine weitgehend autonome Versorgung mit Eigenenergie gewährleistet. Die Zentrale der Eigenenergieversorgung ist das Maschinenhaus. Dort werden über Gasmotoren die für den biologischen Teil erforderlichen Luftgebläse und Generatoren betrieben. Der Klärschlamm wird in den Speicherbehältern gelagert und über das Klärwerk I zur Verbrennung in das Kraftwerk Nord gepumpt. Auch das Rechen- und Sandfanggut wird in das Kraftwerk München Nord transportiert und verbrannt.

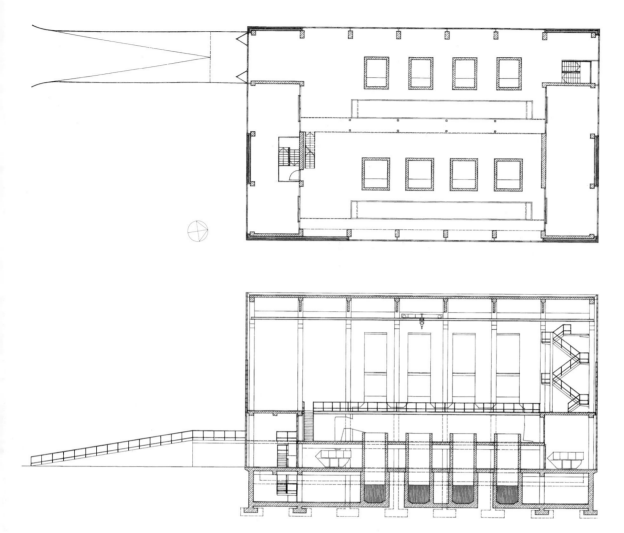

Links oben: Rechenhaus. Grundriß und Längsschnitt. Mechanische Reinigung des Abwassers von groben Schadstoffen durch zwei Rechenanlagen mit unterschiedlicher Maschenweite

Top left: screening chamber. Plan and longitudinal section. Mechanical removal of harmful solid matter from the sewage by passing it through two screens of different mesh sizes

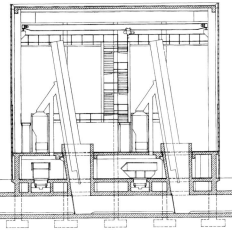

Querschnitt durch
das Rechenhaus

Cross-section through
the screening chamber

based on the use of industrialized methods and materials, which were left untreated. As a result, the appearance of the plant is characterized by the functional forms of the various parts and by the overall technical aesthetic. The structural supporting members are in steel and reinforced concrete. The materials used – bright metal, glass and facing bricks – establish a unifying theme that links the visible structures.

The structures for the purification of the sewage, the mechanical plant and the works building are cubic forms in reinforced concrete construction with a column grid spacing of 5.5 m (4.8 m in the works building). The façades consist of a grid of natural-colour aluminium elements based on dimensions of 1.2 x 0. 6 m and 1.375 x 0.6 m, with areas of clear glazing, thermally insulating glass, opening lights, doors, gates, panels and robust facing brickwork that will retain its attractive appearance after weathering.

The sapropel tanks are laid out radially. The reinforced concrete truncated cones are covered with gleaming sheet aluminium braced by the standing seams. The access and viewing tower, which is square on plan, is linked

to the octagonal lanterns of these containers by three bridges in a lightweight steel construction with beams trussed on the underside. The access tower itself is a steel structure consisting of cruciform-section columns at the internal and external angles, and I-beams supporting trapezoidal-section ribbed metal sheeting to the floors. Steel rods were used to provide wind bracing.

The consolidation and receiver basins are in the form of flat reinforced concrete cylinders with truncated conical covers in aluminium. Like the cylindrical gasholder, they are clad with silver-grey aluminium with horizontal standing seams.

Over the entire site, the external areas were planted with 800 trees and 170,000 bushes. Originally, lanes were to be left free between the plantings to afford views of the buildings and to allow them to be experienced visually from various points. The technological content of this complex was to establish a counterpoint to and form a unity with the natural surroundings. Strict conditions imposed by the local authority, however, required the buildings to be screened from sight by the landscaping.

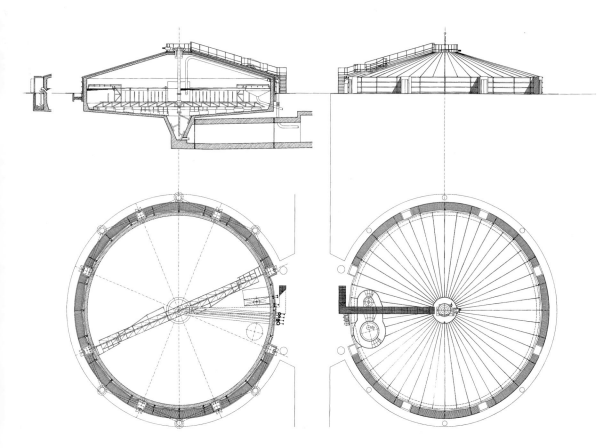

Eindicker. Schnitt, Ansicht und Grundrisse. Durch die verschiedenen Reinigungsgänge fällt Klärschlamm an. In den flachen Behältern wird er eingedickt und anschließend in den Faulbehältern ausgefault.

Sludge consolidation tank: section, elevation and plans. The various stages of treatment result in sludge deposits that are consolidated in the flat containers and then digested in sapropel chambers.

Verfolgt wurde ein einfaches, rationales Entwurfsprinzip. Klare und einprägsame geometrische Formen drücken die jeweiligen Funktionen aus. Kuben, Kegel, Kegelstümpfe und Zylinder sind die Grundelemente, die mit industriellen Mitteln und naturbelassenen Materialien hergestellt oder verkleidet wurden. Die Anlage erhielt so ein Erscheinungsbild, das durch die funktionale Gestalt der Bauteile und durch technische Ästhetik geprägt ist. Stahl und Stahlbeton als Tragwerkselemente stützen die Form, helles Metall, Glas und Sichtziegel fassen die Hochbauten zusammen.

Die Hochbauten für Abwasserreinigung, Maschinentechnik und die Betriebsgebäude sind kubische Körper in Stahlbetonkonstruktionen im Stützraster von 5,5 m und 4,8 m bei den Betriebsgebäuden. Die Fassaden bestehen aus naturfarbenem Aluminiumgitterwerk im Raster von 1,2 m x 0,6 m bzw. 1,375 m x 0,6 m mit eingesetzten Flächen aus Klarglas, Wärmeschutzglas, Fensterflügeln, Türen, Toren, Paneelen und aus robustem Sichtmauerwerk, das sich auch im Alterungsprozeß bewährt. Die Faulbehälter sind sternförmig

angeordnet. Die Außenwände der Kegelstümpfe aus Stahlbeton sind mit hellen, durch Aufkantungen versteiften Aluminiumelementen verkleidet. Der im Grundriß quadratische Aufgangs- und Aussichtsturm hat drei Verbindungsbrücken in einer leichten, unterspannten Stahlkonstruktion zu den drei achteckigen Laternen auf den Faulbehältern. Der Aufgangsturm ist eine Stahlkonstruktion: Kreuzstützen an den Innen- und Außenecken, IPE- und IPB-Profile als Deckenträger mit Trapezblechauflage, alle Windverbände in Rundstahl ablesbar.

Eindicker und Vorlagebecken sind flache Zylinder aus Stahlbeton mit kegelstumpfförmiger Alu-

miniumeindeckung. Sie tragen entsprechend dem zylinderförmigen Gasbehälter silbergraue, waagrecht abgekantete Aluminiumverkleidungen.

Die Freianlagen des Gesamtareals wurden mit 800 Bäumen und 170 000 Sträuchern aufgeforstet. Ursprünglich sollten Schneisen die bauliche Anlage der Kläranlage von verschiedenen Standpunkten aus sicht- und erlebbar machen. Natur und das von der Technik geprägte Klärwerk sollten eine kontrapunktische Einheit bilden. Die strengen Auflagen der Gemeinde machten jedoch das »Weggrünen« der Gebäude zur Auflage.

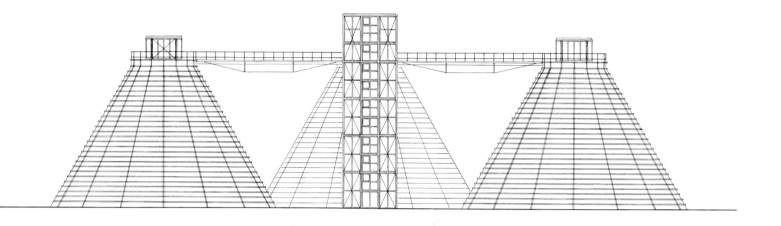

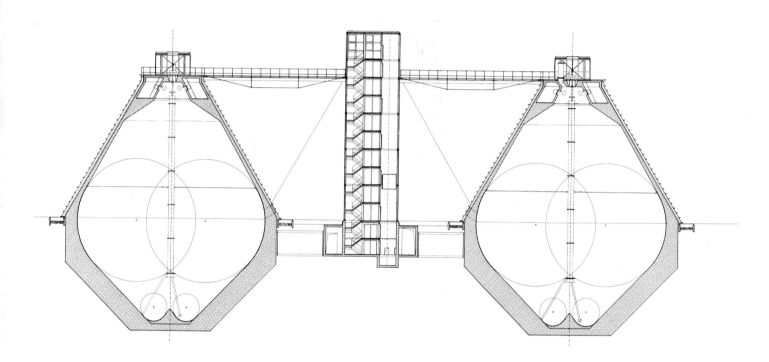

Faulbehältergruppe und Aufgangsturm. Ansicht und Schnitt. Das Innenvolumen der Faulbehälter wurde auch nach außen in eine klare geometrische Form umgesetzt. Nutzung, Konstruktion und Form bilden eine Einheit. Die dicken, schweren Außenwände unter Geländeniveau verhindern ein Aufschwimmen der leeren Faulbehälter.

Group of sludge digestion (sapropel) chambers with access tower: elevation and section. The internal shape of the digestion chambers generated a clear geometric form externally. Here, function, structure and form are united into a single whole. The thick, heavy outer casing below ground level prevents the chambers floating up when empty.

Rechte Seite: Stahldetails der Treppe im Aufgangsturm

Opposite page: details of steel staircase construction in access tower

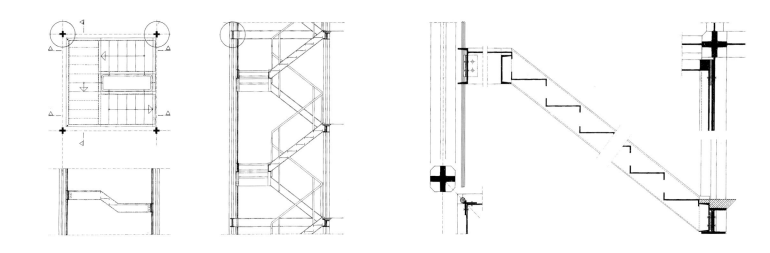

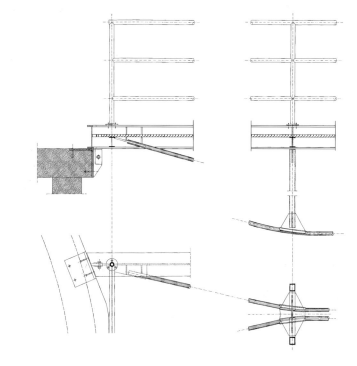

"The architect and the landscape architect have to reconcile this extremely unnatural industrial ensemble with its natural surroundings. They have to design the heterogeneous buildings in such a way that these may enter into a dialogue with the landscape that will overcome all differences. . . .

In the sewage treatment plant on the Marienhof Estate near Dietersheim, all these requirements were met in almost ideal manner. The architects commissioned to design the scheme, Kurt Ackermann and Partners, together with the landscape architect Karl Kagerer, have not attempted to create an embarrassing liaison between the clearly technical content of the sewage treatment machinery and the river meadows of the Isar, which form part of a landscape conservation area. Instead, using technical means and materials, they have helped the structures to stand in their own right in these alien surroundings. . . .

The most powerful architectural image of the Marienhof Estate is the group of three silvery, gleaming pyramids of the sludge digestion towers. It is almost a miracle that they stand there in such a splendid configuration; for if the thinking of the building and sewage technicians had triumphed, a row of bloated concrete balloons would have been stuck into the ground one after another as in Grosslappen and would have been extremely difficult to mask. . . .

On the Marienhof site, the architects took the unattractive theme of a sewage plant seriously and treated it as a genuine design challenge. They have cleverly separated the extremely different uses and arranged the many individual structures into three groups, each of which forms a functional entity in itself. Seen as a whole, the structures demonstrate their cohesion through their unobtrusive symmetry and the unity of their materials and forms. . . .

The quality of the architecture is the outcome . . . of an imaginative use of industrial materials and the creativity with which the technological forms were developed and structurally refined."
Gottfried Knapp, *Süddeutsche Zeitung*, 21/22 October 1989

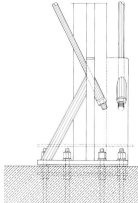

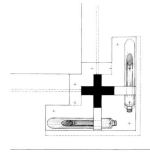

Linke Seite: Unterspannte
Stahlbrücken zu den
Faulbehältern mit Stahl-
rosten. Details der
Brückenkonstruktion

Opposite page: steel
bridges to lanterns of
sapropel chambers. The
construction is trussed
on the underside; the
walkway consists of steel
gratings laid between
steel beams. Details of
bridge construction

Aufgangsturm. Details
der Aussteifungen am
Fußpunkt des Aufgangs-
turmes

Access tower. Details of
bracing at foot of access
tower

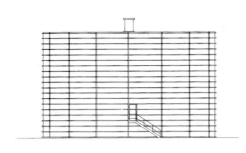

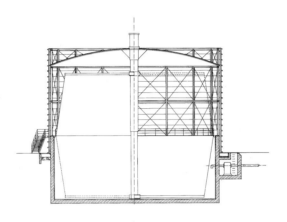

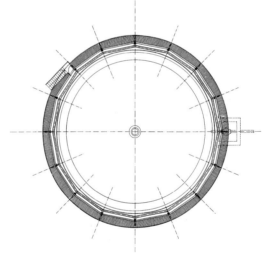

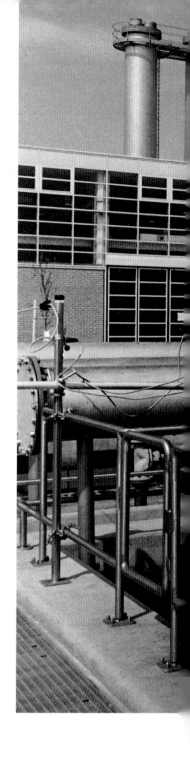

Gasbehälter. Ansicht, Schnitt und Grundriß

Gasholder: elevation, section and plan

Rechte Seite: Maschinenhaus Grundriß

Opposite page: plan of powerhouse

Das Klärgas wird im Gasbehälter gespeichert und betreibt im Maschinenhaus die Gasgeneratoren; die autonome Stromversorgung ist rund 90 %.

Digester gas given off during the sewage treatment process is stored in the gasholder and used to operate the generators in the powerhouse. Autonomously produced electricity accounts for about 90 per cent of overall consumption.

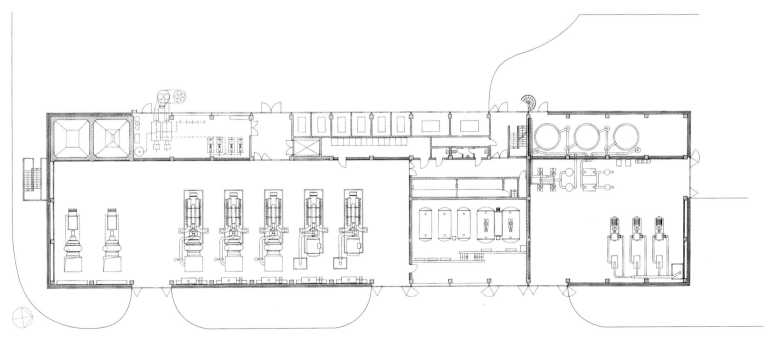

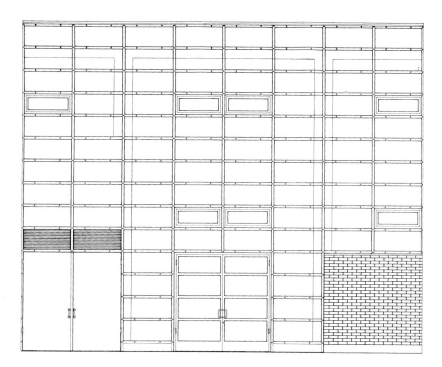

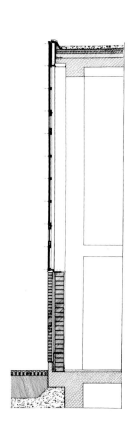

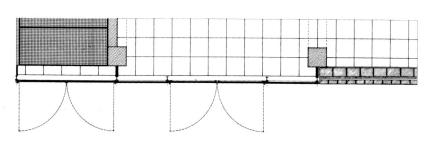

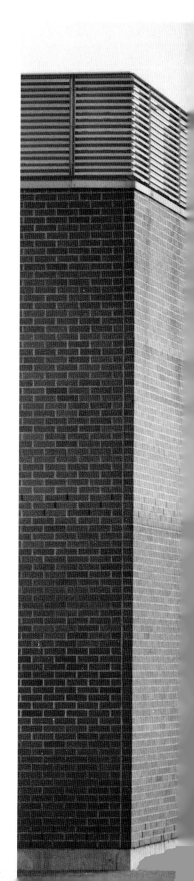

Die Fassaden aller Hochbauten folgen einem auf die Nutzung abgestimmten Prinzip aus Grundelementen im Raster 1,2 x 0,6 m bzw. 1,375 x 0,6 m. In ein naturfarbenes Aluminiumgitterwerk sind Flächen aus Klarglas, Wärmeschutzglas, Fensterflügel, Türen, Tore und Paneele eingesetzt. Geschlossene Wandflächen sind in einem robusten, zweischaligen Sichtmauerwerk ausgeführt.

The façades of all buildings are based on a single design principle, which was adapted to meet the functional needs of the individual structures. The basic grid dimensions are 1.20 x 0.60 m and 1.375 x 0.60 m. The framework of natural-coloured aluminium mullions and transoms is filled with areas of clear glass, thermally insulating glass, opening lights, doors, gates and other panels. The closed wall areas are in a robust, two-leaf facing brick construction.

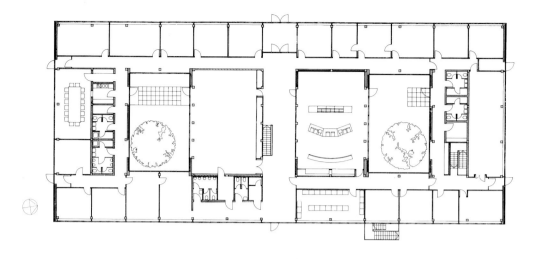

Labor und Verwaltungs-
gebäude. Oben: Grundriß.
Mitte: Von der zentralen
Leitwarte wird das gesam-
te Klärwerk elektronisch
gesteuert und überwacht.
Links: Der mit Oberlich-
tern ausgestattete Flur
der Elektrowerkstatt

Laboratory and adminis-
tration building. Top:
plan. Above: the entire
sewage treatment plant
is electronically operated
and monitored from a
central control room.
Left: corridor in the
electrical workshop with
continuous roof light

»Architekt und Landschaftsplaner müssen das extrem unnatürliche Industrieensemble mit seiner naturhaften Umgebung versöhnen, sie müssen die heterogenen Bauten so gestalten, daß über die Gegensätze hinweg ein Dialog mit der umgebenden Landschaft möglich ist.

All diese Anforderungen wurden beim Klärwerk im Gut Marienhof bei Dietersheim auf fast ideale Weise erfüllt. Das mit dem Entwurf betraute Architekturbüro Kurt Ackermann und Partner und der Landschaftsarchitekt Karl Kagerer haben keine peinliche Annäherung zwischen der eindeutig technischen Klärwerksmaschinerie und den unter Landschaftsschutz stehenden Isarauen versucht; sie haben vielmehr den technischen Bauten mit technischen Mitteln und Materialien zu einem angemessenen Auftritt in der fremden Umgebung verholfen. ...

Das architektonisch stärkste Zeichen im Gut Marienhof setzen aber die drei silbrig glänzenden Pyramiden der Faultürme. Daß sie in so brillanter Konfiguration dastehen, muß man fast als Wunder bezeichnen, denn wenn der Fachverstand der Bau- und Abwassertechniker sich durchgesetzt hätte, wären, wie in Großlappen, ballonartig aufgedunsene Betonblasen, die sich nur schwer verkleiden lassen, in einer Reihe hintereinander in den Boden gerammt worden. ...

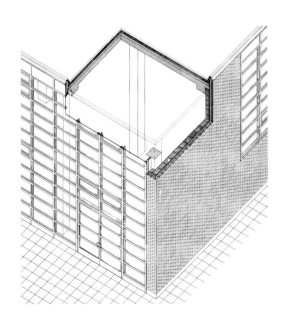

Beim Gut Marienhof haben die Architekten das unappetitliche Thema Klärwerk als Gestaltungsaufgabe ernstgenommen. Sie haben die extrem gegensätzlichen Funktionen geschickt voneinander getrennt und die vielen Einzelbauten zu drei Gruppen zusammengefaßt, die in sich funktional eine Einheit bilden und nach außen durch eine unaufdringliche Symmetrie und durch einheitliche Materialien und Formen ihre Zusammengehörigkeit zeigen. ...

Die Qualität der Architektur ergibt sich ... aus der Phantasie, mit der industrielle Baustoffe eingesetzt, und aus der Kreativität, mit der technologische Formen weiterentwickelt und konstruktiv verfeinert wurden.«
Gottfried Knapp, *Süddeutsche Zeitung*, 21./22. Oktober 1989

Brandkalkaufbereitung.
Verladebänder,
1978–79 gebaut,
dahinter Kalkofen 2

Preparation of anhydrous
lime. Conveyor loading
plant, built in 1978–79,
with limekiln 2 to the rear

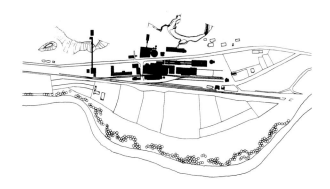

Der Lageplan oben zeigt
die Ausdehnung des
Werks im Jahr 1960 am
Beginn der langfristigen
Werksplanung. Rechts
der Zustand 1998. Oben:
Gesamtansicht des
Zement- und Kalkwerks
von Norden

The site plan at the top
shows the extent of the
works in 1960, when
long-term plans were
being drafted. On the
right, the plant in 1998.
Top right: overall view of
the cement and lime
works from the north

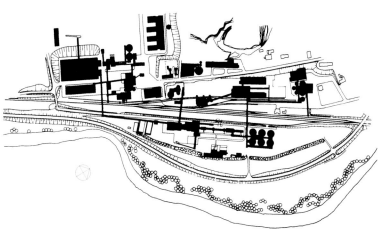

Märker Zementwerk, Harburg/Schwaben

Planungsbeginn: 1958
Bauzeit: 1978 –1979 Kalkwerk,
1992 –1996 Werkstätten

Märker Cement
Works, Harburg,
Swabia

Commencement of
planning: 1958
Construction period:
1978–79
lime works
1992–96
workshops

Kalkschachtofen 3,
1979 in Betrieb ge-
nommen

Vertical limekiln 3,
taken into operation
in 1979

When the planning of the Märker plant began 40 years ago, the works produced 900 tonnes of cement a day in a wet process. The highway ran through the middle of the site, and the sequence of work was based more on the dictates of the old buildings than on technical needs.

At the outset, an overall concept was drawn up for the long-term planning of the works. The production capacity was to be increased nearly fourfold to 3,500 tonnes of cement a day; the main road was to be rerouted further east outside the works area; and the building programme for the plant was to be based on two main design principles.

The first related to space-enclosing structures – halls to protect machinery and materials from the elements, but also to protect the environment from emissions. All machinery that was a source of noise, and materials that could spread dust were to be enclosed.

The second principle was that of designing the buildings to suit the functional layout of the machinery or groups of machines. The enclosing structures were to be tailor-made to fit the equipment, while at the same time allowing the original form and function to remain legible. Changes were to be made only where absolutely necessary. At the same time, the buildings were to be given a more pronounced sculptural quality and have their own characteristic forms. These design principles largely determine the appearance of the works today.

As a result of the expansion, the workshops and the various stores for spare parts were removed to a less central position. The new and centrally located workshops with ancillary high-bay stores were a necessary and logical step. The comb-like layout of the complex ensures excellent functional links, short routes and simple orientation. The high-bay store tract forms the spine of the complex. The four legs house two metalworking shops with training areas and two workshops. All areas are reached via an internal access route. The load-bearing structures reflect the different uses they serve.

A quality-conscious client and an efficient engineering department within the works provided the guarantee that the long-term developmental and works planning would be carried through to the desired goal. The principle of the architectural design was to regard the entire plant as a functioning machine, in which silos, grinding plant, kiln and conveyor belts were to be laid out in relation to each other in a conceptionally ideal and functionally efficient manner. At the same time, it was to respect the needs of the environment and the landscape. A consistent functional image was to be created. This concept led to a degree of variety within the uniform overall appearance of the works.

Reparaturwerkstatt
für Schwerlastkipper
des Steinbruchs

Repair workshop for
heavy-duty quarry
tipper trucks

Vor 40 Jahren wurde mit den Planungsarbeiten für das Märkerwerk begonnen, das damals 900 Tonnen Zement pro Tag im Naßverfahren produzierte. Die Bundesstraße führte mitten durch das Werk. Der Betriebsablauf richtete sich außerdem mehr nach der alten Bausubstanz als nach technischen Erfordernissen.

Zuerst wurde ein ganzheitliches Konzept für eine langfristige Werksplanung entwickelt, die Kapazität der Tagesproduktion sollte auf 3500 Tonnen Zement erhöht und damit vervierfacht werden. Die Bundesstraße wurde aus dem Werk weiter nach Osten verlegt. Die Bauaufgaben des Werkes sollten mit zwei Gestaltungsprinzipien gelöst werden:

Ein Prinzip ist als das der Hülle zu bezeichnen, also Hallen für Maschinen und Materialien, die vor Witterungseinflüssen, aber auch die Umgebung vor Emissionen schützen. Alle Maschinen mit großer Geräuschentwicklung und Materialien, die Staub verursachen, werden eingehaust.

Das andere Prinzip ist das der Maßschneiderei. Die Gebäudeteile sollen den funktionellen Aufbau der Maschinengruppe wie ein Maßanzug umschließen, aber die ursprüngliche Form und Funktion sichtbar lassen. Dabei soll nur das Notwendigste umbaut werden; die Baukörper erhalten mehr Plastizität und charakteristische Gestalt. Diese Gestaltungsprinzipien prägen das Erscheinungsbild des Werks.

Die Werkstätten und die unterschiedlichen Ersatzteillager werden durch die Expansion des Werks in dezentrale Standorte gedrängt. Neue und zentrale Werkstätten mit angeschlossenem Hochregallager sind eine notwendige und folgerichtige Disposition. Das System einer kammartigen Organisation des Grundrisses bringt optimale Funktionszusammenhänge, kurze Wege und eine gute Orientierung. Der Komplex des Hochregallagers bildet das Rückgrat der Bauanlage. In den vier Fingern liegen zwei Schlossereien mit Lehrwerkstatt und je eine Werkstatt für die Steinbruchgeräte und für die Elektroabteilung. Alle Bereiche werden über die dazwischengelegte innere Werkstattstraße erschlossen. Die Tragwerke sind auf die Nutzung ausgerichtet.

Ein qualitätsbewußter Bauherr und eine gut funktionierende Ingenieurabteilung im Werk schafften die Voraussetzungen, um die langfristigen Entwicklungs- und Werksplanungen zum gesteckten Ziel zu führen. Die Einheit von Funktion, Konstruktion, Material und Form zu erreichen und bestmögliche Rücksicht auf die Umwelt und Landschaft zu nehmen, war Entwurfsabsicht. Es sollte ein durchgängiges funktionales Erscheinungsbild geschaffen werden. Dieses Konzept hat zu Vielfalt im einheitlichen Gesamtbild des Werks geführt.

Werkstätten für Elektroabteilung und Schlosserei, Kraftfahrzeuge und Ausbildung, 1992–96. Rechts im Bild die Kalkverladeanlage

Workshops for electrical and metalworking trades, vehicles and training, 1992–96. On the right of the picture is the lime loading plant.

Endpunkt der Schotterförderanlage aus dem Steinbruch Bräunlesberg

End of conveyor plant for stone from the Bräunlesberg quarry

Canal Bank and
Bridge Construction
Main-Danube Canal,
Kelheim
Pedestrian Bridge

Competition: 1980
First prize
Commencement of
planning: 1981
Construction period:
1985 – 88

The competition proposals for
the pedestrian bridge over the
Main-Danube Canal at Torhausplatz in Kelheim were drawn
up in collaboration with Jörg
Schlaich and his office in Stuttgart.

The construction of the new
ship canal decisively altered the
urban situation in Kelheim.
The image of the town and the
attractive landscape of the river
meadows were subject to major
changes, not only of scale.
A newly designed paved court
marks the entrance to the town
through the tower of the Altmühl
Gate. Between the bank of the
canal and the historical buildings
on the periphery of Kelheim,
routes with panoramic views
were laid out with avenues of
plane trees and landscaped
areas.

With the construction of the
canal, a number of new bridges
were needed. They were to be
distinguished in their appearance
by broad spans, innovative load-
bearing systems and a technical
aesthetic. These design goals
resulted in an exciting contrast
between old and new. Navigation
on the canal required a clear
height beneath the bridges of
10 m. The difference in height
was overcome in a form that is
acceptable even for disabled
people. Lightly inclined ramps,
that seem to grow out of the

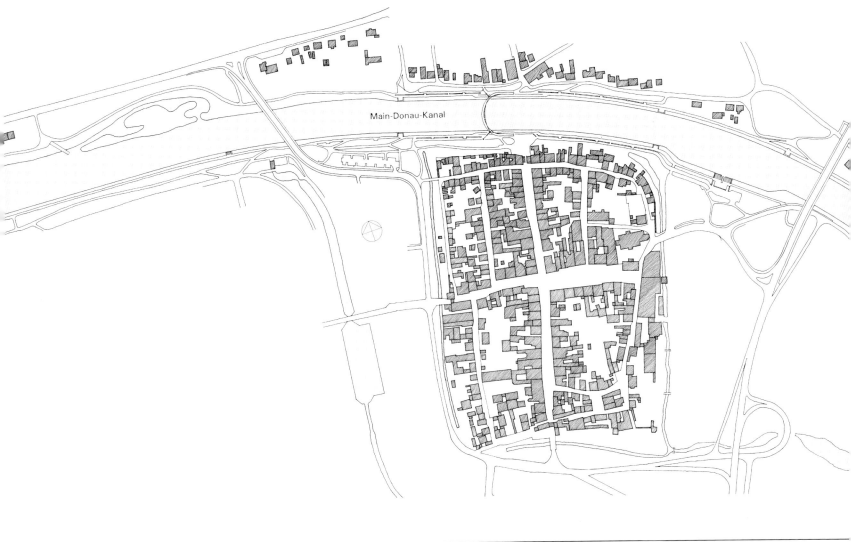

Uferanlage mit Brücken, Main-Donau-Kanal, Kelheim
Fußgängerbrücke

Wettbewerb 1980
1. Preis
Planungsbeginn: 1981
Bauzeit: 1985–1988

Der Wettbewerb für die Fußgängerbrücke am Torhausplatz über den Main-Donau-Kanal in Kelheim wurde zusammen mit Jörg Schlaich und seinem Stuttgarter Büro bearbeitet.

Die veränderte städtebauliche Situation in Kelheim ist durch den neuen Schiffahrtskanal geprägt. Das landschaftlich reizvolle Auengelände und das Stadtbild wurden nicht nur im Maßstab durch den neugebauten Kanal stark verändert. Der Stadteingang durch den Torturm des Altmühltores erhielt einen neu gestalteten, gepflasterten Platz. Zwischen der Kanaluferzone und der historischen Stadtrandbebauung wurden Panoramawege mit Platanen-Alleen und Grünanlagen angelegt. Der Main-Donau-Kanal als technisches Verkehrsbauwerk erhielt neue Brücken, die in ihrem Erscheinungsbild durch große Stützweiten, innovative Tragsysteme und

technische Ästhetik geprägt sind. Aus dieser Symbiose entstand ein spannungsreicher Gegensatz zwischen Alt und Neu. Die Schifffahrt auf dem Kanal verlangte eine lichte Durchfahrtshöhe von 10,0 m. Diese Höhenlage wird behindertengerecht mit leicht geneigten Rampen überwunden, die aus den Ufermauern herauswachsen und dann nahtlos in den korbbogenförmigen Grundriß der Brücke übergehen. Die halbrunde Führung der Grundrisse ermöglicht für die Fußgänger schöne Rundblicke zu den aufsteigenden Hängen, zur Stadt und zur Befreiungshalle.

Die Fußgängerbrücke, eine Hängebrücke, überspannt stützenfrei die Lichtraumprofile des Kanals und die beidseitigen Be-

Fußgängerbrücke. Die
Durchfahrtshöhe von
10 m für die Schiffahrt
wird mit behindertenge-
rechten Rampen zur korb-
bogenförmigen Gehbahn
erreicht.

Pedestrian bridge.
The 10 m clear height
required for navigation
resulted in a considerable
difference of levels.
This was overcome by
designing the bridge as
a large elliptical ramp
structure that is also
easily accessible to dis-
abled people.

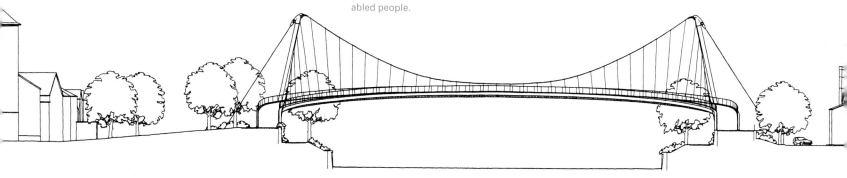

embankment, were designed to
flow into the elliptical curve of
the bridge. This curved layout
also affords pedestrians attractive panoramic views of the
surrounding slopes, the town
and the Hall of Liberation, the
Befreiungshalle.

The pedestrian bridge is a
suspension structure without
intermediate piers. It spans a
width of 62 m across the canal
and the service paths on both
sides. The service routes can be
used as footpaths. The curved
plan form of the bridge lent itself
to the design of an ideal load-
bearing system. The elliptically
curved inner ring girder acts as
the load-bearing member for the
cantilevered slab construction.
The bridge is supported – i. e.
suspended – on one side only.
Instead of the double cables that
are usually required in suspension bridge construction, a single
cable on the inner side of the
curve is sufficient. The cable is
suspended from two 18-metre-
high tubular steel masts with a
diameter of 0.66 m. These are
restrained and anchored in abutments on the banks of the canal.
The bridge has an overall width
of 4.18 m and an effective width
of 3.50 m. Floodlights were
installed at the feet of the socketed masts and directed upwards

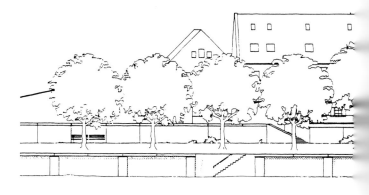

triebswege, die auch als Spazier-
wege genutzt werden. Die Spannweite beträgt 62,0 m. Die Form
der Brücke als liegender Bogen
läßt sich statisch-konstruktiv gesehen als ideales Tragsystem nüt-
zen. Der korbbogenförmige, innere Ringträger wird zum Kragträger
und muß nur auf einer Seite ge-
stützt, also aufgehängt werden.
Statt der üblichen zwei Seile bei
Hängebrücken wird nur ein Seil
auf der Innenseite des Korbbo-
gens geführt. Das Tragseil ist an

zwei abgespannten, 18 m hohen
Pylonen aus Stahl mit einem
Durchmesser von 0,66 m aufgehängt. Die Brücke hat eine Ge-
samtbreite von 4,18 m, die Nutz-
breite beträgt 3,50 m. Am Fuße
der Masten, die Pendelstäbe sind,
wurden Scheinwerfer angeordnet,
die zu den Mastköpfen strahlen.
Unter den Mastköpfen aus Gußstahl wurde ein Kreis von reflektierenden Spiegeln mit unterschiedlichen Neigungen montiert,
die die halbrunde Gehwegplatte
gleichmäßig und ohne Blendung
ausleuchten.

Die Brücke wurde vor der Fer-
tigstellung des Kanals auf Gerü-
sten gebaut und durch Anheben
der Masten und Spannen der
Tragseile ausgeschalt.

Details der Pylonabspan-
nung und Scheinwerfer-
beleuchtung zum Spiegel-
kranz am Mastkopf

Details of anchoring for
mast cable stays and
floodlights trained on
the ring of mirrors at
the heads of the pylons

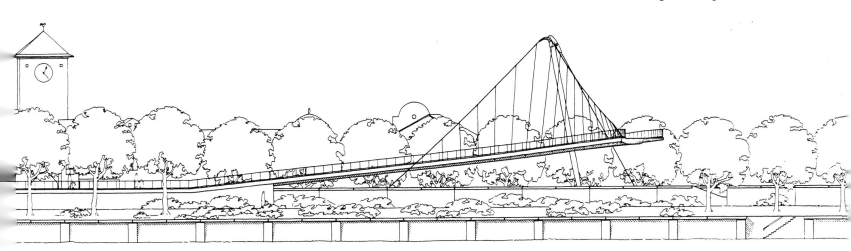

to the tips. Fixed beneath the cast-steel heads of each of the masts and tilted at various angles is a circle of mirrors that reflect the light down to illuminate the curving path of the bridge evenly and without glare.

The bridge was built on supporting scaffolding before the completion of the canal. The shuttering was removed in the process of hoisting the masts into position and tensioning the cables.

"Of all the entries submitted, this design is furthest removed from the old bridge and from the line of the tower. It shifts the pedestrian bridge roughly 60 m further west. The area round the

and 13.5 m wide. The central section is in a double prestressed box-girder construction. At the ends, where it is penetrated by circular openings for the service roads, it has a monolithic cross-section. No unnecessary projections above the carriageway or artificial embankments around the abutments were to be allowed to detract from the compact, three-dimensional form of the bridge. All structural concrete elements were poured in smooth-faced plastic-lined formwork. Sawn timber formwork was used for the approach ramps.

All other visible structures, including the canal and flood

Die Brückenplatte wächst aus den Ufermauern und schwingt über den Kanal.

The inclined ramp of the bridge grows from the embankment and flows in a broad curve over the canal.

Altmühl Gate and the attractive silhouette of the town are affected as little as possible. The height of the bridge structure with its suspension cables, hangers and pylons is perfectly acceptable in view of the elegant form of construction. The irresistible aspects of this design are the complete unity achieved between the ramp and the bridge itself, and the strikingly innovative form of construction."
Excerpt from jury report

The reinforced concrete road bridge that forms the extension of the tangential route to the west of the town is 120 m long

walls, are in reinforced concrete. The canal walls were sandblasted; the flood walls were treated with a rough-cast rendering and planted. Depending on their function, other surfaces are in exposed concrete with a smooth formwork finish. Through the work of the landscape architect, Karl Kagerer, the new canal zone has been carefully integrated into the existing urban fabric and the surrounding landscape.

Die klare, kubische Gestalt der Straßenbrücke sollte nicht durch eine übergreifende Fahrbahnplatte oder durch schräge Böschungen gestört werden.

No unnecessary carriageway projections or splayed embankments were to be allowed to detract from the clear cubic form of the road bridge.

»Der Entwurf rückt von allen eingereichten Arbeiten am entschiedensten von der alten Brücke und der Turm-Achse ab und verschiebt die Fußgängerbrücke um 60 m nach Westen. Der Bereich auf das Altmühltor und die reizvolle Stadtsilhouette ist so wenig wie möglich beeinträchtigt: Die Höhenentwicklung des Brückenbauwerkes mit den Tragseilen, Hängern und Pylonen ist bei der eleganten Konstruktion durchaus vertretbar. Was an dem Entwurf besticht, ist die völlige Einheit von Rampe und Brückenbau und die Neuartigkeit der bemerkenswert innovativen Konstruktion.«
Aus dem Jury-Protokoll

Die Straßenbrücke an der Westtangente, eine 120 m lange und 13,5 m breite Brückenanlage aus Stahlbeton, ist in ihrer Tragkonstruktion in Feldmitte als zweizelliger, vorgespannter Hohlkasten ausgeführt. Im Bereich der Brückenwiderlager und der kreisrunden Durchfahrten für die Betriebswege ist der Querschnitt monolithisch. Die plastische Gestalt der Brücke sollte nicht durch unnötige Überstände der Fahrbahnplatte oder durch künstliche Anböschungen der Widerlager gestört werden. Alle konstruktiven Bauteile wurden mit glatten Kunststoffschalungen, die Anfahrtsrampen mit rauher Holzbrettschalung betoniert.

Alle sonstigen Hochbauten, Kanal- und Hochwassermauern bestehen aus Stahlbeton, die Oberflächen je nach Funktion aus Sichtbeton mit gehobelter Schalung. Die Kanalmauern sind sandgestrahlt und die Hochwassermauern grob gespritzt und begrünt. Behutsam hat der Landschaftsarchitekt Karl Kagerer die neue Kanalzone landschaftsgärtnerisch in die Stadtlandschaft eingebunden.

Anlegetreppen für Sportboote der Ruderer und Segler

Landing stage for rowing boats, yachts, etc.

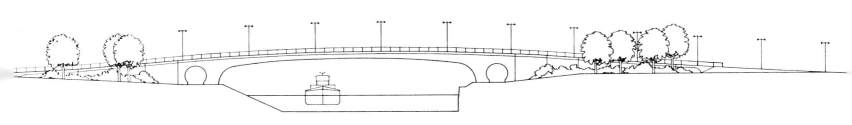

Tent Roof over
Ice-Skating Rink
in Olympia Park,
Munich

Commencement of
planning: 1980
Construction period:
1982–83

The Olympia Park in Munich is
dominated by the structures
erected for the Olympic Games in
1972, and in particular the tent
roofs over the stadium, the
sports hall and the swimming
hall. The various sporting facilities, open spaces, transport and
circulation routes, and the planting of the external areas were
conceived as a unified whole,
based on a principle of inte-
grating landscape and architecture. This formed the urban
context for the design of the
roof structure over the open-air
ice-skating rink.

Der Münchner Olympiapark wird durch die Bauten für die Olympischen Spiele 1972 geprägt, vor allem durch die Zeltdächer des Stadions, der Sport- und Schwimmhalle. Sportanlagen, Freiflächen, Verkehrswege und Vegetation wurden als Einheit geplant und realisiert. Die Integration von Landschaft und Architektur ist das prägende Prinzip des Olympiaparks und bildete den städtebaulichen Rahmen für die Überdachung der Freieisfläche.

Die Grundbedingung war, die Freieisfläche ganzjährig für den Eislauf nutzbar zu machen. Von verschiedenen Entwurfsalternativen, die zusammen mit dem Ingenieur Jörg Schlaich erarbeitet wurden, erwies sich die Zeltkonstruktion in Form eines leichten Flächentragwerkes, das an einer bogengestützten Tragkonstruktion aufgehängt ist und die auftretenden Kräfte über ein Betonwiderlager ableitet, als das wirtschaftlichste und originellste. Für die Fundierung dieses hybriden Tragwerks neben der vorhandenen Eisfläche gab es erhebliche Vorteile. Durch den über die Längsseiten über 97,42 m abgespannten Dreigurtbogen mit einer Bogenhöhe von 18,92 m wurden die Fundamente der vorhandenen Eissporthalle in keiner Weise beeinflußt. Auch die vorhandene

Betonplatte mit allen Kälteeinrichtungen für die Eisgewinnung wurde nicht beeinträchtigt.

Der schwebende Charakter des Eislaufs korrespondiert mit dem Charakter der vorgespannten Seilnetzkonstruktion, die den Ausdruck von Leichtigkeit vermittelt und für große Spannweiten in funktionaler und konstruktiver Hinsicht eine optimale Lösung darstellt.

Wichtig war, die ausladende Dimension der Überdachung von über 4500 qm mit der inneren Scheitelhöhe von 16,6 m möglichst klein zu halten, um nicht in Konkurrenz zur Nachbarschaft zu treten und um die Einfügung in die vom Landschaftsarchitekten Günther Grzimek geschaffene Topographie zu gewährleisten.

A basic requirement of the brief was that the ice rink should be open for use throughout the year. Of the various design alternatives for the roof, which were drawn up in collaboration with the engineer Jörg Schlaich, a lightweight, large-area tent construction suspended from an arched girder proved to be the most economical and original solution. The 97.42 m triangular arched truss has an arch rise of 18.92 m. The loads are transmitted to concrete abutments. There were decisive reasons for placing the foundations of this hybrid

Eislaufzelt im Olympiapark, München

Planungsbeginn: 1980
Bauzeit: 1982 – 1983

Das hybride Tragwerk:
Der Dreigurtbogen wird
durch die rein zugbean-
spruchten parallelen Seil-
netzflächen stabilisiert.

Hybrid suspension
structure: the triangular
arched truss is stabil-
ized by the network of
parallel cables, which
are subject purely
to tension stresses.

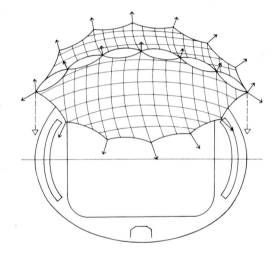

structure outside the existing ice rink. By spanning the arched truss over the length of the arena, the foundations of the existing ice-skating hall were not affected, and the existing concrete slab of the open-air ice rink – which contains all the ice-making equipment – was left intact.

The essential nature of skating, the sense of floating over the ice, is reflected in the modern technology of the network of pre-stressed roof cables. The roof conveys an impression of lightness and also provides an ideal functional and structural solution for covering large areas without intermediate columns.

With an internal height of 16.6 m at the crown and an area of over 4,500 m^2, the expanse of the roof had to be restricted as much as possible so as not to compete with the neighbouring building. Furthermore, the new roof structure had to be integrated into the topography of the site, which had been created by the landscape architect Günther Grzimek. The original plan to cover the roof with perspex – the same material as had been used for the roofs over the Olympic sports stadiums – was abandoned, partly because of the costs involved. The desired effect, which was to ensure natural indoor lighting conditions as close as possible to those of an open-air ice rink, could, therefore, be achieved only by using a translucent plastic membrane. A polyester base fabric with a PVC coating on both faces was chosen. The light-coloured skin was laid on a 75 x 75 cm timber grid, which in turn was mounted on a cable net. At the edges, where

the roof is flatter, the spacings of the timber grid were reduced to bear the much greater snow loads that may be expected here and to diminish the spans of the PVC skin, which acts as a load-bearing membrane. This reduction of the timber spacings at the edge accentuates the sweeping, upward curve of the roof. The saddleback form of suspension of the two cables along the arched crest of the roof resulted in 12 oval openings. These eye-shaped roof lights, which are covered with clear polycarbonate sheets fixed above the crest cables, form a vital part of the natural ventilation system of the hall. Through these openings, one also has a view of the triangular arched truss and the structural suspension of the cable net. The hybrid load-bearing system of the arched truss, stabilized by the two sheaves of cables, is clearly legible from beneath. The entire tent structure is ventilated without mechanical equipment. The behaviour of the thermal up-currents was investigated in wind-tunnel tests.

Blick vom Olympiaturm
auf Eislaufzelt, Eissportstadion und Leistungszen-
trum für Eiskunstlauf

View from the Olympic
Tower: in the foreground,
the ice rink with its tent
roof; beyond this, the
ice-sports stadium and
the ice-skating training
centre

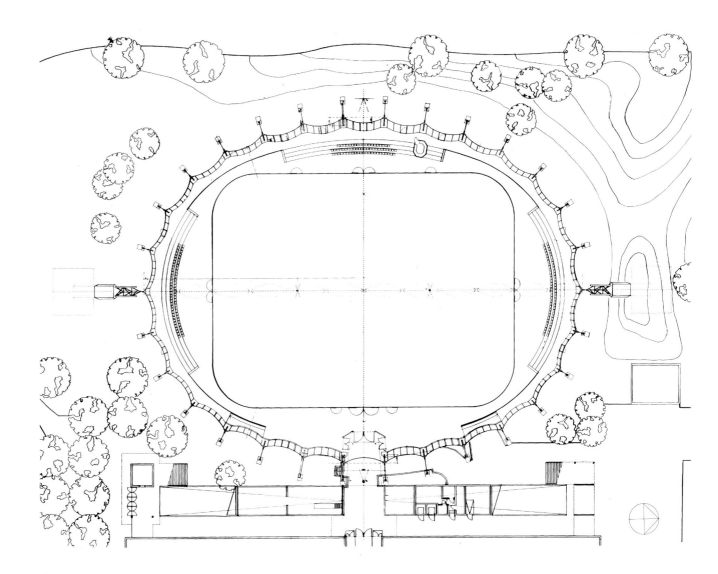

Das Eislaufzelt wird vom
bestehenden Eissport-
stadion, wo sich Kassen,
Umkleide- und Nebenräu-
me befinden, erschlossen.
Die notwendige direkte
Anbindung wurde mit
einem verglasten Verbin-
dungsgang geschaffen.

Access to the tent-
covered rink is from the
existing ice-sports stadium, where the ticket
office, changing rooms
and ancillary spaces are
also located. The two
structures are directly
linked by a glazed strip.

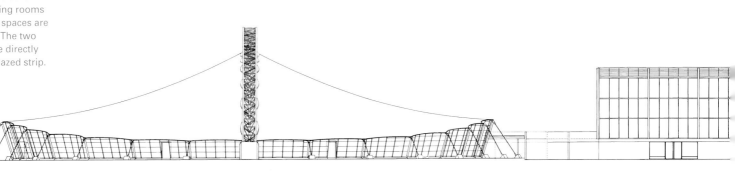

In collaboration with Jörg Schlaich, a new kind of membrane façade was also developed. It represents an ideal solution in respect of the structural behaviour of the two elements between which it is fixed: at the top, a network of cables suspended from the central arched truss and subject to deformation; and at the bottom, the rigid concrete foundations. This new façade system was modelled on the principle of lead-jointed Gothic windows. The membrane-like quality of stained-glass construction was applied to the design of the façade. Double cables are spanned from the flexible cables at the edge of the roof to the rigid peripheral foundations. The panes of glass, which can move laterally within the horizontal glazing bars, are attached to these pairs of cables with specially designed fixing elements. This constructional detail allows optimum freedom of movement between the load-bearing cables and the enclosing walls in both a vertical and horizontal direction. The technical and structural effectiveness and the functional design of this newly developed membrane façade were investigated in trials, using full-scale models.

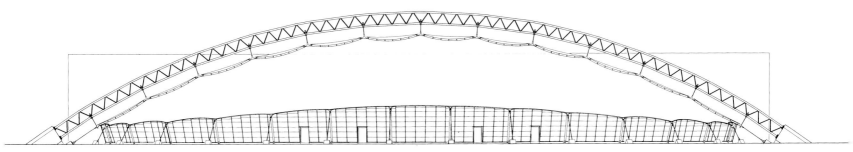

Die ursprünglich geplante Eindeckung mit demselben Acrylglas, das für die Olympiabauten verwendet wurde, scheiterte u. a. an den Kosten. Die angestrebte Wirkung, die den natürlichen Lichtverhältnissen einer Freieisfläche am nächsten kommt, war deshalb nur durch die Eindeckung mit einer transluzenten Kunststoffolie zu erreichen. Gewählt wurde ein Polyester-Trägergewebe mit beidseitiger PVC-Beschichtung. Die helle Folie wurde auf einen Holzrost von 75 x 75 cm im Quadrat aufgebracht, der auf ein Seilnetz montiert ist. Der Holzrost wird der Schneelast wegen an den Dachrändern mit den wesentlich flacheren Neigungen dichter, die Spannweiten für die Kunststoffolie, die in ihrer Tragfunktion als Membrane wirkt, werden verkürzt. Die Verdichtung der Hölzer an den Rändern verdeutlicht das schwingende Aufsteigen der Dachflächen. Die beiden oberen Gratseile bilden durch ihre Sattelaufhängung zwölf ovale Öffnungen. Diese augenförmigen Oberlichter sind mit Polycarbonat-Glasklar-Platten abgedeckt und mit Abstand auf die Gratseile montiert. Sie garantieren die natürliche Lüftung der Halle. Durch diese Augen wird der Blick auf die konstruktive Aufhängung der Seilnetze und auf den Dreigurtbogen frei. Die hybride Tragwirkung des Bogens, durch die beiden Seilnetzscharen stabilisiert, ist so auch von innen deutlich ablesbar. Das ganze Eislaufzelt wird ohne mechanische Ausrüstung be- und entlüftet; in Windkanalversuchen wurde der thermische Auftrieb untersucht.

Mit Jörg Schlaich wurde eine neue Fassadenkonstruktion entwickelt, eine Membranfassade, die für das konstruktive Verhalten der an einem Bogen aufgehängten, verformbaren Seilnetze und der starren Betonfundamente eine optimale Lösung bildet. Das Leitbild waren die historischen Konstruktionen von gotischen Fenstern mit Bleiverglasung. Das Membranhafte der Bleifenster wurde auf die Konstruktion der Fassade übertragen. Von den oberen weichen Randseilen zu den starren Randfundamenten wurden zweifache Seilscharren gespannt. Die verschiebbaren Glasscheiben in den horizontalen Metallsprossen wurden mit den vertikalen Seilscharren durch entsprechend ausgebildete Befestigungselemente verbunden. Diese konstruktive Ausbildung läßt eine optimale Bewegungsmöglichkeit von Seiltragwerk und Raumabschluß in vertikaler und horizontaler Richtung zu. In Modellversuchen im Maßstab 1:1 wurde die technisch-konstruktive Wirkungsweise und die funktionale Gestalt der neuentwickelten Membran-Fassade überprüft.

An den etwa 7,75 m
voneinander entfernten
Umlenkpunkten der
Randseile werden die
Kräfte aus den Seilnetzen
gesammelt und mit Stahl-
gußsätteln über Pendel-
stützen zu den Funda-
menten weitergeleitet.

At node points at roughly
7.75 m centres along the
peripheral roof cables,
loads from the cable
network are bundled
and transmitted via cast-
steel saddle pieces and
hinged columns to the
foundations.

Oben: Stützenkopf als
Gußstahlsattel. Die funk-
tionale Gestalt macht
die statisch-konstruktive
Aufgabe des Bauteils
ablesbar. Mitte: Fußpunkt
der Pendelstützen

Top: head of column as
cast-steel saddle piece.
The constructional pur-
pose of this element is
revealed in the functional
form. Centre: foot of
hinged column

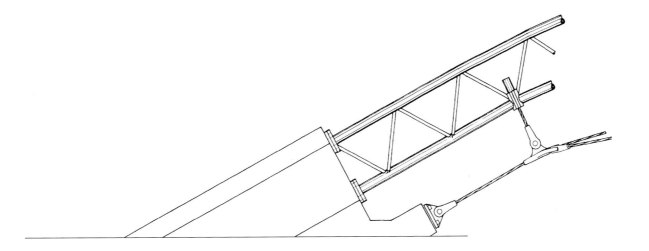

Die zwei Gratseile der beiden Seilnetze werden gemeinsam über Gratseilsättel und die Hänger am Bogen aufgehängt. Die Hänger sind kurze Stahlseile mit 60 mm Durchmesser. Sie sind mit aufgegossenen Gabelseilköpfen verankert.

The two cables along the crest of the roof, to which the cable networks are attached, are jointly suspended from saddle pieces and hangers fixed to the central truss. The hangers consist of short lengths of 60 mm diameter steel cable with forked cable heads cast on.

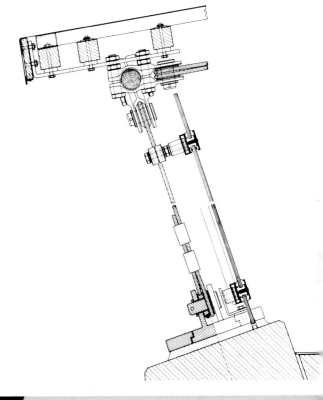

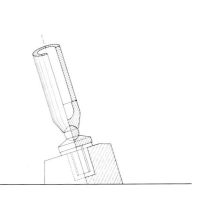

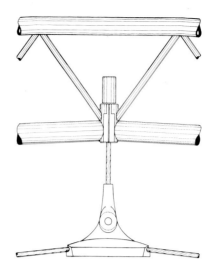

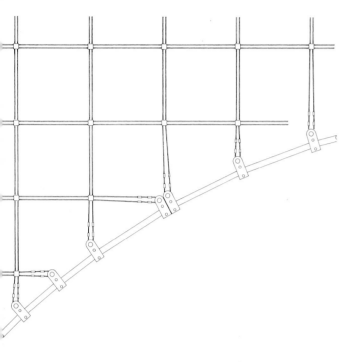

Der Dreigurtbogen mit einer Spannweite von rund 100 m hat eine Bauhöhe von nur 1,45 m. Der Bogen wurde mit den bereits eingebauten Hängern in fünf Schüssen montiert und dann vermessen. Die Hängerkoordinaten mußten eine hohe Genauigkeit erreichen.

The triangular arched truss, which spans a distance of approx. 100 m, is only 1.45 m deep. The five sections of the truss, with inbuilt hangers, were assembled on site and then levelled. The coordinates for the hangers had to be extremely precise.

An dem Netzknoten sind die Befestigungselemente für den Holzrost sichtbar. Die Rollen und Seile für den hydraulischen Hebevorgang der Seilnetze hängen am Bogen.

The fixings for the timber grid can be seen at the node points of the cable network. The pulleys and cables for the hydraulic lifting of the network are suspended from the arched truss.

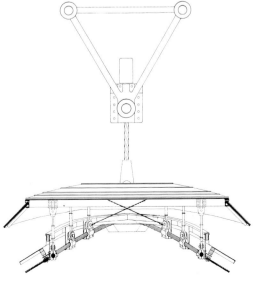

Die beiden Gratseile bil-
den durch ihre Aufhän-
gung an den Gratsätteln
zwölf ovale Öffnungen.
Diese augenförmigen
Oberlichter sind autonome
Bauteile, die ›schwim-
mend‹ auf die Gratseile
aufgesetzt sind. Sie geben
einen freien Ausblick auf
den freigespannten Drei-
gurtbogen und machen
die Tragwirkung der hybriden Seilnetzkonstruktion
deutlich ablesbar.

The saddleback form of
suspension of the two
cables along the crest of
the roof results in 12 oval
openings. These eye-
shaped roof lights are
independent construc-
tional elements that
"float" on the cables.
They allow a clear view
of the triangular arched
truss and reveal the
load-bearing function
of the hybrid cable-net
structure.

"To enable the open-air ice rink to the west of the worthy but somewhat bulky ice sports stadium to be used all year round, regardless of weather conditions, a lightweight and obviously column-free covering was required. The architects and engineers jointly found an inspired solution to this problem in the form of a tent roof, 100 m long and roughly 19 m high at the crown, suspended from a triangular arched trussed girder. All the loads from this girder are transmitted to two massive concrete abutments. . . . The logic of this structure, its beauty, elegance and extraordinary daring convey the impression that true functionalism, born of technical intelligence, results in effective aesthetic expression. This is what makes the continued development of wide-span, large-area, lightweight load-bearing structures one of the outstanding phenomena of the post-Olympics period in Munich, a phenomenon that is of more than just local significance."
Christoph Hackelsberger in *Stahl und Form*, Munich, 1983, p.1

Windkräfte bewirken eine horizontale Verschiebung zwischen Randseilen und Baugrund – eine biegeweiche Membran-Fassade ist daher erforderlich. Zwischen Randseil und Ringfundament sind Fassadenseile gespannt. Verschiebungen senkrecht zu den Fassadenglasscheiben werden leichter durch liegende Formate mit geringer Höhe der Glaselemente aufgenommen.

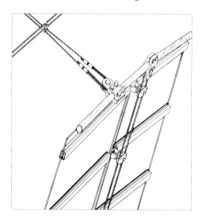

The horizontal deflection of the peripheral roof cables caused by wind loads necessitated an elastic membrane façade construction. Façade cables run between the cable at the edge of the roof and the peripheral foundations. The deformation caused by wind is easily absorbed by a construction using panes of glass of horizontal format and limited height.

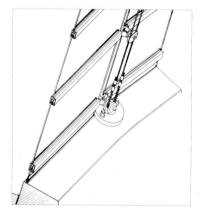

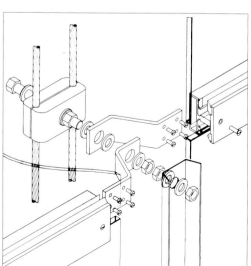

Die Verschiebungen in der Fassadenebene machen erforderlich, daß jedes Glaselement an einem der horizontalen Befestigungspunkte in Längsrichtung auf Bürsten gleiten kann. An den Fassadenseilen werden horizontale Aluminiumprofile im Abstand von 60 cm befestigt, in denen die Scheibe im unteren Profil geklemmt werden und im oberen Profil horizontal gleiten kann.

To allow for deformation within the plane of the façade, every pane of glass was set in a brush bed along one horizontal edge to permit lateral movement. The horizontal aluminium glazing sections were fixed to the façade cables at 60 cm centres. The lower edges of the panes of glass are clamped in these sections and are free to glide horizontally in the upper glazing bars.

»Um die westlich des eher klobig-
biederen Eissportstadions gelegene Freieisfläche ganzjährig und
wetterunabhängig nutzen zu können, suchte man nach einer leichten, selbstverständlich stützenfrei-
en Überdachung. Architekten und
Ingenieure lösten gemeinsam dieses Problem auf geniale Weise
durch einen 100 m überspannenden, im Scheitel ca. 19 m hohen

stählernen Dreigurtfachwerkbogen, der imstande ist, alle auftretenden Kräfte auf zwei mächtige
Betonwiderlager abzutragen. ...
Die Logik der Konstruktion, ihre
Schönheit, Eleganz und außeror-
dentliche Kühnheit vermitteln den
Eindruck, wirkliche Funktionalität,
erfunden von technischer Intelligenz, führe zu ästhetischer
Wirkung. Dies macht die Weiterentwicklung der Idee eines weit-
gespannten leichten Flächentrag-
werks zu einem der größten

baulichen Ereignisse der Münchner Nacholympiazeit, deren Auswirkungen weit über das Lokale
hinausgehen.«
Christoph Hackelsberger, in: *Stahl
und Form*, München 1983, S. 1

"One simply has . . . to look at the roof to see that the architect who covered this large ice-skating rink understood his task – like the sportspeople who use it – above all as a question of elegance. The hall could have assumed this and no other form, I thought. That is not entirely the case, but it is nevertheless true. . . .

From the outside, the white, turtle-shaped roof seems almost frail alongside the box-like form of the old hall; no, more than that: it looks graceful. Inside, one is surprised by the sheer breadth of space, an impression evoked by the serene brightness that floods the interior, without the white light seeming cold to the eye. The 12 oval openings along the crest of the roof are meant to afford visitors a glimpse of the

sky: but even more importantly, they allow fresh air to enter. Glass covers over the openings protect the hall against rain, and nets at the side prevent birds straying inside.

The large expanse of the arena was to be covered as originally, as lightly and as economically as possible – and without supporting columns, of course. The easy elegance of the hall reflects

in a most wonderful manner the evidently so pleasurable sporting sensations of gliding, leaping and dancing that take place within it.

In view of such a sound expression of architecture that seeks to derive aesthetic profit from its primary constraints, slogans such as 'postmodern' are simply superfluous."
Manfred Sack in *Stàhl und Form*, Munich, 1983, p.1

»Man braucht sich nur in der Halle umzusehen, das Dach zu betrachten, um zu meinen, daß der Architekt, der den großen Eislaufplatz überdacht hat, seine Aufgabe wie die Sportler vor allem als eine Affäre der Eleganz verstand. Diese Halle, dachte ich, hatte nur so und keinen Deut anders werden können. Das stimmt zwar nicht, aber es ist wahr. . . .

Von außen wirkt das weiße Schildkrötendach neben der kastenförmigen alten Halle beinahe zierlich, mehr: graziös. Innen ist man überrascht von der Weite, ein Eindruck, der durch die auffallend heitere Helligkeit hervorgerufen wird, die sie durchflutet, ohne mit ihrem weißen Licht die Augen zu erkälten. Die zwölf ovalen Öffnungen im Dachfirst sollen den Blick zum Himmel öffnen, vor allem aber strömt da frische Luft herein; Glashauben schützen gegen Schlagregen, Netze an ihren Seiten hindern Vögel daran, sich ins Innere zu verirren.

Die ausladenden Dimensionen der Halle sollten so originell, so leicht, so einfach, so preiswert wie möglich überspannt werden, stützenfrei. Ihre gelassene Eleganz spiegelt auf wunderbare Weise den so offensichtlich lustbaren Sport, der darin gelaufen, gesprungen, getanzt wird.

Schlagwörter wie ›postmodern‹ machen sich angesichts einer so soliden Architektur, die versucht, aus ihren primären Bedingungen ästhetischen Gewinn zu ziehen, überflüssig.«
Manfred Sack, in: *Stahl und Form*, München 1983, S. 1

Wettbewerbsmodell.
Links im Bild die Nationalgalerie von Ludwig Mies
van der Rohe. Die Sockel-
zone wird um zwei Atrien
erweitert. Von Baumstüt-
zen getragene Glasflächen
zur Belichtung der Aus-
stellungsräume, wobei
das Zenitlicht ausgeblen-
det wird. Die kammförmig
ausgebildeten Wohnge-
bäude für die Mitarbeiter
der Neuen Nationalgalerie
schließen den Komplex
ab.

Rechts: Ansicht und
Längsschnitt. Die aus
Rundrohren konstruierten
Baumstützen gewähren
nahezu stützenfreie
Ausstellungsräume
durch Kräftebündelung.

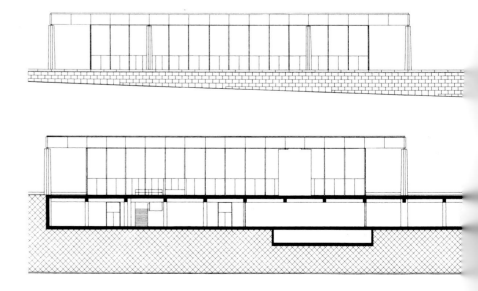

Competition model.
On the left: the National
Gallery by Ludwig Mies
van der Rohe. The raised
plinth was extended to
form two new courtyards.
Large areas of glass sup-
ported by tree-like structures allow daylight to
enter the exhibition
spaces. Zenith light is
nevertheless deflected
away from the gallery.
The complex is termin-
ated at the opposite
end by the comb-like
layout of the housing
for the staff of the New
National Gallery.

Bottom: elevation and
longitudinal section. The
tree-like tubular supporting system concentrates
the loads at certain points
and thus ensures exhibi-
tion spaces that are virtually free of intermediate
columns.

Im Rahmen der Internationalen Bauausstellung – IBA wurde ein engerer internationaler Wettbewerb ausgeschrieben, der vor allem die Erweiterung der Neuen Nationalgalerie zum Ziel hatte. Außerdem sollten 24 Wohnungen für die Mitarbeiter am Kulturforum geschaffen werden.

Eingeladen waren die Büros, Max Bill, Alexander von Branca, Harald Deilmann, Fehling und Gogel, Hölzinger und Goepfert, Christine Jachmann, Al Mansfeld, Richard Meier, Gerd Neumann, Renzo Piano, Barna von Sartory, Peter C. von Seidlein und Kurt Ackermann.

Das Urteil der Jury zu der vorliegenden Arbeit lautete: »Der Entwurf schafft klare und eindeutige stadträumliche Beziehungen. Die kammartige Wohnbebauung im Westen definiert den Straßenraum an der Hitzigallee und markiert die Ecke zur Sigismundstraße, ohne durch Kleinteiligkeit die in diesem Stadtgebiet gegebenen Größenordnungen herunterzuspielen. Dem bestehenden Bau der Nationalgalerie wird voller Respekt erwiesen, die Pavillons des Erweiterungsbaus sichern andererseits auch dem Neubau Ablesbarkeit. Mit zwei Spangen nördlich und südlich des Skulpturenhofes ist der Neubauteil so an die Nationalgalerie angeschlossen, daß sich auf dem Niveau des Untergeschosses ein logischer Rundgang herstellt, der für den aus der Nationalgalerie kommenden Besucher keine Orientierungsprobleme aufgibt. Im Erweiterungsbau bietet der Verfasser in einer logischen Grundrißfigur zwei Rundgänge durch günstig geschnittene Säle und Räume an. Die Baumstützen legen die Räume nicht so weit fest, daß sich für ihre Nutzung Probleme ergäben. Nicht ganz leicht auffindbar ist der Zugang des Neubaueingangs durch Treppenläufe von der Plattform. Sowohl die Museums- wie die Wohnbauten nehmen durch ihre noble und großstädtische Form für sich ein.«

Erweiterung der Neuen Nationalgalerie
Wohnen am Kulturforum, Berlin

Wettbewerb 1981
2. Preis, ein 1. Preis wurde nicht vergeben

Planungsbeginn: 1982
Bauzeit: 1984–1986

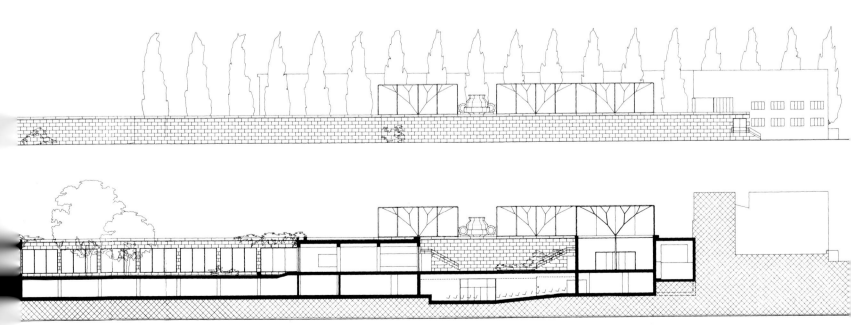

Extension of New
National Gallery
Housing in the
Kulturforum, Berlin

Competition: 1981
Second prize; no first
prize awarded
Commencement of
planning: 1982
Construction period:
1984 – 86

In the context of the International
Building Exhibition, IBA, in
Berlin, an international architectural competition was held for
the extension of the New National Gallery and the erection of 24
staff dwellings in the Kulturforum.

The following architects were
invited to participate in the
competition: Max Bill, Alexander
von Branca, Harald Deilmann,
Fehling and Gogel, Hölzinger and
Goepfert, Christine Jachmann,
Al Mansfeld, Richard Meier,
Gerd Neumann, Renzo Piano,
Barna von Sartory, Peter C. von
Seidlein and Kurt Ackermann.

spaces. The tree-like column supports do not restrict the use of
the rooms to such an extent as to
be problematic. The entrance to
the new development is not so
easily found. It is reached via
staircases from the platform. In
their noble metropolitan form,
both the museum and the housing are convincing urban developments."

The expansion of the New
National Gallery was cancelled
without explanation, but plans
for residential development were
carried out.

The aim of this development
was to build a mixture of owner-

Lageplan zum Wett-
bewerbsentwurf für
die Erweiterung der
Nationalgalerie

Site plan: part of
competition entry for
the extension of the
National Gallery

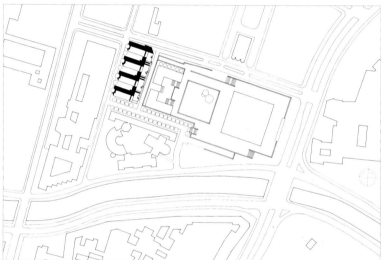

According to the assessment of
the jury, "The design creates a
set of clear, unequivocal urban
spatial relationships. The comb-
like layout of the housing to the
west defines the street space
along Hitzigallee and articulates
the corner at the junction with
Sigismundstrasse, without reducing the urban scale of the area
through a fragmentation of the
structure. Due respect is also
shown to the existing National
Gallery, although the extension
pavilions ensure that the new
development is legible as an
independent entity. With two
tracts flanking the sculpture
courtyard to the north and south,
the new development is linked to
the National Gallery in such a
way that a coherent circulation
route is created at lower ground
floor level. For visitors coming
from the gallery, the route presents no problems in terms of
orientation. In the extension, with
its logical overall layout, the
architect offers two alternative
routes through a series of well-
proportioned halls and other

occupied flats and publicly assist-
ed rented units. The programme
comprised some 60 –70 two- and
three-room dwellings and a number of studio flats. In the end,
75 dwellings were built. In urban
planning terms, the scheme was
meant to enliven the Kulturforum
and create a clear, unambiguous
set of relationships between the
open spaces. The comb-like
arrangement of the buildings led
to the development of a series
of courtyard spaces that open
on to the street and provide a
high degree of habitable quality.
The increase in the number of
dwellings, however, meant that
it was not possible to retain the
pleasingly low eaves heights
as originally planned, and a
greater building volume had to
be accepted.

Gegenüber dem Wettbe-
werbsentwurf wurden die
Wohngebäude deutlich
erhöht; im Hintergrund die
Nationalgalerie. Der für
die Erweiterung der Nationalgalerie vorgesehene
Platz blieb unbebaut.

View of the housing
development, consider-
ably heightened in
comparison with the
competition design. In
the background is the
National Gallery. The
space foreseen for
the gallery extension
remains undeveloped.

Die Erweiterung der Neuen Nationalgalerie wurde ohne Angabe
von Gründen ganz aufgegeben.
Die Wohnungen wurden ausgeführt.

Die Zielsetzung war, Wohnungen im Eigentum und Mietwoh-
nungen im öffentlich geförderten
sozialen Wohnungsbau zu schaffen. Es sollten 60 – 70 Wohneinheiten mit Zwei- und Dreizim-
merwohnungen sowie einige
Atelierwohnungen entstehen;
realisiert wurden schließlich
75 Wohneinheiten. Die städtebauliche Vorgabe war, das Kulturforum zu beleben und gleichzeitig
klare, eindeutige Stadtraumbezie-
hungen zu schaffen. Durch die
kammartige Anordnung der Baukörper entstanden zur Straßenseite hin offene Höfe, die eine hohe
Wohnqualität gewähren. Durch
die Erweiterung der Zahl der Wohnungen mußten die städtebaulich
angenehmeren, niedrigen Traufhöhen aufgegeben und das größere Bauvolumen hingenommen
werden.

In Material, Form und Gestalt
nimmt die Wohnbebauung die

Berliner Tradition des Neuen Bauens der zwanziger Jahre auf und
führt sie mit einfachen Mitteln
zu einem zurückhaltenden Erscheinungsbild fort. Weiße, klare
Baukörper, ruhige Putzfassaden
mit eingeschnittenen Fenster-
öffnungen vermitteln zur Nachbarschaft der Kulturbauten und
heben den Gegensatz Kultur und
Wohnen auf. Die Laubengänge
sind aus funktionalen und gestalterischen Gründen verglast. Die
Anlage besitzt bewußt keine
spektakuläre Formenvielfalt und
Details; Material und Bauweise
stimmen überein. Die Wohnbauten erhielten einen Granitsockel,
um die Korrespondenz zur Umgebung herzustellen. Die Nationalgalerie von Ludwig Mies van der
Rohe bleibt die beherrschende
Dominante der Gesamtanlage.
Auch die Solitärsituation des
Wissenschaftszentrums von
James Stirling wird nicht beeinträchtigt.

In its use of materials, in its form and design, the housing scheme represents a continuation of the tradition of the Modern Movement in Berlin in the 1920s. Simple materials are used to create a development of restrained appearance.

Clear, white cubic forms, with undemonstrative rendered façades and rectangular openings cut into them, ease the transition to the nearby cultural buildings and help to resolve the opposition between structures for the arts and housing. The access galleries are glazed for functional and formal reasons. The development deliberately avoids extravagant details and spectacular formal variety. The materials and the form of construction are attuned to each other. The housing tracts are set on a granite plinth layer that establishes a relationship to the surrounding developments. Mies van der Rohe's National Gallery remains the dominant structure in the area, and the special position assumed by James Stirling's science centre is not affected in any way.

Die Wohnungen in den Kämmen sind über verglaste Laubengänge direkt erschlossen. Im Hintergrund zwei Verwaltungshochhäuser von Paul Baumgarten.

Glazed galleries provide direct access to the dwellings in the teeth of the comb. The two high-rise office blocks to the rear are by Paul Baumgarten.

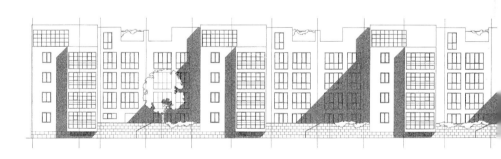

Grundriß Erdgeschoß mit den Freianlagen

Ground floor plan with external areas

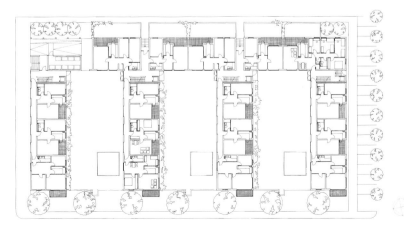

Wohnanlage Gottfried-Böhm-Ring, München

Planungsbeginn:
Bauteil A, B, C, 1981;
D, E, 1983

Bauzeit: A, B, C, 1983 –1986,
D, E, 1985 –1988

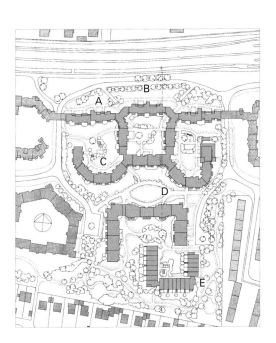

Das 16 ha große, zusammenhängende Baugebiet der BHB südlich der Heckenstallerstraße – ein Abschnitt des Mittleren Rings – wurde als allgemeines Wohngebiet ausgewiesen. Damit konnten dort Verwaltungen, Büros, Praxen, Gaststätten und Läden untergebracht werden. Der den Architekten vorgegebene Bebauungsplan war in den Bauteilen A, B, C in der Figuration der Einzelgebäude stark bewegt. Im Rahmen der genehmigten Baulinien wurden die Gebäudeformen gestrafft. Die nördliche sechsgeschossige Randbebauung wirkt als aktiver Lärmschutz und schirmt das neue Quartier nach Süden von der stark belasteten Emissionsquelle des Mittleren Rings ab.
   Die von der Fassade deutlich abgesetzten Laubengänge geben der geschlossenen Hauszeile eine deutlich gegliederte Kontur und wirken als abwechslungsreiche Bauelemente der einzelnen Häuser. Alle Aufenthaltsräume in den parallel zum Ring liegenden Bauteilen sind nach der lärmabgewandten Südseite, also zu den Wohnhöfen hin, orientiert. Die zusammenhängenden Baukörper wurden so geplant, daß nach Süden großzügig gestaltete, ruhige Gartenhöfe von unterschiedlicher Intimität entstehen. Durch die Abstaffelung der Häuser nach

Housing Development on Gottfried-Böhm-Ring, Munich

Commencement of planning: sections
A, B, C 1981;
D, E 1983
Construction period: sections
A, B, C 1983 – 86;
D, E 1985 – 88

Grundrisse Bauteile A, B. Die Erschließung der Wohnungen an der verkehrsreichen Ringstraße erfolgt über abgesetzte Laubengänge. Wohn- und Schlafräume orientieren sich zu den ruhigen Gartenhöfen.

Plans of sections A and B. Access to the dwellings situated on the busy ring road is via galleries that are set off against the façade. Living rooms and bedrooms are oriented to the quiet courtyard gardens to the south.

The 16-hectare BHB site south of Heckenstallerstrasse, which forms part of the middle ring road round the city, was designated as an area for general housing construction. This meant that administration buildings, offices, professional practices, restaurants and shops could be erected there as well. In the development plan for this site, an irregular configuration was foreseen for the buildings in sections A, B and C. The design straightened the layout within the approved building lines. The six-storey peripheral development to the north functions as an acoustic screen that shields the new neighbourhood to the south from the high levels of noise from the busy ring road.

The access galleries, clearly set off against the façade, articulate the continuous housing strips and lend them a three-dimensional quality. All living spaces in the tract parallel to the ring road are oriented to the quieter courtyard areas to the south. The continuous strips of housing were laid out in such a way that, on the south-facing aspects, generous, quiet garden courtyards are created that allow various degrees of intimacy. By stepping down the limbs extending to the south by two storeys, it was possible to achieve ideal sunlight conditions. In the central zone, the arms of a four-storey U-shaped development interlock with those of a two-storey tract of terrace housing that is also laid out in a U-form. All ground floor dwellings have small gardens that are screened from view. The dwellings on the upper floors have loggias. Those at the top of the building are protected by glass roofs. The flats in the roof storey have planted and partially covered roof gardens. In their layout, all dwellings were oriented to the sun. The single-storey basement garage is separate from the housing blocks, but is easily accessible. The entrance and exit ramps are covered with wired-glass enclosures.

The external walls of the development are in rendered brickwork and, like the reinforced concrete access galleries and loggias, are painted white. The protective glass roofs are supported by a galvanized steel construction. The external works were designed by the landscape architect Paul Schraudenbach.

"On a site with all kinds of disadvantages, Kurt Ackermann has succeeded in creating a cheerful, lively housing estate that lets one forget that only a few metres away thousands and thousands of cars are driving past every day. He achieves this without sealing off the development hermetically from the road. He does not give the cold shoulder to the car drivers who are stuck here in traffic jams every day, but conveys an impression of a housing development where life is worth living."
Lilli Thurn und Taxis, "Architektur in Bayern" in *Prosekt Revus Slovenskes Architektury* 3/1993

Die landschaftsgärtnerisch
gestalteten Innenhöfe der
Wohnanlage wurden vom
Autoverkehr freigehalten.

The landscaped residen-
tial courtyards were kept
free of vehicular traffic.

Süden um je zwei Geschosse
werden optimale Verhältnisse zur
Besonnung erreicht. Die Mittelzone der Anlage bildet ein vierge-
schossiges U, in das die ebenfalls
U-förmig angeordneten zweigeschossigen Reihenhäuser hinein-
greifen. Alle Erdgeschoßwoh-
nungen haben einen kleinen,
sichtgeschützten Vorgarten. Alle
Geschoßwohnungen besitzen
Loggien, die obersten mit
Schutzdächern aus Glas. Die
Dachwohnungen haben begrünte,
ebenfalls teilweise überdachte
Dachterrassen. Die Grundrisse der
Wohnungen wurden zur Sonne
hin entwickelt. Die eingeschossigen Tiefgaragen sind von den
Wohngebäuden getrennt, aber

direkt zu erreichen, die Ein- und
Ausfahrten wurden mit Drahtglas-
dächern abgedeckt.

    Die Außenwände bestehen
aus geputzten Mauerziegeln und
sind wie die Laubengänge und
Loggien aus Stahlbeton weiß
gestrichen. Die Schutzdächer aus
verzinktem Stahl tragen eine Glas-
abdeckung. Die Außenanlagen
stammen von dem Landschaftsarchitekten Paul Schraudenbach.

»Kurt Ackermann ist es hier ge-
lungen, auf einem Grundstück mit
allerlei Standortnachteilen eine
heitere, aufgelockerte Wohnsied-
lung zu errichten, die vergessen
macht, daß einige Meter entfernt
Tag für Tag Abertausende von
Autos vorbeiziehen. Dabei
schließt er die Anlage zur Straße
nicht hermetisch ab, zeigt den
Autofahrern, die hier täglich
im Stau stehen, nicht die kalte
Schulter, sondern vermittelt den
Eindruck einer lebenswerten
Wohnanlage.«
Lilli Thurn und Taxis, *Architektur
in Bayern*, in: *Prosekt Revus
Slovenskes Architektury*, 3/1993

Die abgesetzten Lauben-
gänge verhindern die
direkte Einsicht und
geben den Wohnungen
eine gewisse ungestörte
Intimität.

The inset galleries pre-
vent overlooking and
lend the dwellings a
degree of intimacy.

Bauteil D. Alle Erdge-
schoßwohnungen haben
kleine Vorgärten, die
Geschoßwohnungen
Loggien, den Dachwoh-
nungen sind Dachterras-
sen vorgelagert.

Section D. All ground
floor dwellings have
small attached gardens.
The flats on the upper
floors were designed
with open loggias. The
dwellings on the top
storey have partially
covered roof gardens.

Grundriß Bauteil D.
Obergeschoß

Upper floor plan,
section D

Der verglaste Zugang zur
Tiefgarage im Innenhof
des Bauteils E

Glazed enclosure to
basement garage access
ramp in the courtyard of
section E

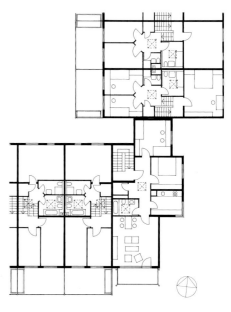

Bauteil E. Grundrisse der
Reihen- und Eckhäuser,
Obergeschoß

Section E. Upper floor
plan of terrace houses
with corner dwellings

Bauteil E. Grundrisse der
Reihen- und Eckhäuser,
Erdgeschoß

Section E. Ground floor
plan of terrace houses
with corner dwellings

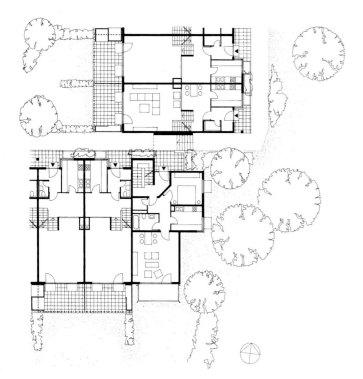

Die Bauweise der Reihen-
häuser ist an den ruhigen,
weiß verputzten Lochfas-
saden ablesbar.

The form of construction
of the terrace houses is
legible in the calm white
rendered façades with
punched openings.

Die Vorgärten sind vor
Einsicht geschützt,
die Sitzplätze sind mit
Glasdächern überdeckt.

The attached gardens are
screened from view. The
sitting areas are covered
with glass roofs.

Post Office
Regensburg 1

Competition: 1983
First prize
Commencement of
planning: 1984
Construction period:
1988 – 91

This new distribution centre was erected to improve the efficiency of postal operations in eastern Bavaria. The post office contains a large number of complex functional areas. Its main purpose, however, is to sort and distribute the incoming and outgoing letters and parcels in the region of east Bavaria. Other facilities accommodated in the building are a customer zone, postal deliveries for the Regensburg area, a training centre, administration offices, social functions and a canteen.

The design of the development reflects the translation of these different uses into visual form.

The five-storey post office building is 218 m long, 43 m wide and up to 18 m high. It is divided into four main functional realms. The three-storey head structure, in which the counter areas, deliveries department and training rooms are located, forms an urban closing element to the station square. The canteen is situated in the slightly set-back roof storey, which affords an open view over the historical city centre of Regensburg.

The two-storey mail-handling tract, 22 m deep and roughly 168 m long, is laid out along the railway lines to the rear of the development. Here, all post arriving by road or rail – parcels on

Postamt Regensburg 1

Wettbewerb 1983
1. Preis

Planungsbeginn: 1984
Bauzeit: 1988 – 1991

Um die Dienstleistung der Post in
Ostbayern effektiver zu gestalten,
wurde ein neues Verteilerzentrum
errichtet. Das Postamt beherbergt
eine Vielzahl komplexer Funktionsbereiche. Seine Hauptaufgabe ist
es, die gesamte ankommende
und abgehende Brief- und Paket-
post des ostbayerischen Raumes
zu sortieren und zu verteilen.
Auch der Kundenbereich und die
Postzustellung für die Regensburger Zustellbezirke, ein Schulungszentrum, Verwaltung, Sozialbe-
reiche und Kantine sind in diesem
Gebäude untergebracht. In der
formalen Umsetzung ist die Gestalt des Gebäudes durch die
Visualisierung der vielfältigen
Funktionen geprägt.
    Das fünfgeschossige, 218,0 m
lange, 43,0 m breite und bis zu
18,0 m hohe Postamt gliedert sich
im wesentlichen in vier Nutzungsbereiche. Der am Bahnhofsplatz

the ground floor, letters on the first floor – is sorted, reloaded on to lorries or trains and dispatched. The heavy loads that have to be handled, the wide spans, and the requirements of fire regulations necessitated a heavy reinforced concrete skeleton-frame structure, which at the same time functions as a thermal storage mass.

The protective roof and façade of the unheated loading hall are designed as a lightweight, transparent steel and glass construction. The load-bearing structure, consisting of slender steel trussed beams, was located externally and left visible, in order to articulate the great length of this tract. The façade is clad with storey-height point-fixed panels of single glazing with open joints. The transparency of this part of the building allows its internal operations to be seen from outside and also facilitates naturally lighted workplaces, with daylight penetrating into the depth of the space. The relatively small load require-

ments of the administration tract on the top floor allowed it to be built in a lightweight steel construction set on top of the main structure. Most of the office spaces are oriented to the quiet, planted internal courtyards. Between the head structure and the loading hall, the free-standing glazed main staircase forms a striking vertical element that articulates the functional design of the overall complex.

The curtain-wall façade – a white glass and metal skin, consisting of prefabricated elements to a 140 x 70 cm grid – establishes a visual unity between the individual functional realms. The proportion of the areas of transparent glazing in relation to opaque panels can be adjusted at any time to accommodate later changes of use. Large areas of thermally insulating glazing, in conjunction with the internal storage mass of the concrete structure, facilitate the passive exploitation of solar energy and help to reduce the energy requirements of the building.

Additional artificial lighting is necessary in only a few areas. The external, translucent blinds, which provide optimum protection against insolation and glare, form a second layer to the façade and thus lend it a three-dimensional quality.

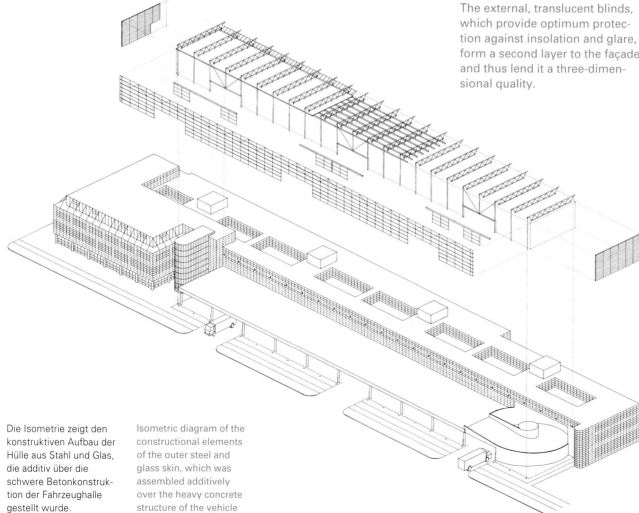

Die Isometrie zeigt den konstruktiven Aufbau der Hülle aus Stahl und Glas, die additiv über die schwere Betonkonstruktion der Fahrzeughalle gestellt wurde.

Isometric diagram of the constructional elements of the outer steel and glass skin, which was assembled additively over the heavy concrete structure of the vehicle hall.

Lageplan. Nördlich des
Postamts liegt die Bahn-
hofstraße, südlich der
Gleiskörper der Bahn,
rechts der Hauptbahnhof
mit dem Bahnhofsvorplatz.

Site plan. The road to the
main station runs along
the northern side of the
post office development.
To the south, the com-
plex is flanked by the railway tracks. The station
itself with its forecourt is
situated to the east.

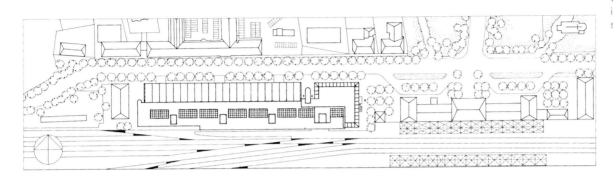

gelegene, dreigeschossige Kopfbau bildet den städtebaulichen
Abschluß des Platzes und beherbergt die Schalterbereiche, den
Postzustellungsbereich und die
Schulungsräume. Im leichten,
zurückgesetzten Dachgeschoß
liegt die Kantine, mit freiem Blick
über die Altstadt von Regensburg.

Der zweigeschossige, 22,0 m
tiefe und rund 168,0 m lange
Betriebsteil erstreckt sich entlang
der Bahnanlage. Alle mit der Bahn
oder mit Straßenfahrzeugen an-
kommenden Sendungen – Paket-
post im Erdgeschoß, Briefe im
ersten Obergeschoß – werden
sortiert, neu zusammengestellt,
auf Bahn oder Lkw verladen und
verschickt. Die großen Verkehrs-
lasten des Betriebsteils, die be-
trächtlichen Spannweiten und der
geforderte Brandschutz machten
eine schwere Stahlbetonskelett-
konstruktion notwendig, die
gleichzeitig als Speichermasse in
bauphysikalischer Hinsicht genutzt
wird. Das Dach und die Fassade

der unbeheizten Verladehalle sind
Wetterschutz und als leichte,
transparente Stahl-Glas-Konstruktion konzipiert. Das Stahltragwerk
mit seinen filigranen Fachwerkträ-
gern ist zur maßstäblichen Gliederung des langgestreckten Baukörpers sichtbar nach außen gelegt.
Die Konstruktion der Fassade
ist eine punktweise gehaltene,
geschoßhohe Einfachverglasung
mit offenen Fugen. Die Betriebsabläufe sind nach außen transparent und ablesbar; sie ermöglichen
für die Tiefe des Raumes noch
natürlich belichtete Arbeitsplätze.
Der Verwaltungsbereich im obersten Geschoß ist wegen der ge-
ringeren Eigenlasten eine leichte,
aufgesetzte Stahlkonstruktion. Die
Büroräume sind überwiegend zu
den ruhigen, begrünten Innenhöfen orientiert. Zwischen dem
Kopfbau und der anschließenden
Verladehalle setzt das freistehende, gläserne Haupttreppenhaus
einen deutlichen Akzent und
gliedert vertikal die funktionale
Gestalt der einzelnen Nutzungsbereiche.

Zusammenfassendes, opti-
sches Bindeglied der einzelnen
Funktionsbereiche ist die vorgehängte weiße Metall-Glas-

Die Baumallee entlang der
Bahnhofstraße übernimmt
eine Filterfunktion zwi-
schen Gehsteig und Fahr-
straße.

The trees along the sta-
tion road act as a filter
between the pavement
and the carriageway.

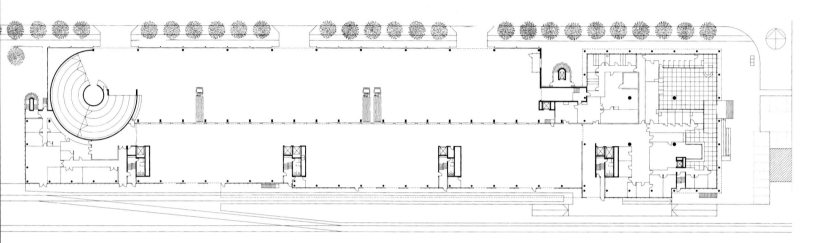

Grundriß
Erdgeschoß

Ground floor
plan

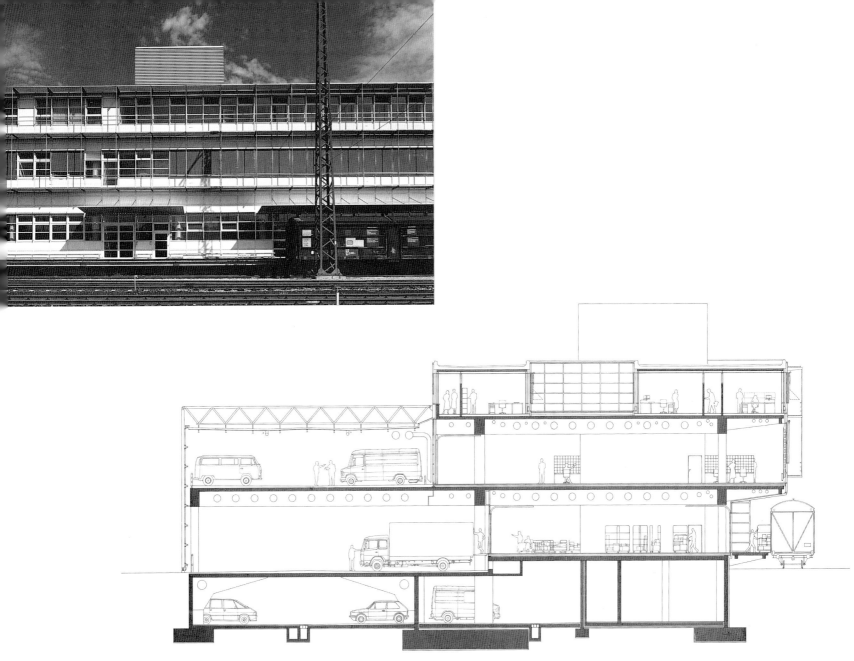

Hülle aus elementierten Teilen mit einem Rastermaß von 140 cm x 70 cm. Die Anteile der Fenster- und Paneelflächen können jederzeit ausgewechselt und späteren Nutzungsänderungen angepaßt werden. Großflächige Wärmeschutzverglasungen ermöglichen in Verbindung mit den inneren Speichermassen der Betonkonstruktion eine passive Sonnenenergienutzung und Energieeinsparung.

Zusätzliche künstliche Beleuchtung ist nur in ganz wenigen Bereichen notwendig. Außenliegende, transluzente Markisen bieten einen optimalen Sonnen-Blendschutz und bilden eine zweite Schicht, die der Fassade eine bestimmte Plastizität verleiht.

Querschnitt Betriebsteil. Briefe und Pakete werden in den beiden Betriebsgeschossen von der Straße auf die Bahn und umgekehrt befördert. Im obersten Geschoß, als leichtes Stahlskelett mit Innenhöfen ausgebildet, befinden sich die Räume für die Verwaltung.

Cross-section through mail-handling tract. Letters and parcels arriving by road or rail are sorted, reloaded and dispatched. The administration is situated on the top floor, which consists of a lightweight steel skeleton frame structure with internal courtyards.

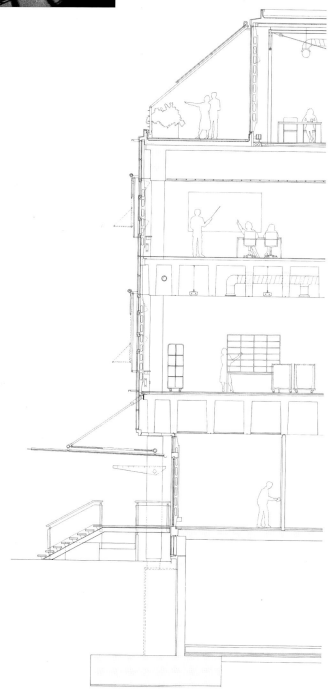

Schnitt Kopfbau. Die additiv angeordneten Markisen geben den Fassaden und Dachterrassenbereichen eine gewisse plastische Tiefe.

Section through head building. The additive sunblind system lends the façades and the roof garden areas a three-dimensional quality.

Der glasüberdeckte
Eingang zum Postamt
ist behindertengerecht
ausgebildet.

The glass-covered
entrance to the post
office is also designed
for disabled people.

Grundriß 1.Obergeschoß
mit Briefverteilerzentrum

First floor plan with
letter-sorting centre

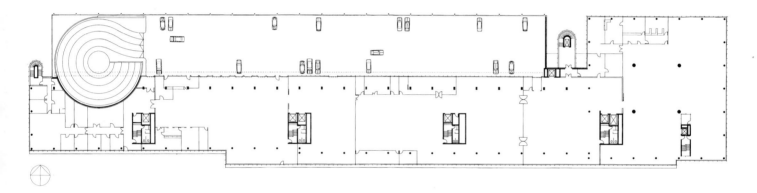

Von der Kantine im ober-
sten Geschoß bietet sich
ein schöner Blick über die
Regensburger Altstadt
und den Bahnhofsvorplatz.

The canteen on the top
floor affords a fine view
over the old city centre
of Regensburg and the
station forecourt.

Die Büroräume der Ver-
waltung im zweiten Ober-
geschoß sind ruhig und
um begrünte Innenhöfe
angeordnet.

The administrative
offices on the second
floor are oriented to
quiet, landscaped
internal courtyards.

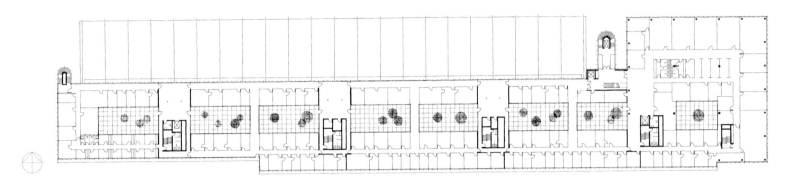

Die geschoßhohe, punkt-
weise gehaltene Ein-
fachverglasung macht
die Betriebsabläufe nach
außen transparent.

The storey-height, point-
fixed panels of single
glazing allow the oper-
ations to be seen from
outside.

Das Stahltragwerk der
Verladehalle mit seinen
filigranen Fachwerk-
trägern liegt außen und
gliedert den Baukörper.
In den breiten Zufahrts-
bereichen sind die Luft-
stützen als abgespannte
Hängestützen ausge-
bildet.

The steel structure of the
loading hall, with its finely dimensioned trussed
beams, is situated on the
outside of the building,
where it serves to articulate the great length of
this tract. The columns
over the broad entrance
openings are designed
as braced suspension
members.

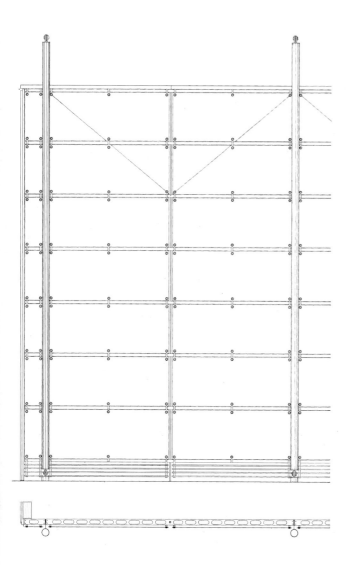

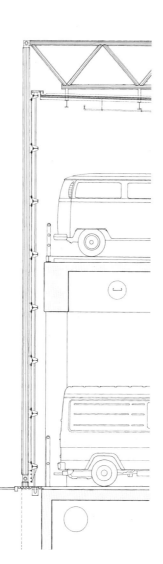

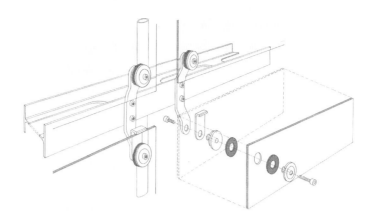

Die Endscheiben des
Betriebsgebäudes sind
mit gehämmerten
Edelstahlelementen
verkleidet.

The end walls of the
mail-handling tract are
clad with hammered
stainless-steel elements.

Die Fassade hat eine punktweise gehaltene Einfachverglasung mit offenen Fugen, die eine Durchlüftung zulassen. Die großflächige Verglasung vermittelt zu den Nachbargebäuden.

The façade is clad with point-fixed panels of single glazing with open joints that permit cross-ventilation. The large areas of glazing also establish a link with the neighbouring buildings.

Student Hostel in
Freimann, Munich

Competition: 1982
First prize
Commencement of
planning: 1983
Construction period:
1986 – 88

A clear, simple form was chosen for the Georg Lanzenstiel House, a student hostel belonging to the German Protestant Church. One of the aims of the design was that the complex should assert itself amid the chaotic variety of the surrounding developments. Two linked L-shape tracts are laid out about a generous landscaped courtyard. To the north and east, they screen off the noise from the suburban railway *S-Bahn* line. The slightly sunken entrance area is clearly located in the south-west front at the point of transition from a double-bay to a single-bay layout. The entrance and the small foyer to the hall are oriented to the internal court-yard. The staircases, situated at diagonally opposite corners of the building, encourage communication between the residents. For the same reason, the kitchen facilities and dining areas are distributed about the building on all floors. The foyer can also be used as a common recreational space and can be extended into the courtyard when the weather permits. Most of the 135 student rooms are oriented to the south and west – to the quiet courtyard. Planted areas with trees were laid out in front of the rooms on the street faces. The well lit corridors and staircases widen at certain points to provide opportunities for communication between students. The rooms for disabled persons are distributed about the building on all storeys. There are three communal kitchens on every floor.

Der Vortragssaal im Erdgeschoß hat mit seiner Foyerzone direkte Verbindung zum begrünten, ruhigen Innenhof.

The lecture hall on the ground floor is directly linked, via a foyer zone, to the quiet landscaped courtyard.

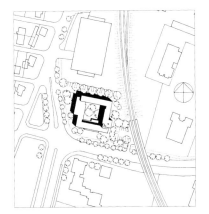

Studentenwohnheim, München-Freimann

Wettbewerb 1982
1. Preis

Planungsbeginn: 1983
Bauzeit: 1986–1988

Die in der Höhe abgestuf- | The stepped-down vol-
ten Baukörper lassen | umes of the hostel permit
eine optimale Besonnung | an optimum insolation of
der Studentenzimmer zu. | the students' rooms.

Für das Georg-Lanzenstiel-Haus, ein evangelisches Studentenwohnheim, wurde eine klare, einfache Form gewählt. Die Bautengruppe sollte sich in der chaotischen Vielfalt der umgebenden Bebauung behaupten. Um einen großzügigen, begrünten Innenhof sind zwei winkelförmige Baukörper gegeneinander gestellt, die den Lärm der S-Bahn nach Norden und Osten abschirmen. Durch den Übergang von einem zweibündigen in einen einbündigen Grundriß entsteht an der Süd-Westseite ein gut auffindbarer, leicht abgesenkter Zugang. Der Eingangsbereich und das kleine Foyer für den Saal sind zum Innenhof orientiert. Durch die diagonal angeordneten Treppenhäuser wird die Kommunikation unter den Bewohnern gefördert. Deshalb werden die Koch- und Eßräume auf alle Geschosse dezentral angeordnet. Das Foyer ermöglicht auch eine Nutzung als Gemeinschaftsbereich, der beim schönem Wetter in den Innenhof erweitert werden kann.

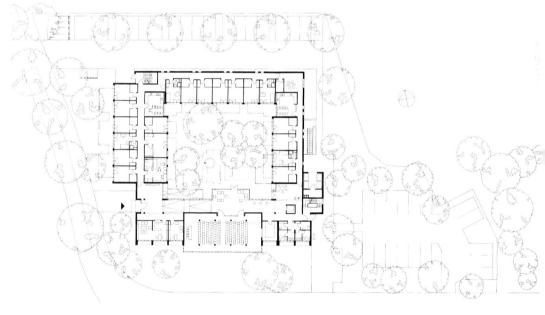

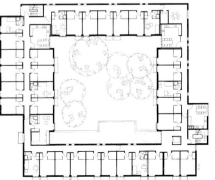

Die zwei winkelförmigen Baukörper erhielten durch unterschiedliche Raumanordnung eine plastische Ausformung.

The different arrangement of the rooms in the two L-shape tracts ensured the plasticity of the building's appearance.

A reinforced concrete cross-wall construction provided the ideal structural solution for the building. The cross-walls, which form the divisions between the students' rooms, ensure excellent sound insulation.

The white rendered brick external walls are articulated by white metal-framed casements and suspended balconies with inset steel gratings. The option of locating the French windows next to either of the cross-walls dividing the rooms helped to relieve the façade of any sense of austerity. In the tracts exposed to traffic emissions, the corridors were located along the outer faces, with only small openings to admit light. The modest range of design elements is used in such a way that all sense of regimentation or repetition is avoided.

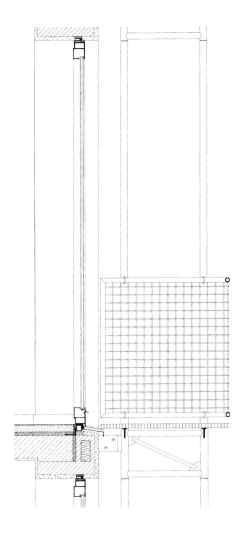

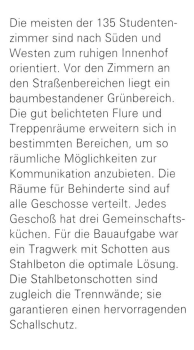

Die Studentenzimmer
im Erdgeschoß erhiel-
ten Schiebeläden aus
Alu-Jalousetten.

The windows to the
students' rooms on
the ground floor can
be screened off with
sliding aluminium-
louvre elements.

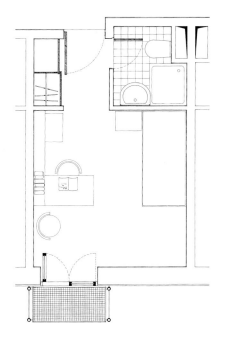

Die meisten der 135 Studentenzimmer sind nach Süden und
Westen zum ruhigen Innenhof
orientiert. Vor den Zimmern an
den Straßenbereichen liegt ein
baumbestandener Grünbereich.
Die gut belichteten Flure und
Treppenräume erweitern sich in
bestimmten Bereichen, um so
räumliche Möglichkeiten zur
Kommunikation anzubieten. Die
Räume für Behinderte sind auf
alle Geschosse verteilt. Jedes
Geschoß hat drei Gemeinschafts-
küchen. Für die Bauaufgabe war
ein Tragwerk mit Schotten aus
Stahlbeton die optimale Lösung.
Die Stahlbetonschotten sind
zugleich die Trennwände; sie
garantieren einen hervorragenden
Schallschutz.

Die weiß verputzte Ziegelfassade
ist durch weiße Metallfenster und
vorgehängte Metallbalkone, eine
leichte, verzinkte Stahlrohrkon-
struktion mit eingelegten Stahl-
rosten, gegliedert. Die Freiheit,
die Fenstertüren entweder an die
eine oder die andere Trennwand
der Zimmer zu plazieren, nimmt
den Fassaden jede Strenge. Die
Flure mit kleinen Belichtungs-
öffnungen wurden an die emis-
sionsbelasteten Fassaden gelegt.
Die wenigen Gestaltungsele-
mente der Gebäude sind so eingesetzt, daß jede kasernenhafte
Addition vermieden wurde.

District Centre in
Laim, Munich

Commencement of
planning: 1984
Construction period:
1985 – 87

This local centre has a restrained
but friendly appearance. Openness and transparency, rather
than civic display, are the main
features. The simple, industrially
produced materials used in the
scheme, its clearly legible structure, its light colours and formal
discipline all help to create an
inviting and lively atmosphere.
The underlying aim of the design
is to arouse visitors' curiosity and
to stimulate them to enter the
building, which houses a large
number of municipal services.
These include a public library,
a branch of the adult education
institute, local government
offices, a registration office and
social counselling facilities.

The complex consists of a five-
storey main block in Fürstenrieder Strasse with an elongated,
single-storey library tract adjoining it to the rear. The library is
closed off at its eastern end by
a demountable wall slab, which
can be easily removed for the
planned extension of the building
in the second phase of development. To the north, the building
abuts the wall of a department
store, the height of which is taken
up by the sloping skylight on the

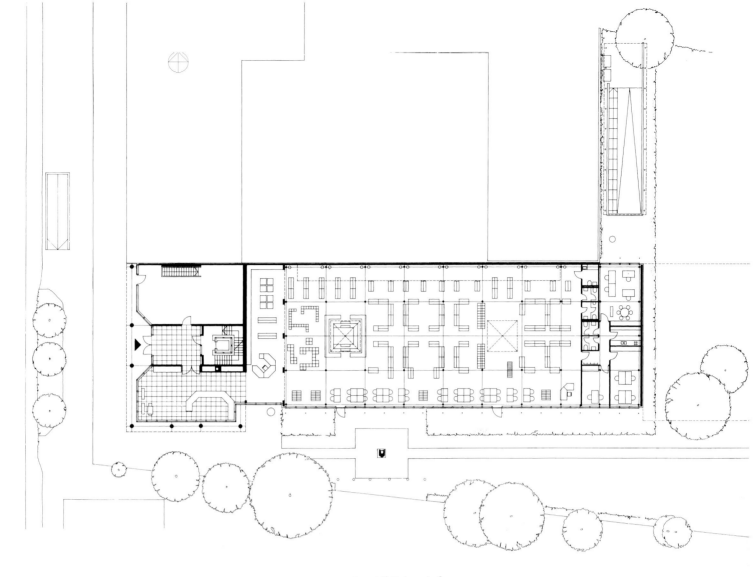

Grundriß Erdgeschoß
mit dem dreischiffigen
Bibliotheksbereich zum
Grünbereich orientiert

Ground floor plan with
three-bay library tract
oriented to landscaped
area

Das Stadtteilzentrum mit seinen vielfältigen Dienstleistungsfunktionen
zeigt ein zurückhaltendes, freund-
liches Erscheinungsbild. Nicht Reprä-
sentation, sondern Offenheit und
Transparenz herrschen vor. Einfache,
industriell hergestellte Materialien,
klare ablesbare Konstruktionen,
lichte Farben und formale Disziplin
machen die Atmosphäre einladend
und lebendig. Das Haus soll Besucher neugierig machen und Auffor-
derungscharakter haben. Der Bau
wird von zahlreichen städtischen
Behörden genutzt: als Stadtbücherei, Volkshochschule, Bezirks-
inspektion, Meldestelle, Soziale
Beratungsstelle.

Stadtteilzentrum München-Laim

Planungsbeginn: 1984
Bauzeit: 1985 – 1987

library roof. Along the south face a space was left between this development and the neighbouring building, partly to allow access to the eastern end of the site, but also to preserve the existing stock of trees. The flat areas of the library roof are planted.

The main entrance to this district centre is in Fürstenrieder Strasse. From here, a visual link has been created to the bright, open, ground floor library to the rear. The other municipal facilities and the caretaker's flat on the upper floors of the main block are reached via a glazed staircase or via a lift for disabled people. The glass-covered ramp

to the basement garages is reached from Hogenbergstrasse. The garage area itself is situated beneath the library tract.

The public library along Fürstenrieder Strasse is easily accessible for local residents. Beyond the foyer and the lending counter, this south-facing tract extends into the quiet rear area of the site. It contains an open-shelf library section, working rooms for the staff and sanitary facilities.

On the third floor of the main building are the office of the principal of the adult education institute, a room for child care, a teaching room and two work-rooms with ancillary spaces. The fourth floor accommodates a four-room caretaker's flat with a roof garden and a gymnastics room for the adult education institute.

Längsschnitt Haus an der Fürstenrieder Straße und Bibliothek. Unten: Querschnitte

Longitudinal section through main structure in Fürstenrieder Strasse and library tract to rear. Bottom: cross-sections

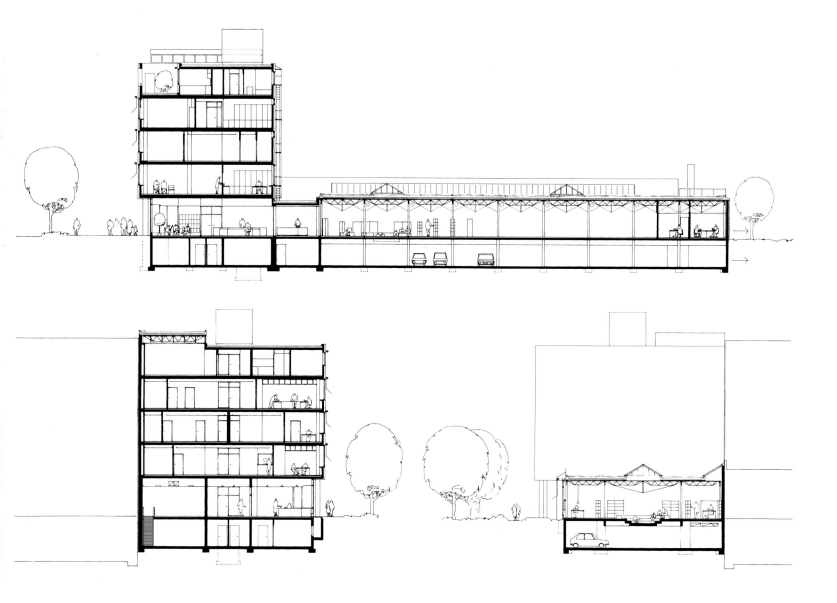

Skulptur aus rostendem
Stahl von Lothar Fischer

Sculpture in rusting steel
by Lothar Fischer

Der Teil des Mehrzweckgebäudes an der Fürstenrieder Straße besteht aus einem fünfgeschossigen Kopfbau und einem rückwärtig anschließenden, eingeschossigen Gebäudeteil für die Bibliothek. Den Abschluß des langgestreckten Bibliotheksgebäudes bildet eine montierbare Wandscheibe; dadurch ist eine Fortführung des geplanten zweiten Bauabschnittes problemlos möglich. Der Baukörper lehnt sich im Norden an das benachbarte Kaufhaus an und nimmt dessen Höhenentwicklung durch ein schräges Oberlicht auf. Im Süden wird ein Gebäudeabstand gehalten, damit die Durchgängigkeit zum östlichen Grundstücksteil erhalten und der vorhandene Baumbestand nicht beeinträchtigt wird. Das Flachdach ist begrünt.

Der zentrale Eingangsbereich des Laimer Stadtteilzentrums liegt unmittelbar an der Fürstenrieder Straße. Schon vom Gehsteig gibt es eine Blickverbindung zur offenen, lichtdurchfluteten ebenerdigen Bibliothek. Die übrigen städtischen Einrichtungen und die Hausmeisterwohnung sind über ein verglastes Treppenhaus und den behindertengerechten Aufzug erreichbar. Die Ein- und Ausfahrt zur Tiefgarage erfolgt über eine glasüberdachte Rampe an der Hogenbergstraße, die Tiefgarage selbst liegt unter dem Bibliotheksbereich.

Die Stadtbücherei entlang der Fürstenrieder Straße ist für die Bürger leicht zu finden. Die Büchereifläche setzt sich im Anschluß an Foyer und Buchausgabe in einen rückwärtigen, ruhigen, nach Süden orientierten Grundstücksteil fort. Dort befinden sich die Freihandausleihe, personalinterne Arbeitsräume und Sanitäreinrichtungen.

Im dritten Obergeschoß liegen das Leiterbüro der Volkshochschule, ein Raum für Kinderbetreuung, ein Unterrichtsraum und zwei Werkräume mit Nebenräumen. Das vierte Obergeschoß enthält neben einem Gymnastikraum für die Volkshochschule eine Vierzimmerwohnung mit Dachterrasse für den Hausmeister.

The five-storey block in Fürstenrieder Strasse has a reinforced
concrete skeleton frame with
ventilated, white-coated aluminium curtain-wall façades. The
load-bearing structure of the
single-storey library tract is in
steel. The girders over the central
bay are trussed on the underside,
which made it possible to use
standard girders over a double-
span width.

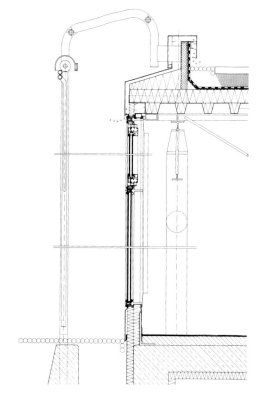

Im Bibliothekstrakt ist der
Sonnenschutz von der
Fassade abgesetzt und
nach oben offen, um durch
Hinterlüftung einen Hitze-
stau zwischen Markisen
und Glas zu vermeiden.

The sunscreening to the
library tract projects
beyond the façade. The
ventilated space thus
created is open at the top
and helps to avoid any
build-up of heat between
the blinds and the glass.

In der Raumtiefe der
Bibliothek wird das
nach Süden geneigte
Oberlicht spürbar.

The south-facing roof
light allows natural
light to penetrate to the
internal areas of the
library.

Der fünfgeschossige Bauteil an
der Fürstenrieder Straße ist als
Stahlbetonskelettbau mit vor-
gehängter hinterlüfteter, weiß-
beschichteter Alufassade ausgeführt, der eingeschossige
Bibliotheksbau ist eine Stahlkonstruktion. Die Fachwerkträger
im Mittelschiff sind unterspannt;
so konnte mit den Standardträ-
gern die doppelte Spannweite
überbrückt werden. Der Biblio-
theksraum ist in ein Mittel- und
zwei Seitenschiffe unterteilt.

Die geschoßhohe Glas-
wand ist mit einem
äußeren, ausklappbaren
Sonnenschutz und mit
einem inneren Blend-
schutzrollo ausgestattet.

The storey-height
glazed skin is fitted with
an external, upward-
pivoting sunscreen
system and internal
anti-glare blinds.

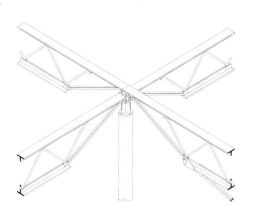

Das Dachtragwerk der Bibliothek besteht aus gleichen R-Trägern, wobei die beiden Mittelträger durch eine Luftstütze getragen werden. Es entsteht ein dreischiffiges Tragwerk mit unterschiedlichen Stützweiten, die den Raum prägen.

Although the library is laid out in three bays of different spans, the distinctive roof structure consists of identical prefabricated girders. This was made possible by trussing the central pair of girders on the underside with a suspended braced column in the middle.

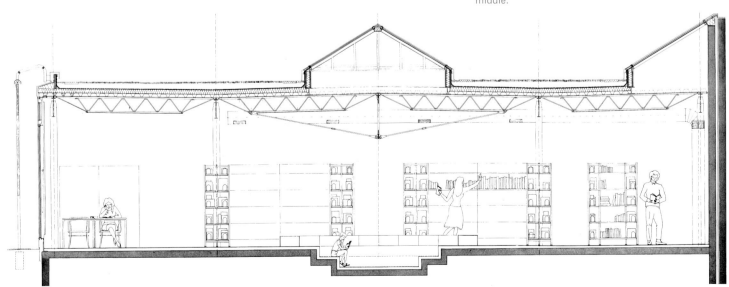

Pedestrian Bridge in
Berching, Upper
Palatinate

Competition: 1986
First prize
Commencement of
planning: 1987
Construction period:
1989 – 91

The construction of the Main-Danube Canal severed many traffic routes and urban structures that had evolved over a long period of time.

In 1986, when the town of Berching and the Rhein-Main-Donau AG held a competition for the reorganization of the urban, transport and landscape structure in the area, both parties were aware that the headroom necessary for shipping under the new canal bridges would result in changes in the landscape and urban skyline. The participants in the competition were, however, encouraged to regard the bridges not as a necessary evil, but as an opportunity to seek exceptional solutions.

Berching has a well-preserved townscape with brick-covered medieval walls. The insertion of a pedestrian bridge in the small-scale structure of the urban environs, therefore, required a great deal of care. Surprisingly enough, the huge dimensions of the Main-Danube Canal did not conflict with the modest scale of the six-metre-high ring of walls as much as had originally been

feared. The siting of the bridge in relation to the town, and the decisive way in which the urban environment is now turned towards the water of the canal help to establish a lively dialogue of opposites.

The location of the bridge at the south-west corner of the town was determined largely by the presence of the old earth bulwark. The embankment was raised slightly to provide an approach ramp to the bridge in harmony with the topography. The route to the bridge appears to follow a natural path from the gateway in the town walls along the redesigned waterside promenade. Major changes to the historical approach to the town between the embankment, the fosse and the walls were avoided. The fortified backdrop remains intact over its entire

Die Brücke überspannt den Main-Donau-Kanal als halbe Hängebrücke. Die Pylonhöhe ordnet sich den Türmen der Stadt unter.

The bridge spans the Main-Danube Canal in the form of a suspension bridge with a mast support at one end only. In its height, the mast is subordinated to the towers of the town fortifications.

Fußgängerbrücke Berching, Oberpfalz

Wettbewerb 1986
1. Preis

Planungsbeginn: 1987
Bauzeit: 1989 – 1991

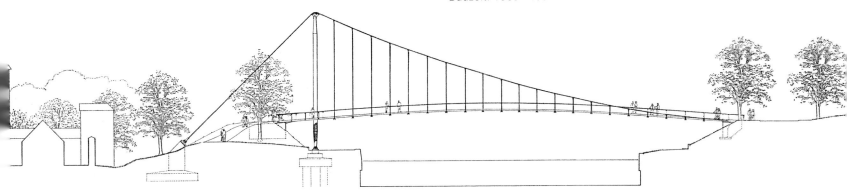

Durch den Bau des Main-Donau-Kanals wurden vielerorts über Generationen gewachsene städtebauliche Strukturen und Verkehrswege durchschnitten.

Als im Jahre 1986 die Stadt Berching und die Rhein-Main-Donau AG einen Wettbewerb zur Neuordnung der städtebaulichen, verkehrlichen und landschaftlichen Beziehungen auslobten, waren sich die Verantwortlichen darüber im klaren, daß durch die für die Schiffahrt notwendigen Höhenlagen der neuen Brücken eine Veränderung der Landschafts- und Stadtsilhouette erfolgen würde. Die Wettbewerbsteilnehmer wurden ermutigt, die Brücken nicht als notwendiges Übel zu betrachten, sondern als Chance für besondere Lösungen.

Das sehr gut erhaltene mittelalterliche Stadtbild verlangte nach einer rücksichtsvollen Einfügung der Fußgängerbrücke in das städtebaulich kleinmaßstäbliche Umfeld von Berching. Erstaunlicherweise beeinträchtigen die mächtigen Dimensionen des Main-Donau-Kanals den kleinstädtischen Maßstab des mittelalterlichen, 6 m hohen, ziegelgedeckten Mauergürtels weniger stark als befürchtet. Die Lage der Brücke zur Stadt und die entschiedene Zuwendung zum Kanal ergeben sogar spannungsreiche Gegensätze.

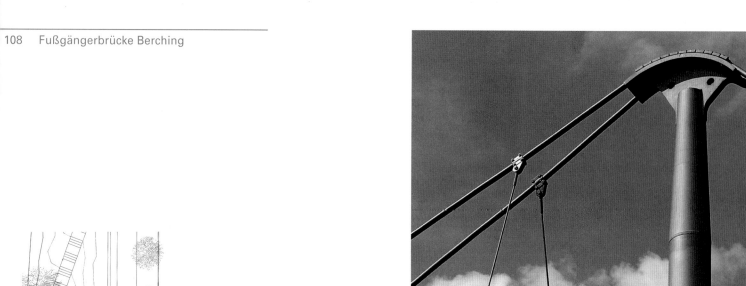

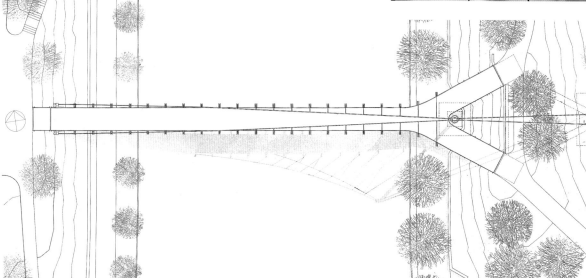

Die beiden Tragseile
werden über einen guß-
eisernen Umlenksattel
des 17 m hohen Pylons
umgeleitet.

The two suspension
cables are drawn over a
cast-iron saddle at the
top of the 17-metre-high
mast.

Die Zugkräfte der Trag-
seile werden über
Zylinderverankerungen
als Druckkräfte in die
Stahlbetonbrückenplatte
zurückgeleitet, also
rückverankert.

The tension forces
exerted on the suspen-
sion cables are trans-
mitted, via cylindrical
anchors, as compression
loads to the reinforced
concrete bridge slab,
which is fixed to founda-
tions in the bank of the
canal.

Die Situierung der Brücke an der südwestlichen ›Stadtecke‹ resultiert aus der vorhandenen alten Wallanlage, die geringfügig erhöht wurde, um als topographisch natürliche Aufgangsrampe für den Fußgängersteg zu dienen. Die Wegeführung ergibt sich wie selbstverständlich aus den Toren der Stadtmauer, entlang der neugestalteten Uferpromenade und der Stadtmauer zur Brücke. Größere Eingriffe in den historischen Vorraum der Altstadt zwischen Wall und Stadtmauer und dem Stadtgraben wurden vermieden. Die befestigte Stadtkulisse bleibt in der ganzen horizontalen Ausdehnung unberührt; der Pylon der Brücke ordnet sich in der Höhe den Türmen der Stadtmauer unter.

Der 3,5 m breite Fußgängersteg spannt sich als ›halbe Hängebrücke‹ über fast 70 m. Die Aufzweigung der Brückenplatte am Pylon resultiert aus den Wegeführungen auf der Wallanlage. Die leichte Seilkonstruktion mit dem nur 17 m hohen Pylon ist über eine Zylinderverankerung über die Stahlbetonbrückenplatte rückverankert. Die Zugkräfte der Tragseile werden also als Druckkräfte in die Brückenplatte zurückgeleitet. Im wesentlichen werden nur Vertikalkräfte in den Baugrund eingeleitet. Durch das überzeugende Konstruktionsprinzip konnte der Ingenieur Jörg Schlaich für die Brücke den Materialaufwand auf ein Minimum reduzieren. Das erzielte Ergebnis ist ein Maximum an Transparenz, das der empfindlichen Situation am Rande der Altstadt gerecht wird. Die Jury dazu: »Der klare konstruktive Aufbau gibt der Brücke eine hohe gestalterische Qualität.«

Durch die geringen Dimensionen der Tragseile mit ø 55 mm und der Hängeseile mit nur ø 16 mm wird das Baumaterial in der Festigkeit hoch beansprucht. Gleichermaßen haben Seile und Brückenplatte optimale Dimensionen für die filigrane und transparente Gestalt der Brücke. Die 30 cm starke, in Blech geschalte Gehwegplatte liegt auf zwei 16 cm hohen U-Profilen, die von den Hängern getragen werden. Der Pylon aus Stahl hat einen Durchmesser von 60 cm und steht auf seinem allseitig drehbaren Lager auf der Neoprene-Kopfplatte einer Pfahlgründung.

Auf der Pylonseite werden die Zugkräfte der Tragseile über Stahlbetonfundamente in den Baugrund eingeleitet.

At the mast end of the bridge, tension forces in the suspension cables are restrained by reinforced concrete foundations anchored in the ground.

length. Even the pylon of the bridge is subordinated to the height of the towers in the town walls.

The pedestrian walkway is 3.5 m wide. It is designed as a suspension bridge with a mast support at one end only and spans a width of almost 70 metres. The bifurcation of the slab around the pylon is a response to the routes along the embankment. The light cable construction and the pylon itself, which is only 17 metres high, are tied to a cylindrical anchor fixed to the reinforced concrete slab of the bridge. Tension forces in the suspension cables are, therefore, transmitted

to the slab in the form of compression loads, and virtually all loads are transmitted vertically to the ground. This convincing load-bearing principle enabled the structural engineer, Jörg Schlaich, to reduce the material dimensions to a minimum. This, in turn, resulted in a maximum degree of transparency, which is in the interests of the sensitive situation at the edge of the old town centre.

In the words of the competition jury: "The clear structural concept results in a bridge with a high design quality."

The slender dimensions of the suspension cables, 55 mm diameter, and the hangers, 16 mm diameter, mean that the materials are subject to relatively great loads. On the other hand, in terms of a finely drawn, transparent bridge design, the cables and the slab are optimally dimensioned. The 30 cm thick walkway slab, cast in metal forms, is supported by pairs of 16 cm high channel sections suspended from the hangers. The steel pylon has a diameter of 60 cm and stands on a 360°-pivoting bearer on the neoprene head of the pile foundation.

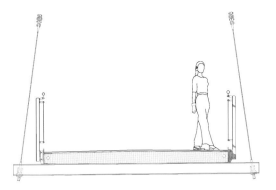

Die 30 cm starke, in Stahl-
blech betonierte Gehweg-
platte liegt auf zwei 16 cm
hohen U-Profilen, die von
den Hängern getragen
werden.

The 30 cm thick concrete
walkway was cast in
sheet steel forms and is
supported by pairs of
16 cm high channels sus-
pended from the main
cables by hangers.

Durch die optimale
Bemessung aller Stahl-
bauteile wird die an-
gestrebte Leichtigkeit
erreicht.

The slender dimension-
ing of all steel members
helped to achieve
the required sense of
lightness.

Hauptzugang vom Holländischen Platz in das Wissenschaftliche Zentrum der Universität

Main entrance to Scientific Centre of the Comprehensive University from Holländischer Platz

Auf dem ehemaligen Werksgelände der Lokomotiven produzierenden Firma Henschel wurde zu Beginn der achtziger Jahre die neue Gesamthochschule Kassel errichtet. Letzter Baustein zur Stadt hin sollte ein Institutsgebäude für die technischen Fachbereiche Bauingenieurwesen, Maschinenbau und das Wissenschaftliche Zentrum werden. Der längs der Kurt-Wolters-Straße entwickelte Baukörper führt die Blockrandbebauung des Hochschulquartiers konsequent weiter und stellt durch ausgeprägte, klare Raumkanten und eine dem Straßenraum angemessene, maßvolle Höhenentwicklung einen signifikanten städtebaulichen Auftakt zum Hochschulgelände dar. Die Eingangssituation am Holländischen Platz wird räumlich herausgestellt, sowohl als Eingang zur Hochschule von der Stadt als auch als Abschluß der Hochschuldiagonale. Der durch das dreieckige Grundstück entstehende Freibereich nördlich des Institutsgebäudes öffnet sich zum historischen Gießhaus und zur Halle K13, der ›Henschelei‹, und bezieht diese technischen Baumonumente in das Konzept der Freiraumgestaltung mit ein; in diesem ergänzen sich mechanische Objekte, Materialprüflinge, Bäume und Grün zu einer technischen Landschaft.

Das 170,0 m lange, bis zu 39,0 m breite und über Gelände 22,0 m hohe Gebäude ist nach seinen Funktionen in zwei lineare Bauteile organisiert, die durch das Rückgrat der Erschließung miteinander verbunden sind.

Im niederen Gebäudeteil entlang der verkehrsreichen Kurt-Wolters-Straße liegen die Versuchshallen – Lärm zu Lärm – ein Hörsaal für dreihundert Personen und Wissenschaftliches Zentrum in zwei Geschossen. Diese Räume sind entweder gegen Lärm unempfindlich oder, wie Hörsaal und Wissenschaftliches Zentrum, durch eine introvertierte Grundrißorganisation und zweischalige Fassade vor Immissionen geschützt. Da tragfähiger Boden erst in 8 m Tiefe vorhanden war, konnten diese Bereiche flächenoptimierend und wirtschaftlich gestapelt werden.

Im nördlichen, höheren Baukörper liegen auf fünf Geschossen die Lehrstuhl-, Labor- und Meßräume der einzelnen Institute. Alle Räume, die sich zum Hochschulgelände, der ›Technischen Landschaft‹ hin orientieren, sind durch die Zone der Hallen vor Lärm geschützt. Die vertikal geknickte Fassade mit der Schräge in den beiden untersten Geschossen resultiert aus der Forderung nach großen Raumtiefen für die Labor- und Meßräume.

Technik III der Universität GhK Kassel

Wettbewerb 1985
1. Preis

Planungsbeginn: 1986
Bauzeit: 1990–1995

Technology Centre III of the Comprehensive University, Kassel

Competition: 1985
First prize
Commencement of planning: 1986
Construction period: 1990 – 95

The new Comprehensive University in Kassel was built at the beginning of the 1980s on the site of the Henschel company's former locomotive manufacturing works. The final element of the university complex was erected at the end nearest to the city and houses the technical institutes for building and mechanical engineering, as well as the Scientific Centre. The structure, extending along Kurt-Wolters-Strasse, represents a logical continuation of the existing street block development of the university district. With its distinctive, clearly defined contours and moderate height, which take up the scale of the existing street space, the development represents a striking urban overture to the university complex. The entrance situation in Holländischer Platz is spatially accentuated both as the point of access to the university from the city and as the termination of the diagonal axis of the university layout. The space to the north of the institute building – resulting from the triangular shape of the site – opens on to the historical

Giess building and Hall K13 of the "Henschelei". The space also serves to integrate these built monuments to technology into the overall urban spatial concept, in which mechanical objects, test materials, trees and other plantings coalesce to form a technical landscape.

The structure, 170 m long and up to 39 m wide, rises over 22 m above ground level. It is functionally organized into two linear tracts linked by an access spine.

Situated in the lower part of the building along the Kurt-Wolters-Strasse traffic artery are the testing halls, a lecture hall for 300 persons and the Scientific Centre, which extends over two storeys. These spaces are either not particularly sensitive to noise, or, like the lecture hall and Scientific Centre, are shielded from it by their introverted position in the layout and by the

Längsschnitt durch das Wissenschaftliche Zentrum mit introvertiertem Hörsaal und Versuchshallen, die gleichzeitig als aktiver Lärmschutz zur Kurt-Wolters-Straße wirken

Longitudinal section through Scientific Centre with introverted lecture hall and the testing halls. These spaces serve as an active acoustic buffer zone that screens off noise from Kurt-Wolters-Strasse.

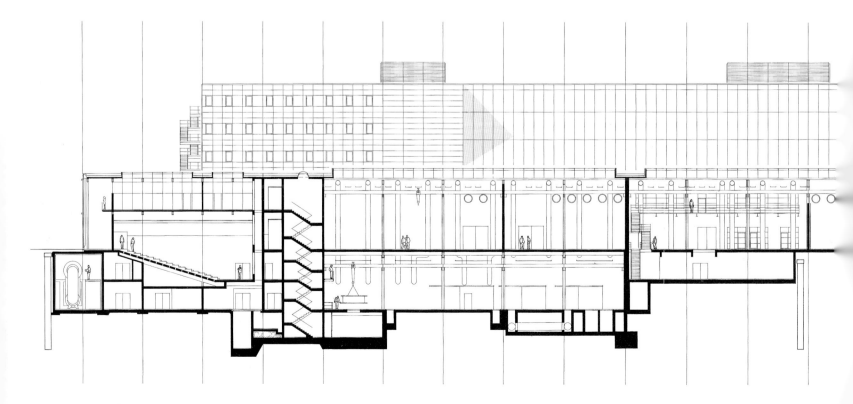

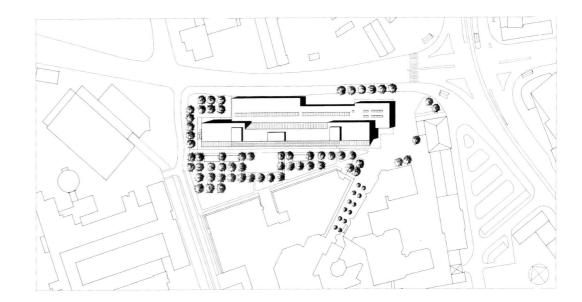

Lageplan. Das Technikge-
bäude bildet das städte-
bauliche Tor von der Stadt
zum südlich gelegenen
Hochschulgelände.

Site plan. For visitors
approaching from the
town, the building con-
taining the technical
institutes forms an
urban gateway to the
university campus to
the south.

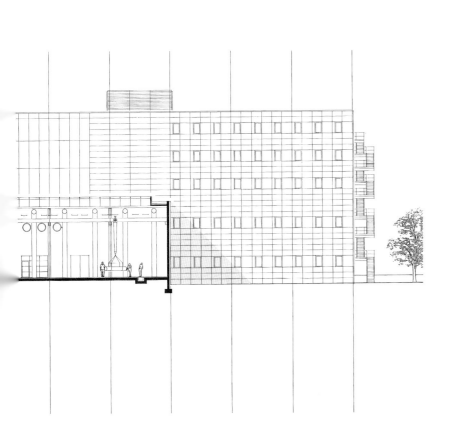

Der Hauptzugang liegt am Holländischen Platz. Durch ein zwei-
geschossiges, verglastes Foyer
gelangt man über eine Treppe in
eine zentrale, viergeschossige
Halle. An dieses Rückgrat ist auch
das Wissenschaftliche Zentrum
angeschlossen. Durch die zentrale
Lage werden fachbereichüber-
greifende Kooperation und Kommunikation wesentlich erleichtert.

Das äußere Erscheinungsbild
des Bauwerkes mit den großzügigen Fensterflächen und seinen
Fassadenverkleidungen aus natur-
farben eloxierten Aluminium-
Paneelen entspricht in seiner
technischen Ästhetik dem Erscheinungsbild eines modernen
Forschungsgebäudes. Seine verschiedenen Funktionen in Gestalt
und Material sind auch von außen
ablesbar.

Das Tragwerk der Büro-,
Labor- und Meßraumbereiche
wurde als Stahlbetonskelett entworfen. Die erforderlichen großen
Massen tragen zur Verhinderung
von möglichen Erschütterungen
aus dem Straßenverkehr oder den
Versuchshallen bei. Das Haupt-

achsmaß beträgt 8,4 m, die Raumtiefen staffeln sich in 1,2 m-Schrit-
ten von 6,0 m auf 9,6 m im Erdgeschoß.

Von diesem Bereich abge-
trennt und aus Brandschutzgrün-
den in Stahlbetonverbundbau-
weise relativ leicht gebaut, sind
die Maschinenhallen. Die leichte,
betonunterstützte Stahlbauweise
ermöglicht eine flexible Anpas-
sung des Hallenbereichs an mögliche spätere Nutzungsänderungen
wie Zwischendecken, Lagerrega-
le, zusätzliche Kranbahnen oder
Containereinbauten.

Die in einem Forschungsgebäude notwendigerweise aufwen-
dige Installation zur unterschiedlichen Konditionierung der Räume
folgt dem Prinzip größtmöglicher
Flexibilität. Das bedingt eine
Zugänglichkeit zu den einzelnen
Medientrassen. Der Hauptteil aller
nachrüstbaren Installationen ist
deshalb offen und sichtbar ausgeführt und kann in einem regel-
mäßigen Raster abgegriffen
werden. Eine technische Beson-
derheit ist das Prozeßkühlwasser-
system im gesamten Haus, mit
dem Prozeßabwärme aufgefangen
und über eine Kälteanlage an die
Lufttechnik abgegeben wird.

double-skin outer walls. The location of the testing halls next to the road is an example of the way noisy uses can be placed adjacent to each other. Since load-bearing soil was found only at a depth of eight metres, it was practical to stack these areas economically on top of each other and thus save valuable space.

The five-storey building to the north contains areas for the various study departments as well as laboratories and measuring rooms for the individual institutes. All spaces facing on to the university grounds – the "technical landscape" – are shielded from noise disturbance by the hall zone. The vertically angled façade on the lower two floors answers the need for greater depth in the laboratories and measurement spaces.

The main entrance is in Holländischer Platz. After passing through the two-storey glazed foyer and up the stairs, one reaches a central, four-storey spine hall, to which the Scientific Centre is also attached. The central position of this hall stimulates co-operation and communication between the various faculties.

With its technical aesthetic and its large areas of fenestration and natural-anodized aluminium façade cladding, the complex complies with the image of a modern research centre. Its various functions are legible in its outward form and use of materials.

Der charakteristische
Knick der Südfassade
resultiert aus den unter-
schiedlichen Nutzungen.
Die funktionsbedingten
Raumtiefen zwischen
Lehrstuhlräumen und
Labors werden ablesbar.

The distinctively angled
south face is an expres-
sion of the various uses
to which the building
is put. The different
depths of the rooms for
the individual depart-
ments and the labora-
tories are made legible
in this way.

In den Querschnitten werden die multifunktionalen Nutzungen deutlich. Oben: Bereich der Versuchshallen und der viergeschossigen Treppenhalle. Unten: Bereich Hörsaal. Tragfähiger Grund steht bei 8 m unter Gelände an. So wurden die Untergeschosse für weitere Versuchshallen genutzt und das oberirdische Bauvolumen entsprechend verringert.

The cross-sections reveal the multi-functional use of this structure. Top: testing halls and the four-storey staircase hall. Bottom: lecture hall area. Soil with an adequate load-bearing capacity was found only at a depth of about eight metres. A number of testing halls were, therefore, located in basement storeys. In this way, it was possible to reduce the volume of the structure above ground.

The load-bearing structure of the office, laboratory and measuring tract is a reinforced concrete skeleton frame. The large mass that was necessary helps to absorb any potential vibrations from road traffic or from the testing halls. The principal grid dimension is 8.4 m. Rooms are graduated in depth in 1.2 m steps from 6.0 m, to 9.6 m on the ground floor.

The machine halls are separated from this tract and built in a relatively lightweight reinforced concrete composite form of construction for reasons of fire protection. The light steel structure in combination with concrete allows the hall areas to be flexibly adapted to subsequent changes of use, facilitating the insertion of elements such as intermediate floors, shelves for storage, additional crane tracks or container units.

The elaborate mechanical services needed for research buildings, where different indoor climatic conditions are required in different spaces, are also based on the principle of maximum flexibility. This necessitates ready access to the individual services and media runs. As a result, most of the installations that may have to be modified or extended in the future were left exposed and are grouped in a regular grid. A special technical feature of the mechanical services is a process cooling-water system for the entire building, in which process heat is collected and fed via the cooling plant into the air-conditioning system.

"In this building, which not only houses technology, but seeks to give it an appropriate form of expression, the care taken in the design is evident in

the details. The corridors on the office floors are an example of this. In order to reduce their length visually, they were articulated with a series of recesses. Many achievements, however, such as the hydraulic-engineering hall, become apparent only when one goes down into the bowels of the building, which extends as far as 12 metres into the ground. Here is final proof of the fact that this house of technology is not only a typological masterpiece, but a functional one as well."
Wolfgang Jean Stock in
Baumeister 11/1996, p. 42

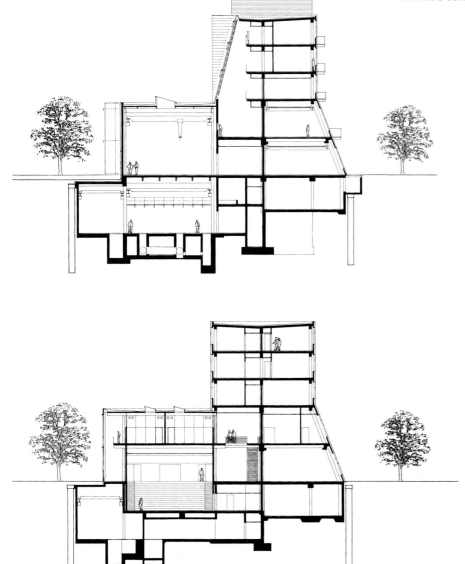

Grundrisse. Unten: Erdge-
schoß mit Hörsaalebene.
Mitte: Erstes Ober-
geschoß. Oben: Zweites
bis viertes Obergeschoß

Plans. Bottom: ground
floor with lecture hall
level. Middle: first floor.
Top: second to fourth
floors

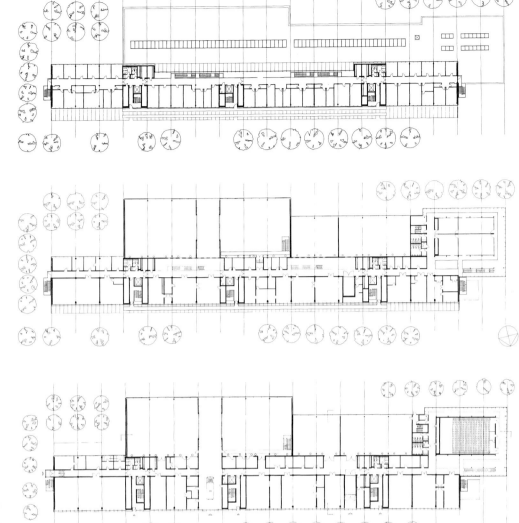

»Bei diesem Gebäude, das nicht
nur Technik enthält, sondern
angemessen zum Ausdruck bringen will, zeigt sich die gestalterische Sorgfalt im Detail. Ein
Beispiel sind die Flure in den
Bürogeschossen: Um ihre Länge
optisch zu mindern, wurden sie
durch Rücksprünge gegliedert.
Viele Leistungen, etwa die Was-
serbauhalle, lassen sich aber nur
erfahren, wenn man sich in den
Bauch des Bauwerks begibt, das
bis zu zwölf Meter in die Erde
reicht. Hier zeigt sich endgültig,
daß dieses Haus der Technik nicht
nur ein typologisches, sondern
auch ein funktionales Meisterwerk
ist«.
Wolfgang Jean Stock, in:
Baumeister 11/1996, S. 42

Die zweischaligen Um-
gänge um Hörsaal und
Seminarräume schützen
vor den Emissionen der
verkehrsreichen Kurt-
Wolters-Straße.

The lecture hall and
seminar rooms are
protected against traffic
emissions from Kurt-
Wolters-Strasse by a
double-skin construc-
tion with a peripheral
circulation route that
acts as a buffer zone.

Der Sicht- und Blend-
schutz erfolgt über
individuell steuerbare
Markisen. In den
Versuchshallen wird
blendfreies Tageslicht
über Oberlichter in
die hohen Räume der
Versuchshallen einge-
leitet.

Visual screening and
protection against glare
are achieved by indi-
vidually operated blinds.
Top lights guarantee
non-glare daylight condi-
tions in the high testing
halls.

Die Gebäudeecke des
Hörsaaltraktes mit den
sichtbaren Auskreuzungen
und ablesbarem Konstruk
tionsaufbau. Die Ver-
suchshallen sind zum
Gehsteig geöffnet und
gewähren Einblick in
die Forschungsarbeit
der Ingenieure.

Corner detail of lecture
hall tract with exposed
diagonal bracing and
legible structural system.
The testing halls open
on to the road, thus
allowing a view of the
engineering research
work conducted inside.

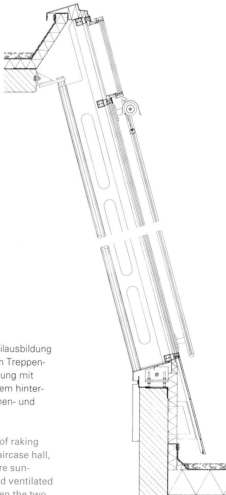

Rechts: Detailausbildung
der geneigten Treppen-
hallenverglasung mit
davorliegendem hinter-
lüfteten Sonnen- und
Blendschutz

Right: detail of raking
glazing to staircase hall,
with anti-glare sun-
screening and ventilated
cavity between the two
layers

Die Funktion der Bau-
elemente wird in ihrer
Gestalt sichtbar. Die
zentrale Treppenhalle,
gleichzeitig Ort der Kom-
munikation, verbindet
Versuchshallen, Labor-
und Bürobereiche.

The function of the indi-
vidual constructional
elements is revealed
through their form. The
central staircase hall
creates a link between
the testing halls, the laboratory and office tracts.
It also functions as a
place for communication.

Seminarraum mit Umgang;
nach außen geneigte Fassade
der Labors und Meßräume

Outer corridor to seminar
rooms. Bottom: raking
outer face of laboratory
and measuring tract

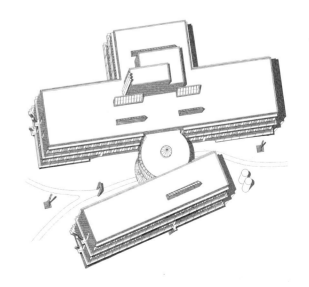

Die archaisch anmuten-
den Skulpturen von
Lothar Fischer stehen in
einem spannungsreichen
Gegensatz zum techni-
schen Erscheinungsbild
des Institutsgebäudes.

The archaic-looking
sculptures by Lothar
Fischer create an exciting
contrast to the technical
aesthetic of the institute
building.

Die ins Tal abfallende Topographie, die Erschließung vom All-
mandring, die Lernstraße und die
freie Landschaft zum Büsnauer
Tal sind Kriterien der städtebaulichen Lage des Gebäudes. Der
Neubau für die Bioverfahrenstechnik, eine hochspezialisierte Bauaufgabe, verlangt nach einer ähnlich spezialisierten Infrastruktur.
Das Bauvolumen von rund 90000
cbm umbauten Raumes auf dem
eher kleinen Grundstück stellte
die Entwurfsplanung vor eine
schwierige, aber interessante Aufgabe. Die Räume für die technische Gebäudeausrüstung umfas-
sen allein 57 % des Gesamt-
volumens. Da auf die umgebende
Bebauung Rücksicht zu nehmen
war, war es angestrebtes Ziel, die
sichtbare Baumasse gering zu
halten: Die Gebäudehöhe sollte
zwei Vollgeschosse nicht über-
schreiten.

Ein weiteres Entwurfsziel war
es, dem Institutsbau als naturwis-
senschaftlicher Arbeitsstätte ein

durch Technik geprägtes Erscheinungsbild zu geben und ihn für
zukünftige Entwicklungen offenzuhalten. Das geringe, ablesbare
Bauvolumen wurde durch die
Verlagerung der überwiegenden
Teile der Technik unter die Erde
erreicht.

An der Grundrißlösung ist
erkennbar, daß es galt, neben den
Forderungen der fünf Institute an
einen funktionalen Zusammenhang auch einen kommunikativen
Mittelpunkt für die Nutzer zu finden. Die angemessene Form für
Begegnungen der Wissenschaftler
mit den Studenten wurde in der
zentralen, runden Eingangshalle
als gemeinsamem Foyer gefunden. Zwei lineare Baukörper

Forschungszentrum Bioverfahrenstechnik
der Universität Stuttgart

Planungsbeginn: 1986
Bauzeit: 1989–1993

Centre for Biological
Process Engineering,
Stuttgart University

Commencement of
planning: 1986
Construction period:
1989–93

The main criteria for the location
of this complex and its integration into the existing urban
fabric were the topography of
the site on the sloping flank
of a valley, the line of access
from the Allmand ring road, the
Lernstrasse and the open landscape to the Büsnauer Valley.
A new structure for biological
process engineering represented
a highly specialized design task
and also required a specialized
infrastructure. Accommodating
the 90,000 m³ volume of the
building on the relatively small
site was a challenging but
interesting assignment. The
technical equipment alone occupies 57 per cent of the overall
space. Since the design also had
to take account of the surrounding developments, the architects
sought to keep the visible mass
of the building as small as
possible. The height above
ground was not to exceed two
full storeys.

   Further design goals were to
identify the institute as a centre
for scientific work through its
decidedly technical appearance
and to ensure that it would be
able to adapt to future developments. It proved possible to limit

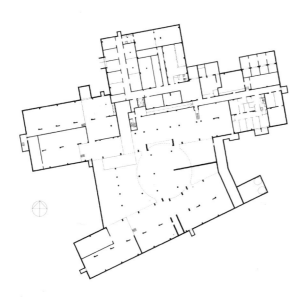

Oben: Grundriß Unter-
geschoß mit den ausge-
dehnten Technikflächen.
Links: Luftaufnahme des
Geländes der Universität
Stuttgart in Vaihingen. In
der Bildmitte links das
Forschungszentrum.
Rechte Seite: Grundriß
Erdgeschoß

Above: plan of basement
level with extensive areas
for technical uses. Left:
aerial view of University
of Stuttgart site in Vaihingen. In the middle of the
picture on the left is the
research centre. Opposite
page: ground floor plan

berühren die gläserne Rotunde, werden trichterförmig aufgeweitet und leiten fast selbstverständlich zum Haupteingang. Die Nutzungen der einzelnen Funktionsbereiche sind ablesbar und geben dem Gebäude einen unverwechselbaren Charakter. Neben einem durchgängigen Maßstab wurde in allen Bereichen eine formale Durchgängigkeit angestrebt. Das gewählte Baumaterial – in der Regel industriell hergestellte Produkte – wurde werkgerecht verarbeitet und farblich aufeinander abgestimmt. In Zusammenarbeit mit den Ingenieuren wurde ein logisches Tragwerk mit vertikalen, feuersicheren Schächten über alle Stockwerke entwickelt, das den Anforderungen der komplexen haustechnischen Installationen entspricht und Raum für spätere Nachrüstungen läßt. Knappe Details verdeutlichen die funktio-

nale Gestalt der einzelnen Bauteile. Durch den Raumabschluß der vorgesetzten Fluchtbalkone aus Glas und Metall staffelt sich die Fassade in zwei Ebenen und ist so von graphisch geometrischer Plastizität. Das tages- und jahreszeitlich bedingte unterschiedliche Licht verändert den visuellen Ausdruck der Fassaden ständig.

Das Kunstkonzept von Lothar Fischer, schon früh gemeinsam zwischen Nutzern, Universitätsbauamt, Kunstkommission der Oberfinanzdirektion und Architekten abgestimmt, ist der integrale Blickpunkt der Gesamtanlage. Die eisernen, archaisch anmutenden

the visible scale of the complex and to create a number of clearly legible volumes by placing the bulk of the technical facilities underground.

In addition to providing a functional link between the five institutes, the layout reveals an attempt to establish a central point of communication for the various users. The circular central entrance hall, which serves as a common foyer, has an appropriate form for a place where scientists may come together with students. This glazed rotunda is intersected by two linear structures. Set at an angle to each other, they funnel users and visitors automatically to the main entrance. The different uses of the individual realms are clearly legible and lend the building an unmistakable character. In addition to finding an acceptable scale for the complex, a consistent formal language was sought for all areas. The materials selected – mainly industrially manufactured products – were processed in an appropriate form and colour coordinated with each other.

In collaboration with the structural engineers, a logical load-bearing structure was developed with vertical fire-resisting shafts extending over all storeys. This system facilitated the installation of the elaborate mechani-

cal services and provided scope for future additions and modifications. The concise design details illustrate the functional nature of the individual components of the building. The escape balconies, projecting as a second layer in front of the glass and metal outer skin, lend the façade a geometric, three-dimensional quality and a sense of depth. The changes of light, depending on the time of day and the season, result in constant variations in the appearance of the façade.

The artistic concept by Lothar Fischer, which was endorsed at an early stage of the development by the users, the university construction office, the art commission of the regional financial administration and the architects themselves, creates an integral visual focus for the entire complex. The iron sculptures, with their archaic appearance, form an exciting counterpoint to the technical aesthetic of the façades.

Skulpturen stehen in spannungs-
reichem Gegensatz zu der durch
Technik geprägten Ästhetik der
Fassaden.

Die Anforderungen, die die
Wissenschaftler an die technische
Gebäudeausrüstung stellten, verlangten nach vielfältigen Ver- und
Entsorgungssystemen. Allein im
Bereich der technischen Medien
wurden 25 Ver- und Entsorgungs-
systeme installiert, z. B. für technische Gase, unterschiedliche Was-
ser- und Dampfqualitäten sowie
diverse Abwassersysteme. In den
Standardlabors wurden außer den
notwendigen Be- und Entlüftungsanlagen noch zusätzlich sieben
Sonderabluftsysteme eingebaut.
Spezielle Forderungen wurden

an die Sonderlabors für Isotopen,
S3 Labors und an die Biotech-
nikhalle gestellt. Grundsätzlich
mußte die gesamte Haustechnik
folgende Kriterien erfüllen: absolute Betriebssicherheit, Nach-
rüstbarkeit ohne Betriebsstö-
rung, Hygiene durch einsehbare
Installationen, leichte Wartung
unter weitgehendem Verzicht
auf abgehängte Decken. Alle
vertikalen und horizontalen offenen Leitungsführungen wurden
von den Architekten koordiniert.
Die überaus komplexe Gebäude-

ausrüstung bedeutete eine intensive Kooperation zwischen Architekten und Ingenieuren.

Das Tragwerk der Technikräume ist ein Stahlbetonskelett unter
der Erdoberkante. Die Instituts-
bauten wurden wegen der Instal-
lationsführungen in Stahlbeton-
verbundbauweise realisiert. Die
Rotunde ist ein reiner Stahlbau.

Ein kompliziertes Gebäude,
ein strenger, vielleicht ein spröder
Bau, nicht spektakulär, aber einfach, klar und solide, und von
den Professoren und Studenten
mit großer Zustimmung angenommen.

The needs of the scientists in terms of technical equipment required the installation of an elaborate array of supply and discharge systems. Alone in the realm of technical media, 25 supply and disposal systems were installed; for example, for technical gases, different qualities of water and water vapour, and for various waste and soil-water systems. The standard laboratories required not just air-supply and extract plants, but seven additional special ventilation systems. Specific requirements also had to be met in the special laboratories for isotopes, in the S3 laboratories and in the hall for biological engineering. The entire mechanical services had to comply with the following criteria: they had to guarantee absolute

Schnitt durch Biotechnikum, Institute und zentrale Halle. Deutlich zu erkennen ist das große Bauvolumen der technischen Gebäudeausrüstung im Untergeschoß.

Section through the biological engineering centre, the institute building and the central hall. The large underground volume of the building accommodating technical installations is clearly visible.

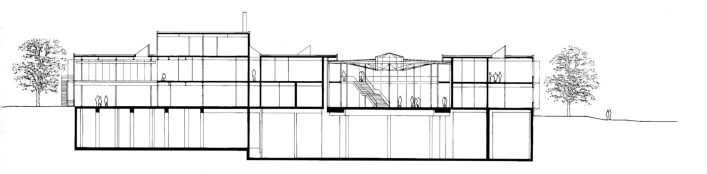

Die zweigeschossige Eingangshalle mit umlaufender Galerie im Obergeschoß bietet Raum für Begegnung und Kommunikation, Vorträge, Veranstaltungen und Ausstellungen.

The two-storey entrance hall with a peripheral gallery level provides a central space used as a meeting place and for lectures, exhibitions and other events.

operational safety; be capable of modification or extension without interrupting operations; be capable of inspection as a guarantee of hygiene; be easy to maintain and, therefore, not be concealed beneath suspended ceilings. All exposed service runs, both vertical and horizontal, were co-ordinated with each other by the architects. As a result of the extremely complex equipment and service installations required in the building, a close collaboration between architects and engineers was essential.

The load-bearing structure for the technical areas below ground was designed in the form of a reinforced concrete skeleton frame. Because of the service runs in the buildings for the various technical institutes, a reinforced concrete composite form of construction was chosen for these areas. The rotunda has an all-steel structure.

The result was a complex development, an austere, perhaps somewhat reserved building that does not reward the first, quick glance; an unspectacular building that is nevertheless simple, clear, sound and accepted enthusiastically by professors and students alike.

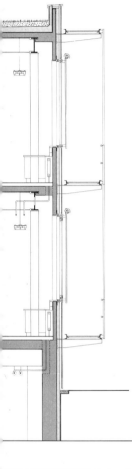

Den hinterlüfteten Raum-
abschluß bilden Stahlbe-
tonfertigteilbrüstungen.
Aluminiumfensterbänder
und die Brüstungsverklei-
dungen aus Aluminium-
wellblech sind silberbe-
schichtet.

Precast concrete parapet
wall elements with rear
ventilated cavities form
part of the outer skin.
The strip windows and
the corrugated sheet
cladding to the parapet
walls are in silver-coated
aluminium.

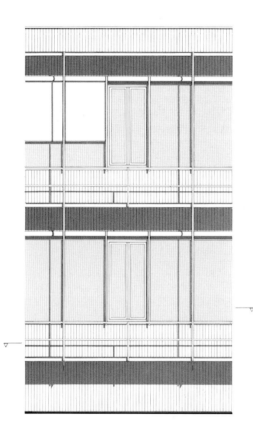

Durch die vorgesetzten
Fluchtbalkone, die addi-
tiven Sonnenschutzan-
lagen und die Flucht-
treppen erhält die Fassade
in der Tiefe versetzte
Ebenen und damit eine
vorbestimmte graphische
Plastizität.

The projecting escape
balconies, the additive
sunscreen system and
the escape stairs create
a series of layers that
lend the façade a vivid
three-dimensional quality.

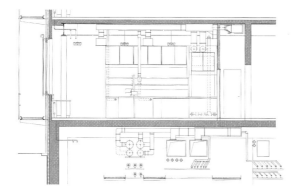

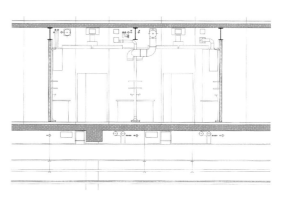

Längs- und Querschnitt
durch ein Standardlabor
mit Laboreinrichtung und
der vertikalen sowie horizontalen Führung der
Installationen

Longitudinal section and
cross-section through a
standard laboratory,
showing technical instal-
lations and vertical and
horizontal service runs

Links: Das Herzstück des Forschungszentrums ist die zweigeschossige Großfermenterhalle, die von allen Instituten genutzt wird. Rechts: Grundriß eines Standardlabors mit den senkrechten Installationsschächten an den Flurwänden, in denen die 25 Medien in die Labors geführt werden.

Left: the two-storey main fermentation hall used by all institutes forms the heart of the research centre. Right: plan of standard laboratory. Along the corridor walls are vertical services shafts, in which 25 technical media are fed into the laboratories.

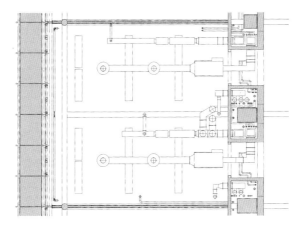

In den Technikräumen des Untergeschosses werden alle Haus- und Gebäudetechnischen Installationen unter der Decke zu den Laborräumen geführt.

All mechanical services and special installations are routed to the laboratories beneath the soffits of the technical spaces in the basement.

Alle Institutsflure im Obergeschoß erhalten von oben natürliches Tageslicht. In den Institutsfluren sind Lichtbänder angeordnet, die auch eine natürliche Belichtung der Erdgeschoßflure ermöglichen.

All institute corridors on the upper floor receive natural light from above. Strip windows also allow daylight to enter the ground floor corridors.

Williamsburg Bridge,
New York

Competition: 1988
First prize

As part of its programme to renew Williamsburg Bridge, which was in a dilapidated state, the City of New York held an international engineering competition. From a total of 62 groups of engineers throughout the world, 21 teams were chosen to participate. Twenty-five competition entries were submitted.

The existing suspension bridge, dating from 1903, links Manhattan with Brooklyn across the East River. It has an overall length of 918 m, with a free-spanning middle section 488 m long. Every day, some 240,000 persons cross the bridge on its eight road lanes and two urban railway lines. The competition brief required a reduction of the road to six lanes and the addition of a third railway line. The most important aim, however, was to develop a concept that would allow the construction of a new bridge with a minimum of disturbance to the flow of traffic. In other words, ideally the old bridge was to be removed and replaced with a new one without causing any disruption.

The competition team, led by Jörg Schlaich and Rudolf Bergermann, produced a design for a suspension bridge that met the requirements of the brief in optimum form. The cable-stayed bridge type usually favoured for large spans was not appropriate in this urban situation because of the great rigidity. A suspension bridge, with all the advantages it implies in terms of design and scale, provided a more restrained solution and fitted much better into the world-famous ensemble of the nearby Brooklyn and Manhattan Bridges.

Other features of the design include additional diagonal cables in the main span to restrict deformation, the orthotropic slab laid on the steel bridge structure, and steel pylons filled with concrete. The existing abutments were still in good condition and could be used for anchoring the main cables.

The project proposed the construction of two new segments – one on each side of the existing bridge – without interrupting the flow of traffic. During the phase of dismantling the old bridge structure, the new sections were to be used to keep the traffic moving. After the removal of the existing lanes, the two new segments were to be pushed together and aligned with the former axis of Williamsburg Bridge. The interruption to traffic for this shifting process was scheduled to last only two weeks. What is more, no existing buildings had to be demolished.

The competition design was not realized, however, and the old Williamsburg Bridge is at present being refurbished. In the context of the American tradition of large-scale bridge-building, this, of course, has its positive aspects.

Client: New York City Department of Transportation

Structural design: Consulting Engineers Schlaich, Bergermann und Partner, Stuttgart; Walther & Mory, Basle

Architectural advisers: Myron Goldsmith, Chicago; Kurt Ackermann und Partner, Munich

Zur Erneuerung der baufälligen Williamsburgbrücke wurde von der Stadt New York ein internationaler Ingenieurwettbewerb ausgeschrieben. Weltweit wurden aus zweiundsechzig Ingenieurgruppen einundzwanzig teilnehmende Wettbewerbsteams ausgewählt. Fünfundzwanzig Wettbewerbsbeiträge wurden zur Beurteilung eingereicht.

Die 918 m lange, mit einem Mittelfeld von 488 m freigespannte Hängebrücke über den East River aus dem Jahre 1903 verbindet Manhattan mit Brooklyn. Täglich gibt es hier eine Verkehrsbelastung von etwa 240 000 Passanten auf acht Straßenspuren und zwei Stadtbahngleisen. In der Wettbewerbsausschreibung der Brücke wurden nur noch sechs Spuren, aber drei Gleise für die Stadtbahn gefordert. Wichtigstes Ziel des Wettbewerbs war es, ein Konzept zu entwickeln, das es erlaubt, mit geringstmöglicher Verkehrsunterbrechung eine neue Brücke zu realisieren. Die alte Brücke sollte einfach ausgetauscht werden.

Das Wettbewerbsteam, unter Federführung von Jörg Schlaich und Rudolf Bergermann, erarbeitete den optimalen Entwurf für eine Hängebrücke. Die für große Spannweiten bevorzugte Schrägkabelbrücke war für diesen Ort und in dieser städtebaulichen Umgebung mit der bestimmten rigiden Steifheit nicht befriedigend. Die Hängebrücke mit ihren gestalterischen und maßstäblichen Vorteilen fügt sich besser und behutsamer in das weltbekannte Ensemble der benachbarten Brooklyn- und Manhattan-Brücken ein.

Weitere Merkmale des Entwurfs sind die zusätzlichen Schrägseile im Hauptfeld zur Verformungsbegrenzung sowie der Überbau der Stahlbrücke mit orthotroper Platte und ausbetonierten Stahlpylonen. Die vorhandenen, gut erhaltenen Widerlager wurden zur Rückverankerung der Hauptkabel verwendet.

Zwei neue Brückenhälften sollten beiderseits der vorhandenen Brücke bei weiterlaufendem Verkehr neu gebaut werden. Während des konstruktiven Rückbaus der alten Brücke übernehmen die neuen Brückenteile den laufenden Verkehr. Nach dem Abbruch der alten Fahrbahnen werden die beiden neuen Brückenhälften auf die jetzige Achse der Williamsburgbrücke zusammengeschoben. Die Verkehrsunterbrechung für den Verschiebevorgang beträgt nur zwei Wochen; kein Gebäude muß abgebrochen werden.

Der Wettbewerbsbeitrag wird nicht realisiert. Die alte Williamsburgbrücke wird renoviert, was sicher für die amerikanische Tradition im Großbrückenbau als positiver Beitrag zu werten ist.

Auftraggeber: New York City Department of Transportation; Konstruktiver Entwurf: Beratende Ingenieure Schlaich, Bergermann und Partner, Stuttgart, Walther & Mory, Basel; Architektonische Beratung: Myron Goldsmith, Chicago, Kurt Ackermann und Partner, München

Städtebauliche Situation der Williamsburgbrücke über den East River; im Hintergrund Manhattan und Brooklyn

Urban context of Williamsburg Bridge across the East River; in the background, Manhattan and Brooklyn

Williamsburgbrücke, New York

Wettbewerb 1988
1. Preis

Directorate-General 2
of the European
Patent Office, Munich

Commencement of
planning: 1979
Construction period:
1988 – 93

The former Hacker-Pschorr brewery site in Munich is steeped in tradition. It is bounded by Bayerstrasse, Zollstrasse and Grasserstrasse and by the railway lines leading out of Munich main station. After the relocation of the brewery, this valuable city-centre site with excellent traffic links was to be put to a new use. As early as 1979, the developer Josef Schörghuber commissioned designs for a scheme comprising a 300-room hotel and freehold housing. In a second phase, the project was extended by a congress centre for trade fairs, but during the development stage, Munich city council decided to move the trade fairs venue to a location in Riem outside the centre. The next planning brief for the former brewery site proposed a commercial complex with dwellings. This, in turn, was followed by a scheme for a purely leasehold office development, with smaller units up to 300 m² in area. Construction of the first phase of the project began in Zollstrasse, at which point the European Patent Office decided to purchase the entire commercial content. The outcome was a further revision of the planning – the fifth scheme in all – with a new spatial programme to meet the special needs of the patent organization.

The urban planning concept comprised a five-storey development along Bayer-, Grasser- and Zollstrasse, where the moderate eaves height took account of the older buildings in the neighbourhood. The land-use plan drawn up by the architects proposed

**Generaldirektion 2
des Europäischen Patentamtes EPA**
München

Planungsbeginn: 1979
Bauzeit: 1988 –1993

Von der Hackerbrücke zur Bayerstraße entsteht eine neue Fußgängerverbindung – Pschorrgasse – durch die Anlage des EPA. Der Stadtteil Neuhausen wird dadurch direkt mit der Theresienwiese verbunden.

A new pedestrian link – Pschorrgasse – was created across the European Patent Office site between Hacker Bridge and Bayerstrasse. It connects the district of Neuhausen with the Theresienwiese, where the Oktoberfest is held.

Das Brauereigelände der traditionsreichen Hacker-Pschorr-Brauerei wird begrenzt von der Bayerstraße, Zoll- und Grasserstraße und den Gleisanlagen des Münchner Hauptbahnhofes. Nach Auslagerung der Brauerei sollte das wertvolle Areal in der Innenstadt mit bester Verkehrserschließung einer neuen Nutzung zugeführt werden. Bereits im Jahre 1979 erteilte Josef Schörghuber den Auftrag zur Erarbeitung von Entwürfen für ein Hotel mit 300 Zimmern und Wohnungen im Privateigentum. In einer zweiten Phase wurde das Projekt um ein Kon-

greßzentrum für die Münchener Messe erweitert. Während der Bearbeitungsphase faßte der Stadtrat der Landeshauptstadt München den Beschluß, die Messe nach München-Riem zu verlagern. Das neue Planungsziel war nun ein Bürozentrum mit Wohnungen; darauf folgte eine weitere Planungsstufe für reine Mietbüros mit kleinen Einheiten bis zu 300 qm. Mit dem Bau des ersten Bauabschnitts wurde an der Zollstraße begonnen, bis sich das Europäische Patentamt zum Kauf aller gewerblichen Nutzungen entschloß.

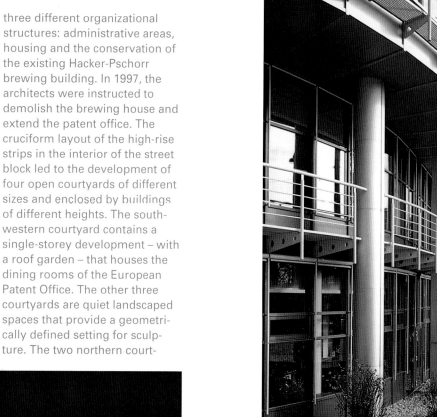

three different organizational
structures: administrative areas,
housing and the conservation of
the existing Hacker-Pschorr
brewing building. In 1997, the
architects were instructed to
demolish the brewing house and
extend the patent office. The
cruciform layout of the high-rise
strips in the interior of the street
block led to the development of
four open courtyards of different
sizes and enclosed by buildings
of different heights. The south-
western courtyard contains a
single-storey development – with
a roof garden – that houses the
dining rooms of the European
Patent Office. The other three
courtyards are quiet landscaped
spaces that provide a geometri-
cally defined setting for sculpture. The two northern court-

Die Form des Gebäudes
wird bestimmt durch die
für diesen Stadtteil typische Blockstruktur.

In their form, the build-
ings adopt the typical
street block structure of
the neighbourhood.

yards contain a group of stelae
by Nikolaus Gerhart and a granite and steel sculpture by Markus
Stangl. In the large entrance
court is Max Bill's meandering
granite sculpture "rhythm in
space", through which visitors
can walk.
    At Hacker Bridge, at the end
of the newly created Pschorrgasse pedestrian lane, is a tree-
lined square with space for a
beer garden. The lane, which
leads from the bridge to Bayerstrasse, forms a link with the
Theresienwiese where the
Oktoberfest is held and is a
much-frequented route during
that festival. Unfortunately, the
pedestrian bridge proposed
by the architects over Bayerstrasse was not realized. Also
in Pschorrgasse, the sculptor

Damit begann die fünfte Umplanung nach einem neuen Raumprogramm, diesmal für die speziellen Bedürfnisse der Europäischen Patentorganisation.

Grundlage für die städtebauliche Disposition war die fünfgeschossige Randbebauung entlang der Bayer-, Grasser- und Zollstraße. Durch die maßvollen Traufhöhen wurde auf den Altbestand der Nachbarschaft Rücksicht genommen. Der von den Architekten entwickelte Bebauungsplan hatte drei organisatorisch unterschiedliche Strukturen der Nutzung: Verwalten, Wohnen und Bestandsschutz für das zu belassende Sudhaus der Hacker-Pschorr-Brauerei. 1997 erhielten die Architekten den Auftrag, das Sudhaus abzureißen und das EPA zu erweitern. Durch die kreuzförmige Anordnung der im inneren Bereich situierten Hochhausscheibe entstehen vier unterschiedlich dimensionierte, auch in der Höhenentwicklung differenzierte, offene Innenhöfe. Der südwestliche für das Casino des EPA wurde erdgeschossig überbaut und mit einem Dachgarten versehen. Die drei anderen ruhigen Höfe wurden gärtnerisch gestaltet und bilden einen geometrisch definierten Raum für Skulpturen. In den beiden nördlichen Höfen stehen eine Stelengruppe von Nikolaus Gerhart und eine Granit-Stahl-Skulptur von Markus Stangl. Den großen Eingangshof bereichert die begehbare, mäanderförmige Granitskulptur ›rhythmus im raum‹ von Max Bill.

An der Hackerbrücke wurde als Auftakt für die neu entstandene fußläufige Pschorrgasse ein

Das Europäische Patentamt ist ein Förderer moderner Kunst. Ein umfangreiches Konzept der Architekten zur Ausgestaltung wurde von verschiedenen Künstlern umgesetzt. Linke Seite: Nikolaus Gerhart, ›Ohne Titel‹; oben: Hannsjörg Voth, ›Zwischen Sonnentor und Mondplatz‹; links: Max Bill, ›rhythmus im raum‹

The European Patent Office demonstrates its role as a patron of modern art. The architects drew up a comprehensive concept for complementing the scheme with works of art. It was implemented by a number of artists. Opposite page: stelae "Untitled" by Nikolaus Gerhart; top: Hannsjörg Voth's "Between Sun Gate and Moon Square"; left: Max Bill's "rhythm in space"

In der Luftaufnahme ist
die städtebauliche Ein-
fügung in die Münchner
Blockstruktur deutlich
zu erkennen. Im Lageplan
ist die Erweiterung des
EPA 1997–99 bereits
dargestellt.

Aerial view, showing
the integration of the
development in the urban
street block structure.
The site plan includes
the patent office exten-
sion, 1997–99.

Kontrastreiche Akzente
setzen die gestreiften
Markisen des außenlie-
genden Sonnenschutzes.
Die Erdgeschoß- und
Mezzaninzonen sind zwei-
geschossig zurückgenom-
men, an der Bayerstraße
wurde eine begleitende
Pappelallee gepflanzt.
Eingangsskulptur von
Christian Hinz

The striped external sun-
blinds form a bold con-
trast to the façade. The
ground floor and mezza-
nine zone is set back. A
row of poplars has been
planted along the Bayer-
strasse front. The sculp-
ture at the entrance is by
Christian Hinz.

Hannsjörg Voth has created an austere yet aesthetically convincing spatial experience with his large-scale sculpture "Between Sun Gate and Moon Square".

The slender proportions of the silvery metal elevations along the perimeter street development adopt the scale of the rendered façades opposite. The legible load-bearing structure, the additive sunscreen blinds fixed at a distance to the façade, the three-dimensional quality of the recesses and projections of the vertical elements, and the set-back ground floor zones all help

The standard floors have a dual aspect, while the ten-storey central tracts are organized about a three-bay layout. The offices along the busy street face of Bayerstrasse are mechanically ventilated. All office areas have cooling soffits, although the windows can be opened individually. Even the automatically operated external sunblinds or louvres can be singly controlled. The ten conference rooms had to be air-conditioned because of the acoustic insulation that is necessary there. They are also equipped with simultaneous interpreting equipment for international patent-law meetings.

The offices of the European patent organization provide 1,500 workplaces designed to the most exacting standards. In the two-storey basement garage, which has a separate entrance and exit, there is space for 1,442 cars.

The working drawings were prepared to the architects' standard details by the architectural practice of Klaus Bellmann in Munich.

Ablesbare Tragstrukturen und feingliedrige Fassadenteilung gehen auf den Maßstab der umgebenden Bebauung ein.

The legible load-bearing structure and the slender façade divisions adopt the scale of the surrounding developments.

to articulate the imposing ensemble of the European Patent Office with its almost 80,000 m² gross floor area.

The strict articulation of the silver-grey aluminium panels gives the entire complex a uniform, semi-lustre skin that is subject to different effects at different times of day and with the changing seasons.

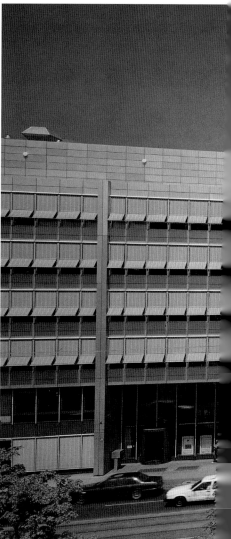

Hannsjörg Voths ›Sonnentor‹ bildet den südlichen Abschluß der Pschorrgasse. Die eingelegte Bodenlinie entspricht dem Sonnenstand zur Mittagszeit.

Hannsjörg Voth's "Sun Gate" forms a closing piece to Pschorrgasse at its southern end. The line inset in the pavings marks the ray of light cast by the midday sun.

baumbestandener Platz für einen Biergarten geschaffen, eine optimale Fußgängerverbindung zur Theresienwiese. Leider wurde die von den Architekten entworfene Fußgängerbrücke über die Bayerstraße nicht realisiert. Der Bildhauer Hannsjörg Voth hat in der Pschorrgasse mit seiner Großskulptur ›Zwischen Sonnentor und Mondplatz‹ einen strengen, ästhetisch überzeugenden Erlebnisraum zwischen Hackerbrücke und Bayerstraße gestaltet, der allerdings nur in der Oktoberfestzeit stark frequentiert ist.

Die feingliedrigen silbernen Metallfassaden entlang der Straßenrandbebauung nehmen den Maßstab der gegenüberliegenden Putzfassaden auf. Die ablesbare Tragstuktur, die additiven, im Abstand montierten Sonnenschutz-Rollos, die plastischen Vor- und Rücksprünge der vertikalen Bauteile und die zurückgenommenen Erdgeschoßzonen gliedern die stattliche Bauanlage des Europäischen Patentamtes mit einer fast 80 000 qm großen Bruttogeschoßfläche.

Die strenge Gliederung der silbergrauen Aluminium-Paneele gibt der ganzen Anlage eine einheitlich matt glänzende Hülle,

die bei unterschiedlichen Tages- und Jahreszeiten von jeweils anderer Wirkung ist.

Die Grundrisse der Normalgeschosse sind zweihüftig, der zehngeschossige Mittelteil dreihüftig. Die Büros entlang der verkehrsreichen Straßenrandbebauung der Bayerstraße sind zwangsgelüftet. Alle Büros haben Kühldecken, wobei die Fenster individuell geöffnet werden können; auch die automatisch gesteuerten außenliegenden Markisen oder Lamellen sind individuell regelbar. Die zehn Sitzungssäle sind aus Schallschutzgründen klimatisiert und mit Simultananlagen für internationale Patentrechtssitzungen ausgestattet.

Das Dienstgebäude des Europäischen Patentamtes bietet 1500 Arbeitsplätze, die höchsten Ansprüchen genügen. In einer zweigeschossigen Tiefgarage mit getrennten Ein- und Ausfahrten sind 1442 Stellplätze für Pkw untergebracht.

Für die Ausführungsplanung zeichnete nach den Regeldetails der Architekten das Münchner Architekturbüro Klaus Bellmann verantwortlich.

Gartner Construction Office, Gundelfingen on the Danube

Commencement of planning: 1988
Construction period: 1989 – 91

The new premises for the Gartner construction company in the Bavarian-Swabian town of Gundelfingen were designed to provide a suitable office environment for the company's engineers, who work mainly in groups. All workplaces were to be of roughly the same quality and be suitable for both drawing-board and computer activities. The building was, therefore, designed with an open structure that would facilitate communication and teamwork.

The development took the form of two pavilions 42 m long and 21 m wide, each of which consists of a large undivided space extending over two storeys and containing bridges and gallery areas. The visual and acoustic links between the spaces mean that they are not subject to any hierarchical order. Furthermore, they are ideally suited to concentrated mental work, communication or group activities. Each of the pavilions contains 75 workplaces. The complex can be extended by adding a third pavilion.

The technical installations served as an experimental area for new developments in the fields of thermal and solar insulation, temperature control and daylighting. The control of the lighting quality was of special importance in view of the high degree of flexibility required.

Das Entwurfsziel für den Bau des Konstruktionsbüros Gartner im bayerisch-schwäbischen Gundelfingen war, geeignete Räume für vorwiegend in Gruppen arbeitende Ingenieure zu schaffen. Alle Arbeitsplätze sollten annähernd die gleiche Qualität haben und für Reißbrett wie Bildschirm tauglich sein. Um diese Bedingungen zu erfüllen, wurde eine offene Gebäudestruktur gewählt.

Es entstanden zwei Pavillons mit 42,0 m Länge und 21,0 m Tiefe, die jeweils aus einem sich über zwei Stockwerke erstreckenden Großraum bestehen, in dem Flächen für Brücken oder Galerien angeordnet sind. Der optisch wie akustisch verbundene Raum hat keine hierarchische Gliederung und eignet sich bestens für Denkarbeit, Kommunikation und Teamwork. Jeder Pavillon hat 75 Arbeitsplätze. Ein dritter Pavillon als Erweiterung kann hinzugefügt werden. Die technische Gebäudeausrüstung dient als Experimentierfeld für neue Entwicklungen des Wärme- und Sonnenschutzes, der Temperatursteuerung und der Belichtung, wobei der Steuerung der Lichtqualität wegen der hohen Flexibilität besondere Bedeutung zukommt.

Der Grundgedanke beim Tragwerk ist ein freistehender Tisch für die Untergeschoßdecke in Stahlverbundbauweise mit geneigter schwebender Dachkonstruktion, die einen maximalen Lichteinfall zuläßt und optimale Reflexionsflächen ermöglicht. Das Haupttragsystem bilden Y-Stahlrahmen aus Rohrstützen mit Kragträgern, die im Abstand von 6,8 m über zwei Geschosse reichen. Die Spannweite zwischen den Y-Stützen beträgt 13,6 m, die Kragarmlänge 3,4 m zum Rand und 4,2 m zur Mitte. Deckenriegel und Dachkragträger werden über die Fassadenstützen abgespannt.

Für den äußeren Raumabschluß wurde eine integrierte Fassade gewählt. Die wasserdurchströmten Stahlrohrquerschnitte der Pfosten-Riegel-Konstruktion dienen zum Heizen oder Kühlen.

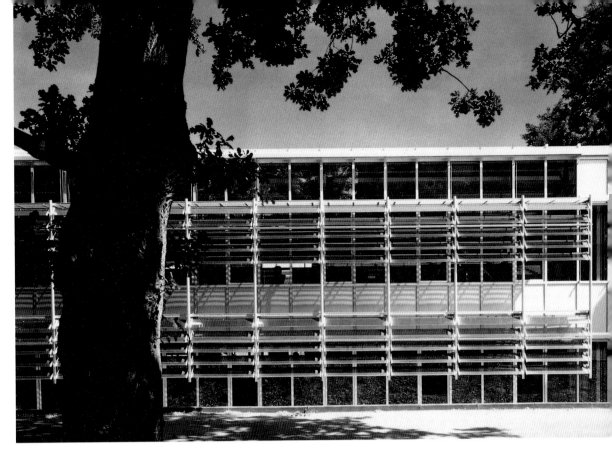

Additiv vor die Fassade gehängte gläserne Lichtumlenksysteme gliedern die Längsfassaden der beiden Pavillonbauten und nehmen die Wartungsbalkone mit Gitterrosten als Belag auf.

Maintenance balconies with metal grating walkways are suspended from the long faces of the two pavilion structures. Integrated into them are additive light-deflecting systems in glass that also serve to articulate the façades.

Konstruktionsbüro Gartner, Gundelfingen/Donau

Planungsbeginn: 1988
Bauzeit: 1989–1991

The concept of a free-standing table formed the basic model for the floor structure over the lower level. The structure is in a steel composite form of construction and supports a "floating", sloping roof that ensures a maximum entry of daylight and optimum reflective surfaces. The main load-bearing system comprises a series of steel Y-frames that extend over two floors. Spaced at 6.80 m centres, the Y-frames consist of tubular columns with cantilevered arms. The lateral span between the columns is 13.6 m. The cantilevered arms extend 3.4 m to the outer edge of the building and 4.2 m to the centre. The floor beams and cantilevered roof beams are anchored to the façade columns.

An integrated façade system was chosen for the outer skin. Water flowing through the tubular steel post-and-rail construction serves as a means of heating or cooling.

The roof was designed as a "fifth façade" and covered with the same sandwich elements as were used for the façades themselves. Aluminium composite sections with a twofold thermal separation were developed as frames for the glazing and façade panels. Three-layer thermally insulating glazing with two infrared reflecting layers and an inert gas filling was used for the transparent areas of the façade and the glass roof. Compared with conventional double glazing, this kind of glazing can reduce thermal losses through transmission by up to 70 per cent.

The escape and maintenance balconies attached to the north and south faces filter the light that enters the building. They also support the frameless, pivoted glass louvres that function as a sunscreening system and a means of deflecting light. The louvres are 10 mm thick and 300 mm wide and are fixed with their pivoting axis parallel to the outer face of the building. By adjusting the position of the louvres when the façade is exposed to direct sunlight, an even shading of the windows is possible without creating a banding effect. In contrast to conventional systems with non-transparent louvres, the present sunscreen installation allows an unimpeded view from the interior to the world outside, even when the louvres are closed. When the sky is overcast, when the sun is high

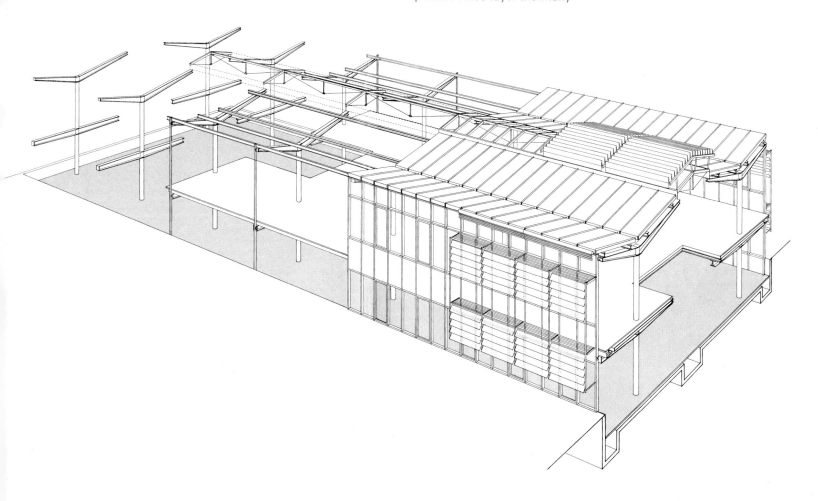

Das Tragwerk aus zwei gegenüberstehenden Y-förmigen Stahlrahmen mit dazwischengehängtem Glassatteldach gibt dem Bau einen durch die Funktion geprägten, charakteristischen Gebäudequerschnitt.

The main load-bearing structure consists of two parallel rows of Y-shape steel frames, between which a glazed pitched roof light is suspended over the entire length of the pavilions. The distinctive cross-sectional form of the building is, therefore, the outcome of functional needs.

Das Dach wurde als fünfte Fassade mit den gleichen selbsttragenden Sandwich-Elementen wie die vertikalen Fassadenelemente eingedeckt. Als Rahmen für die Verglasung und die Paneele der Fassade wurden Verbundprofile aus Aluminium mit doppelter thermischer Trennung entwickelt. Im transparenten Bereich der Fassade und des Glasdaches ist eine Dreifach-Wärmeschutzverglasung mit zwei infrarotreflektierenden Schichten und Edelgasfüllungen eingebaut. Gegenüber einer konventionellen Zwei-Scheiben-Isolierverglasung lassen sich mit diesen Gläsern die Transmissionswärmeverluste um 70 % reduzieren.

Der an der Nord- und Südfassade vorgehängte Flucht- und Wartungsbalkon filtert das Licht und ist gleichzeitig Konstruktionsträger der Glaslamellen für Sonnenschutz und die Lichtumlenkung. Der Sonnenschutz besteht aus rahmenlosen, schwenkbaren Glaslamellen mit einer Stärke von

10 mm und einer Breite von 300 mm, deren drehbare Achsen parallel zur Fassade angeordnet sind. Damit wird bei entsprechender Stellung der Lamellen eine streifenfreie Abschattung der Fensterflächen gegenüber direkter Sonneneinstrahlung sichergestellt. Im Gegensatz zu herkömmlichen Systemen mit nichttransparenten Lamellen ermöglicht diese transparente Sonnenschutzvorrichtung eine unbeeinträchtigte Sichtverbindung von innen nach außen, auch wenn die Lamellen aufgrund des Sonneneinfallswinkels geschlossen sein müssen. Bei vollständig bedecktem Himmel wie bei hohem Sonnenstand oder in Zeiträumen, in denen die Fassade von direkter Sonnenstrahlung nicht getroffen wird, können die Lamellen in eine horizontale Stellung geschwenkt werden und garantieren eine maximale Durchsicht. Weiter läßt sich über die

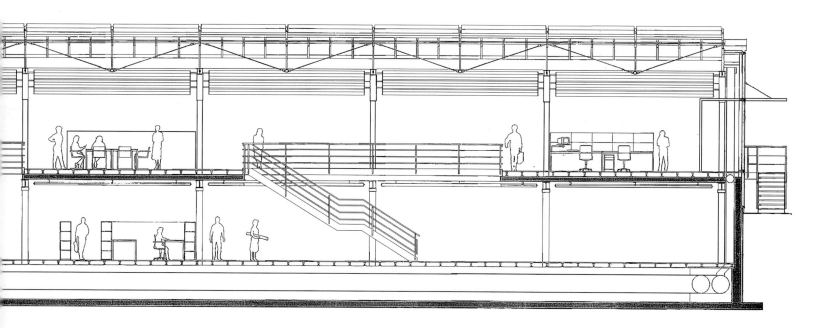

in the sky, or when the façade is not subject to direct insolation, the louvres can be turned to a horizontal position and thus guarantee maximum transparency and unimpeded views out. The reflective coating of the louvres also permits daylight to be deflected on to the diffusely reflecting internal soffits and thus improve the natural lighting conditions of areas further away from the windows.

Glass roofs were installed over the entire length of both pavilions to ensure optimum lighting conditions even in the middle of the internal spaces. The roofs can be shaded by a computer-operated sunscreen system, consisting of natural anodized aluminium pivoting louvres. When the angle of incidence of the sun is low, the louvres are moved to a vertical position; when the sun is high, the louvres are tilted slightly to the north. The effect is similar to that of a north-light roof, where direct insolation is screened off, but diffused light from the north can enter the building. The degree of light-transmission of this construction is optimized by using louvres with a slender cross-section, 60 mm, and a light-coloured, diffusely reflecting surface.

To improve the daylighting of the lower storey, which was sunk into the ground for urban planning reasons, large gallery-like openings were formed in the floor above. The workplaces beneath these light wells receive direct daylight through the glass roof.

Reflective cooling soffits help to achieve an even distribution of light even in the areas furthest removed from the windows. These soffits consist of white powder-coated aluminium sheeting and hollow sections through which water is fed. The cooling or heating effect is achieved by means of radiation, so that there are no unpleasant draughts, as are sometimes experienced with dynamic cooling systems. Provision is made for individual ventilation via the windows. This is complemented by fresh-air inlets in the façade balustrade panels. At night, depending on temperature forecasts, the building can be cooled. To ensure an agreeable indoor atmosphere, great importance was attached to allowing users individual control over all service facilities.

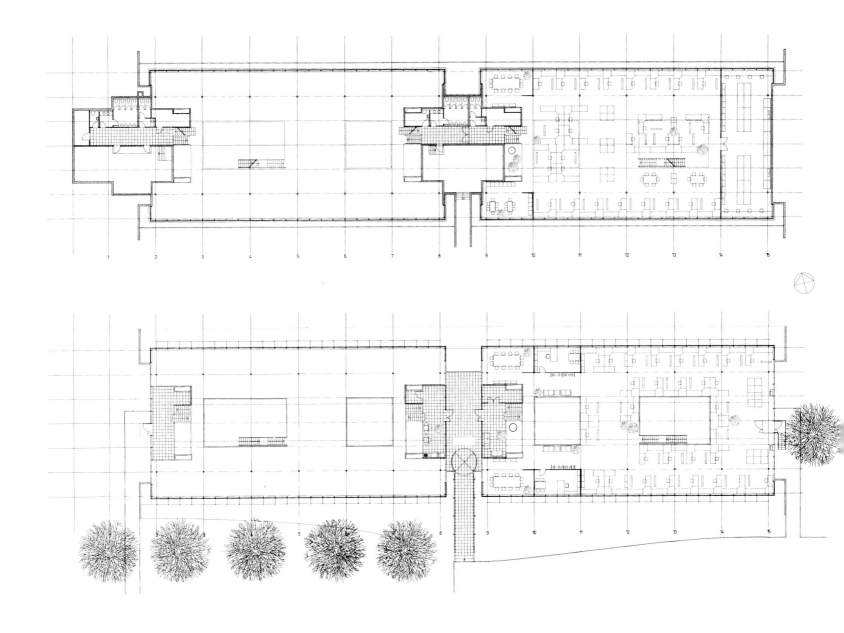

Reflexionsbeschichtung Tageslicht an die diffus reflektierenden Raumdecken lenken, wodurch auch die tieferliegenden Arbeitsbereiche des Gebäudes aufgehellt werden.

Um auch in der Raummitte optimale Lichtqualität zu erreichen, liegt über der gesamten Länge jedes Pavillons ein Glasdach. Dieses läßt sich durch einen computergesteuerten Sonnenschutz aus schwenkbaren, im Naturton eloxierten Aluminiumlamellen verschatten. Bei niedrigem Sonnenstand stehen die Lamellen vertikal, bei hohem Sonnenstand leicht nach Norden geneigt. Dadurch wird, ähnlich wie bei einem Nord-Sheddach, die direkte Sonnenstrahlung ausgeblendet, die diffuse Strahlung von Norden kann in das Gebäude ein-

dringen. Der Lichttransmissionsgrad der Konstruktion wurde durch einen schlanken Lamellenquerschnitt von 60 mm und eine helle, diffus reflektierende Oberfläche optimiert.

Zur Erhöhung der Tageslichtnutzung in dem aus städtebaulichen Gründen abgesenkten Untergeschoß wurde die Geschoßdecke durch großflächige galerieartige Öffnungen unterbrochen. Die Arbeitsplätze im Bereich dieser Lichthöfe erhalten Tageslicht durch das Glasdach.

Für eine gleichmäßige Lichtverteilung über die Tiefe des Raumes hinweg sorgen reflektierende Kühldecken. Die Konstruktion der Kühldecke besteht aus

weißen, pulverbeschichteten Aluminiumblechen mit wasserführenden Profilen. Die Kühl- und Heizwirkung wird durch Strahlung erreicht. Unangenehme Zugerscheinungen wie bei dynamischen Kühlsystemen gibt es nicht. Neben der Möglichkeit der individuellen Lüftung über die Fenster erfolgt die Frischluftversorgung durch Quellüftung. Die Luftaustrittsöffnungen sind in die Brüstungsverkleidungen der Fassade integriert. In der Nacht kann das Gebäude der vorhergesagten Temperatur der Wetterberichtslage entsprechend gekühlt werden. Um ein behagliches Raumklima zu erreichen, wurde bei allen gebäudetechnischen Einrichtungen größter Wert auf die individuelle Regelbarkeit durch die Benutzer gelegt.

Die Form des Innenraumes ist auch durch die doppelten Y-Stützen und durch das Satteldachoberlicht geprägt.

The internal spatial form is partly determined by the double row of Y-columns and the pitched roof light.

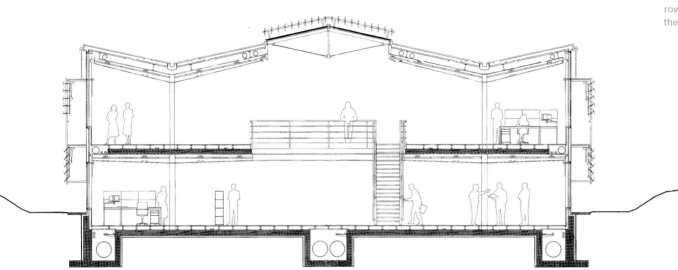

Leider wurde die von den Architekten vorgeschlagene Einrichtung mit dem USM-Haller-System nicht ausgeführt.

Unfortunately, the architects' proposal using the USM-Haller-System was not executed.

Die offenen Räume der beiden Pavillons lassen unterschiedliche Arbeitsplatzsituationen mit individueller Ausprägung und die für die Teamarbeit notwendige Flexibilität zu.

The undivided internal spaces of the two pavilions permit a variety of working situations. All workplaces have their own distinct character. At the same time, they possess the necessary flexibility to allow group activities.

Die verspiegelten Glaslamellen werden elektronisch gesteuert und ermöglichen einen optimalen Lichteinfall.

The electronically controlled reflective glass louvres permit an optimum penetration of daylight.

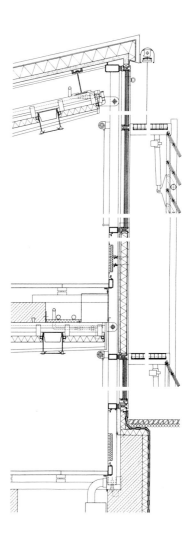

Die Glaslamellen bieten einerseits die Möglichkeit, bei Computerarbeitsplätzen Licht auszublenden, andererseits, bei dem manuellen Arbeitsplatz am Zeichentisch Licht in den Raum einzuspiegeln.

The glass louvres provide the option of screening light from computer workplaces or of deflecting daylight into areas where staff work manually at drawing boards.

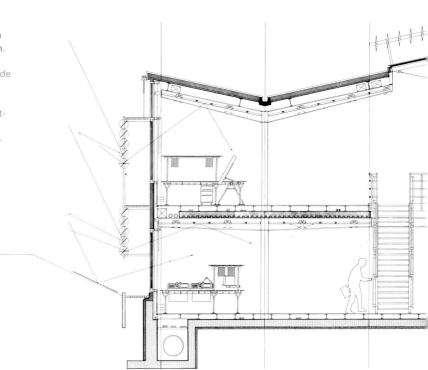

German Pavilion,
World Exposition '92,
Seville

Competition: 1990

"What and how the united Federal Republic of Germany will be in 1992 and how it will wish to present itself are things no one knows today, two years before the event. For that reason, no attempt has been made to formulate indefinable contents in the design. An open architectural concept has been developed that can be varied up to the very last minute."
From the architects' explanatory notes to the competition submission

A compact, six-storey rectilinear volume was designed, the structure of which allows a high degree of variation. The house-within-a-house principle on which the pavilion is based guarantees a pleasant indoor climate and an optimum energy balance. The 65,000 m³ inner volume is enclosed within a climate-regulating outer skin. Nine concave membrane mirror elements were installed on the roof for the supply of energy.

They are mounted on tracks in such a way that they can be steered to follow the course of the sun. Suspended at their focal points are energy transformers that convert solar heat into electricity.

The building is 54 m wide, 91 m long and 27 m high. A load-bearing structure consisting of a space-frame laid out to a 7 x 7 m grid was proposed. The design was largely determined by the following criteria. The pavilion was to be assembled quickly. It had to be capable of extension or reduction in size during the exposition to accommodate the needs of changing exhibitions; and the structure was to be easily demounted afterwards and be suitable for reuse in other locations.

»Was und wie die vereinigte Bundesrepublik Deutschland im Jahr 1992 sein wird oder sich darstellt, weiß heute, zwei Jahre zuvor, keiner. Deshalb wurde auf die gestalterische Konzeption noch nicht definierbarer Inhalte verzichtet. Es wurde ein offenes architektonisches Konzept entwickelt, das bis zum letzten Augenblick variabel genutzt werden kann«.
Aus dem Erläuterungsbericht des Wettbewerbs

Der Entwurf sieht einen kompakten, kubischen, sechsgeschossigen Baukörper vor, dessen Konstruktion sich durch große Variabilität auszeichnet. Das Haus im Haus garantiert ein angenehmes Raumklima und eine optimale Energiebilanz: Ein innerer Baukörper von 65000 cbm ist von einer Klimahülle umhüllt. Zur Energieversorgung sind neun Membranhohlspiegel auf dem Dach angebracht. Diese sind so aufgehängt und auf Schienen gelagert, daß sie der Sonne nachgeführt werden können. In ihrem Brennpunkt hängt ein Energiewandler, der die Sonnenwärme in elektrischen Strom umwandelt.

Für die tragende Konstruktion des Baukörpers – Breite 54,0 m, Länge 91,0 m, Höhe 27,0 m – wird ein Raumfachwerk mit einem Raster von 7,0 x 7,0 m vorgeschlagen. Dabei waren folgende

Bedingungen wesentlich: schnelle Montierbarkeit, die Möglichkeit der einfachen Ergänzung oder Reduzierung während der Expo bei wechselnden Ausstellungen, eine einfache Demontage nach der Expo und die Wiederverwendbarkeit an anderer Stelle.

Die Deckenträger bilden ein orthogonales Raster, auf dem in beliebiger Richtung gespannte Kassettendeckenelemente oder auch Treppen eingehängt werden können. Die Träger sind an einen Typenknoten, der aus Gußstahl nach dem Kraftfluß geformt wird, mit einer Steckverbindung und Bolzen angeschlossen. Die Stahlrundstützen werden mit diesen Knoten biegesteif verbunden.

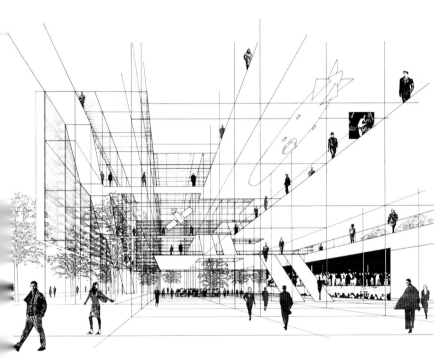

Die Fassaden weisen an den Verglasungen keine Sonnenschutzmaßnahmen auf. Diese Aufgabe wird der vorgelagerten Konstruktion zugewiesen, in der gläserne prismatische Lamellen dem Sonnenstand elektronisch nachgeführt werden.

No immediate sunscreening is foreseen for the glazed façades. They are protected by an outer skin with electronically controlled prismatic glass louvres that can be moved in accordance with the position of the sun.

Deutscher Pavillon, Weltausstellung Expo '92, Sevilla

Wettbewerb 1990

The floor beams form an orthogonal grid in which coffered floor slabs or staircase elements can be inserted, spanning in either direction. The beams are fixed with bolted socket connections to standardized cast-steel nodes, the form of which reflects the flow of forces. The round steel columns are rigidly jointed to these node points.

The structure is glazed on all faces. The façades are, nevertheless, not equipped with integrated sunscreen or anti-glare systems. This function is assumed by a construction projecting beyond the face of the building. Solar shading is provided by prismatic glass louvres that can be adjusted in accordance with the position of the sun. This system allows a high degree of sunscreening combined with maximum light transmittance. Behind the louvres, a second layer, consisting of glass or metal elements, deflects the zenith light that penetrates the sunscreening into the interior of the pavilion.

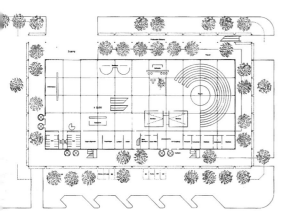

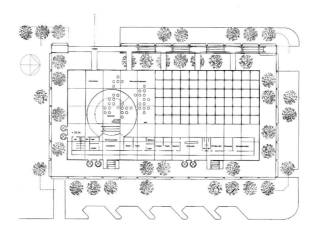

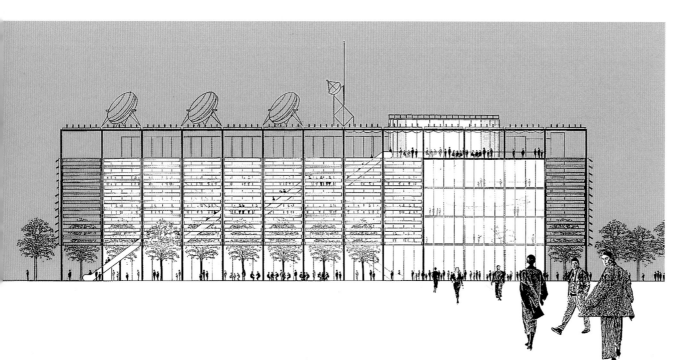

Die Gestalt des Pavillons wird durch die klare Geometrie – industrieller Vorfertigung – geprägt.

The design of the pavilion is distinguished by its clear geometry and industrial prefabrication.

Für die Energieversorgung
sind neun Solarkraftwerke
mit je 50 kW Leistung auf
dem Dach aufgestellt,
deren Membranhohlspie-
gel einfallendes Licht in
Strom umwandeln.

Mounted on the roof are
nine solar energy units,
each with a capacity of
50 kW. Light falling on
the concave membrane
mirror elements is con-
verted into electricity.

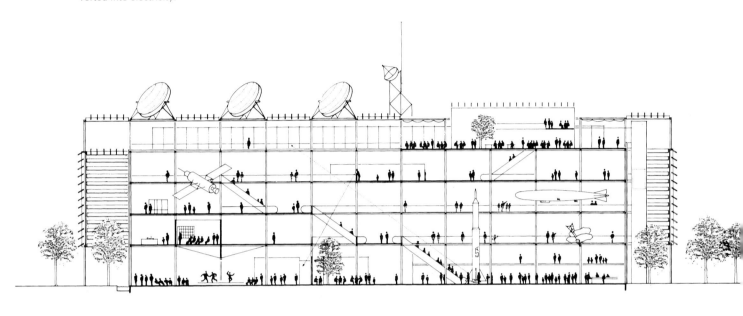

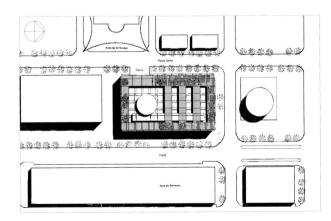

Die Fassaden weisen in den
rundum durchgehenden Verglasungen keine Sonnen- und Blend-
schutzmaßnahmen auf. Diese
Aufgabe wird der vorgelagerten
Konstruktion zugewiesen. Der
Sonnenschutz besteht aus gläsernen prismatischen Lamellen,
welche der Sonnenposition nachgeführt werden. Sie stellen einen
hochwertigen Sonnenschutz bei
maximaler Lichtdurchlässigkeit
dar. Hinter dieser Sonnenschutz-
ebene ist eine zweite Ebene zur
Umlenkung des Tageslichtes vorgesehen. Diese Fläche besteht
aus gläsernen oder metallischen
Elementen, welche das steil durch
den Sonnenschutz durchtretende
Zenitlicht ins Innere des Pavillons
leiten.
    Für die Nachtsituation sind
integrierte Kunstlicht-Systeme in
die Umlenkfläche vorgesehen.
Mittels engstrahlender Werfer,

die mit hochlumigen Lichtquellen
bestückt sind, wird Licht in ähn-
licher Art und Weise wie das
Tageslicht an die Deckenbereiche
des Pavillons gestrahlt. Gezielt
eingesetztes Streulicht wird für
die Aufhellung der gläsernen
Sonnenschutz- und Umlenkebene
verwendet.

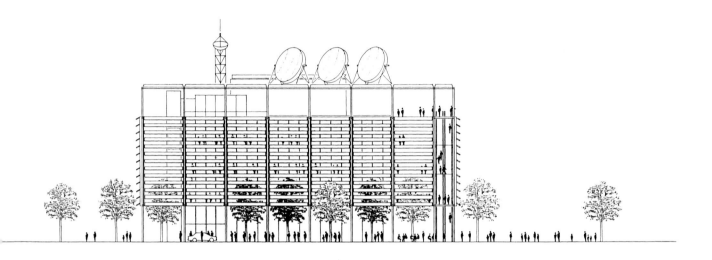

Artificial lighting systems are integrated into the light-deflecting layer for night-time use. The light from high-luminosity spotlights is cast on the ceiling areas of the pavilion, creating a similar effect to that of the deflection of daylight. Carefully controlled diffused lighting is used for illuminating the glass sunscreening and light-deflecting layers. The pavilion is protected on all faces with an external screening system against the effects of direct insolation. The building is, therefore, exposed to only about 15 per cent of overall solar radiation – in the form of diffused radiation. This system also ensures an even level of lighting in the internal spaces. A two-layer façade, consisting of glass and aluminium elements with water trickling down the face and an intermediate planted zone, creates a climatic buffer that shields the cool exhibition spaces within the pavilion from high external temperatures. The water running down the outer face evaporates. The heat required for this process is drawn from the air and from the elements in contact with the water, thus ensuring an adiabatic cooling of the façade and the adjacent air. In addition to the water-cooling façade system, non-centralized air-conditioning appliances, functioning with a heat-transfer process via cooling water, ensure pleasant indoor temperatures within the pavilion.

Die Vorfertigung in
Deutschland und der
Transport der einzelnen
Teile bestimmen das
Konstruktionsprinzip des
Pavillons, dessen unter-
schiedliche Komponenten
additiv zusammengesetzt
und je nach Funktion
ausgewechselt werden
können.

The design is based on
an additive constructional
system, using compo-
nents prefabricated in
Germany and transported
to the site for assembly.
The structure can be
extended or modified to
meet a variety of chang-
ing needs.

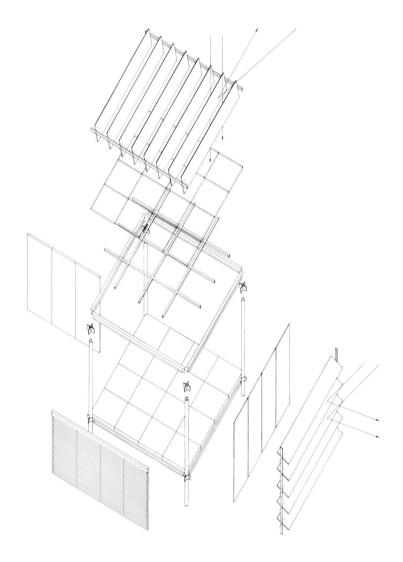

Das Gebäude ist allseitig mit
einem außenliegenden Sonnenschutz vor direkter Sonneneinstrahlung geschützt. Es wird
somit nur noch der Diffusstrah-
lung mit ca. 15% aus der Gesamt-
strahlung ausgesetzt. Hiermit verbunden ist eine gleichmäßige
Ausleuchtung der Innenräume.
Eine wasserberieselte Fassade
aus Glas- und Aluminiumelementen sowie eine Begrünung dieses
Zwischenraumes ergeben eine
Klima-Pufferzone zwischen der
hohen Außentemperatur und den
kühlen Ausstellungsräumen im
Pavillon. An der Fassade verdun-
sten die Wasseranteile, wobei die
für die Verdunstung erforderliche
Wärme den wasserberührten Bauteilen und der wasserberührten
Luft entzogen wird. Das ergibt
eine adiabate Abkühlung der Fassade und der angrenzenden Luft.
Zusätzlich zu der wasserberiesel-
ten Fassade sorgen dezentral auf-
gestellte Klimageräte mit Wärme-
transport über Kühlwasser für
angenehme Raumtemperaturen
im Pavillon.

Bereits im Frühjahr 1989 hatte Abt Dr. Odilo Lechner die geplanten Veränderungen im Benediktinerkloster Andechs formuliert. In der Rückbesinnung auf die alte klösterliche Tradition sollte die religiöse und kulturelle Bildungsarbeit des Klosters stärker gefördert werden. Um dies räumlich leisten zu können, war der Ausbau von Bereichen des Konvents erforderlich. Wertvolle historische Repräsentationsräume sollten zukünftig kulturellen Nutzungen zugeführt und für die Öffentlichkeit freigegeben werden; für die Wallfahrer sollten Unterkunftsmöglichkeiten in einem Pilgerdorf geschaffen werden; eine neue Kerzenkapelle war notwendig. Alle Maßnahmen verlangten vor der Realisierung nach einer städtebaulichen Untersuchung des gesamten Klosterbereiches einschließlich des Klostergartens, der Bierterrassen, des landwirtschaftlichen Gutsbetriebes und der Klosterbrauerei. Ein langfristig angelegtes Umbaukonzept sollte in Abschnitten realisiert werden.

Bei dem geplanten Umbau mußte das Klostergebäude den dringend notwendigen baupolizeilichen Sicherheitsanforderungen gerecht werden. Die behördlichen Auflagen forderten gesicherte Fluchtwege und den Einbau eines Aufzuges für die behindertengerechte Erschließung. Für zu erwartende Besucher mußten neue Garderoben und WC-Anlagen eingerichtet werden. An der Frage, wie diese Anforderungen zu verwirklichen seien, entzündete sich eine langwierige denkmalpflegerische Diskussion. Nach Überzeugung der Architekten galt es, die historische Substanz der barocken Klosteranlage unberührt zu lassen.

Die nach alternativen Untersuchungen schließlich gefundene Entwurfslösung sah folgende drei baulichen Veränderungen vor:

Überdachung des Pfortenhofes zwischen Kirche und Kloster mit einem leichten, transparenten, offenen Stahl-Glas-Dach gegen die direkten Witterungseinflüsse;

Einbau einer zusätzlichen, filigranen, einläufigen Treppenanlage als gerade freitragende Stahlkonstruktion in den Pfortenhof;

Einbau eines Aufzugs für Behinderte im Konventgebäude. Der Aufzug sollte die historische Bausubstanz nicht beeinträchtigen, transparent sein und keine Aufbauten über dem Dach zeigen.

Kloster Andechs

Pfortenhof und Konvent-Revitalisierung

Planungsbeginn: 1989
Bauzeit: 1992–1993

Andechs Monastery
Refurbishment of
Entrance Courtyard
and Monastic
Buildings

Commencement of
planning: 1989
Construction period:
1992 – 93

As early as the spring of 1989, Dr Odilo Lechner, the abbot of the Benedictine monastery of Andechs in Upper Bavaria, had drawn up a programme of alterations for the complex. In a re-avowal of old monastic traditions, greater emphasis was to be placed on the monastery's work in the realms of religious and cultural education. The additional space required for this purpose necessitated the extension of certain areas. Valuable historical rooms used for formal occasions were to be opened for cultural events and made accessible to the public. A special village was to be created to accommodate pilgrims; and a new candle chapel was required. The implementation of these measures required a preliminary urban study of the entire monastery, including the gardens, the beer terraces, the agricultural estate and the brewery. A long-term concept for the conversion work was to be implemented in a series of stages.

The proposed changes meant that the monastery complex had to comply with public safety regulations for buildings. These required the provision of escape

routes and the installation of a lift for disabled access. New cloakrooms and toilet facilities for visitors had to be provided, too. A protracted conservational discussion ensued as to how these requirements were to be realized. The architects firmly believed that the historical substance of this Baroque monastery should be left intact. After exploring many alternative solutions, they proposed the following changes to the buildings:

The erection of a lightweight, transparent open steel and glass roof over the entrance courtyard

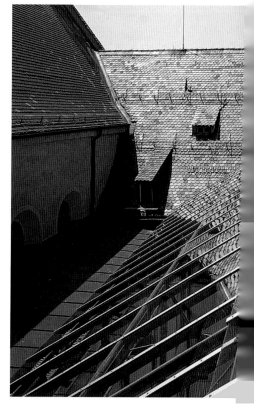

Das über dem Ostufer des Ammersees gelegene Kloster Andechs ist eine der ältesten und bedeutendsten Benediktinerabteien nördlich der Alpen.

Andechs Monastery, rising above the eastern shore of Ammersee and commanding a fine view of the lake, is one of the oldest and most important Benedictine abbeys north of the Alps.

between the church and the monastery buildings to protect this space against the immediate effects of the weather;

The insertion of a finely articulated staircase in the entrance courtyard in a straight free-standing steel construction;

The installation of a lift for disabled people in the monastery buildings. Two conditions were attached to this addition: the historical substance was not to be affected in any way; and the lift was to be transparent and not to require any visible structure above roof level.

Pfortenhof

Der 170 qm große, trapezförmige Pfortenhof wurde mit einer leichten Stahl-Glas-Konstruktion überdacht. Die Binder des Dachtragwerks sind nach dem Konstruktionsprinzip des Ponceauträgers gelenkig auf Stahlrohrstützen unterschiedlicher Höhe mit Abstand vom Dachfuß der Ziegeldächer – also aufgeständert – gelagert. Die Traufhöhenunterschiede zwischen dem Seitenschiff der Kirche und der Klosteraußenwand konnten damit ausgeglichen werden. Der Zwischenraum übernimmt gleichzeitig die natürliche Durchlüftung. Das Regenwasser wird in den vorhandenen Regenrinnen abgeführt. Punktlasten aus den Stützen werden über einen Ringbalken aus Stahlbeton in das bestehende Mauerwerk eingeleitet.

Die Entlüftung und Entrauchung ist durch Firsthauben auf dem Glassatteldach gewährleistet. Der Pfortenhof bleibt ein offener, aber überdachter Freiluftraum. Lichtwerfer auf dem romanischen Kirchenseitenschiff strahlen sieben Spiegel an, die unter dem First des Glasdaches angebracht sind. Sie reflektieren das Licht nach unten in den Pfortenhof; dabei wird das Seitenschiff der Kirche deutlich hervorgehoben.

Die beiden Treppenläufe mit einmal 24 und einmal 45 Stufen werden durch Antrittspodeste aus Granit aus dem einfachen Kopfsteinpflaster herausgehoben.

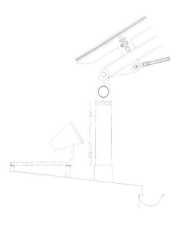

Das Satteldach aus Sicherheitsglas über dem Pfortenhof ist auf den Traufen der vorhandenen Dächer mit einem Luftzwischenraum aufgeständert.

The pitched roof over the entrance courtyard is covered with toughened safety glass. It is raised on columns over the eaves of the flanking buildings, leaving an open space between the edge of the new structure and the existing roof slopes.

Entrance courtyard:
The 170 m² trapezium-shaped courtyard was covered with a lightweight steel and glass roof. The roof trusses were designed according to the structural principle of a Polonceau truss and are fixed with hinged joints to tubular steel columns of different heights – i.e. on raising pieces – inset from the eaves of the existing tiled roofs. In this way it was possible to accommodate the difference in eaves height between the church and the monastery building. The gap between the edge of the new roof and the surface of the existing coverings ensures natural cross-ventilation and allows rainwater to flow down to the existing gutters. The point loads from the columns are transmitted to a peripheral reinforced concrete beam in the existing walls.

Vitiated air and smoke are extracted via hoods along the ridge of the glass pitched roof. The entrance yard remains an open space, but at the same time is protected by a light glazed skin. Floodlights on the Romanesque side wall of the church are directed to seven mirrors beneath the ridge of the glass roof, from where the light is reflected down to the courtyard below, articulating the wall of the church at the same time.

The two flights of stairs – one with 24 steps, the other with 45 – are accentuated at the base by granite plinths that rise from the simple cobblestone pavings.

Durch die Überdachung ist der Pfortenhof für die verschiedensten kulturellen Veranstaltungen nutzbar.

The glazed roof allows the entrance courtyard to be used for a wide range of cultural activities.

Der Kirchenumgang entstammt einer alten bayerischen Pilgertradition, die durch die Öffnung und Neugestaltung des Umgangs wiederbelebt wurde.

The ambulatory around the outside of the church is an important feature of the old tradition of pilgrimage in Bavaria. The redesign of the processional route lent this tradition a new lease of life.

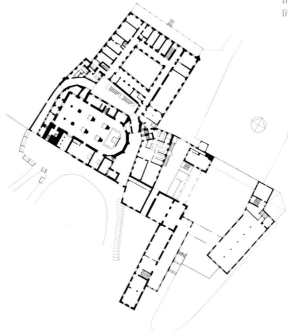

Die einläufigen, frei in
den Pfortenhof einge-
stellten Treppen erinnern
an die alte Form der
Himmelsleitern, wie sie
auch genannt werden.

The straight flights of
stairs that stand indepen-
dently in the entrance
courtyard recall the old
image of the heavenly
ladder and indeed bear
that name.

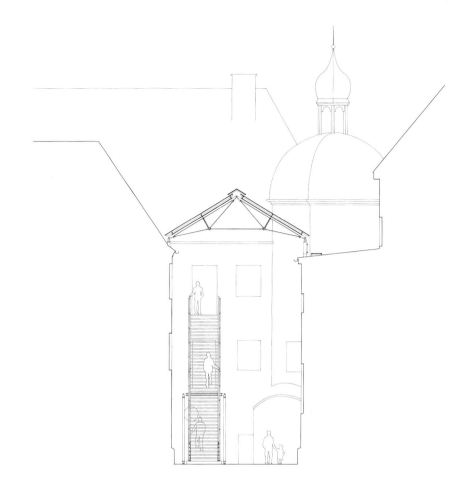

Die alte Pflasterung des
Zu- und Umgangs der
Kirche wurde stets im
rechten Winkel zu den
angrenzenden Wänden
neu verlegt; dadurch
entstanden die reißver-
schlußartigen Verschnei-
dungen.

The old pavings to the
forecourt of the church
and along the ambulatory
were relaid with joints
at right angles to the adjoining walls. The inter-
locking forms created at
intersections resemble
the pattern of a zip
fastener.

Pilgrims' processional route:
The continuous processional
route for pilgrims round the
church is an old Bavarian tradition and represents a genuine
enrichment of the life of the
monastery. The old granite
pavings were laid orthogonally to
the adjoining walls. Intersections
inevitably occurred at changes of
direction and these were laid out
in an interlocking pattern resem-
bling the form of a zip fastener.

The steps up to the
monastery church were cut to
slope and thus ease the ascent.
Even vehicles can drive up them
without difficulty. From the top,
the steps appear as an uninterrupted paved area.

Along the processional route
round the church, an opening
was created in the wall to allow a
view to Ammersee, the nearby
lake. In front of the opening
stands the stela of the Three
Hosts by the sculptor Blasius
Gerg.

Monastery building:
The renewed awareness of the
cultural aspects of monastic life
invoked by Abbot Odilo Lechner
and the congregation of monks
finds visual expression in the
addition of the new elements

described above. The construction of escape routes and the
refurbishment of the splendid
Baroque chambers allowed the
Prince's Tract to be made available for public use. As far as the
conservation of the monastery
is concerned, the historical
building fabric remains intact.

Senior civil servants responsible for construction in Bavaria
expressed the following reserva-
tion towards this concept: "In
spite of its great architectural
quality and the fact that no alterations are made to the substance
of the historical monastery buildings, the rural Bavarian atmosphere of the entrance courtyard
is fundamentally changed." Ultimately, however, the Bavarian
Minister of Culture, Education
and Church Affairs and the Minister of the Interior overruled these
objections and decided in favour
of the scheme.

Pilgerumgang

Einer alten bayerischen Tradition folgend, ist der freie Umgang um die Kirche als Pilgerweg eine echte Bereicherung des kirchlichen Lebens. Die alten Granitpflastersteine wurden im rechten Winkel zu den begrenzenden Hauswänden neu verlegt. Fast wie selbstverständlich ergaben sich in der Mitte Verschneidungen wie bei einem Reißverschlußsystem. Die Pflasterstufen beim Aufgang zur Klosterkirche verschleifen sich zur Erleichterung des Anstiegs und können problemlos befahren werden. Von oben nach unten blickend, erscheinen sie als reine Pflasterfläche. In den Kirchenumgang wurde ein Ausblick zum Ammersee eingelassen, davor steht die Drei-Hostien-Stele von Bildhauer Blasius Gerg.

Konventgebäude

Die von Abt Dr. Odilo Lechner und dem Konvent angestrebte verstärkte Rückbesinnung auf die kulturellen Aspekte des klösterlichen Lebens ist durch die Hinzufügung der beschriebenen neuen Bauelemente optisch wahrnehmbar.

Durch den Ausbau der Fluchtwege und die bauliche Revitalisierung der schönen barocken Fürstenräume wird die öffentliche Nutzung des Fürstentraktes ermöglicht. In denkmalpflegerischer Hinsicht wurde keine alte Bausubstanz zerstört.

Diesem sinnvollen Konzept wurde von obersten bayerischen Hochbaubeamten entgegengehalten: »Trotz hoher architektonischer Qualität und ohne Eingriff in die materielle Substanz der historischen Klosteranlage wird der ländlich-bayerische Zugangshof in seiner substantiellen Atmosphäre verändert.« Der Kultus- und der Innenminister entschieden sich schließlich für die Umsetzung des vorgelegten Konzeptes und gegen die vorgetragenen Bedenken.

Rahmenlose Ganzglastüren zum Schutz gegen Verrauchung unterteilen kaum merklich die schönen, großzügigen Gänge. Ein gläserner Lift für die behindertengerechte Erschließung macht den Gegensatz von Baukunst und Technik deutlich.

The beautiful, spacious corridors of the monastery remain virtually uninterrupted by the frameless, fully-glazed smoke-stop doors. A glazed lift structure, which allows access for disabled people, elegantly contrasts architecture and technology.

Ice-Skating Training Centre in Olympia-park, Munich

Commencement of planning: 1989
Construction period: 1990 – 91

In 1989, plans were put forward for a second ice-skating arena in the Olympia Park in Munich. The structure was built as a training hall for the ice-skating championships in 1992. The area of the site, to the east of the ice hockey hall, was extremely tight for the construction of a standard-size rink and the retention of the existing number of parking spaces. The skating hall was, therefore, raised above the ground to leave space for parking underneath. On its western side, the new structure was connected to the ice hockey hall by a tract that contains the ventilation plant, the ice-making equipment and a hydraulic lift. At the northern end of this tract is a ramp up to the rink for the ice-making vehicles, and at the southern end, a staircase that provides access to the hall. The ice rink itself is situated on an indepen-

dent raised reinforced concrete slab, over which the free-spanning roof structure, with its five enclosing planes, is fitted like a lid. In other words, the ice-skating hall consists of two independent structural systems that nevertheless form a unified whole. By placing the load-bearing structure on the outside of the building, it was possible to reduce the eaves height and the volume of the space to be air-conditioned – a major factor in the operation of this building.

Seating for 300 spectators is laid out along the ends of the arena in rows that are tilted upwards. The top of the "table" that forms the actual rink – a 78 x 35 m concrete slab with

1989 wurde im Münchner Olympiapark eine zweite Eislaufhalle als Trainingshalle für die Eislaufweltmeisterschaft 1992 geplant und realisiert. Eine äußerst knapp bemessene Baufläche östlich der Eishockeyhalle bildete das Grundstück für eine genormte Eisfläche und die Beibehaltung der bisherigen Zahl der Parkplätze. Daraus folgte eine Aufständerung der Eislaufhalle. An der Westseite wurde ein Verbindungsbau zwischen der Eishockeyhalle und der Trainingshalle angeordnet. Hier liegen die Be- und Entlüftungsanlagen, die Maschinen für Eisaufbereitung und der hydraulische Aufzug. An der Nordseite verläuft eine betriebsbedingte Rampe, an der

Südseite eine Treppenanlage als Zugang zur Halle. Die Eisfläche liegt auf einem eigenständigen Stahlbetontisch, über den das freigespannte Dachtragwerk der fünf Raumabschlüsse als unabhängiges Konstruktionsteil gestülpt ist. Damit entstanden zwei unabhängige Konstruktionssysteme, die zusammen die Eislaufhalle bilden. Durch das nach außen gelegte Tragwerk reduziert sich die Traufhöhe und, was für den Betrieb besonders wichtig ist, das zu konditionierende Raumvolumen.

An den ansteigenden Stirnseiten liegen die Zuschauertribünen für je 300 Personen. Die 78,0 m x 35,0 m große Stahlbetonplatte des Tisches mit vorgespannter Bewehrung ist auf vorgefertigten Stahlbetonstützen im Achsraster von 10,8 m x 5,4 m aufgelagert. Unter dem Stahlbetontisch blieben die bisherigen Parkplätze erhalten.

Das Leistungszentrum für Eiskunstlauf ist östlich an das bestehende Eissportstadion angebaut. Im vorgelagerten gläsernen Rundpavillon wird der gesamte Kartenverkauf für den Olympiapark abgewickelt.

The ice-skating training hall was erected immediately to the east of the existing ice-sports stadium. The ticket office for all events in the Olympia Park is housed in the circular glazed pavilion in front of the new hall.

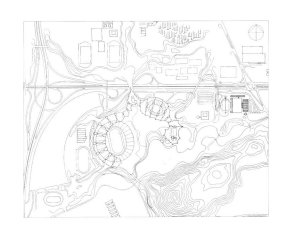

Leistungszentrum für Eiskunstlauf im Olympiapark, München

Planungsbeginn: 1989
Bauzeit: 1990–1991

prestressed reinforcement – is supported by prefabricated re-inforced concrete columns set out to a 10.8 x 5.4 m grid. This enabled the existing parking spaces to be retained at ground level below the arena.

The steel roof construction is suspended from Vierendeel gird-ers that span a width of 36 m. They consist of two steel sheets 22 mm thick and 2.7 m high, bolt-ed and welded together. The rec-tangular openings with rounded corners in the webs of these girders reflect the distribution of forces, which permit larger openings towards the points of support. In conjunction with the double channel-section columns, the girders form a structural frame. Longitudinal bracing is provided by steel rods that can be post-tensioned and that also serve to stabilize the girders. The roof construction itself, sus-pended below the Vierendeel girders, consists of a grid of longitudinal and lateral beams with trapezoidal-section ribbed metal sheeting and integrated thermal insulation.

The façades to the hall are in a post-and-beam construction with translucent triple glazing.

The glass-fibre quilt inlay between the middle and outer panes of glass prevents the pene-tration of direct insolation and thus helps to avoid marked varia-tions in temperature on different areas of the ice. To allow skaters a clear view of the outside world, the lower part of the façade was glazed with clear glass and fitted with an external sunscreening system.

The temperature in the ice sports hall is maintained at +15 °C. A special technical con-struction was installed to prevent moisture dripping from the ceil-ing on to the ice. A soffit of reflective, polished natural-anodized aluminium panels was suspended over the arena. It ensures good acoustics and reflects the cold radiation from the surface of the ice down-wards, thus preventing the for-mation of condensation on the

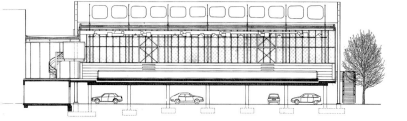

Die 36,0 m langen und
2,7 m hohen Vierendeel-
Träger aus zwei 22 mm
starken Stahlblechen wur-
den in zwei Teilen gelie-
fert und an Ort und Stelle
verschweißt und montiert.

The Vierendeel girders,
consisting of two 22 mm
steel plates, have an
overall length of 36 m
and a height of 2.7 m.
Prefabricated in two
sections, they were
assembled and welded
together on site.

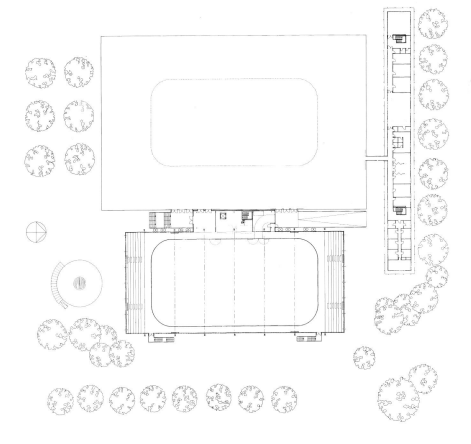

An den Vierendeel-Trägern aus
zwei miteinander verschraubten,
22 mm starken und 2,7 m hohen
Stahlblechen, verschweißt zu
einer Spannweite von 36,0 m,
hängt die stählerne Konstruktion
des Daches. Die ovalen Aus-
sparungen in den Stahlblechen
der Vierendeel-Träger folgen dem
statisch-konstruktiven Kräftever-
lauf. Er läßt zu den Auflagern hin
größere Öffnungen zu. Diese
Träger bilden zusammen mit den
zweischnittigen Stützen aus
U-Profilen in statischer Hinsicht
einen Rahmen. Die Längsausstei-
fung erfolgt über nachjustierbare
Abspannungen aus Rundstäben,
die gleichzeitig die Träger stabilisieren. Unter den Vierendeel-Trägern hängt das Dach – ein Rost
aus Längs- und Querträgern sowie
Trapezblechen – mit integrierter
Wärmedämmung.
   Die Fassade ist eine Pfosten-
Riegel-Konstruktion mit einer
transluzenten Dreischeiben-Isolier-
verglasung. Die Glasvlieseinlage
der äußeren Scheiben verhindert
eine direkte Sonneneinstrahlung
und damit auch starke partielle
Temperaturveränderungen auf der
Eisfläche. Um den Eisläufern den

direkten Sichtbezug zur Außen-
welt zu erhalten, wurde der
untere Teil der Fassade mit transparentem Klarglas und außen-
liegendem Sonnenschutz ausgestattet.
   Die Eissporthalle ist auf 15°C
temperiert und verlangt in bauphysikalischer Hinsicht eine besondere technische Ausrüstung.
Deshalb wurde an den oberen
Raumabschluß eine reflektierende
Decke aus natureloxierten und
polierten Aluminiumplatten
gehängt. Sie bewirkt eine optimale Raumakustik und reflektiert
die Kältestrahlung der Eisfläche;
eine Tauwasserbildung am
abgehängten Trägerrost wird
somit verhindert.

Durch die transluzenten Glaselemente mit weißer Glasvlieseinlage wird die direkte Sonneneinstrahlung auf die Eisfläche verhindert. Das unten transparente Glasfeld macht die optische Kommunikation nach außen möglich.

The translucent glazing elements, with an intermediate layer of white glass-fibre quilt, screen the surface of the ice from direct sunlight. The transparent lower strip of façade glazing creates a visual link between inside and outside.

An den sieben Vierendeel-Trägern ist das Dach aufgehängt. Die notwendigen Seilverspannungen stabilisieren die Träger in ihrer Lage und verkürzen die Spannweiten der Aufhängungen der minimierten Konstruktion.

The roof is suspended from the seven Vierendeel girders. Tension cables stabilize the girders in their plane and reduce the spans of the suspension members of this minimized structure.

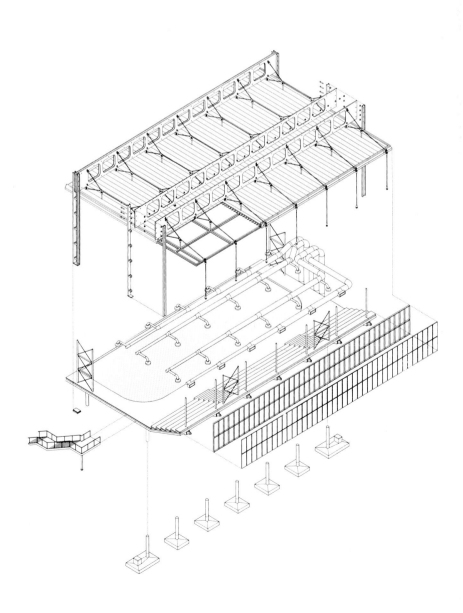

supporting structure. Integrated into the ceiling are adjustable light fittings and electro-acoustic equipment. All conduits for the control of the air temperature in the hall are housed in the space between the suspended soffit and the supporting grid.

Unlike the arena for amateur ice-skating, which takes place beneath a broad open tent roof, the training centre requires an enclosed hall. The two projects were comparable in nature, but the different constraints resulted in structures that are strongly contrasted in appearance.

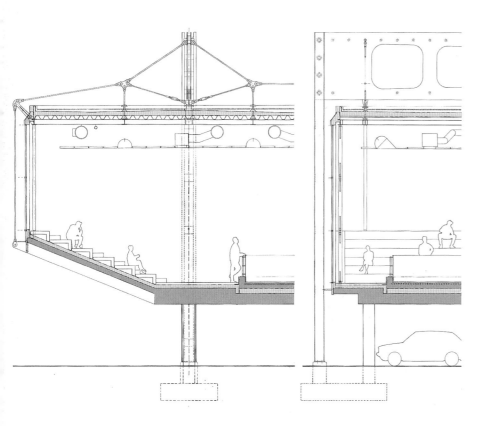

In die Decke sind die steuerbare Beleuchtung und die elektroakustischen Anlagen integriert. Zwischen der abgehängten Decke und dem Trägerrost verlaufen sämtliche Lüftungsleitungen für die Regelung der Raumlufttemperaturen.

Der Amateureislauf findet unter dem offenen Flächentragwerk des Eislaufzeltes statt; das Leistungszentrum braucht eine geschlossene Halle. Zwei an sich gleiche Bauaufgaben kommen aufgrund der unterschiedlichen Anforderungen deshalb zu ganz unterschiedlichen Erscheinungsbildern.

Fire Station 8 in Unterföhring, Munich

Commencement of planning: 1991
Construction period: 1994 – 95

The site lies to the south of the northern power station, to the east of a partly completed commercial development and close to a new housing area on the northern edge of Munich.

The two-storey fire station is 65.5 m long and 14.1 m wide and has a basement under part of its area. The striking triangular projection in the entrance face was designed to afford the operations centre a view of the rest of the station. The two main functional realms – the firemen's tract and the vehicle hall – are clearly separated.

The bedrooms for the firemen are situated on the ground floor, so that, in the event of night-time operations, the fire engines can be reached without hindrance.

The ground floor also houses sanitary facilities, rooms for boots and large-scale cleaning, and the vehicle master's office, which has immediate access to the engine hall. The news and communications centre in the entrance area adjoining the vehicle hall commands an uninterrupted view of the alarm exits.

On the upper floor, with a gallery and open staircase, are the instruction areas, reading and seminar rooms, a dining room and lounge, the ancillary kitchens and canteen, plus offices and bedrooms for the chief officers.

The upper floor is additionally linked to the ground floor by two vertical shafts with slide poles. Daylight penetrates to all floors via the roof light over the gallery.

Feuerwache 8
der Landeshauptstadt München, Unterföhring

Planungsbeginn: 1991
Bauzeit: 1994 –1995

Die Fahrzeughalle hat eine durch Technik geprägte, vorgefertigte Hülle. Der abstrahierte Neonschriftzug von Dietmar Tanterl soll die FW 8 symbolisieren.

The vehicle hall has a prefabricated outer skin with an explicitly technological appearance. The emblem by Dietmar Tanterl is a stylized representation of the fire station logo, FW 8.

Das Grundstück liegt südlich des Heizkraftwerks Nord, östlich eines teilweise realisierten Gewerbegebiets und in der Nähe neuer Wohngebiete am nördlichen Rande Münchens.

Das 65,5 m lange und 14,1 m breite Wachgebäude ist zweigeschossig und teilweise unterkellert. Der markante dreieckige Vorsprung resultiert aus den geforderten Blickbeziehungen der Einsatzzentrale. Die zwei Funktionsbereiche Mannschaftsgebäude und Fahrzeughalle sind klar voneinander getrennt.

Die Schlafzimmer für die Feuerwehrleute liegen im Erdgeschoß. Bei Alarmfall in der Nacht sind die Wege zu den Löschfahrzeugen direkt und ohne jede Behinderung zu erreichen. Im Erdgeschoß befinden sich außerdem die Sanitärräume, Räume für Stiefel- und Großreinigung und nahe der Fahrzeughalle das Büro des Kfz-Meisters. Am Eingangsbereich, der Nahtstelle zur Kraftfahrzeughalle, liegt die Nachrichtenzentrale mit ungestörtem Blick auf die Alarmausfahrten.

Im Obergeschoß mit einer Galerie und offener Treppe befinden sich die Schulungs-, Seminar- und Leseräume, ein Eß- und Aufenthaltsraum mit dazugehörigen Küchen- und Kantinenbereichen sowie Büro- und Schlafräume für die Führungskräfte. Zusätzlich sind die Erd- und Obergeschoßbereiche mit zwei vertikalen

The presence of natural lighting also accentuates the spatial link between the various levels.

Mechanical services, showers, equipment stores, a caretaker's workshop and store, a drying room and a naturally lit fitness room are housed in the basement.

The vehicle hall accommodates four fire engines, with a repair lanc providing space for a further vehicle. The folding gates to the rear entrances are mechanically operated. Those to the front exits are operated automatically, to avoid any delays when there is a fire alarm.

An open drill tower was erected to the south of the fire station building. It is in the form of a steel skeleton frame and has three levels, which are equipped with dry risers, balustrades for ladder access, a swivelling beam for roping down, and removable balustrades for rescue drill.

The load-bearing structure of the staff tract consists of reinforced concrete floors supported by a primary structure of longitudinal steel beams on round steel columns. The steel structure remains exposed internally. The roof over the vehicle hall is supported by a series of open steel trussed girders, which save headroom and allow a simple routing of mechanical services.

The façades are clad with natural-anodized aluminium sheeting with a rear ventilated cavity. The layout is based on vertical grid dimensions of 25 cm for the metal panels and 50 cm for the windows. This ubiquitous metal and glass skin serves to unify the quite different functions of the vehicle hall and the staff tract.

The extensive areas of paving that inevitably dominate any fire station complex were relieved – but not greatly reduced – by islands of planting.

The neon light installation designed by the artist Dietmar Tanterl reflects the technical aesthetic of the fire station.

Rutschstangenschächten verbunden. Das Oberlicht über der Galerie sorgt für Helligkeit und die räumliche Verknüpfung der Geschosse.

Im Untergeschoß befinden sich die Räume der Haustechnik, Duschräume, Ausrüstungslager, eine Hausmeisterwerkstatt mit Lager, ein Trockenraum und ein natürlich belichteter Konditionsraum.

Die vier Löschfahrzeuge stehen in der Fahrzeughalle mit einer Reparaturgasse als fünftem Fahrzeugstand. Die rückwärtig gelegenen Einfahrten sind mit mechanischen Falttoren versehen, die Ausfahrten nach vorne besitzen sich automatisch öffnende Falttore für den schnellen Einsatz.

Südlich der Feuerwache wurde ein offener Übungsturm errichtet. Die Stahlskelettkonstruktion hat drei Ebenen, die mit Löschwassersteigleitungen, Brüstungen zum Anleitern, einem schwenkbaren Galgen zum Abseilen und aushängbaren Geländern für Rettungsübungen ausgestattet sind.

Das Tragwerk des Wachgebäudes besteht aus längslaufenden Stahlträgern auf runden Stahlstützen. Auf der primären Stahlkonstruktion liegen die jeweiligen Geschoßdecken aus Stahlbeton, das Stahltragwerk bleibt innen sichtbar. Das Dachtragwerk der Fahrzeughalle wird durch offene Stahlfachträger gebildet, die Höhe sparen und eine gute Führung der Installationen bieten.

Die hinterlüftete Fassade ist mit natureloxiertem Aluminium verkleidet. Die Höhenrasterung der Metallelemente beträgt 25 cm im Brüstungsbereich und 50 cm im Fensterbereich. Die sehr unterschiedlichen Funktionsbereiche Fahrzeughalle und Wachgebäude werden durch die Hülle aus Metall und Glas zu einer Einheit zusammengefügt.

Die Dominanz der funktionsbedingten großen befestigten Freiflächen wird durch die Pflanzinseln aufgelockert, aber nicht gemindert.

Die künstlerische Installation aus Neonröhren von Dietmar Tanterl korrespondiert mit der technischen Ästhetik der Feuerwache 8.

Linke Seite oben: Der offene Stahlturm ist ein Trainingsgerät der Feuerwehrleute, an dem die Rettung von Menschen geübt wird. Rechts: Die Mittelzone des Mannschaftsbereichs hat ein gläsernes Oberlicht. Unten: Die helle Halle zur Fahrzeugwartung

Opposite page, top: on the open steel tower, which forms part of the training apparatus, firemen undergo life-saving drill. This page, right: over the central area of the staff tract is a glazed roof light. Below: the brightly lit vehicle maintenance hall

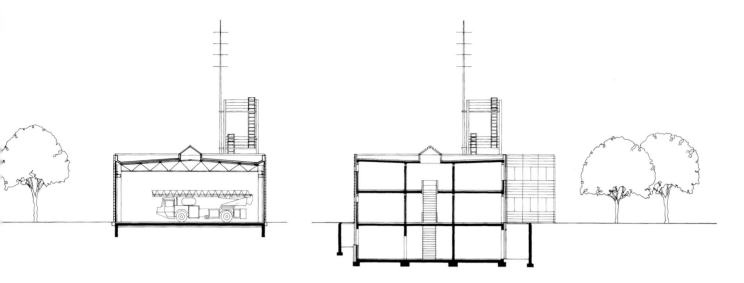

An der Gartenfassade
wurden die Fenster nach
funktionalen Gesichts-
punkten angeordnet.
Querschnitte. Links:
Kraftfahrzeughalle.
Rechts: Mannschafts-
gebäude

The windows in the gar-
den front were located
according to functional
needs. Cross-sections.
Left: vehicle hall. Right:
staff building

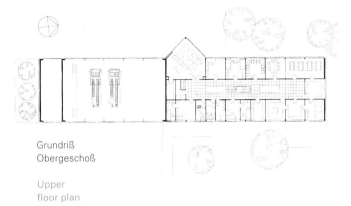

Grundriß
Obergeschoß

Upper
floor plan

Grundriß
Erdgeschoß

Ground
floor plan

Ansicht des neuen Pump-
werks von der Hofseite;
rechts im Bild der Ziegel-
bau des alten Pumpwerks,
das als Museum genutzt
werden sollte.

Courtyard elevation of
new pumping station; on
the right of the picture is
the old brick machine
hall, which was to have
been converted into a
museum.

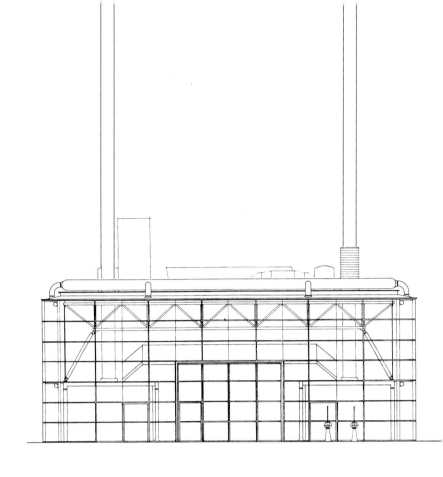

Hauptpumpwerk, Berlin-Wilmersdorf

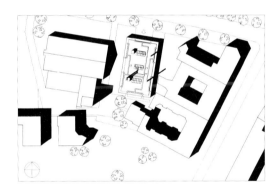

Wettbewerb 1991
1. Preis

Planungsbeginn: 1991
Bauzeit: 1993–1998

Die Berliner Wasser-Betriebe
ersetzen das 1903–06 errichtete
Hauptpumpwerk am Hohenzollerndamm durch einen Neubau.
Die repräsentativ gestaltete, denk-
malwerte Maschinenhalle mit
ihrer industriegeschichtlich be-
deutsamen Pumpenanlage sollte
Technisches Museum der BWB
werden.

   Das neue Pumpwerk macht
durch seine transparente Doppelfassade die technischen Abläufe
im Inneren ablesbar. Eine Galerie
über den Arbeitsbereichen erlaubt
den Besuchern – in der Mehrzahl
Schüler – Einblicke in den ökologischen Kreislauf heutiger Stadt-
technik.

   Das Tragwerk wird von vier
autonomen, in sich ausgesteiften
Tragwerksböcken gebildet. Die
20,0 m langen Dreigurtbinder mit

Auslegern überspannen den Ober-
bau des Pumpwerks. Das Tragwerk demonstriert im Gegensatz
zum massiven Unterbau, der über
dem Erdboden gefertigt und dann
abgesenkt wurde, filigrane Leichtigkeit, die durch die Ganzglas-
fassaden deutlich sichtbar wird.
Der doppelte Fassadenaufbau
muß Anforderungen des Schallschutzes und der passiven Solar-
energienutzung gerecht werden.
Die Glashülle soll gleichzeitig das
40,0 m lange und 20,0 m breite
Bauwerk in dem dicht überbauten
Stadtgebiet transparent machen.
Gezielte Tageslichteinspiegelung
ersetzt Kunstlicht auch in den
Bereichen des bis zu 18,0 m unter
Gelände liegenden Unterbaus.

Main Pumping Plant
in Wilmersdorf,
Berlin

Competition: 1991
First prize
Commencement of
planning: 1991
Construction period:
1993–98

The Berlin water authority, BWB,
is replacing its main pumping
plant in Wilmersdorf with a new
building. The existing structure,
erected between 1903 and 1906
in Hohenzollerndamm, is an
architectural monument to the
industrial past. The stately old
machine hall and the pumping
plant it contains were, therefore,
to have been converted into a
technical museum for the BWB.

The transparent double
façade of the new pumping
house allows the technical processes that go on within it to be
seen from the outside. From a
gallery over the working areas,
visitors – mostly schoolchildren –
will be able to obtain an insight
into the ecological cycle of modern urban technology.

The load-bearing structure
comprises four rigid trestle-like
elements with cantilevered arms
and 20-metre-long triangular
trusses that span the width of
the pumping station. In contrast
to the solid substructure, the
structure of the building above
ground exhibits a quality of slen-
derness and lightness and is
clearly visible through the fully
glazed outer skin. The two-leaf
façade construction is designed
to provide sound insulation and

to facilitate a passive exploitation
of solar energy. At the same
time, the transparency of the
glass skin serves to reduce the
bulk of this 40 x 20 m structure at
the heart of a densely developed
urban district. The controlled
deflection of daylight into the
interior replaces artificial lighting
even in the deepest parts of the
building, which are as much as
18 m below ground level.

There are no permanent
workplaces in the pumping station. It was not necessary, therefore, to create a specific indoor
climate. More important was the
avoidance of extremes of temperature. Even under exceptional
weather conditions, with an
external temperature of roughly
15 °C, the two-layer climate-control buffer façade means that the
199 kW waste heat emitted by
the six electric and two diesel
pumps – with a total capacity of
20,000 m³/hour – should be sufficient to maintain internal temperatures at +14 °C without the use
of additional energy. The double-
skin façade consists of a 9 mm
layer of toughened safety glass

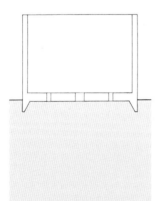

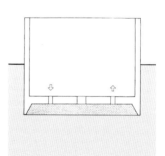

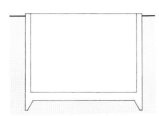

Da der Berliner Sandboden
eine Senkkastenbauweise,
also die Bauweise mit
einem Caisson, zuläßt,
wurde der Unterbau des
Pumpwerks oberirdisch
betoniert und in den Bau-
grund abgesenkt. Die
Abbildungen zeigen drei
Phasen der Absenkung.

The sandy soil of Berlin
permits a caisson form
of construction that could
be sunk into the ground.
That concrete substruc-
ture of the pumping
station was, therefore
poured above ground
and lowered to the re-
quired level. The illustra-
tions show three phases
of the lowering process.

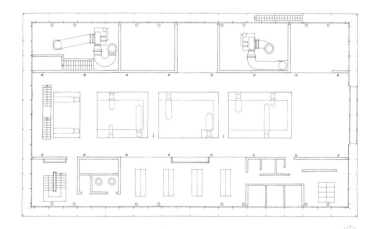

Grundriß Erdgeschoß des Pumpwerks. Die Außenfassade wurde aus Gründen des Schallschutzes als belüftete Doppelfassade ausgebildet. Sie ermöglicht gleichzeitig den notwendigen und sicheren zweiten Fluchtweg.

Ground floor plan of pumping station. To provide acoustic insulation, the outer façade was designed as a two-leaf ventilated enclosure. The space between the two skins also provides a necessary and safe second escape route.

externally, an intermediate space 0.7 m wide and an internal layer of double glazing with a 50 mm cavity between the two panes. This form of construction allows thermal gains to be made in the spring and autumn and even on sunny winter days. Heated air in the intermediate space can escape into the interior of the pumping house via ventilation flaps in the upper part of the internal skin of the façade. The corresponding intake of fresh air occurs via openings in the lower part of the outer façade. The internal heat gains resulting from the operation of the pumping plant are stored in the concrete substructure.

Noise emission from the centrifugal pumps is 80 dB, and 102 dB from the diesel pumps. During the day, the noise level in the street is roughly 55 dB, and at night 40 dB. The required noise reduction during the day is,

therefore, approximately 50 dB and at night 62 dB. To reduce the level of noise transmitted through the concrete caisson structure, it was acoustically separated from the machine foundations. The two-layer façade reduces airborne noise emissions by 63 dB. The insulating effect is based on an elastic mass principle, to which the inner layer of double-glazing contributes a 44 dB reduction and the outer layer of single glazing a reduction of 19 dB.

In den Innenräumen des Pumpwerkes befinden sich keine stän-
digen Arbeitsplätze. Ein spezifisch
definiertes Raumklima ist also
nicht angestrebt, es gilt vielmehr,
extreme Temperaturschwankun-
gen zu vermeiden. Die Pumpenab-
wärme von 199 kW – verursacht
durch sechs Elcktro- und zwei
Dieselpumpen mit einer Förderlei-
stung von insgesamt über 20.000
cbm in der Stunde – soll mit der
zweischaligen Klimafassade als
Puffer auch bei extremen klimati-
schen Bedingungen – etwa bei
minus 15 °C Außentemperatur –
ohne zusätzlichen Energieaufwand
Innentemperaturen von 14 °C ermöglichen. Die Doppelfassade –
außen 9 mm starkes Einscheiben-
sicherheitsglas, ein Fassadenzwischenraum von 0,7 m, innen
Isolierverglasung mit einem Schei-
benzwischenraum von 50 mm –
gewährt in Übergangszeiten und
an sonnigen Wintertagen einen
zusätzlichen Wärmegewinn. Im
oberen Teil der Innenfassade kann
die im Fassadenzwischenraum
erhitzte Luft über Lüftungsklappen
in das Innere des Pumpwerks
gelangen. Die Nachströmöffnun-
gen im unteren Bereich der äußeren Fassade führen frische Luft
nach. Die betriebsbedingten inter-
nen Wärmegewinne werden im
Betonunterbau gespeichert.
    Die Geräuschabgabe der Krei-
selpumpen liegt bei 80 dB, die der
Dieselpumpen bei 102 dB. Das
Umgebungsgeräusch im Straßen-
bereich beträgt tagsüber ca. 55 dB
und nachts 40 dB. Die Schallre-
duktion muß also nachts 62 dB
und 50 dB tagsüber betragen. Zur

Verminderung des Körperschalls
werden die Maschinenfundamen-
te vom Betonbau des Caissons
akustisch entkoppelt. Die Luft-
schallemission wird durch die
Doppelfassade um insgesamt
63 dB reduziert. Zum Feder-Mas-
se-Dämmprinzip trägt die innere
Isolierverglasung mit 44 dB und
die äußere Einfachverglasung mit
19 dB bei.

»Das wohltuend großzügig dimensionierte neue Pumpwerkgebäude
formuliert durch seine zeitgemäße
transparente Gestaltung und
durch seine entschiedene ortho-
gonale Anordnung ein straffes
städtebauliches Konzept, das
sowohl in der heute offenen
Blocksituation als auch mit einer
zusätzlichen Randbebauung trag-
fähig ist. Ohne Anbiederung,
durchaus in der Tradition guter
Stadttechnikbauwerke, wird ein
Baukörper in den Blockinnenbe-
reich selbstbewußt und verträg-
lich eingestellt. Die Idee einer gläsernen und damit transparenten
Industriehalle mit einer Höhenentwicklung knapp unter der
Traufhöhe des alten Pumpwerkes
findet ungeteilte Zustimmung.
Dadurch entsteht ein zeitgemäßes
Pendant zur Architektur der alten
Pumpstation. Den Museumsbesu-
chern wird damit ein unmittelbarer
Vergleich gestriger und heutiger
Abwassertechnik geboten.«
Aus dem Jury-Protokoll

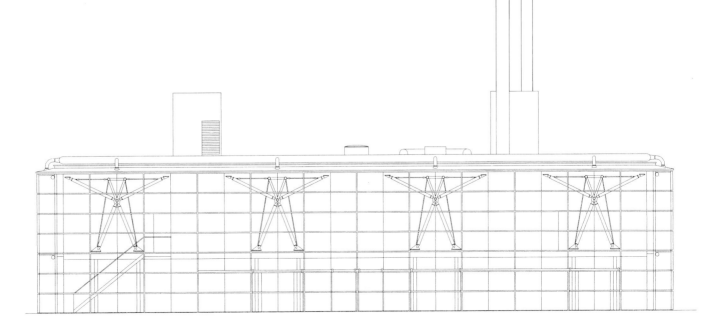

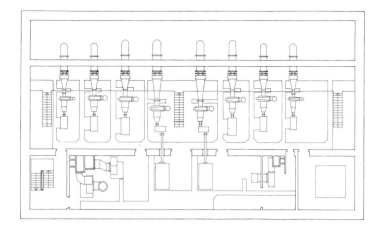

Oben: Grundriß eines Untergeschosses. Durch Lichtumlenkung werden die Untergeschosse durch galerieartige Öffnungen belichtet. Rechts: Querschnitt. Die Rahmen des Dachtragwerks stehen auf den beiden massiven Seitentrakten des Erdgeschosses.

Top: basement plan. By means of a system of light deflection and openings in the floors, even the levels below ground receive natural light. Right: cross-section. The framed roof structure is supported by the two solid side tracts on the ground floor.

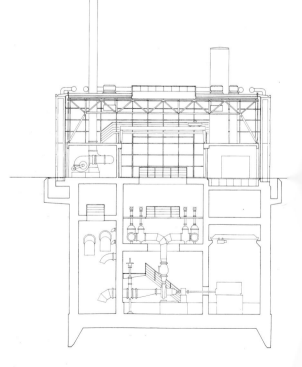

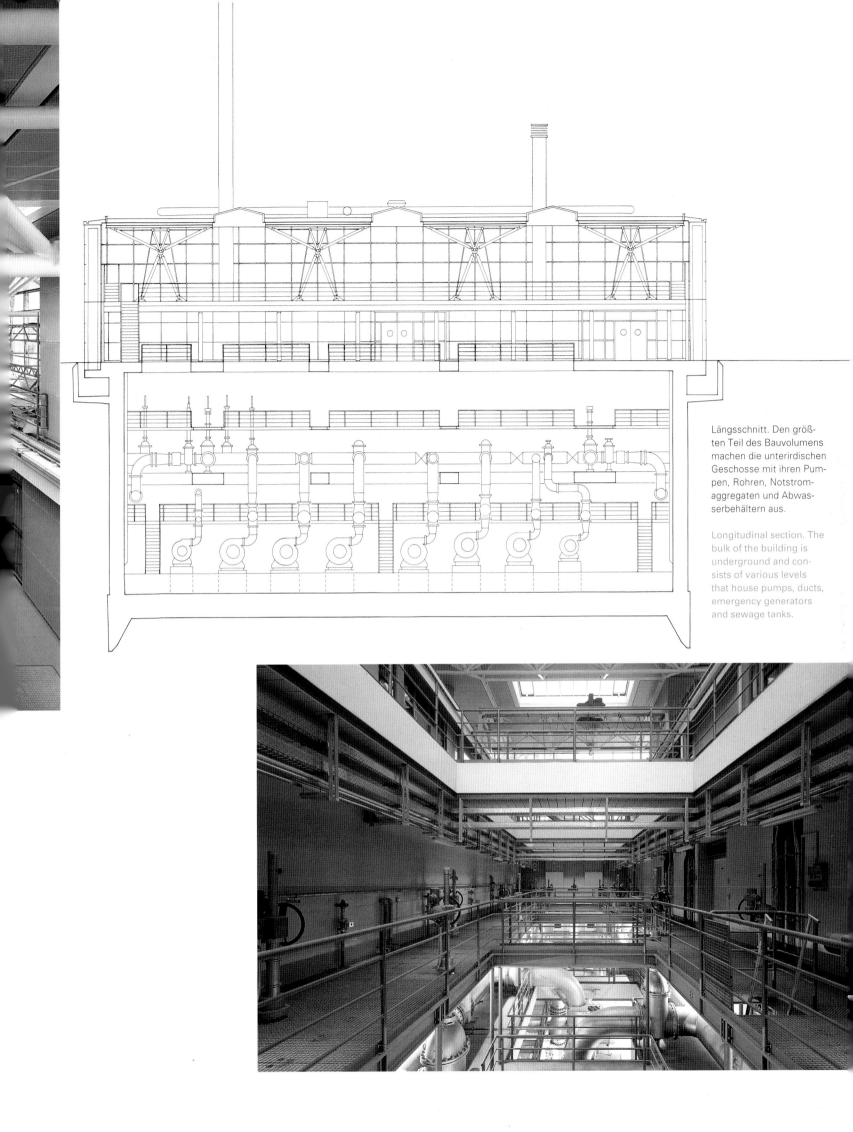

Längsschnitt. Den größten Teil des Bauvolumens machen die unterirdischen Geschosse mit ihren Pumpen, Rohren, Notstromaggregaten und Abwasserbehältern aus.

Longitudinal section. The bulk of the building is underground and consists of various levels that house pumps, ducts, emergency generators and sewage tanks.

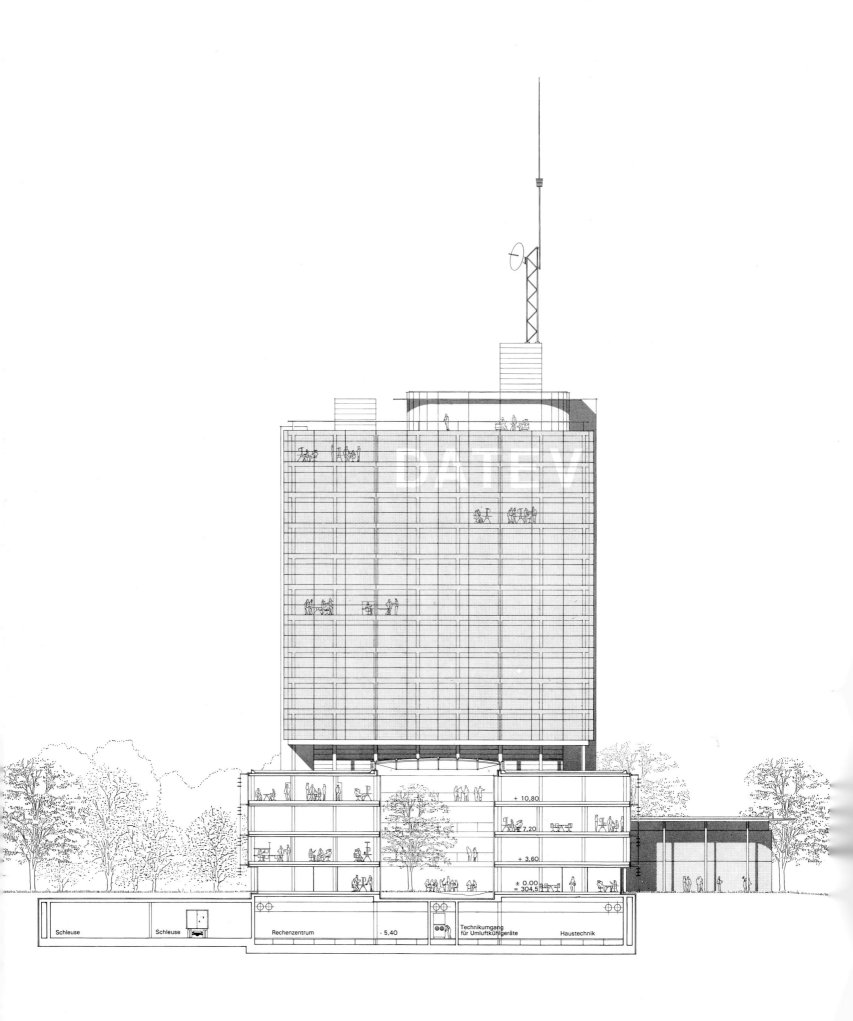

DATEV

+ 10,80

+ 7,20

+ 3,60

± 0.00
= 304,5

Schleuse   Schleuse   Rechenzentrum   - 5,40   Technikumgang   Haustechnik
                                                            für Umluftkühlgeräte

Das Baugrundstück liegt am Stadtrand von Nürnberg in einem Gebiet, dessen städtebaulicher Charakter mit dem Entwurfskonzept des Wettbewerbs neu definiert wird. Gegenüber der bisherigen niedrigen Bebauung mit ihrem hohen Flächenverbrauch ist die Hochhausgruppe kompakt. Durch den reduzierten Flächenbedarf bleiben ökologisch wertvolle Freiflächen erhalten.

Im ersten der drei Bauabschnitte sind die meisten Parkplätze ebenerdig gefordert; in weiteren Bauabschnitten wird die Tiefgarage stufenweise realisiert. Wegen der hohen Sicherheitsanforderungen wird auf eine Unterkellerung des Rechenzentrums verzichtet.

Der Wunsch nach flexibler Unterteilbarkeit der Büroflächen führte zu klar organisierten Grundrissen. Einzel-, Gruppen-, Großraum- und Kombibüros können nach Bedarf eingerichtet werden. Gleichbleibende Arbeitsplatzqualität ist gewährleistet, Gruppenbüros bleiben ohne Durchgangsverkehr.

Alle Arbeitsbereiche sind natürlich belichtet und belüftet. Büroflächen mit größeren Raumtiefen erhalten natürliches Licht, das durch ein bewährtes System zur Einspiegelung des Tageslichtes ergänzt wird.

Ansicht des ersten Bauabschnitts. Lageplan der Gesamtanlage

Section and elevation of first phase of development. Site plan of entire development

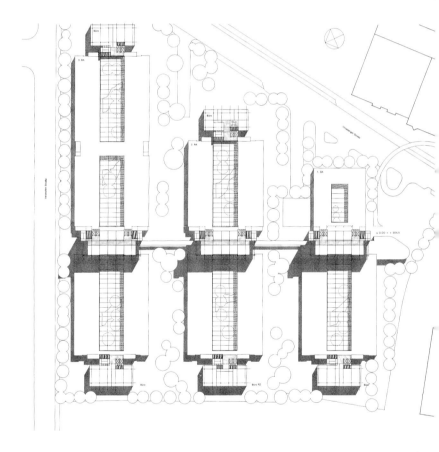

Hauptverwaltung der Datev, Nürnberg

Wettbewerb: 1992
2. Preis

Administrative Headquarters of Datev, Nuremberg

Competition: 1992
Second prize

The site lies on the outskirts of Nuremberg, in an area whose urban character has undergone a redefinition as a result of the competition scheme. Compared to the existing low-rise developments and their extensive use of land, the group of high-rise buildings represents a compact solution. The smaller land coverage meant that ecologically valuable open spaces could be retained.

In the first of the three phases of construction, most of the parking spaces were required to be at ground level. In the subsequent phases, a basement garage will be built in a series of stages. Because of the high security requirements, it was decided not to build a basement beneath the computer centre.

The brief required flexible office spaces that could be divided up in various ways. This led to a clear organizational layout, allowing the creation of single and group office spaces, open-plan and combination offices, according to needs. At the same time, workplaces of equal quality are guaranteed. The group offices do not suffer from through traffic.

All working areas are naturally lighted and ventilated. Offices with greater room depths receive natural light by means of an efficient system of daylight deflection into the interior.

Modellansicht der gesamten Anlage mit den begrünten Innenhöfen

Model of entire development with landscaped courtyards

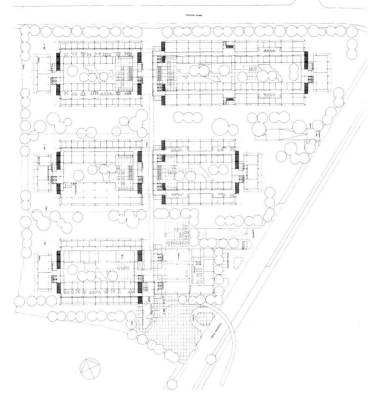

Grundriß der Gesamt-
anlage mit den Außen-
anlagen

Plan of overall develop-
ment with external areas

Grundriß Erdgeschoß des
ersten Bauabschnitts

Ground floor plan of first
phase of development

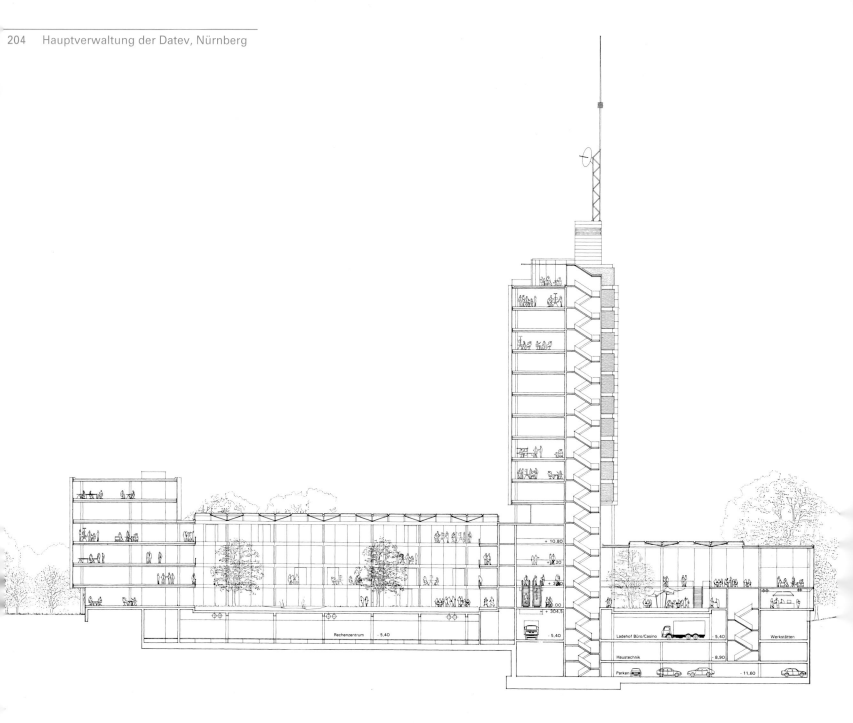

The in situ reinforced concrete structure is based on a column grid of 8.4 x 5.0 m. Concrete flat-plate floors with mild steel reinforcement provide an adequate heat-storage mass and allow an uncomplicated installation of technical services. The façade construction is in metal and glass, with interchangeable modular elements of uniform size. A two-layer climate-control façade with an external skin of toughened safety glass and a daylight deflection system was designed for the high-rise blocks and the satellite buildings.

"The first phase of the development provides a solution that is both significant and convincing in its own right."
Excerpt from jury report

Schnitt durch den ersten Bauabschnitt

Section through first phase of development

Die Gebäude sind als durchge-
hende Ortbetonkonstruktionen mit
einem Stützraster von 8,4 x 5,0 m
geplant. Schlaff bewehrte Flachdecken bieten ausreichend Speichermasse und ermöglichen die
problemlose Installation der technischen Gebäudeausrüstung. Die
Fassaden sind als Metall-Glaskon-
struktion in austauschbaren, einheitlich großen Modul-Elementen
konzipiert. Bei den Hochhäusern
und den Satellitengebäuden
kommt eine zweischalige Klimafassade mit außenliegender Ein-
scheibensicherheitsglas-Vergla-
sung und Tageslichtumlenkung
zum Einsatz.

»Der erste Bauabschnitt stellt
eine für sich allein schon signifikante und überzeugende Lösung
dar.«
Aus dem Jury-Protokoll

Grundriß Obergeschoß
des ersten Bauabschnitts
mit den Freianlagen

Upper floor plan of first
phase of development,
showing external areas

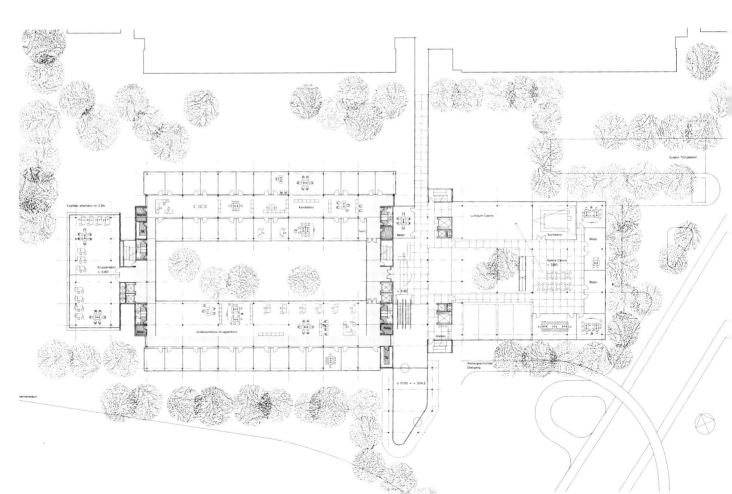

Generations in
Dialogue

Kurt Ackermann and
Peter Ackermann
interviewed by
Ingeborg Flagge

IF: To start with, the obligatory question: why
did you both become architects?

KA: As a small boy, I was acquainted with the
process of building by my father. My father
was not an architect. Among other things, he
had a small farm, and every year he did a bit
of building, which annoyed my mother. I was
allowed to help him, and so I became familiar
with the still purely crafts side of construction
at a very early age. That went on till 1941.
During his leave from the front, my father
demolished parts of our house, and in three
weeks – that was all the time he had – he had
rebuilt the carcass. Unfortunately, he never
returned from the war.

PA: I grew up, of course, in an architect's
family. Many of my holidays were architectural holidays, and that left its mark at a very
early age. One developed subconsciously, so
to speak, a relationship to architecture.
What's more, doing things on a building site
is fun for any boy, I imagine. It's tremendous-
ly exciting. After completing my civilian
service, I did consider studying medicine;
but not for long.

IF: What were the beginnings of the Kurt
Ackermann office?

KA: I obtained a degree and went to the University of Technology in Munich. In 1953, I
set up in practice on my own. I've never been
employed. In 1951, I built my first house.
The beginnings were tough: no telephone,
no secretary, no assistants.

IF: It was the time when Germany was still in
ruins, just at the beginning of the period of
reconstruction. How did one obtain commissions in those days?

KA: There was a mood of enterprise, of setting out for new horizons, but I never
received a commission for the reconstruction
of damaged houses or industrial works. My
first buildings were single- and two-family
houses. They became known and led to further commissions. My first larger scheme,
following a competition, was the hop store
Hopfenhalle in Mainburg in 1957. I visited
my first building sites on a bicycle and later
on a Vespa.

IF: Is site supervision a regular activity of the
office?

KA: Yes. For 40 years now, we have attempted to do the site supervision within our own
office. The reason for this is that quality is
possible only if we retain control ourselves.
That still applies today.

PA: If possible, it should stay that way,
although in the future it is likely to become a
problem. The position today, unfortunately, is
that in many cases only stages one to four of
the fee scales for architects and engineers are
awarded; sometimes the fifth, too – for the
detailed design. Site supervision is excluded.
We were entrusted with the site supervision
for the trade fair hall in Hanover. For me as a
young architect it is of enormous help in
understanding how a concept is translated
into reality. It's true: site supervision allows
one to intervene on site and make improve-
ments up to the very end.

IF: Is the increasing use of computers in
architects' offices changing the nature of site
supervision?

PA: No. The two have nothing to do with
each other. Working on the computer, one is
faced with the problem that a drawing has no
scale. You have to be particularly careful in
this respect when designing. On the computer, you can enlarge and reduce sizes at will,
but the section of the plan you are working
on is always limited by the size of the screen.
That distorts the real size of the task in hand.
One has to be aware of that and constantly
make checks.

IF: Am Anfang steht die obligatorische Frage, warum sind Sie beide Architekt geworden?

KA: Ich habe das Bauen von meinem Vater schon als kleiner Junge gelernt. Mein Vater war kein Architekt. Er hatte unter anderem eine kleine Landwirtschaft und baute jedes Jahr, was meine Mutter ärgerte. Ich durfte ihm helfen und bin so sehr früh auf das noch rein handwerkliche Bauen gestoßen. Das ging bis 1941. Mein Vater hat im Fronturlaub Teile unseres Hauses abgerissen und in drei Wochen, so lange hatte er Zeit, im Rohbau wiederaufgebaut. Leider kam er vom Krieg nicht zurück.

PA: Ich wuchs ja in einer Architektenfamilie auf; viele Urlaube waren Architektururlaube; das prägte schon sehr früh. Man entwickelt sozusagen im Unterbewußten einen Bezug zur Architektur. Hinzu kommt, daß wohl jedem Buben die Tätigkeit auf der Baustelle Spaß macht, das ist unheimlich spannend. Sicher habe ich auch einmal nach meinem Zivildienst daran gedacht, Medizin zu studieren, aber das legte sich rasch wieder.

IF: Wie sahen die Anfänge des Büros Kurt Ackermann aus?

KA: Ich habe graduiert und bin dann an die TH München gegangen. 1953 habe ich mich selbständig gemacht; angestellt war ich nie. 1951 habe ich mein erstes Haus gebaut. Die Anfänge waren hart: kein Telefon, keine Sekretärin, keine Mitarbeiter.

IF: Es war noch die Zeit eines kaputten Deutschlands, die unmittelbare Wiederaufbauzeit. Wie kam man damals an Aufträge?

KA: Es herrschte Aufbruchstimmung. Ich habe jedoch nie einen Auftrag für den Wiederaufbau von zerstörten Häusern oder Werkstätten bekommen. Meine ersten Bauten waren Ein- und Zweifamilienhäuser. Die wurden bekannt und zogen andere Aufträge nach sich. Der erste größere Auftrag, nach einem Wettbewerb, war die Hopfenhalle in Mainburg 1957. Die ersten Baustellen wurden mit dem Fahrrad und später mit der Vespa abgeklappert.

IF: Ist die Bauleitung eigentlich ein durchgängiges Thema für das Büro?

KA: Ja. Wir versuchen seit über vierzig Jahren, im eigenen Büro die Bauleitung zu machen. Der Grund: Qualität ist nur möglich, wenn wir selbst die Kontrolle haben. Das gilt bis heute.

PA: Das soll, wenn möglich, auch so bleiben. Allerdings wird das in Zukunft ein Problem. Heute ist es leider so, daß oft nur die Stufen eins bis vier der Honorarordnung für Architekten und Ingenieure, vielleicht noch die fünfte, die Werkplanung, an die Architekten gegeben werden. Die Bauleitung wird ausgeschlossen. Bei der Messehalle Hannover hatten wir die Bauleitung. Mir als jungem Architekten hilft es ungemein zu verstehen, wie das Erdachte umgesetzt wird. Und es ist richtig, die Bauleitung gibt einem die Möglichkeit, bis zum Schluß auf der Baustelle eingreifen und verbessern zu können.

IF: Verändert der zunehmende Einsatz von Computern in Architekturbüros die Bauleitung auf der Baustelle?

PA: Nein, beides hat nichts miteinander zu tun. Am Computer entsteht das Problem, daß es in der Zeichnung keinen Maßstab gibt. Beim Entwerfen muß man hier besonders aufpassen. Am Computer kann man willkürlich vergrößern, verkleinern, aber der Planausschnitt bleibt immer durch die Größe des Bildschirms definiert. Das verfälscht die reale Größe einer Bauaufgabe. Das muß man wissen und stets kontrollieren.

KA: Seit wir Computer im Büro haben, hat sich die Arbeit im Modellbau verdreifacht. Wir versuchen, die Entwurfsergebnisse, die mit dem Digitalen des Computers entstanden, an dem Analogen der Modelle zu überprüfen. Das geht so weit, daß wir Detailpunkte, die wir lösen

Generationen im Dialog   Ein Gespräch zwischen
Kurt Ackermann und Peter Ackermann
mit Ingeborg Flagge

KA: Since we have had computers in the office, the amount of work done on models has increased threefold. We try to test the outcome of design work that has been done digitally with the computer on analogue models. We go as far as to build models of the details we have to resolve parallel to the drawings. We investigated, modified and perfected the cast metal nodes for the fairs hall in Hanover on the basis of full-size models. When the drawings go on site, our planning is, as a rule, fully worked out and complete. Afterwards, only corrections are possible, although these can sometimes be quite decisive.

IF: Let's go back to the beginnings. The student digs you had in 1953 were your office and your home – the place where you worked, slept and ate. Everything took place in one room. When did that change?

KA: It was in 1956 that I could first afford an office for myself and a separate little flat with

the subsidy for building costs that was generally available in those days. And the first assistants, like Richard Martin, came, too. In 1997, after 41 years' work, he retired. Jürgen Feit and Peter Jaeger came in 1960. We moved to the Malsenstrasse in 1968; and in 1969, the assistants of many years' standing became partners.

PA: In my case, it was somewhat different, of course. I studied in Munich, went to the Academy of Fine Arts in Vienna and completed my studies with a diploma at the University of

Technology in Munich. I took part in my first competition here in the office. Afterwards I went to Renzo Piano in Italy. I couldn't speak a word of Italian, but at that time the office had an international staff. English and French were spoken more than Italian. We worked in a big team on the conversion of the Fiat Lingotto factory in Turin and planned the first modern concert hall in Italy with seating for 2,400 people. It was a highly interesting, but very difficult project. After a bit more than a year, I went to New York, to Richard Meier. The work there was completely different from that with Piano. Here, creative chaos; there, a cool, perfect division of labour. At Piano's, everyone did everything. With Meier, one did what one was good at. What impressed me most was the professionalism of the Americans and the way this affects the running of the office. Apart from that, though, it was lovely just to live in New York.

IF: And your first building project?

PA: I designed it for my sister. She was setting up a physiotherapy practice in Munich. We get on well together. She was the client, I the architect. The site supervision was done by a fellow student from the office. It was a good project and a lot of fun.

IF: Didn't Kurt Ackermann regret not having had opportunities of this kind as a young architect: an education like this, stays abroad?

KA: Not in those days. Later I sometimes envied Peter. When I was younger, Egon Eiermann was an important man for me. He was a guiding light. Mies van der Rohe was another person I revered, and Scharoun was no stranger either.

IF: Having a model is one thing; but surely it's much more exciting to work personally with big architects.

KA: Yes, of course. I occupied myself in a quite concrete form with Eiermann. I attended lectures he gave; but I spoke to him for the first time when my Gartner House was published in *Bauen + Wohnen* in 1956. I met him in the editorial offices in Munich.

IF: How important were publications in the early years?

KA: Very important. I published a lot of things, and that resulted in quite a bit of animosity towards me at the Technological University in Munich. My professor, Franz Hart, regarded it almost as an insult at the time that I, as a student, should be publishing things. *Bauen + Wohnen* was the journal for the avant-garde. It was not popular in Munich. The journal for Munich architects, of course, was the sober, traditionalist *Baumeister*.

IF: Why did you wish to publish so much? Was it a question of vanity, or was it a means of acquiring commissions?

KA: When something appeared in print, you had a much greater chance of getting a commission from clients. If an expert audience recognized our work, the client felt a certain security.

IF: What do you do about competitions at times when you have a lot of work? Do you take part only in competitions where you are invited to do so?

PA: There is, naturally, far less risk for the office in competitions in which participation is by invitation. One knows the rival offices, and there are fewer participants. On the other hand, we have just taken part in the competition for the trade fair site in Düsseldorf. It was an open competition, and there one can approach the matter in a much freer way.

KA: For me, a restricted competition is a much greater spur than an open one. You know whom you're up against. You make a greater effort. In general, though, the competition scene today, with the enormous numbers of participants, is a disaster. The organizers and the judges are overburdened by the sheer numbers of competitors. Quality suffers as a result of quantity.

IF: In the 1950s, what form did the discussion take about the architectural profession, about architecture and politics, about the Third Reich?

müssen, neben der Zeichnung auch im Modell bauen. Die Gußknoten für die Messehalle in Hannover haben wir im Modell 1:1 untersucht, verändert, vervollkommnet. Wenn die Pläne auf die Baustelle gehen, ist unsere Planung in der Regel ausgereift und abgeschlossen. Denn dort lassen sich nur noch Korrekturen anbringen, aber manchmal doch noch ganz entscheidende.

IF: Zurück zu den Anfängen. Die Studentenbude 1953 war Büro, Wohnen, Arbeiten, Schlafen, Essen – alles fand in einem Zimmer statt. Wann änderte sich das?

KA: Erst 1956 konnte ich mir ein Büro und eine separate kleine Wohnung mit dem damals obligaten Baukostenzuschuß leisten. Damit kamen auch die ersten Mitarbeiter, wie Richard Martin. Er ist 1997 nach 41 Jahren in den Ruhestand gegangen. Jürgen Feit und Peter Jaeger kamen 1960. In die Malsenstraße sind wir 1968 gezogen. 1969 wurden die langjährigen Mitarbeiter Partner.

PA: Bei mir sah das natürlich anders aus. Ich habe in München studiert, nach Wien an die Akademie der Bildenden Künste gewechselt und in München an der TU mit dem Diplom abgeschlossen. Meinen ersten Wettbewerb habe ich hier im Büro gemacht. Danach bin ich zu Renzo Piano nach Italien gegangen. Ich konnte kein Wort Italienisch, aber das Büro war zu der Zeit international besetzt. Englisch und Französisch wurden mehr gesprochen als Italienisch. Wir haben in einem großen Team die Fiat-Fabrik Lingotto in Turin umgebaut und den ersten modernen Konzertsaal Italiens mit 2400 Plätzen geplant, ein hochinteressanter, aber sehr schwieriger Auftrag. Nach über einem Jahr bin ich dann nach New York zu Richard Meier gegangen. Das war ein völlig anderes Arbeiten als bei Piano. Hier kreatives Chaos, dort kühle und perfekte Arbeitsteilung. Bei Piano machte jeder alles, bei Meier machte man das, worin man gut war. Am meisten hat mich die Professionalität der Amerikaner beeindruckt und wie sich diese auf die Büroführung auswirkt. Abgesehen davon war es einfach schön, in New York zu leben.

IF: Und Ihr erster Bau?

PA: Den habe ich für meine Schwester gemacht. Sie richtete sich damals eine Praxis für Physiotherapie in München ein. Wir können gut miteinander, sie war die Bauherrin, ich der Architekt. Die Bauleitung vor Ort machte ein Studienkollege aus dem Büro. Eine schöne Arbeit, die viel Spaß gemacht hat.

IF: Hat Kurt Ackermann als junger Architekt solche Möglichkeiten, solche Bildung, solche Aufenthalte im Ausland nicht vermißt?

KA: Damals nicht. Später habe ich Peter manchmal beneidet. Für mich war damals ein wichtiger Mann Egon Eiermann; er hat einen Maßstab vorgelebt. Auch Mies van der Rohe habe ich sehr verehrt, und Scharoun war mir nicht fremd.

IF: Ein Vorbild ist eine Sache; mit großen Architekten selbst zu arbeiten aber viel spannender.

KA: Ja, natürlich. Ich habe mich mit Eiermann ganz konkret auseinandergesetzt. Ich habe

einen Auftrag zu bekommen. Wenn die Fachöffentlichkeit unsere Arbeiten anerkannte, gab das dem Bauherrn auch eine bestimmte Sicherheit.

IF: Wie sieht es mit Wettbewerben in gut beschäftigten Zeiten aus? Nehmen Sie nur noch an eingeladenen Wettbewerben teil?

PA: Natürlich sind die Chancen bei eingeladenen Wettbewerben für das Büro risikoloser, man kennt die Konkurrenz, und die Zahl der Teilnehmer ist kleiner. Andererseits haben wir gerade den Wettbewerb für die Messe Düsseldorf mitgemacht. Das war ein offener Wettbewerb, da kann man sehr viel freier an die Sache herangehen.

Vorlesungen von ihm gehört. Gesprochen habe ich mit ihm das erste Mal, als ich das Gartner-Haus in ›Bauen + Wohnen‹ 1956 veröffentlicht habe. Ich traf ihn in der Münchner Redaktion.

IF: Wie wichtig waren in den Anfängen Veröffentlichungen?

KA: Ganz wichtig. Ich habe viel publiziert. Das hat mir an der TH München sehr viel Verdruß gebracht. Mein Lehrer Franz Hart hat es damals fast als eine Beleidigung empfunden, daß ich als Student publizierte. ›Bauen + Wohnen‹ war die Zeitschrift der Avantgarde. In München wurde sie nicht geliebt. Die Zeitschrift der Münchner Architekten war natürlich der solide, traditionsbewußte ›Baumeister‹.

IF: Warum die Versuche, so viel zu publizieren? War es eine Frage von Eitelkeit, war es ein Mittel der Auftragsbeschaffung?

KA: Wenn etwas gedruckt war, gab es bei den Bauherren weitaus größere Möglichkeiten,

IF: What do all these names mean to you?

PA: I know them all, of course, but my generation sees them differently from the way people in the 50s and 60s saw them.

KA: In 1992, I went to New York and offered Peter a partnership. The discussion took place in the Four Seasons. In that light, our work together began in Mies's Seagram Building.

PA: When I was studying, Postmodernism was at its height. The persons my father mentioned had receded into the background. Aldo Rossi was greatly in favour.

IF: Your father not only didn't participate in Postmodernism. He ridiculed it. Did that make any difference to you?

KA: A discussion did take place, but it was not far-reaching enough. My teacher at the Oskar von Miller Polytechnic, Carl Erdmannsdorfer, showed us that terrible postcard montage, in which the Weissenhof Estate is depicted as an Arab village with camels. He was a Bavarian regionalist, and as such he was firmly convinced that the architecture was degenerate. At university, we first heard about modern architecture from Döllgast. I heard about Eiermann from him. But there was certainly no systematic discussion of these topics.

IF: One discussed the pros and cons of reconstruction. One talked about education, schools and universities, about simple architecture and so on. Were these subjects also discussed in the office, or was it just a place of work?

KA: When we built our first church, in Bad Füssing in 1968, there were debates about the spatial concepts of Otto Bartning and Rudolf Schwarz. I was familiar with their buildings and writings. In the office, Scandinavian architecture was also discussed a lot. We made our first visits to Finland, where I met Alvar Aalto and Aarne Ervi. During my first trip to America in 1961, I made the personal acquaintance of Mies van der Rohe. We talked about Eero Saarinen, and Louis Kahn. We were fascinated by the architecture of Le Corbusier. The discussions were hefty and contentious.

PA: No. At that time, I moved from the vast University of Technology in Munich to Vienna, to Gustav Peichl at the academy. He set high standards of quality and sought to communicate them. For him, Otto Wagner and Adolf Loos were important, not Hans Hollein and the other Postmodernists.

KA: Didn't you once say, when a woman student asked you whether Kurt Ackermann was your father, that you were distantly related to him...?

PA: That's right. I didn't go to Vienna to play the part of your son. That was also one of the reasons I left Munich. And anyway, Kurt Ackermann's views are not particularly close to those of the Viennese. Those who know him, appreciate him. My teacher, Gustav Peichl, speaks of eroticism in architecture, not of rationalism.

IF: What was so different in Vienna from the large-scale operations of Munich?

PA: One had a lot of independence. Everyone had to look for his own design projects. You looked for a site and considered what you could put on it. I drew up my own spatial programme and had my own ideas. But it might take months before one could even begin with the design. There were big discussions and debates, though. We always worked in the school, in the studio. Everyone had his own drawing board. There were 47 students in Peichl's master school, extending over all terms.

IF: How did your appointment as a professor at the University of Stuttgart in 1973/74 affect the office? Did it lead to changes?

KA: Yes. When I went to Stuttgart we had 35 people in the office. Within a year, the number of colleagues had been reduced to 12. I became aware that I couldn't cope with running a big office and working at the university at the same time. It was the time after 1968. Some assistants were of the opinion that the office should be socialized. There were heated debates. On the one hand, we had just built the open school in Weilheim and had been discussing the issue of co-determination; and then came all these dismissals. It was a tough test. On the other hand, I got on very well with the students. I had a lot of discussions with them, but these were rarely political. I had my own opinion as a liberal, and that was not questioned or subjected to discussion. But there were heated debates about education and training, about architecture, about quality.

PA: My father is certainly a liberal person, even as an architect. But he manages to get his opinions accepted. He is strong. On occasion, when he considers it necessary, he can be authoritarian.

KA: Mich spornt der engere Wettbewerb stärker an als der offene. Du weißt, gegen wen du antrittst; du strengst dich mehr an. Aber im übrigen ist das heutige Wettbewerbswesen mit den riesigen Bewerberzahlen eine Katastrophe. Die Auslober und die Preisrichter sind mit der großen Masse der Teilnehmer einfach überfordert. Die Qualität kommt durch Quantität zu kurz.

IF: Wie war die Diskussion in den fünfziger Jahren über das Berufsbild des Architekten, über Architektur und Politik, über das Dritte Reich?

KA: Es gab die Diskussion, aber nicht umfassend genug. Mein Lehrer am Oskar-von-Miller-Polytechnikum, Carl Erdmannsdorfer, hat uns noch diese furchtbare Postkarten-Montage mit den Kamelen in der Weißenhofsiedlung als

arabisches Dorf gezeigt. Als bayerischer Regionalist war er der festen Überzeugung, daß dies eine abartige Architektur sei. Erst von Döllgast an der TH haben wir von der modernen Architektur gehört. Von ihm hörte ich von Eiermann. Von systematischer Diskussion dieser Themen konnte nicht die Rede sein.

IF: Man diskutierte das Für und Wider des Aufbaus, man sprach über Bildung und Schulen, über einfache Architektur u. a. Waren das auch Themen im Büro? Oder arbeitete man nur?

KA: Bei unserer ersten Kirche in Bad Füssing 1968 ging es um die Raumvorstellungen von Otto Bartning und Rudolf Schwarz. Deren Bauten und Aufsätze kannte ich. Im Büro gab es zudem viele Diskussionen über skandinavische Architektur, es gab die ersten Reisen nach Finnland. Dort lernte ich Alvar Aalto und Aarne Ervi kennen. Bei meiner ersten Amerikareise 1961 bin ich auch Mies van der Rohe persönlich begegnet.
Wir diskutierten über Eero Saarinen und Louis Kahn. Die Architektur von Le Corbusier faszinierte. Es ging durchaus heftig und streitbar her.

IF: Was sagen Ihnen alle diese Namen?

PA: Natürlich kenne ich sie alle, aber meine Generation sieht sie anders als die der fünfziger und sechziger Jahre.

KA: Ich flog 1992 nach New York und habe Peter die Partnerschaft angetragen. Dieses Gespräch fand im Four Seasons statt. So gesehen hat unsere gemeinsame Arbeit im Seagram Building von Mies angefangen.

PA: Als ich studierte, war die Postmoderne gerade auf ihrem Höhepunkt. Die von meinem Vater erwähnten Leitfiguren waren in den Hintergrund getreten, Aldo Rossi hatte Hochkonjunktur.

IF: Ihr Vater hat die Postmoderne nicht nur nie mitgemacht, er hat sie verhöhnt. Hat Ihnen das etwas ausgemacht?

PA: Nein. Ich habe damals von der großen TU München nach Wien zu Gustav Peichl an die Akademie gewechselt. Er hat einen hohen Qualitätsanspruch und den sucht er zu vermitteln. Für ihn waren Otto Wagner und Adolf Loos wichtig, nicht Hans Hollein und die anderen Postmodernen.

KA: Stammt von dir nicht der schöne Ausspruch, als eine Studentin dich gefragt hat, ob der Ackermann dein Vater sei, du seist weitläufig mit ihm verwandt…?

PA: Das stimmt. Aber ich bin nicht nach Wien gegangen, um als dein Sohn aufzutreten. Auch deshalb bin ich ja aus München weg. Im übrigen, der Ackermann steht in seiner Auffassung nicht unbedingt den Wienern sehr nahe. Die ihn kennen, schätzen ihn. Mein Lehrer Gustav Peichl aber spricht von Erotik in der Architektur und nicht über Rationalität.

IF: Was war in Wien gegenüber dem Großbetrieb München so anders?

PA: Man war sehr selbständig. Jeder mußte sich seine Entwurfsaufgabe selber suchen. Man suchte ein Grundstück, überlegte, was kann man darauf machen; ich habe mir ein Raumprogramm erarbeitet und dies stellte ich mir vor. Es konnte Monate dauern, bis man den Entwurf überhaupt anfangen konnte. Aber die Diskussionen, die Auseinandersetzungen waren groß. Wir haben immer an der Schule gearbeitet, im Atelier, jeder hatte seinen Zeichentisch. Die ganze Meisterschule von Peichl hatte 47 Studenten über alle Semester.

IF: Welche Auswirkungen auf das Büro hatte eigentlich die Berufung 1973/74 an die Universität Stuttgart? Hat sie zu Veränderungen geführt?

KA: Ja. Als ich nach Stuttgart ging, hatten wir 35 Leute im Büro. Innerhalb eines Jahres sind wir schließlich auf 12 Mitarbeiter zurückgegan-

gen. Ich spürte, daß ich mit einem großen Büro und der Hochschule gleichzeitig nicht fertig wurde. Wir befanden uns in den ausgehenden 68er Jahren, das Büro sollte nach Ansicht einiger Mitarbeiter sozialisiert werden, es gab heiße Auseinandersetzungen. Einerseits hatten wir gerade die offene Schule in Weilheim gebaut, hatten über Mitbestimmung diskutiert, und dann diese Kündigungen. Das war eine recht harte Bewährungsprobe. Mit den Studenten dagegen kam ich gut aus. Ich habe viel mit ihnen diskutiert, selten in politischer Hinsicht. Als Liberaler hatte ich meine Meinung; die wurde nicht in Frage und zur Diskussion gestellt. Aber über Lehre, über Architektur, über Qualität gab es hitzige Debatten.

PA: Sicher ist mein Vater ein liberaler Mensch, auch als Architekt. Aber er setzt seine liberale Meinung auch durch; er ist stark. Er kann auch manchmal, wenn er es für notwendig hält, autoritär sein.

IF: Gab es eine Rückwirkung aus der Arbeit an der Universität Stuttgart auf das Büro? Oder war es nur umgekehrt?

KA: Natürlich sind interessante Wechselwirkungen entstanden. Denn die Studenten hinterfragen ja die Lehrer, und sie erwarten Antworten. Bei den Korrekturen und in der Zusammenarbeit mit den Studenten entstanden gleichzeitig neue Fragen. Die trägt man wieder ins Büro. In den Vorlesungen und Korrekturen lernt man präzises Fragen und genaues Antworten. Intensive Korrekturen sind eine Herausforderung, die einem oft den höchsten Einsatz abverlangt, die aber auch Ansporn für die Arbeit im Büro ist.

IF: Wie ist eigentlich der Führungsstil im Büro? Wer entscheidet?

PA: Eine Hierarchie gibt es nicht. In der Arbeitsweise sind wir offen, frei, wir mischen unsere Teams, jeder muß bei uns seine Meinung äußern. Wir sind ein kreativer Verein.

KA: Our principle of friendly leadership in the office has proved its worth. We both take our assistants seriously, share their joys and sorrows, success and failure. We do attempt to guide things in a certain direction, however, to motivate, to arouse enthusiasm and to convince people. Sometimes, of course, a decision will be taken that goes against the opinion of the whole team, but only when we two are convinced that this approach promises a better result. We always justify the decisions we take, however.

IF: Collegiality as the basis of the work?

KA: Yes. Our division of labour prevents the formation of hierarchic orders. The various activities in the office all have the same value in terms of the results. Site supervision, preparing production and detail drawings, and the preliminary design are of equal importance for the outcome of a scheme. The results of the work are subjected to a critical discussion within the group. Objective and, if necessary, hard criticism – which must always be constructive for the solution – is more than beneficial for a project. One of my mottos is not to talk the team into doing something, but to convince them with objective arguments. Assistants and clients willingly accept this approach. Spectacular ideas, designs that are immediately pleasing, that are smooth and appealing tend to put me on my guard. If our clients like something from the word go, I become suspicious. I need debate and a certain opposition.

IF: And how is the collaboration with other building professions and disciplines? To what extent do they contribute ideas and help to determine the solution?

KA: We start working with other disciplines at a very early stage. Their knowledge – mostly in the field of the natural sciences – is incredibly important for our work. We don't regard them just as technical assistants, but as partners, and we integrate them into the design process. As a result, they are on our side and uphold the concept jointly with us. Planning and building thus become a truly common task.

IF: Was there any feedback for the office from your work at Stuttgart University, or did it happen only in the opposite direction?

KA: Of course there was an interesting reciprocal action. The students question their teachers, and they expect answers. At the correction stage and in working together with students, new questions arose; and these, in turn, are brought back to the office. In lectures and criticisms, one learns how to ask precise questions and give precise answers. An intense correction process represents a challenge that often demands the utmost of one. But this is also a spur for the work in the office.

IF: What is the management style in your office? Who makes the decisions?

PA: There is no hierarchy. We are open in our method of work, free. We mix our teams. Everyone has to express his or her opinion. We're a creative outfit. Everyone attempts to present his ideas, but that functions only if everyone gives his best. We have a lot of young people, but we are fortunate also to have experienced long-time assistants and project managers in the office. An open exchange of views is important for our work together.

PA: It fits in with the office's method of work that we are open and seek open structures and wish to integrate engineers in our work, in our design team, in the same way as we do architects and people from other disciplines. That makes it enjoyable; it motivates people. I learn things that others know better.

KA: We choose the representatives of other disciplines according to the nature of the project. In that way, we usually know what we may expect of them.

PA: We select them at a very early stage indeed, sometimes when we are still not certain what we intend to do. Initially, there is a general discussion of ideas without everyone having an appointed role.

KA: Jörg Schlaich has been working with us as a genuine partner for a long time now. Our first project together was the pedestrian bridge in Kelheim. Then came the tent roof over the ice-skating rink, then the ice-sports hall in Munich. At present we are building a bridge over the Danube in Ingolstadt.

PA: In schemes such as Andechs Monastery, atmospheric things can be more important than high-performance structures. In such cases, our main discussion partner, with whom we consult, exchange ideas and develop the project, may be a sculptor like Blasius Gerg.

KA: The specialists with whom we work most are engineers, though. Our design principle, as I said, is to make the contents of the scheme legible and to achieve a congruence between structure and form. In that respect, a study of modern architecture – which I mean in a broad sense – can yield a rich source of ideas. The planning for ideal factories by Ledoux or Robert Owen, or the factory complexes of Tony Garnier and Antonio Sant'Elia all provide food for thought. I have observed with fascination, and not without a certain

Jeder versucht, seine Ideen darzustellen, das klappt nur, wenn jeder sein Bestes gibt. Wir sind viele junge Leute und haben das Glück, auch erfahrene, langjährige Mitarbeiter und Bauleiter im Büro zu haben. Der offene Austausch ist für unsere gemeinsame Arbeit wichtig.

KA: Unser kollegiales Führungsprinzip im Büro hat sich bewährt. Wir nehmen beide unsere Mitarbeiter ernst, teilen Freud und Leid, Erfolg und Mißerfolg. Wir versuchen allerdings zu steuern, zu motivieren, zu begeistern und zu überzeugen. Manchmal wird natürlich auch eine Entscheidung getroffen, die gegen die Meinung des ganzen Teams geht; das aber nur, wenn wir zwei überzeugt sind, daß diese Vorgehensweise für das Ergebnis einfach besser ist. Aber die Entscheidungen, die wir fällen, werden begründet.

IF: Kollegialität also als Voraussetzung für die Arbeit?

KA: Ja. Unsere Arbeitsteilung verneint hierarchische Ordnungen. Die unterschiedlichen Tätigkeiten im Büro haben für das Ergebnis den gleichen Stellenwert. Bauleitung, Werk- und Detailplanung und Entwurfsfindung sind

für das Ergebnis gleich wichtig. Arbeitsergebnisse werden in der Gruppe kritisch besprochen. Sachliche, wenn notwendig harte, für die Lösung aber immer konstruktive Kritik ist für die gestellte Bauaufgabe mehr als förderlich. Nicht das Team überreden, sondern objektiv überzeugen, ist eine Devise meiner Arbeit. Mitarbeiter und Bauherren nehmen dieses Vorgehen gerne an. Spektakuläre Ideen, Entwürfe, die gleich von Anfang an gefallen, die geschmeidig und eingängig sind, machen mich eher hellhörig. Wenn unseren Bauherren auf Anhieb etwas gefällt, werde ich stutzig. Ich brauche die Diskussion und einen gewissen Widerstand.

IF: Und wie ist es in der Zusammenarbeit mit anderen Fächern und Disziplinen am Bau? Wieweit regen sie an, wieweit entscheiden sie bei einer Lösung mit?

KA: Wir arbeiten sehr früh mit den anderen Disziplinen. Deren Wissen – meist ein naturwissenschaftliches Wissen – ist unglaublich wichtig für unsere Arbeit. Wir betrachten sie

nicht als Hilfskräfte, sondern als Partner und binden sie in den Entwurfsprozeß ein. Damit stehen sie zu uns und tragen eine Konzeption mit uns zusammen. So wird Planen und Bauen zu einer wirklichen Gemeinschaftsaufgabe.

PA: Es paßt eben auch zu der Arbeitsweise unseres Büros, daß wir offen sind, offene Strukturen suchen, Ingenieure genauso in unsere Arbeit einbinden, in unser ›Designteam‹, wie Architekten und andere. Das macht Spaß, motiviert, ich lerne, was andere besser wissen.

KA: Wir suchen uns die anderen Disziplinen bewußt nach der Bauaufgabe aus. Damit wissen wir meist, was wir von ihnen zu erwarten haben.

PA: Wir suchen sie sogar sehr früh aus, auch wenn wir noch gar nicht genau wissen, was wir machen wollen. Zunächst wird die Ideenfindung diskutiert, ohne zugewiesene Aufgabenbereiche.

KA: Jörg Schlaich arbeitet als echter Partner schon lange mit uns zusammen. Unser erstes Projekt war die Fußgängerbrücke in Kelheim. Dann kam das Eislaufzelt, dann die Halle für Eiskunstlauf in München. Jetzt bauen wir eine Donaubrücke in Ingolstadt.

PA: Es kann aber auch Aufgaben wie das Kloster Andechs geben, wo es auf atmosphärische Dinge mehr ankommt als auf Hochleistungskonstruktionen. Da ist unser wichtiger Gesprächspartner vielleicht ein Bildhauer wie Blasius Gerg, mit dem wir uns austauschen, diskutieren und entwickeln.

KA: Die Fachleute, mit denen wir am meisten zusammenarbeiten, sind allerdings Ingenieure. Unser Entwurfsprinzip ist es, wie schon ausgeführt, den Inhalt einer Bauaufgabe ablesbar zu machen und eine Übereinstimmung zwischen Konstruktion und Gestalt zu finden. Dabei ist die Auseinandersetzung mit der Moderne – die ich weit gefaßt sehe – eine Fundgrube. Die Planungsarbeiten für Idealfabriken von Ledoux oder Robert Owen und die Fabrikensembles von Tony Garnier und Antonio Sant'Elia geben Denkanstöße. Fasziniert und nicht ohne Genugtuung habe ich die späte Wiederentdeckung der alten Industriebauten und der in der Fabrik vorgefertigten Bauwerke des letzten Jahrhunderts beobachtet. Diese Industrieprodukte von hohem baukünstlerischem Niveau, oft von Ingenieuren entworfen, wurden in ihrer Zeit überhaupt nicht beachtet und lange Zeit in

element of underlying theory. But I have never looked for a universally valid theory that would explain our buildings. I can justify the things I do, make them plausible and comprehensible for others. My thinking is rational.

IF: Can one equate logic in this context with reason?

KA: No. The logic I mean is related more to the structure, which has to be self-consistent. A building doesn't necessarily have to be logical, but it can be rational.

IF: How do you arrive at a design? How does one draw the first line? What inspires you?

KA: The genius loci, the site, the surroundings in sun and rain, snow and fog. The stimulation of the location plays an important role for me. That became really clear to me with the design of our bridges. And, of course, the contents of the brief.

PA: At the very beginning is the site, going to take a look at it, then the discussions. In designing, we get something for nothing from the location. At the beginning there is the gift or the challenge of the location.

KA: We are not visionaries. Finding good architectural concepts is hard work. The solution comes at the end of a protracted design process.

PA: At the outset, the act of seeing, smelling, tasting the location plays the greatest role. One goes to visit it a number of times, develops initial ideas, goes back to the site and senses different, often quite profane things; nothing very remarkable. The sunrise, for example. The sunrise can spark off quite new ideas. If you don't experience things like that, you can't really build.

IF: Among the various buildings realized by the office, are there any that represent personal highlights in 40 years of architecture?

satisfaction, the late rediscovery of old industrial buildings and the structures that were prefabricated in 19th-century factories. These industrial products, of high architectural quality and often designed by engineers, went completely unheeded in their own day, and for a long time their significance remained totally unrecognized. What's important about this change of attitude is not the historical interest shown in these astonishing structures, but the clear difference in quality compared with the products of architectural fashions. The influence of engineering design on architecture in those days is being recognized again today, thank goodness!

IF: Your collaboration with other disciplines requires you to be informed yourselves. Where do you obtain your information?

PA: My father reads a lot, and in this field – structural engineering and architecture – he is "bilingual". I myself talk more with other people. I am extremely inquisitive. If I want to know something, I have no peace till I find it out.

IF: Does Kurt Ackermann see himself as a worker, an originator of ideas, an intellectual, a motivator...?

KA: As a pragmatic craftsman. I have always identified with making things, doing things – in the sense of realizing something. An architect can be measured only by the things he makes. Only by doing things can ideas be tested, assessed and modified. In that respect, I have always identified with the act of building. I was never really worried what other people considered me to be.

IF: Was the act of searching, which is implicit to making things, always related to practice? Or was there ever a search for a theory?

KA: Building and architecture are related to thought. I have never really designed on the basis of emotions. The process of thinking is important to me – and with it, of course, an

KA: For my own part, I would include the hop store in Mainburg, 1957–58, and the Hypo Bank in Munich, 1961–64, among these. We were awarded the first prize of the Federation of German Architects, BDA, for these schemes. Peter M. Bode wrote his first architectural criticism in the *Süddeutsche Zeitung* on the latter. At that time, an architectural column was not an established institution in the paper. There were a number of difficulties with the bank. When the carcass structure was almost complete, the chairman of the board of directors appeared on site and ordered all the apron panels to be bricked up; otherwise people would be able to look up the secretaries' skirts, he said. I wanted to resign the commission, but that was regarded as arrogant, and they gave me a real dressing down. But the apron panels to the windows are all still fully glazed today as they were planned. For the Hypo Bank project, we were very concerned with modern art. Asger Jorn, Emil Schumacher, Rupprecht Geiger, Heimrad Prem and the sculptor Fritz Koenig were all exhibited. Another key building is the Märker Cement Works in Harburg. We have now been working for over 40 years for the plant. In the course of our collaboration, we were kicked out once. Dr Wolfgang Märker had his own ideas. I had a concept for the

ihrer Bedeutung vollkommen verkannt. Nicht das historische Interesse an diesen erstaunlichen Bauten ist bei dieser Sinneswandlung von Wichtigkeit, sondern ihr deutlicher Qualitätsabstand zu den Architekturmoden. Der damalige Einfluß der Ingenieurbaukunst auf die Architektur wird heute, Gott sei Dank, wieder geachtet.

IF: Die Zusammenarbeit mit anderen Disziplinen braucht eigene Informationen. Woher nehmen Sie sie?

PA: Mein Vater liest sehr viel und ist auf diesem Gebiet – dem konstruktiven Ingenieurbau und der Architektur – zweisprachig. Ich unterhalte mich eher mit anderen. Ich bin extrem neugierig. Etwas wissen zu wollen, läßt mich nicht ruhen.

IF: Als was versteht sich Kurt Ackermann: als Arbeiter, Anreger, Intellektueller, Herausforderer?

KA: Als pragmatischer Handwerker. Ich habe mich immer zum Machen bekannt, und zwar im Sinne von Realisieren. Nur am Machen kann ein Architekt gemessen werden. Nur im Machen können Gedanken erprobt, kontrolliert und korrigiert werden. Insofern habe ich mich immer zum Bauen bekannt. Was die anderen meinten, was ich sei, war mir ziemlich egal.

IF: War das Suchen, das ja zum Machen gehört, immer ein praxisorientiertes? Oder gab es da auch die Suche nach einer Theorie?

KA: Bauen und Architektur hängen mit dem Denken zusammen. Ich habe eigentlich nie aus dem Gefühl heraus entworfen. Der Denkprozeß – und damit ein Stück theoretischer Unterbau – ist für mich wichtig. Eine allgemein gültige Theorie, die unsere Bauten erklärt, habe ich nicht gesucht. Was ich mache, kann ich aber begründen, nachvollziehbar und für andere verständlich machen. Mein Denken ist rational.

IF: Meint Logik in diesem Zusammenhang dasselbe wie Ratio?

KA: Nein. Die Logik ist für mich mehr auf die Konstruktion bezogen, die in sich schlüssig sein muß. Aber ein Bauwerk muß ja nicht unbedingt logisch, aber es kann rational sein.

IF: Wie kommt man zum Entwurf, wie zum ersten Strich? Was inspiriert einen?

KA: Der Genius loci, das Grundstück, die Umgebung, bei Sonne und Regen, bei Schnee und Nebel. Die Stimulanz des Ortes spielt für mich eine wichtige Rolle. Am deutlichsten ist mir das erst beim Entwurf unserer Brücken geworden. Natürlich auch der Inhalt der Bauaufgabe!

PA: Ganz am Anfang steht das Grundstück, es erst einmal anschauen gehen, dann diskutieren. Wir bekommen für das Entwerfen etwas vom Ort umsonst… am Anfang steht das Geschenk oder die Herausforderung des Ortes.

KA: Wir sind ja keine Visionäre; gute Architekturkonzepte zu finden, ist harte Arbeit. Am Ende eines langwierigen Entwurfsprozesses steht die Lösung.

PA: Am Anfang spielt das Sehen, Riechen, Schmecken des Ortes die größte Rolle. Man geht öfter hin, entwickelt die ersten Ideen, geht wieder auf das Grundstück, spürt plötzlich anderes, nichts Umwerfendes, oft ganz profane Dinge. Der Sonnenuntergang, der Sonnenaufgang kann dich auf ganz neue Gedanken bringen. Wer das nicht erlebt, kann eigentlich nicht bauen.

IF: Gibt es unter den Bauten des Büros so etwas wie einen persönlichen Höhepunkt in vierzig Jahren Architektur?

gen zuzumauern. Man könne sonst den Sekretärinnen unter die Röcke schauen. Ich wollte meinen Auftrag zurückgeben; das wiederum fand man arrogant, blies mir den Marsch, aber alle Fensterbrüstungen sind heute noch wie geplant voll verglast. Für die Hypobank haben wir uns mit moderner Kunst beschäftigt. Asger Jorn, Emil Schumacher, Rupprecht Geiger, Heimrad Prem und der Bildhauer Fritz Koenig wurden ausgestellt. Ein anderer Schlüsselbau ist das Märker Zementwerk in Harburg. Wir arbeiten inzwischen über vierzig Jahre für das Werk. In der Zusammenarbeit gab es auch einen Rauswurf. Dr. Wolfgang Märker hatte eine Vorstellung und ich ein Konzept für die langfristige Entwicklung des Werkes. Das gefiel ihm nicht, da er die Finanzierung etc. schon in seinem Sinne geregelt hatte. Mir sagte er, ich sei mit dieser Idee einen Monat zu spät gekommen. Ich bestand auf der Idee, und er hat mich hinausgeschmissen. Ich konnte ihm aber diese Idee nicht früher mitteilen, weil ich sie selbst noch nicht hatte. Als weitsichtiger Unternehmer hat er das Konzept realisiert. Wolfgang Märker beschäftigt uns noch heute. Das Werk hat nie etwas ändern oder abreißen müssen. Die gemeinsam gefundene Gesamtkonzeption der Funktion eines Zementwerks war eine richtige und langfristig gute Lösung.

IF: Und was ist ein Schlüsselbau für Sie aus dem Werk Ihres Vaters?

KA: Ich zähle für mich die Hopfenhalle in Mainburg 1957–58 und die Hypobank in München 1961–64 dazu. Für sie bekamen wir den ersten BDA-Preis. Peter M. Bode hat seine allererste Architekturkritik in der Süddeutschen Zeitung geschrieben, die es damals als feste Institution noch nicht gab. Mit der Bank gab es einige Schwierigkeiten. Als der Rohbau fast fertig war, erschien der Vorstandsvorsitzende auf der Baustelle und ordnete an, alle Brüstun-

plus the workshop area, where the enormous fleet of lorries is maintained and where all the vehicles are repaired. Some 74 different nationalities are represented among the dustmen, which makes this complex almost an international meeting place. The centre of the development is the vehicle port with its translucent membrane tent structure. From the road, one has a view into this area. The dustmen and their work, therefore, represent the focus of activities, not the administration, as is usually the case.

PA: The administration building is the formal address of the complex, simply because it is a tall slab block that occupies a prominent position in the street and forms a salient feature in the urban surroundings. But the main attraction will be the vehicle port with its roof. This translucent membrane roof is not a new invention; but the way we have developed it, it will be a most interesting, unmistakable structure.

IF: Let's turn to the client for a moment. Who is a good client; who is a bad one? How intense are your dealings with him?

KA: I can answer this question only very briefly. Märker in Harburg and Gartner in Gundelfingen were very insistent clients. Both were good, because they wanted something from us. The Gartner construction office is distinguished by its complex requirements in terms of the quality of the workplaces and the spatial atmosphere. Every workplace is laid out with a traditional drawing board as well as a computer. Dr Fritz Gartner was interested in the spatial and structural aspects as well as in the details. He wanted ideal working conditions for his technicians. The construction office is an inspiring place for generating ideas, for communication, for teamwork as well as for creative detailing in undisturbed surroundings with ideal lighting conditions. These were our criteria in our search for a solution. The result is a pilot scheme, rather like the prototype of a new car in automobile manufacturing.

IF: Gartner is a client of the old school: personal, with his own opinions. Do you have other clients like that today?

long-term development of the works, but he didn't like it, because he had organized the financing and other aspects of the project around his own plans. He told me I had come up with my idea a month too late. I insisted on the idea, however, and he threw me out. But I hadn't been able to put the idea to him any earlier, because it hadn't occurred to me earlier. As a far-sighted entrepreneur, he did implement the concept in the end. We are still working for Wolfgang Märker today. It has not been necessary to change or demolish anything in the plant. The overall concept for the functioning of a cement works, which we worked out together, was the right one and represented a good long-term solution.

IF: And what is a key building for *you* in your father's oeuvre?

PA: The school for air force officers in Fürstenfeldbruck. It is a relatively civilian development, but a scheme with many facets to it. It's austere, but not boring; and it's interesting because it is not a drill ground.

KA: Only after the building had been officially handed over did the officers notice that we had deliberately offset the corridors and laid out the external paths in an organic form, so that it would not be possible to march there. Some of them smiled with amusement. I even persuaded them to install a Panamarenko – an artistically significant, but unflyable flying machine that stood in the entrance hall.

IF: Is there a more recent building that you see as a key work?

KA + PA: Yes. The Office for Waste Management in Munich, a competition we won. It was a good, but difficult assignment. Some 500 dustmen have to be co-ordinated here. The brief also included a tower block for the administration with space for 850 employees,

PA: I haven't given the matter much thought, quite honestly. I'm more aware of what a bad client is. In a dairy outside Munich, the client was not prepared to discuss the question of the functioning of the building with us. He simply wanted us to obtain building permission for an enclosing structure. He found our questions about the whys and wherefores of the various processes involved superfluous and stupid. We agreed to go our separate ways, although the budget for the building was more than DM 80 million. The new dairy building that has now been completed proves our decision right.

KA: The City of Munich is an excellent client. It demands innovative solutions for its construction schemes. The Deutsche Messe AG, Hanover, is also a consistent and good client that seeks new concepts.

PA: A tough client, but a fair one. The Messe AG does a lot of building. It is a highly qualified and professional organization. In this project, we were faced with a technical department of 70–80 people who were extremely interested in special, innovative solutions. They sought a discussion of their organizational needs. This kind of dialogue is what makes a good client, a client who has the courage to accept unusual architectural solutions. With a good client, you can build up a personal relationship. A feeling of mutual trust develops. The architect is, or is meant to be, the trustee of the client. If this trust does not exist, one shouldn't enter into a collaboration, or one should break it off prematurely.

IF: How do clients generally react to the qualitative and systematic demands that the Ackermann office makes of its architecture?

KA: It can sometimes happen that a client will regard us as an opponent. The client may be irritated by our insistence on certain things. He may think we are authoritarian and are trying to take over from him and pull the wool over his eyes. We explained the concept for the new beer terrace in Andechs Monastery to the congregation of monks. We were of the opinion that the terrace should be of stone; for underneath it, is a three-storey cellar. One of the monks, however, was set on having grass and trees, and at the end of the discussion, he said to us that an architect

PA: Die Offiziersschule der Luftwaffe in Fürstenfeldbruck. Sie ist verhältnismäßig zivil, aber vielschichtig. Sie ist streng, aber nicht langweilig, und sie ist interessant, weil sie kein Exerzierplatz ist.

KA: Die Offiziere merkten erst, daß wir die Flure bewußt versetzt und Außenwege organisch angelegt haben, damit man dort nicht marschieren kann, als der Bau eingeweiht wurde. Einige haben darüber geschmunzelt. Ich habe ihnen ja damals auch noch einen Panamarenko aufgeredet, nämlich ein künstlerisch bedeutendes, aber fluguntaugliches Objekt einer Flugmaschine, das in der Eingangshalle stand.

IF: Gibt es einen neueren Schlüsselbau?

KA + PA: ...doch, das Amt für Abfallwirtschaft in München, ein gewonnener Wettbewerb. Es ist eine schöne und schwierige Aufgabe. Allein fünfhundert Müllfahrer müssen dort koordiniert werden. Zu der Aufgabe gehört ein Verwaltungshochhaus für insgesamt achthundertfünfzig Mitarbeiter und der Werkstattbereich. Dort wird der riesige Fuhrpark gewartet und es werden sämtliche Fahrzeuge repariert. Unter den Müllkutschern gibt es vierundsiebzig Nationen. Das macht das Amt fast zu einer internationalen Begegnungsstätte. Zentrum der Bauanlage ist der Carport mit seiner transluzenten Struktur aus Membran-Schirmen, der von der Straße einsehbar ist. So stehen die Müllkutscher und ihre Arbeit im Mittelpunkt des Geschehens, und nicht wie üblich die Verwaltung.

PA: Das Verwaltungsgebäude gibt zwar die Adresse, allein dadurch, weil es eine Hochhausscheibe ist, die sich prominent im Straßenraum zeigt, städtebaulich einen Akzent gibt, aber das Hauptaugenmerk wird der Carport mit seinem Dach sein. Dieses transluzente Membrandach ist nicht neu erfunden, aber in der Art und Weise, wie wir es weiterentwickelt haben, wird es sehr interessant und unverwechselbar sein.

IF: Thema Bauherr: Wer ist ein guter Bauherr, wer ein schlechter? Wie intensiv ist die Auseinandersetzung mit ihm?

KA: Auf diese Frage kann ich nur sehr verkürzt eingehen. Ein nachdrücklicher Bauherr war Märker in Harburg und Gartner in Gundelfingen. Beide waren gut, weil sie von uns etwas wollten. Das Konstruktionsbüro Gartner ist geprägt durch komplexe Anforderungen an die Qualität der Arbeitsplätze und die Raumatmosphäre. Jeder Arbeitsplatz ist althergebracht mit einer Zeichenmaschine ausgestattet, aber auch mit einem Computer. Dr. Fritz Gartner

interessierte sich für den Raum, die Konstruktion und für das Detail. Er wollte für seine Techniker den idealen Arbeitsplatz. Das Konstruktionsbüro, ein inspirierender Ort für die Produktion von Ideen, für Kommunikation, für kollegiale Teamarbeit und kreative Detailarbeit in ungestörter Umgebung, mit optimalen Lichtverhältnissen. Diese Kriterien wurden zum Leitbild auf der Suche nach der Lösung. Das bauliche Ergebnis ist eine Nullserie wie beim Automobilbau der Prototyp eines neuen Autos.

IF: Gartner ist ein Bauherr alter Prägung, persönlich, mit einer eigenen Haltung. Haben Sie heute noch mehr solcher Bauherren?

PA: Ich habe darüber noch nicht viel nachgedacht. Ich weiß eher, was ein schlechter Bauherr ist. Bei einer Molkerei im Umkreis von München konnten wir den Bauherrn zu keinem Gespräch über das Thema Funktion gewinnen. Er wollte von uns nur eine genehmigungsfähige Hülle; unsere Fragen nach einem Wie und Warum von Abläufen fand er überflüssig und dumm. Wir haben uns getrennt, obwohl die Bausumme über achtzig Millionen DM war. Der jetzt fertiggestellte Neubau der Molkerei hat unsere Konsequenz bestätigt.

KA: Die Landeshauptstadt München ist eine hervorragende Bauherrschaft, die innovative Lösungen für ihre Bauaufgaben fördert. Auch die Deutsche Messe AG Hannover ist ein konsequenter und guter Bauherr, der neue Konzepte sucht.

PA: ... ein harter, aber fairer Bauherr. Die Messe AG baut sehr viel, sie ist hochqualifiziert und professionell. Eine technische Abteilung von siebzig bis achtzig Mann, die sehr interessiert an speziellen und innovativen Lösungen waren, stand uns bei diesem Projekt gegenüber. Sie suchten die Auseinandersetzung über ihre organisatorischen Bedürfnisse. Die-

ser Dialog macht einen guten Bauherrn aus, der auch den Mut zu einer außergewöhnlichen Architektur hat. Zu einem guten Bauherrn kann man ein persönliches Verhältnis aufbauen, es entwickelt sich ein gegenseitiges Vertrauen. Der Architekt ist oder soll ja der Treuhänder des Bauherrn sein. Wenn dieses Vertrauen nicht gegeben ist, sollte man eine Zusammenarbeit nicht anfangen oder frühzeitig beenden.

IF: Wie reagieren Bauherren generell auf den qualitativen und systematischen Anspruch des Büros Ackermann an seine Architektur?

KA: Es kommt manchmal so weit, daß wir zum vermeintlichen Gegner des Bauherrn werden. Der Bauherr wird durch unsere Konsequenz irritiert. Er meint, wir seien autoritär und würden versuchen, ihm das Heft aus der Hand zu nehmen, ihm etwas aufs Auge zu drücken. Das Konzept der neuen Bierterrasse des Klosters Andechs haben wir vor dem Konvent erläutert und waren der Meinung, diese Terrasse sollte steinern werden, denn darunter liegt ein dreigeschossiger Keller. Ein Frater wollte aber unbedingt Grün und Bäume, und am Ende der Diskussion sagte er uns, ein Architekt, der kein Grün wolle, verachte auch die Menschen. So leicht macht sich aber der Konvent das eigene Bauen nicht, die Terrasse

KA: We take costs and the construction time terribly seriously and precisely. In the case of the Marienhof Sewage Treatment Plant for the city of Munich, roughly DM 30 million were left over at the end. Although it was an experiment, the ice-skating tent went only DM 350,000 over the budget; and the Office for Waste Management saw a saving of DM 20 million.

PA: Even with the Hanover trade fair, where we had an extremely short period in which to realize the scheme and a very tight budget, we remained within the cost limits.

IF: Is there a case where things went completely wrong?

KA + PA: No. Not in any of our by now well over 200 executed projects.

IF: Let's return to the architecture of the Ackermann office and the question of design.

who didn't want greenery also despised people. The congregation, however, doesn't make things as simple as that for itself with its building. The terrace is now paved with terracotta and remains without planted areas. Instead, it has a variable roof of white umbrellas.

PA: I acted as an intermediary between two sides that were in a state of deadlock, and we found a reasonable compromise. It wasn't so difficult really. Sometimes my task is mediation.

IF: Clients want security in respect of time and costs. How is the Ackermann office on that score?

Since you never followed any fashion, you are in danger of being regarded as a reactionary. You even reject the classical role of leadership as the architect in charge of things. How do you work?

KA: My attitude of not participating in every trend that comes along in architecture was and still is a gamble. It has meant a lot of reverses for me, as well as the occasional defeat; and it has not always won me friends. The official architectural scene, from which I

deliberately keep my distance, does indeed call me conservative. But I see in that an affirmation of my work. Today, as in the past, our buildings demonstrate my advocacy of technology and the continued development of the Modern Movement. In the speech I gave on receiving the Tessenow Medal in 1994, I said that what links us to Tessenow are aesthetic objectivity, clarity, indeed honesty. The principles we follow in our work are logic, precision, conciseness and lightness. Our idea of architecture is that it should possess a degree of universal validity and timelessness.

PA: As a younger architect, I can endorse that without hesitation. We are not formalists. We are not trying to create a style of our own. We are not interested in a recognizable mode of expression.

KA: In our design work, we are not bogged down with preconceived formal notions or personal stylistic features. In what are seemingly similar buildings, the different briefs and other requirements result in completely different solutions. In that respect, we do not repeat ourselves. What is important for us is the pervasiveness of a concept in an urban planning and design context. We always subordinate the potential variety of architectural form to a clear order. We stick to well-tried technical solutions, but we seek to develop them further in their content, form and design. Depending on its function, every element of a building will be given a recognizable form; in other words, a functional gestalt. The individual elements should show what they do, what their structural and constructional role is. The mutual compatibility of the individual elements is achieved through a choice of suitable materials, through a maximum degree of integration and an appropriate form. All these things are old-fashioned virtues, but we still believe in the idea of honesty in architecture.

PA: We attempt to develop an idea from the essence of the brief, to formulate it and to arrive at a target we can achieve. We are not here just to be the executants of the client, to confirm his prejudices, as in the case of the dairy project.

IF: How is the quality of a design assessed and discussed? How is it improved?

KA: In a very rational way, I think. I have a training in trade skills. I'm a journeyman bricklayer and carpenter; and as such, I learned to recognized clear, simple forms at an early age. I deepened that knowledge during my studies. Every term, I worked on two designs while the other students were doing one. My first buildings were stronger in their detailing than in their design. The quality of the detailing of our buildings is something we have retained. Perhaps it has even become more expressive. You notice the

KA: Mein Standpunkt, nicht jeden neuen Trend in der Architektur mitzumachen, war und bleibt ein Wagnis. Diese Haltung hat mir viele Rückschläge, manche Niederlage und nicht immer Freunde eingetragen. Der offizielle Architekturbetrieb, zu dem ich bewußt Abstand halte, nennt mich in der Tat konservativ. Ich sehe darin eher eine Bejahung meiner Arbeit, denn gestern wie heute belegen unsere Bauten mein Bekenntnis zur Technik und zur Weiterentwicklung der Moderne. In meinem Vortrag bei der Auszeichnung mit der Tessenow-Medaille 1994 habe ich gesagt, daß uns ästhetische Sachlichkeit, Klarheit, selbst Redlichkeit mit Tessenow verbinden. Logik, Präzision, Knappheit und Leichtigkeit sind Prinzipien, denen wir bei unserer Arbeit folgen. Eine gewisse Allgemeingültigkeit und Zeitlosigkeit sind unsere Ideen von Architektur.

PA: Dem kann ich mich auch als Jüngerer ohne weiteres anschließen. Wir sind keine Formalisten; wir streben nach keinem eigenen Stil. Eine erkennbare Handschrift interessiert uns nicht.

KA: Beim Entwerfen belasten uns keine vorgefaßten Formvorstellungen oder eigene Stilmerkmale. Bei scheinbar ähnlichen Bauten kommen durch die unterschiedliche Aufgabenstellung und anderen Anforderungen völlig verschiedene Ergebnisse zustande. Wir wiederho-

Elemente untereinander wird durch adäquate Werkstoffe, eine möglichst optimale Fügung und eine angemessene Form erreicht. Alles dies sind altmodische Tugenden, aber wir glauben noch an die Ehrlichkeit in der Architektur.

PA: Wir versuchen, aus dem Wesen einer Aufgabe eine Idee zu entwickeln, sie zu formulieren und zu einer Zielvorstellung zu kommen, die wir realisieren. Als Erfüllungsgehilfen eines Bauherrn, zur Bestätigung seiner Vorurteile, lassen wir uns, wie am Beispiel der Molkerei geschildert, nicht verbrauchen.

IF: Wie wird die Qualität eines Entwurfs beurteilt und diskutiert? Wie wird sie verbessert?

KA: Ich denke sehr rational. Außerdem habe ich auch eine handwerkliche Ausbildung. Ich bin Maurer- und Zimmerergeselle. Dabei habe ich früh klare einfache Formen kennengelernt. Das habe ich im Studium vertieft. In jedem Semester habe ich immer zwei Entwürfe bearbeitet, wo die anderen einen gemacht haben. Meine ersten Häuser sind im Entwurf nicht so stark wie im Detail. Die Detailqualität unserer Bauten ist geblieben. Sie wurde vielleicht ausdrucksstärker. Qualität spürst du in dem Moment, wo du dich immer mehr mit dem Bauen auseinandersetzt, du spürst, ob eine Fassade sitzt, ob sie ausgewogen ist, ob die

wird jetzt mit Terrakotta belegt und bleibt ohne Grün und erhält dafür ein wandelbares Dach aus weißen Schirmen.

PA: Ich bin als Mittler zwischen zwei festgefahrenen Ansichten tätig geworden, und wir fanden einen tragfähigen Kompromiß. Es war gar nicht so schwierig. Die Vermittlung ist manchmal meine Aufgabe.

IF: Bauherren wollen Zeit- und Kostensicherheit. Wie steht es damit im Büro Ackermann?

KA: Wir nehmen die Kosten und Bauzeiten ungeheuer genau und ernst. Beim Münchner Klärwerk Marienhof sind ca. 30 Millionen DM übriggeblieben. Das Eislaufzelt, obwohl ein Experiment, ist nur 350 000,– DM teurer geworden. Beim Amt für Abfallwirtschaft werden 20 Millionen DM eingespart.

PA: Selbst bei der Messe Hannover, bei dem vorgegebenen extrem kurzen Realisierungszeitraum und ganz engem Budget, sind wir kostenmäßig voll im Rahmen geblieben.

IF: Ist das irgendwo einmal danebengegangen?

KA + PA: Nein. Bei keinem von unseren inzwischen weit mehr als zweihundert ausgeführten Bauten.

IF: Kommen wir einmal zu der Architektur des Büros Ackermann und zum Entwerfen. Da Sie nie eine Mode mitgemacht haben, stehen Sie allmählich in dem Ruf eines Ewiggestrigen. Auch die klassische Kompetenzzuweisung des federführenden Architekten leugnen Sie. Wie arbeiten Sie?

len uns in diesem Sinne nicht. Wichtig ist uns die Durchgängigkeit eines Konzeptes im städtebaulichen und im gestalterischen Sinne. Die mögliche Vielfalt der architektonischen Gestalt unterstellen wir immer einer klaren Ordnung. Bewährte technische Lösungen behalten wir bei, suchen sie aber inhaltlich, in Form und Gestalt, weiterzuentwickeln. Jedem Bauteil geben wir, seiner Aufgabe entsprechend, eine ablesbare Form, also eine funktionale Gestalt. Die einzelnen Bauteile sollen zeigen, was sie leisten, was ihre statische und konstruktive Aufgabe ist. Die Verträglichkeit der einzelnen

IF: How can something like that happen?

PA: In Hanover it was simply the enormous time pressure. There is no building that one has completely under control from beginning to end. One notices certain things only on site. There are also things that you see differently in the plans from on site, where it becomes clear that you can't leave a certain thing the way it is. In the Hönninger House, the client wanted a two-metre-high garden

quality when you become more involved with a building. You notice whether a façade is right, whether it's balanced, whether the openings are in the right place, whether the proportions fit. When we build a model, this becomes even clearer. I always tried these things out with a lot of variations, until I realized that trying out variants doesn't help much. Then I discovered the creation of alternatives. That's our method of working today – with alternatives.

IF: At what stage of the design does the office start thinking in terms of alternatives?

PA: During the design phase we always try out alternatives, just as we do in all phases of the detailed planning. I believe that architecture has much more to do with practical trade skills than with research, than with the natural sciences. As architects, we have a broad training, much broader than disciplines related to the natural sciences.

KA: We are prepared to jam on the brakes on site in an emergency and demolish something if we see that it's not right. In the trade fair hall in Hanover, we got a flight of stairs wrong in two of the cores – wrong, because the stair flights didn't fit. They were torn out and done again.

wall. We were opposed to this. The wall was nevertheless built in concrete and then pulled down again.

IF: I imagine that must be a unique case. What are the criteria for your competition schemes?

PA: In the competition for the Office for Waste Management, the difficult brief and the highly complex functions involved led us to draw up three alternatives. The solution we finally chose was by no means the most spectacular; but it was by far the most rational and the most sensible in the urban context.

KA: The other competitors concentrated on the show face along the road and placed the vehicle port and the workshops there. We did it the other way round. The narrow front of our administration block faces on to the street. That seemed to us to be a good enough address.

IF: With different approaches in respect of the urban planning, I can well imagine alternative solutions. But what form do alternative details take if they basically all have to comply with the needs of economy and reduction?

KA: One of our tougher debates in the office was over the façade for Hanover. We had desiged a façade and were aiming at a certain continuity by using the section we had developed for Andechs. We were looking for an ideal way of jointing the façade sections. The manufacturing company came up with a suggestion that was really a most ingenious solution: a socketed joint.

PA: It was a marvellous solution, technically sound, minimal, really clever ...

KA: All the assistants jumped at this solution. Even Peter began to waver. Would it be fair to say that?

PA: Yes. The sophisticated technical solution completely seduced me.

KA: I repeatedly tried to impress upon the office that the façade needed a certain legibility; one should be able to see how it was made. A certain craft finishing technique should be evident. If we were to adopt the smooth, precision solution of the manufacturers, I argued, the expression of our somewhat Baroque façade would be much too elegant. The noble appearance would have nothing in common with our robust trade fairs hall. The rough steel with the ecological timber roof, and then this smooth, polished façade were opposites that didn't harmonize with each other.

PA: I soon recognized the problem of consistency, though. Today, we are pleased we did it the way we did.

IF: And how was it done, given completely different production requirements?

KA: The specification was written with our section. We were able to meet the deadline, because our steel section was not extruded, as it had been in the case of Andechs. It had to be welded together. Welding suited our needs: one senses the craftsmanship and sees the traces of handwork. The impression is much livelier, more sculptural.

IF: It's certainly not always possible to get a client to accept one's ideas. To what extent can one accept compromises, and when?

KA: Building is always a compromise, I think. But a compromise is acceptable only to the point where the architect does not have to betray his own principles. A compromise has to show a path to the final goal without the result being diluted. If the concept as a whole suffers, one can no longer speak of a com-

Öffnungen richtig sitzen, ob die Proportionen stimmen. Und wenn wir ein Modell bauen, wird es immer noch deutlicher. Das habe ich in vielen Varianten immer wieder ausprobiert, bis ich begriffen habe, daß die Variantenbildung wenig taugt. Dann kam ich auf die Bildung von Alternativen. In Alternativen arbeiten, das ist heute noch unsere Arbeitsweise.

IF: In welcher Phase des Entwurfs setzt im Büro das Denken in Alternativen ein?

PA: Beim Entwerfen entwickeln wir immer Alternativen, ebenso in allen Phasen der Detailplanung. Ich glaube, daß Architektur viel mehr Handwerk ist als Forschung, als eine naturwissenschaftliche Disziplin. Unsere Ausbildung zum Architekten ist breit, viel breiter als bei den naturwissenschaftlichen Disziplinen.

KA: Wir sind bereit, auf der Baustelle die Notbremse zu ziehen und etwas abzureißen, wenn wir sehen, hier stimmt was nicht. In Hannover bei der Messehalle haben wir in zwei Kernen je einen Treppenlauf falsch gemacht. Falsch, weil die Stufenläufe nicht aufgegangen sind. Die wurden herausgerissen und neu gemacht.

IF: Wie kann es zu so etwas kommen?

PA: In Hannover war es einfach der riesige Zeitdruck. Es gibt kein Gebäude, das man von vorn bis hinten zu hundert Prozent im Griff hat. Einige Sachen merkt man erst auf der Baustelle. Aber es gibt auch Dinge, die werden auf dem Plan anders gesehen als auf der Baustelle. Dort wird deutlich, so etwas darf nicht stehen bleiben. Beim Haus Hönninger wollte der Bauherr eine zwei Meter hohe Gartenmauer, wir waren dagegen. Die Mauer wurde trotzdem betoniert und wieder abgerissen.

IF: Das dürfte sicher ein Einzelfall sein. Was sind die Kriterien bei Ihren Wettbewerbsentwürfen?

PA: Beim Wettbewerb für das Amt für Abfallwirtschaft hatten wir wegen der schwierigen Aufgabe und der hochkomplexen Funktionen drei Alternativen erarbeitet. Die dann von uns gewählte Lösung war keineswegs die spektakulärste, aber mit Abstand die rationalste und für die städtebauliche Situation die vernünftigste.

KA: Die anderen Wettbewerbsteilnehmer haben die goldene Seite zur Straße bedient und den Carport und die Werkstätten dort situiert. Wir haben es genau umgekehrt gemacht.

Unser Verwaltungsbau steht mit der Schmalseite zur Straße. Das schien uns Adresse genug.

IF: Bei städtebaulich unterschiedlichen Ansätzen kann ich mir Alternativen gut vorstellen. Aber wie sieht es bei Detailalternativen aus, die alle im Grunde dem Anspruch an Sparsamkeit, an Reduktion genügen?

KA: Eine unserer härteren Auseinandersetzungen im Büro war die Fassade für Hannover. Wir hatten die Fassade entwickelt und suchten mit unserem Andechser Profil nach Kontinuität. Wir wollten eine optimale Fügung der Profile. Die geniale Lösung brachte ein Sondervorschlag der Fertigungsfirma: eine Steckverbindung.

PA: Es war eine tolle Lösung, technisch einwandfrei, minimiert, ganz clever…

KA: Alle Mitarbeiter sind auf diese Lösung aufgesprungen, auch Peter ist dadurch schwankend geworden. Darf ich das so sagen?

PA: Ja, die raffinierte technische Lösung hat mich völlig bestochen.

KA: Ich habe immer und immer wieder versucht, dem Büro beizubringen, die Fassade brauche eine bestimmte Ablesbarkeit des Machens. Eine bestimmte handwerkliche Fertigungstechnik solle spürbar sein. Wenn wir die glatte und hochpräzise Lösung der Firma übernähmen, sei der Ausdruck unserer etwas barocken Fassade viel zu elegant. Das noble Erscheinungsbild habe mit unserer robusten Messehalle nichts mehr zu tun. Der grobe Stahl mit dem ökologischen Holzdach und die geschleckte Fassade, das seien Gegensätze, die nicht miteinander harmonierten.

political power of the local mayor was so great that he didn't allow this. I wanted visual axes to be left open across the site. The plant was meant to be seen, felt, experienced. He wanted to cover it completely with greenery. Today, the green screening belt has grown round it. It's a pity.

IF: Are the compromises your father describes compromises for you as well?

PA: I have a different opinion in some matters. Recently, with a pedestrian bridge over the River Regen, we sensed that the position of the bridge the town council wanted was better than ours. It was easy to make a compromise in that case.

PA: We both want quality. We want to realize outstanding schemes. We want to use technology in the service of architecture. We want to resolve building assignments in a dialectic manner. We are agreed on that. The difference between us is a matter of emotion. I give vent to my temperament much more than my father does. Even if I'm sometimes wrong, I stick to my emotions.

IF: Some people need opposition to rise to the challenge and give their best. Some even need controversy...

PA: I have a strong urge for harmony. I work well when I feel secure. On the other hand, it is necessary and stimulating for the result to have some opposition against which to grapple.

KA: It's much the same with me.

IF: I find that hard to believe. I know a Kurt Ackermann who attacks others, who approaches a subject negatively. That method functions when there is someone taking part in the discussion who is able to absorb this and turn it to a positive end.

promise. The overall goal is impaired. That's something we don't tolerate, or only very rarely.

IF: But where does the point lie between compromise and abandoning one's principles beyond which one doesn't go?

KA: The Marienhof Estate sewage treatment plant in Munich was a compromise in certain areas. According to my concept, the digestion chambers should have been shown more clearly. They should have risen another five to seven metres out of the ground. But the

IF: Do you think, as a young architect, that times are harder today than they were for your father and that you are required to make more compromises than he had to?

PA: If that were the case, we would not be credible any more. One can't begin work on the basis of a compromise. If we do make a compromise, it is one that has been fought over, that has been achieved through negotiations and that, therefore, has its good and justifiable aspects. Compromise is not a matter of giving in or abandoning one's own ideas.

IF: Can one say that in questions of design, father and son are always more or less in agreement, in respect of the aims and the method of approach?

KA: I attack a thing only when it goes completely against the grain with me. Only then do I go on the offensive. But in principle, I'm anything but quarrelsome. I far prefer a good collaboration to continual antagonism.

PA: He likes to test things for their weaknesses. He's tenacious. He keeps turning things over to examine them, to make them better. He's a perfectionist.

KA: With no one have I argued in a more cultivated manner than with Otl Aicher. And yet we were the best of friends.

PA: Ich habe das Problem der Durchgängigkeit dann schnell verstanden. Heute sind wir froh, es so gemacht zu haben.

IF: Und wie ließ sich das dann bei völlig veränderten Anforderungen in der Produktion realisieren?

KA: Die Ausschreibung war mit unserem Profil gelaufen. Den gesteckten Termin konnten wir halten, weil unser Stahlprofil nicht stranggepreßt war, wie bei dem Andechser Profil, sondern es wurde geschweißt. Das Schweißen ist uns entgegengekommen; man spürt die handwerkliche Arbeit und sieht die handwerklichen Spuren. Dadurch ist der Eindruck lebendiger und plastischer.

IF: Sicher kann man gegenüber dem Bauherrn nicht immer seine Vorstellung durchsetzen. Wie weit kann man Kompromisse eingehen und wann?

KA: Ich meine, Bauen ist immer ein Kompromiß. Aber ein Kompromiß kann nur so weit gehen, daß sich der Architekt nicht selbst verleugnen muß. Der Kompromiß muß den Weg zum Ziel zeigen, ohne daß das angestrebte Ergebnis verwässert wird. Wenn die Gesamtkonzeption darunter leidet, kann von einem Kompromiß nicht mehr die Rede sein. Die ganzheitliche Aufgabe nimmt Schaden; das machen wir nicht oder sehr selten mit.

IF: Aber wo zwischen der Selbstaufgabe und dem Kompromiß verläuft die Linie, hinter die man nicht geht?

KA: Ein Kompromiß war in gewissen Bereichen das Klärwerk Gut Marienhof, München. Meiner Vorstellung nach hätten die Faulbehälter deutlicher gezeigt werden sollen, fünf bis sieben Meter höher sollten sie aus dem Boden schauen. Aber die politischen Kräfte des örtlichen Bürgermeisters waren so stark, daß er dieses nicht zuließ. Ich wollte Sichtschneisen. Das Klärwerk sollte sichtbar, spürbar, erlebbar bleiben. Er wollte es total zugrünen, heute ist der Grüngürtel zugewachsen, schade.

IF: Sind die Kompromisse, von denen Ihr Vater spricht, auch für Sie welche, oder nicht?

PA: Ich habe da in manchen Punkten andere Ansichten. Wir haben gerade bei einer Fußgängerbrücke über den Regen die Erfahrung gemacht, daß die Lage der Brücke, die der Stadtrat wollte, die bessere war als unsere. Da konnten wir leicht einen Kompromiß eingehen.

IF: Sind Sie als junger Architekt nicht der Meinung, daß die Zeiten heute schwieriger sind als bei Ihrem Vater und Sie eher Kompromisse machen müssen als er?

PA: Wenn das so wäre, wären wir nicht mehr glaubhaft. Auf der Basis eines Kompromisses kann man keine Arbeit anfangen. Wenn wir einen Kompromiß eingehen, dann ist er erkämpft, erarbeitet und hat dann seine guten und vertretbaren Seiten. Kompromiß hat ja nichts mit Einknicken zu tun oder mit der Aufgabe der eigenen Idee.

IF: Kann man sagen, daß sich Vater und Sohn im Entwurf, im Ziel einer Aufgabe und im Herangehen weitgehend immer einig sind?

PA: Wir wollen Qualität, wir wollen anspruchsvolle Bauaufgaben realisieren, wir wollen Technik als dienendes Element der Architektur, wir wollen Bauaufgaben dialektisch lösen. Da sind wir uns einig. Der Unterschied bei uns ist die Emotion. Ich lasse viel schneller mein Temperament heraus als mein Vater. Selbst wenn ich manchmal daneben liege, stehe ich zu meiner Emotionalität.

IF: Manche Menschen brauchen den Widerspruch, um zu Höchstleistungen aufzulaufen, manche gar den Streit...

PA: Bei mir ist grundsätzlich ein starkes Harmoniestreben vorhanden. Ich bin gut, wenn ich mich aufgehoben fühle. Andererseits ist es von Reiz und für das Ergebnis essentiell, mich mit einem Gegenpol auseinanderzusetzen...

KA: Bei mir ist es ähnlich.

IF: Das fällt mir schwer zu glauben. Ich kenne einen Kurt Ackermann, der andere attackiert, der negativ an eine Sache herangeht. Das funktioniert, wenn es in der mit ihm diskutierenden Gruppe jemanden gibt, der dies auffangen und ins Positive wenden kann.

KA: Ich schlage nur drauf, wenn mir etwas völlig gegen den Strich geht. Erst dann greife ich an. Aber im Prinzip bin ich alles andere als streitsüchtig; mir ist die gute Zusammenarbeit viel lieber als das dauernde Gegeneinander.

PA: Er rüttelt gerne, er ist hartnäckig, er wendet eine Sache hin und her, um sie zu prüfen, besser zu machen, er ist perfektionistisch.

KA: Mit niemandem habe ich so gepflegt gestritten wie mit Otl Aicher. Und doch verband uns eine tiefe Freundschaft.

IF: Eben fiel das Stichwort Technik. Am Ende des 20. Jahrhunderts hat die Technik ein doppeltes Gesicht: Sie hat der Menschheit den gegenwärtigen Stand ihrer Kultur gebracht, sie hat den Globus durch ihre nicht vorhergesehenen Konsequenzen aber auch an den Rand der Katastrophe gebracht. Was bedeutet das für Ihre Architektur?

KA: Am Ende des ausgehenden Jahrhunderts dürfen wir keine geschlossenen Systeme mehr hervorbringen. Die Aufgabe heißt heute, für kommende Generationen flexible, offene Systeme zu entwickeln, die veränderbar, erweiterbar, leicht zerlegbar, die abbaubar sind, die auch künftigen Entwicklungen einen Spielraum lassen. Intelligente Konstruktionen mit minimalisiertem Materialanteil, die auf energetische und ökologische Notwendigkeiten Rücksicht nehmen, das ist es, was wir brauchen. Echte innovative Lösungen, langfristige Wirtschaftlichkeit und architektonische Qualität sind dabei keine Gegensätze, die sich gegenseitig ausschließen. Langzeitig übersteigen die betriebswirtschaftlichen Kriterien die ursprünglichen Investitionen, trotzdem konzentrieren wir uns noch immer auf die reinen Baukosten. Wir brauchen aber Gebäude, die mit umweltverträglichen, energiesparenden Technologien betrieben werden und die sich ändernden Nutzungen anpassen können.

IF: You mentioned the word "technology" just now. At the end of the 20th century, there are two faces to technology. It has brought humankind to its present cultural level. Yet, through its unforeseen effects, it has also brought the world to the brink of disaster. What significance does that have for your architecture?

KA: At the end of the 20th century we should not create any more closed systems. Today, it is our responsibility to develop flexible, open systems for future generations, systems that are adaptable, extendible, easily dismantled, that can be taken apart and that allow scope for future developments. What we need are intelligent structures with a minimal material content that reflect energy-related and eco-logical needs. Whereby, genuinely innovative solutions, long-term economic viability and architectural quality need not be mutually exclusive. In the long term, the question of initial investment is outweighed by the criteria determining operational efficiency. Despite this, we still concentrate our attention on the pure construction costs. What we need are buildings that can be operated with envi-ronmentally sustainable, energy-saving tech-nologies and that can be adapted to changing uses.

IF: We have spoken about alternatives and high-quality solutions. What role do experi-mentation and innovation play in the Acker-mann office?

KA: Two problematic terms. For me they mean much the same thing. To my mind, experimentation means not knowing in advance the outcome of an innovative design.

PA: We are not an office that is obsessed with innovation. We don't create architecture just for the sake of doing something new. Of course, our aim is to develop things, to optimize them. But experimentation as a risk-taking adventure is not our thing.

KA: The load-bearing girder grid we designed for Hall 13 in Hanover is based on a well-known structural principle. This form of grid, which transmits loads in two directions, has existed for a long time. For us, however, the challenge was to reactivate the underlying principle of the grid to span dimensions of 120 x 225 metres in an optimum manner. Giv-ing a new interpretation to a structural tradi-tion that has been forgotten, and realizing it with the means or technology of our times – that is a task that attracts us and leads to new results.

PA: In Hanover, we also exploited the effect of Venturi elements on the roof, which are 30 x 50 metres in size, like the wings of a jum-bo jet. The experimental aspect was to make them of plastic, with a smooth surface, streamlined, supple, light – in other words, appropriate to their function.

IF: Engineers are sometimes sceptical about structures like that. Where do you get your ideas as architects?

KA: From other disciplines: from aircraft con-struction, from ventilation technology and so on. It's something I call "structural intelli-gence". But even today, we have hardly understood how to cultivate the technology to go with it. This is also something I men-tioned in my speech of thanks on receiving the Tessenow Medal. Technology opens up new, undreamed-of possibilities for us. Using standard industrial elements together with products specially manufactured for a partic-ular building, open structures can be devel-oped that will manifest themselves in their outward appearance. The latest technologies, especially computer-controlled manufactur-ing processes – where production is directed from a control panel – facilitate individual production methods that can react quickly to needs and turn out construction components in small series for special purposes. I must admit that we have so far recognized these positive developments only in certain areas and have scarcely applied them in our own projects. This kind of industrial prefabrication

is comparable with early forms of craft manu-facture of individual building elements. Archi-tects have to rethink their position and stop regarding architecture in the first instance as art, in which one tackles each new problem like the creation of the world. One step along this path would be to reactivate the great crafts tradition in the spirit of Heinrich Tessenow and to use his approach, continu-ing it with industrial means and on a broad basis. That would be a true advancement of modern architecture; but it would demand a critical approach – to technology as well – and unreserved commitment. It also means that the appropriate technical solutions would not necessarily have to be beautiful, but that beauty would depend on appropri-ateness. There again, I am speaking in the spirit of Heinrich Tessenow. For him, "sim-plicity is not always the best; but the best is always simple".

IF: What will happen when you take over the office completely? Will you change anything fundamentally?

PA: Naturally, the office will change. That's a perfectly normal process – just as it has constantly changed and developed over the last 45 years. Architecture is always a process of development. The profession gives me tremendous pleasure. We are really lucky to have a lot to do. I see what we are doing, and it pleases me. We have a wonderful team.

KA: Of course the office will change. But Peter will certainly safeguard the continuity of modern architecture with good, fine build-ings, and I thank him for that.

IF: Über Alternativen und Qualitätsfindung haben wir gesprochen. Welchen Stellenwert haben Experiment und Innovation im Büro Ackermann?

KA: Zwei schwierige Begriffe, die für mich weitgehend dasselbe sind. Experimentieren heißt für mich, das Ergebnis, das bei einem innovativen Entwurf herauskommt, vorher nicht zu kennen.

PA: Wir sind kein Büro, das unbedingt nur auf Innovation abstellt. Nicht um des Neuen willen machen wir Architektur. Natürlich ist unser ganzes Bestreben das Entwickeln, das Optimieren; aber das Experiment als Abenteuer mit Risiken ist nicht unsere Sache.

KA: Der Trägerrost in Hannover für die Halle 13 ist ein bekanntes Konstruktionsprinzip. Den Trägerrost, der zweiachsig abträgt, den gibt es schon lange. Aber das Prinzip des Trägerrostes neu zu beleben und zu versuchen, eine Spannweite von 120 mal 225 Metern optimal zu überbrücken, das war für uns die Herausforderung. Eine konstruktive Tradition, die in Vergessenheit geraten ist, neu zu interpretieren und mit den Mitteln oder den Technologien unserer Zeit zu realisieren, das ist für uns eine Aufgabe, die uns reizt und zu neuen Ergebnissen führt.

PA: In Hannover haben wir daneben auch den Effekt der Venturi-Flügel angewendet, die eine Größe von 30 mal 50 Meter, wie Jumbo-Jet-Tragflächen, haben. Das Experiment war, sie aus Kunststoff zu machen, geschmeidig von der Oberfläche, windschlüpfrig, glatt, leicht, also auch funktionsgerecht.

IF: Die Ingenieure sind bei solchen Konstruktionen manchmal durchaus skeptisch. Woher kommen für Sie als Architekten die Anregungen?

KA: Aus anderen Disziplinen, aus dem Flugzeugbau, der Lüftungstechnik usw. Ich nenne das konstruktive Intelligenz. Allerdings haben wir bis heute kaum verstanden, mit ihr die Technik zu kultivieren. Auch dies ist etwas, was ich in meiner Dankrede bei Erhalt der Tessenow-Medaille gesagt habe. Die Technik gibt uns ungeahnte, neue Möglichkeiten. Mit industriellen Standardelementen und mit speziell für eine Bauaufgabe gefertigen Bauprodukten können offene Strukturen gefunden werden, die sich auch im Erscheinungsbild zeigen. Die neuesten Technologien, vor allem die computergesteuerten, vom Steuerpult dirigierten Produktionsprozesse einer rechnergestützten Fertigung, lassen individuelle und reaktionsschnelle Produktionsmethoden zu, die in kleinen Serien, speziell für den Zweck einer Aufgabe gefertigte Bauteile herstellen. Ich gebe zu, wir haben diese positiven Entwicklungen bis heute nur in Teilbereichen erkannt und für unsere Bauaufgaben nicht oder selten genützt.

Diese Art industrieller Fertigung ist mit dem frühen handwerklichen Machen der jeweiligen Bauteile vergleichbar. Die Architekten müssen allerdings umdenken und Architektur nicht in erster Linie als Kunst auffassen, die jedes neue Problem angeht wie die Erschaffung der Welt. Eine Entwicklung auf diesem Weg bedeutet, den Geist einer großen Handwerkstradition im Sinne und in der Haltung von Heinrich Tessenow wiederzubeleben und mit industriellen Mitteln auf breiter Basis fortzuführen. Das wäre eine echte Weiterentwicklung der modernen Architektur, die aber eine kritische Einstellung – auch zur Technik – und ein vorbehaltloses Engagement verlangt. Das bedeutet aber auch, daß das technisch Richtige nicht unbedingt schön sein muß, aber das Schöne ist auf das Richtige angewiesen. Damit bin ich wieder beim Geist von Heinrich Tessenow. Für ihn war »das Einfache nicht immer das Beste. Aber das Beste ist immer einfach.«

IF: Wie wird es, wenn Sie die Leitung des Büros ganz übernehmen. Werden Sie etwas grundsätzlich ändern?

PA: Ändern wird sich das Büro selbstverständlich, ein ganz natürlicher Prozeß; so wie es sich in den letzten fünfundvierzig Jahren immer geändert und entwickelt hat. Architektur ist doch immer Entwicklung. Mir macht der Beruf unheimlichen Spaß; wir haben wirklich Glück, daß wir viel zu tun haben, ich sehe, was wir machen, es gefällt mir, wir haben eine tolle Mannschaft.

KA: Natürlich wird sich das Büro verändern. Peter wird aber sicher die Kontinuität der modernen Architektur mit guten und schönen Bauten fortsetzen. Dafür danke ich ihm.

Physiotherapy
Practice, Katrin
Ackermann, Munich

Commencement of
planning: 1991
Construction period:
1991– 92

The brief required the insertion
of a physiotherapy practice in
a large undivided space in an
existing building. The space
was dominated by two square
columns; and the entrance level
was two steps higher than the
rest of the room. This difference
in level was used to create a
raised reception and waiting
area.

The design sought to retain
the generous spatial character of
the existing structure, yet at the
same time to create an intimate
atmosphere in the treatment
rooms. All inbuilt elements and
partitions, therefore, stop short
of the ceiling. The spaces above
them are either left open, or are
divided by glazed clerestory
strips that provide an acoustic
separation of the rooms. The
columns are integrated into the
central linen and store block and
into a fitness station.

The choice of materials and the
colour concept were developed
in close consultation with the
client. The specific atmosphere is
distinguished by the clear spatial
layout of the different functional
realms in conjunction with the
coloration. Red was chosen as a
warm tone and an active colour.
The parquet flooring and the sliding doors are in pale ash. The
other fittings are white.

The transparent sliding
screen to the street front can be
flexibly integrated into the spatial
layout.

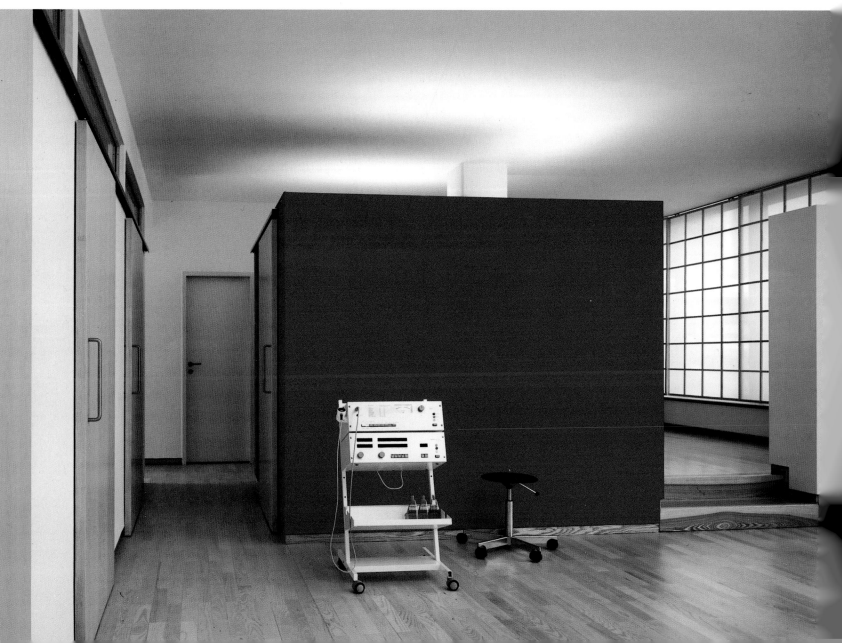

In einem bestehenden Gebäude eine Praxis für Krankengymnastik einzurichten, war die Aufgabe. Der vorhandene Großraum ist durch zwei quadratische Stützen bestimmt. Der Eingang liegt um zwei Stufen höher als die Praxisräume. So wurde der Niveauunterschied genutzt, einen erhöhten Empfangs- und Wartebereich zu schaffen.

Ziel der Planung war es, die Großzügigkeit des Raums zu erhalten und dabei eine private Atmosphäre in den Behandlungsräumen zu schaffen. Aus diesem Grund wurden alle Einbauten und Trennelemente nicht bis zur Decke gezogen, sondern blieben offen oder wurden mit Glasoberlichtern akustisch getrennt. Die Stützen wurden in den zentralen Wäsche- und Lagerblock beziehungsweise in eine Fitneßstation integriert.

Die Wahl der Materialien und das Farbkonzept sind in enger Zusammenarbeit mit der Nutzerin erarbeitet worden. Die klare räumliche Zuordnung der Funktionsbereiche in Abstimmung mit der farblichen Gestaltung bestimmen das Raumgefühl. Als warmer Farbton und aktive Farbe wurde Rot gewählt. Das Parkett und die Schiebetüren sind aus hellem Eschenholz, die restlichen Einbauten wurden in Weiß gehalten.

Der transparente Sichtschutz an der Straßenfront ist verschiebbar und läßt sich flexibel den Raumanordnungen anpassen.

Oben: Grundriß der Praxis.
Links: Blick in den Gymnastikraum. Rechts: Eingang mit Wartebreich

Top: plan of practice.
Left: view of gymnastics area. Above: entrance and waiting area

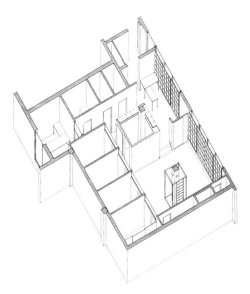

Eine der beiden störenden Stützen wurde mit einem roten Lagerraum umhüllt. Die zweite Stütze dient der Befestigung von Gymnastikgeräten.

One of the two columns in this otherwise unobstructed space was enclosed in a red storage block. The second column is used to support gymnastic equipment.

Praxis für Physiotherapie, Katrin Ackermann, München

Planungsbeginn: 1991
Bauzeit: 1991–1992

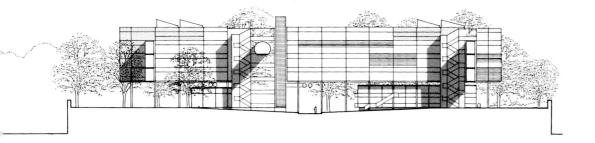

Oben: Ansicht vom Innen-
hof. Mitte: Schnitt durch
die Gesamtanlage. Unten:
Isometrie von Süden mit
der runden Einfriedungs-
mauer

Top: courtyard elevation.
Middle: section through
entire complex. Bottom:
perspective view from
south with the curved
boundary walls

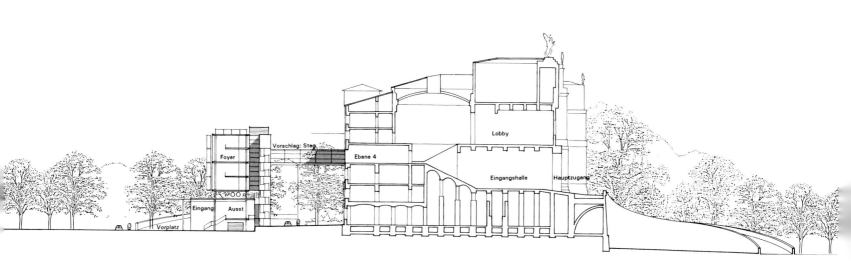

Foyer   Vorschlag: Steg   Lobby

Eingang   Ausst   Ebene 4   Eingangshalle   Hauptzugang

Vorplatz

Die Erweiterung des
Maximilianeums soll
dienender Teil des be-
deutenden Münchner
Baudenkmals sein.

The extension of the
Maximilianeum is con-
ceived as a serving
element of this important
historical building in
Munich.

Am Grüngürtel der Isar liegt das 1857–74 von Friedrich Bürklein im Auftrag von König Maximilian II. errichtete Münchner Baudenkmal, das mit seiner Schauseite nach Westen zum Stadtzentrum die städtebauliche Entwicklung in den angrenzenden Stadtteilen bestimmte.

Der Wettbewerbsbeitrag sieht einen klaren geometrischen Baukörper mit zwei Luftgeschossen und einer relativ geringen Bauhöhe vor. Das Maximilianeum bleibt auch von Osten als Solitär sichtbar. Der viergeschossige Neubau nimmt die Traufhöhen der Flügelbauten auf und steht wegen der Sondernutzungen im Erdgeschoß auf Stützen. Damit konnten die Sonderbereiche mit großzügiger Lockerheit eingeschoben werden, um die optische Durchlässigkeit zum historischen Bestand zu gewährleisten. Die Organisation der Grundrisse sieht eine Trennung der einzelnen Funktionen vor. Der Neubau im Osten stellt sich als Eingangsbauwerk für den Landtagsbereich dar. Ein Steg in der Ebene 4 verbindet ihn direkt mit der Ebene des Plenarsaales, zwei weitere Stege sorgen für kurze Wege.

Das Tragwerk des Gebäudes ist ein Stahlbetonskelett, Achsraster 6,0 x 7,5 m, mit Flachdecken für die einzelnen Geschosse. Mit der doppelten Vorhangfassade erhielten alle Räume natürliche Belichtung und Belüftung. Die Technologie der Fassaden entspricht dem neusten Stand der Lichttechnik; gläserne Umlenkprismen führen das Licht blendfrei in die Tiefe der Räume und fungieren gleichzeitig als blendfreier Sonnenschutz. Neben dem außenliegenden Sonnenschutz ist in den Innenbereichen ein Blendschutz vorgesehen.

Ansicht von Osten, die der
Stadtmitte abgewandte
Seite

East elevation, facing
away from city centre

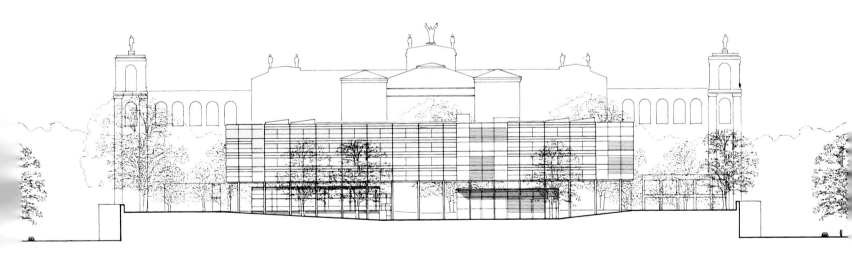

Erweiterung des Maximilianeums,
Bayerischer Landtag, München

Wettbewerb: 1992
3. Preis

Extension of Maxi-
milianeum, Bavarian
State Parliament,
Munich

Competition: 1992
Third prize

Occupying an elevated position in the green belt along the River Isar and overlooking the city centre to the west, the historical Maximilianeum building dominates the surrounding urban areas. It was erected by Friedrich Bürklein between 1857 and 1874 to a commission by King Maximilian II of Bavaria.

The competition scheme for an extension to the east proposed a building with a clear geometric volume of relatively low height and with two open storeys at the base. This four-storey extension adopts the eaves heights of the historical wings and is raised on stilts to accommodate structures for special uses at ground floor level. The generous open spatial form of the extension allows the Maximilianeum to retain its independent character and to remain visible beyond the new structure when viewed from the east. The layout of the various floors provides for a separation of functions. The extension presents itself as an entrance tract to the state parliament. A bridge at level 4 links the new building with the level of the debating chamber. Two further bridges are also foreseen to ensure a network of short routes within the complex.

The load-bearing structure consists of a reinforced concrete skeleton frame, laid out to a 6.0 x 7.5 m grid, with flat plate floors. The two-skin curtain-wall façade ensures that all rooms enjoy daylight and natural ventilation. The façade design reflects state-of-the-art lighting technology. Glass prisms deflect light into the depth of the spaces without causing glare. They also function as a non-glare sunscreen system. In addition to the external solar shading, an anti-glare installation is foreseen internally.

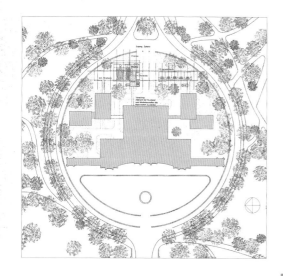

Grundriß
Erdgeschoß

Ground floor
plan

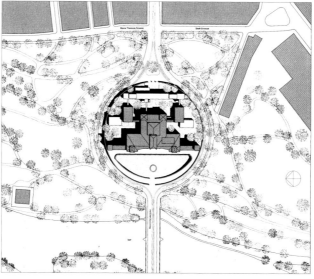

Die Gesamtanlage ist in den landschaftlich reizvollen, parkartigen Hang der Isar eingebettet.

The ensemble is carefully integrated into the attractive park-like landscape of the escarpment rising from the River Isar.

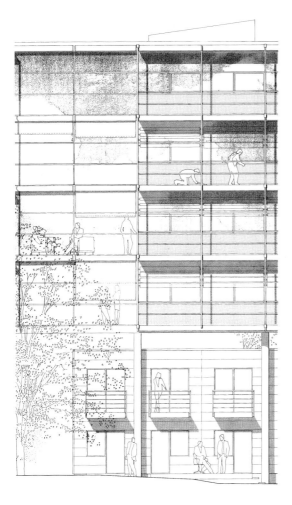

Detailansicht der Fassade.
In den zwei Luftgeschossen sind Ausstellungsräume bzw. Wohnräume für die Stipendiaten des Maximilianeums untergebracht.

Elevation of part of façade. The two open storeys at the base were designed to accommodate special uses such as exhibitions or dwellings for scholarshipholders of the Maximilianeum Foundation.

Der Eingang mit Vordach wurde unter den Baukörper eingeschoben.

The entrance and canopy were inserted beneath the main structure.

Hönninger House,
Grünwald

Commencement of
planning: 1991
Construction period:
1992–94

Designing a single-storey house for a married couple is always an attractive task for an architect. The brief for this project required all areas to be closely linked with the park-like garden. The client is a building engineer and contractor. The form of construction and the materials used were based largely on craft techniques and were thus subject to certain limitations. The 42.5 m long and 11.5 m wide house has a conventional brick structure with reinforced concrete floors. Externally, it is rendered and painted white.

To the north and west, the site is bordered by residential roads. It seemed sensible, therefore, to locate the house along the northern edge of the site, so that the living areas could be screened from the road. The north face contains a series of rectangular openings. To the south, in contrast, the house opens on to the garden with broad areas of glazing.

The clear rectangular form is divided into three functional realms. To the south of the entrance hall and inset into the volume of the house is a covered patio with an open fireplace. This area divides the dwelling into two realms. To the east are the

guest rooms, the garages and a garden tool store. To the west are the living and sleeping areas for the family. The dining and living rooms, the bedrooms and bathroom all have a southern aspect. To minimize the distance from the entrance, the kitchen and utilities room are oriented to the north. Adjoining these areas are the visitors' quarters for the grown-up children of the family.

Stores and rooms for mechanical services are housed in the basement, where there is also a large fitness area with a sauna and steam bath.

At the eastern end of the garden, screened off from the neighbouring site, is the swimming pool, which receives direct sunlight from the east, south and west.

Formally, the strict, white, cubic form of this single-family house is indebted to the tradition of the Bauhaus. The large metal windows have individual openings for ventilation. The white metal louvred elements that can be slid over the areas of glazing

Wohnhaus Hönninger, Grünwald

Planungsbeginn: 1991
Bauzeit: 1992–1994

Die mit einer Mauer abgegrenzte Straßen- und die Gartenseite. Das sich nach Norden öffnende zentrale Oberlicht ist auf der Südseite mit Solarelementen für die Beheizung des Schwimmbades bestückt.

The house has two faces: the street front, which is closed off by a wall; and the garden aspect. The central north-light roof is clad on its south-facing slope with solar panels that heat the water for the swimming pool.

Für ein Ehepaar ein erdgeschossiges Wohnhaus zu entwerfen, ist eine schöne Aufgabe. Alle Bereiche sollten einen intensiven Bezug zum Garten des parkartigen Grundstücks haben. Der Bauherr ist Bauingenieur und Bauunternehmer, die Wahlmöglichkeiten der Bauweise und des Baumaterials waren zwangsläufig auf handwerkliche Methoden ausgerichtet und somit eingeschränkt. Der 42,5 m lange und 11,5 m breite eingeschossige konventionelle Mauerwerksbau mit Stahlbetondecken wurde verputzt und weiß gestrichen. Im Norden und Westen von Wohnstraßen begrenzt, bot sich eine Situierung des Hauses entlang der nördlichen Straße an. Das Haus öffnet sich großzügig mit Glaswänden nach Süden und schirmt sich durch die geschlossenen Lochfassaden zur Straße hin ab. Der rechtwinkelige, klare Baukörper ist funktional in drei Nutzungsbereiche unterteilt. Südlich der Eingangsdiele trennt der überdeckte,

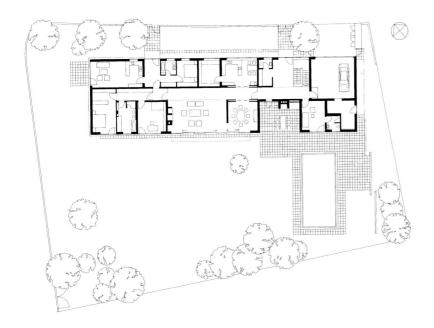

to provide sunscreening also serve as a security measure. The horizontal sunscreen element cantilevered out over the full-height glazing to the living areas functions as a light filter and anti-glare system that provides protection against direct sunlight. The sliding glass doors to the living and dining rooms have additional external sunblinds. Over the central spine of this restrained, rectilinear building is a north-light roof that draws suffused light into the rear part of the large living space. Incorporated in the 45° south-facing slope of this north-light is a solar heating installation that produces enough energy to condition the water in the swimming pool.

Das Nordshed schafft eine gleichmäßige weiche Belichtung, vor allem für die Tiefe des großzügig bemessenen Wohnraumes.

The north-light spine creates soft, even light conditions, especially in the depth of the large living room.

filter und schließen die direkte Blendung durch Sonneneinstrahlung aus. Die Schiebeglaswände vor dem Wohn- und Eßraum haben zusätzlich außenliegende Sonnenjalousetten. Über dem Mittelbereich des strengen, rechteckigen Baukörpers sitzt ein Sheddach, das sich nach Norden öffnet und blendfreies Licht in die Tiefe des großzügigen Wohnraumes bringt. Auf der 45° geneigten Fläche nach Süden ist eine ausreichende Solaranlage zur Konditionierung des Schwimmbades installiert.

eingeschnittene Freisitz mit offenem Kamin die Funktionsbereiche. Im Osten sind der Gastbereich sowie die Garagen und Gartengeräteräume angeordnet, im Westen liegen die Wohn- und Schlafbereiche der Familie.

Die Räume für Essen, Wohnen, Schlafen und das Bad öffnen sich nach Süden. Die Küche und der Hauswirtschaftsraum sind wegen der kurzen Wege zur Eingangsseite nach Norden orientiert. Daran schließt eine Besuchswohnung für die erwachsenen Kinder an. Im Keller liegen die Lager- und Haustechnikräume sowie ein großzügiger Bereich für Fitness mit Sauna und Dampfbad.

Den östlichen Gartenabschluß bildet, abgeschirmt zur Nachbarschaft, das Schwimmbad, das sich zum Grünbereich orientiert und direkte Sonne von Osten, Süden und Westen erhält.

Formal ist das Einfamilienhaus als strenger weißer Kubus der Bauhaus-Tradition verpflichtet. Die Metallfenster sind großflächig verglast mit individuellen Lüftungsöffnungen. Schiebeelemente aus weißen Metall-Lamellen vor den großen Glasflächen dienen als Sonnen- und Sicherheitsschutz. Die waagerecht auskragenden Sonnenschutzlamellen vor dem geschoßhoch verglasten Wohnbereich wirken gleichzeitig als Licht-

Verschiebbare Lamellenelemente aus Aluminium bieten luftdurchlässigen Einbruchschutz und ermöglichen eine Abdunkelung der Schlafräume.

Sliding aluminium louvre elements filter the entry of light and serve to darken the bedrooms. They also function as a safety precaution against burglary.

Academy of Arts,
Pariser Platz, Berlin

Study, 1993
First phase

In the spring of 1993, nine members of the architectural department of the Academy of Arts undertook the task of producing outline proposals for a new academy on the site of the existing building. The designs were to be completed within a short space of time based on only a roughly drafted brief.

In October 1993, the schemes were submitted and assessed by a jury that included members of the Academy of Arts, as well as representatives of the Brandenburg Ministry of Culture, the administration of the Berlin Senate for Cultural Affairs, Urban Development and Environmental Protection, and the Construction and Housing Departments. The schemes submitted, which provided a number of clear responses to the future form of Pariser Platz, sparked off an intense debate within the jury about the design goals for this public open space.

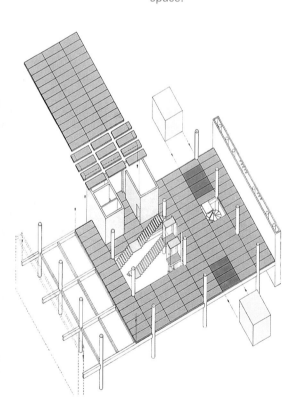

"The unpretentious, unemotional general expression of this structure, its beauty, its objective precision and perfection, its transparency and openness, and the inviting quality the building – the façade – radiates towards the square were all appraised positively."
Excerpt from jury report

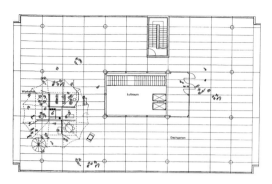

DG

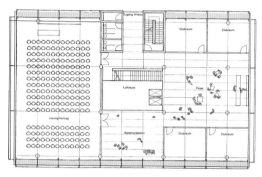

OG

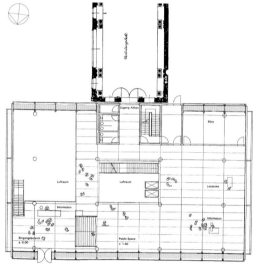

EG

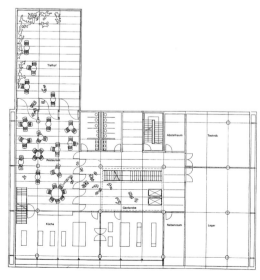

UG

Neun Mitglieder der Abteilung Baukunst der Akademie der Künste ließen sich im Frühjahr 1993 darauf ein, innerhalb kurzer Zeit auf der Basis eines nur andeutungsweise fixierten Programms skizzenhafte Entwürfe für ein neues Haus an alter Stelle auszuarbeiten.

Im Oktober 1993 lagen die Arbeiten vor und wurden von einer Jury beurteilt, der neben Vertretern der Akademie der Künste auch solche des Brandenburgischen Kultusministeriums, der Berliner Senatsverwaltungen für Kulturelle Angelegenheiten, Stadtentwicklung- und Umweltschutz sowie Bau- und Wohnungswesen angehörten. Angeregt durch die Entwürfe mit ihren klaren Stellungnahmen zur künftigen Gestalt des

Platzes, kam es in der Jury zu einer intensiven Diskussion über die geplante Gestaltungssatzung für den Pariser Platz.

»Positiv bewertet wurden der gesamte unprätentiöse, unpathetische Gestus des Gebäudes, seine Schönheit und sachliche Genauigkeit, Präzision und Perfektion, die Transparenz und Offenheit, der einladende Charakter des Hauses – der Fassade – gegenüber dem Platz.«
Aus der Beurteilung der Jury

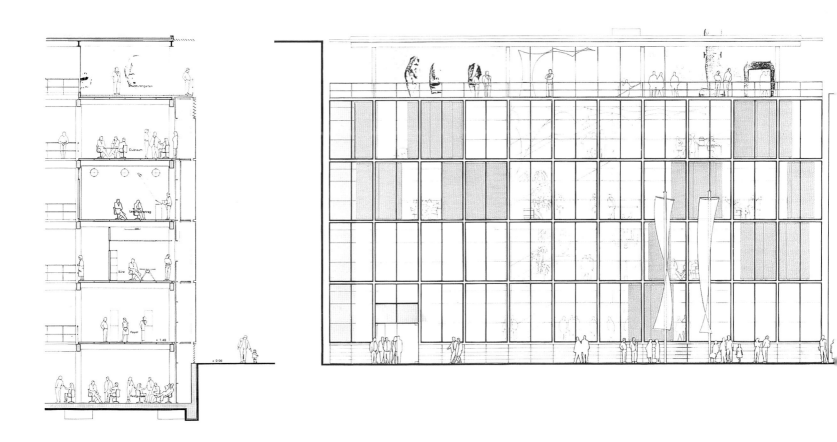

Akademie der Künste Berlin, Pariser Platz

Gutachten 1993
Erste Phase

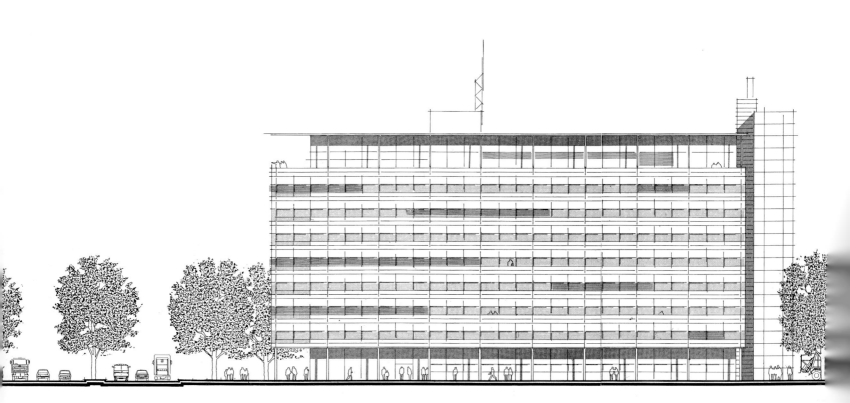

Georg - Brauchle - Ring

Eingang

Das Ziel des von der Landeshauptstadt München ausgelobten Wettbewerbs ist die städtebauliche Neuentwicklung des Bereichs südlich des Georg-Brauchle-Rings zwischen Hanauer Straße und Mittlerem Ring durch eine hochwertige Büro- und Gewerbenutzung. Mit dem Amt für Abfallwirtschaft wurden erste Akzente gesetzt.

Die drei Nutzungsbereiche des Neubaus sollten an ihrer funktionalen Gestalt ablesbar sein. Das Verwaltungsgebäude für 320, der zentrale Betriebshof mit Kfz-Werkstätte für 100 Mitarbeiter und die Abstellhalle für 170 Mülltransporter mit Sozialräumen für die 500 Mitarbeiter des fahrenden Außendienstes mußten in das städtebauliche Konzept integriert werden. Das Verwaltungsgebäude zum Ring hin ist als signifikante Scheibe gleichzeitig Abschluß des Büro- und Gewerbebereichs, der Betriebshof und der zweigeschossige Carport bilden den Abschluß zu dem Grüngürtel im Süden.

Die Verkehrsanbindung zum Georg-Brauchle-Ring erfolgt durch eine interne Stichstraße, flankiert durch das 70,0 m x 13,0 m große, neunstöckige Verwaltungsgebäude. Das Tragwerk ist eine Stahlbetonkonstruktion mit 7,2 m x 7,2 m bzw. 7,2 m x 4,8 m Achsraster. Der äußere Raumabschluß ist als eine vorgehängte Elementfassade aus silberfarbigem Aluminium mit transparentem, im Brüstungsbereich transluzentem Glas und integrierten Schall- und Sonnenschutz konstruiert. Im obersten zurückgesetzten, in Stahl konzipierten Geschoß liegt die Kantine, zu der zwei verglaste Aufzüge führen. Von hier hat man einen freien Blick über den Olympiapark und München bis hin zu den Alpen. Die Kantine ist gleichzeitig Treffpunkt für die Mitarbeiter.

Amt für Abfallwirtschaft, AFA
der Landeshauptstadt München

Wettbewerb 1993
1. Preis

Planungsbeginn: 1994
Bauzeit: 1997–1999

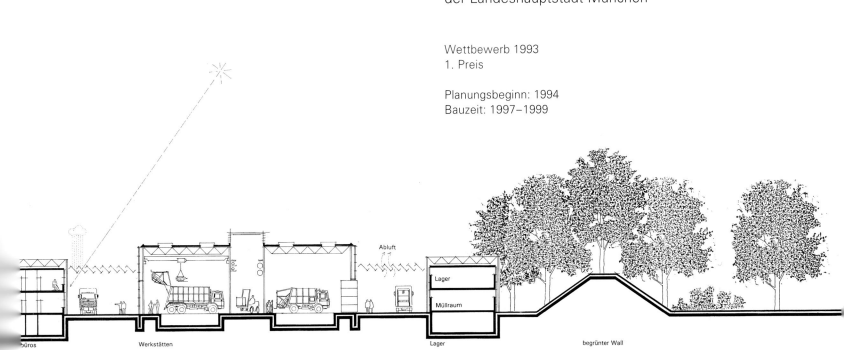

Büros   Werkstätten   Lager   begrünter Wall

Abluft
Lager
Müllraum

Office for Waste
Management AFA
of the City of Munich

Competition: 1993
First prize
Commencement of
planning: 1994
Construction period:
1997–99

The object of the competition
held by the City of Munich was
the urban redevelopment of the
area south of Georg-Brauchle-
Ring, between Hanauer Strasse
and the middle ring road, to
accommodate high-quality office
and commercial uses. An initial
accent was created by the erection of the Office for Waste Management.

The three main sections of
this development were to be
legible in their functional form.
An administration building with
320 workplaces, a central yard
with vehicle workshops for 100
employees, and a hall for 170
refuse lorries, plus social areas
for the 500 members of staff
who work on the road had to be
incorporated into the urban planning concept. The imposing slab
of the administration building
adjoining the ring road marks
the termination of the office and
commercial development on this

side. The southern edge facing
the green landscaped area is
defined by the works yard and
the two-storey vehicle port.

The link to Georg-Brauchle-
Ring is via an internal spur road
flanked on one side by the nine-
storey administration block.
The building is 70 m long and
13 m wide and has a reinforced
concrete structure laid out to a
7.2 x 7.2 m or 7.2 x 4.8 m grid.
It is clad externally with a curtain-
wall façade, consisting of silver-
coloured aluminium elements
with clear glazing, and translucent glass panels to the apron

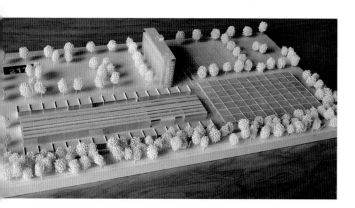

Wettbewerbsmodell. Am
oberen Rand steht die
Scheibe des Verwaltungs-
hochhauses mit der
Schmalseite zum Georg-
Brauchle-Ring. Links
sind die Werkstätten,
rechts davon ist der Car-
port angeordnet.

Competition model. At
the rear is the high-rise
slab of the administration
building, the narrow
end of which faces on to
Georg-Brauchle-Ring.
In front of this on the left
are the workshops and,
on the right, the vehicle
hall/carport.

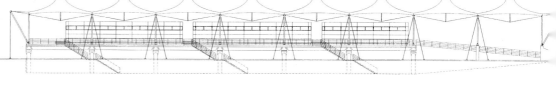

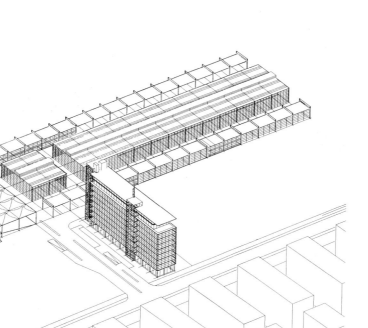

Oben: Der zweigeschos-
sige, mit einer zeltartigen,
transluzenten Membrane
überdachte Carport für die
Müllfahrzeuge. Auf der
oberen Ebene sind an den
Längsseiten die Umklei-
deräume der Mitarbeiter
untergebracht.

Above: two-storey car-
port for refuse vehicles
with a translucent, tent-
like membrane roof.
On the long faces of
the upper level are staff
changing rooms.

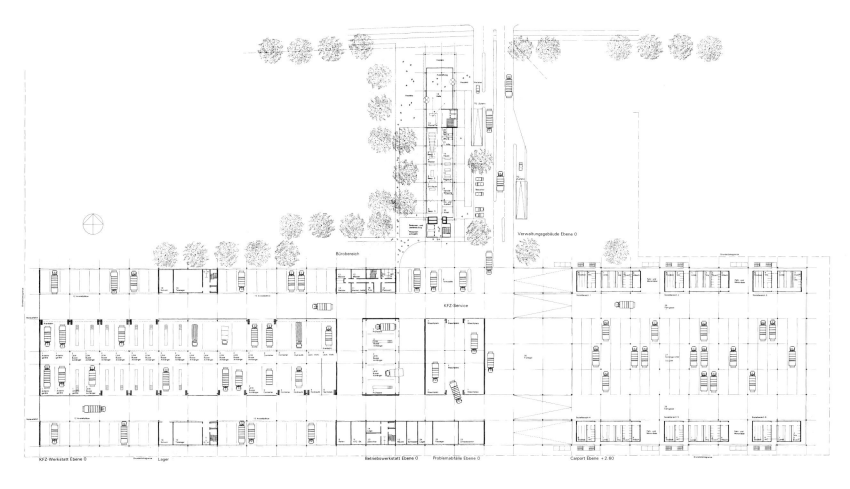

KFZ-Werkstatt Ebene 0   Lager   Betriebswerkstatt Ebene 0   Problemabfälle Ebene 0   Carport Ebene + 2.60

Betriebshof und Carport bilden eine 300,0 m x 70,0 m große, zusammenhängende Einheit. Der 180,0 m lange und 70,0 m breite Betriebshof umfaßt eine Werkstatt für Pkw und Lkw, eine Waschhalle, Tankstelle, den Problemmüllbereich, Freilagerflächen, Kfz-Warteplätze sowie Sozial- und Betriebsbüroräume. Das Tragwerk ist ein Stahlfachwerk mit Stahlstützen im Raster von 12,0 m x 10,0 m. Das Stahlskelett läßt flexible Nutzungen der Einzelbereiche zu.

Im Carport von 120,0 m x 70,0 m werden die Müllfahrzeuge auf zwei Ebenen abgestellt. Die untere Ebene ist zur Hälfte in das Gelände eingegraben. Die obere Ebene ist mit zeltartigen, transluzenten Membranen als Wetterschutz auf einer leichten Stahlkonstruktion im Achsraster von 12,0 m x 10,0 m überdacht. Das transluzente Membrandach gibt der Großgarage eine filigrane Leichtigkeit. Die Buckelzelte sind an ihren Hochpunkten oben offen und garantieren eine natürliche Entlüftung der Parkebenen. Im Kellergeschoß liegen die Technikräume, ein Rechenzentrum, eine Kegelbahn und die Tiefgarage für 250 Pkw.

Das einheitliche Material- und Farbkonzept bindet die drei unterschiedlichen Nutzungsbereiche zu einer baulichen Einheit zusammen. Die Begrünung der Dächer und die sorgfältige Bepflanzung um die Bauten lassen eine freundliche und umweltverträgliche Umgebung erwarten.

Oben: Grundriß Erdgeschoß mit den drei Teilbereichen Verwaltung, Werkstätten und Carport. Unten: Wettbewerbsmodell mit dem Carport im Vordergrund

Top: ground floor plan showing the three main areas - administration, workshops and vehicle port. Above: competition model with the vehicle port in the foreground

walls. Acoustic insulation and sunscreening were incorporated into the construction. The set-back top floor – planned as a steel structure – houses the canteen, access to which is via two glazed lifts. From the top floor one has an unobstructed view over the Olympia Park and Munich to the Alps. The canteen also functions as a meeting place for the staff.

Together, the works yard and vehicle port form a continuous unit 300 m long and 70 m wide. The works yard alone is 180 m long and 70 m wide and contains workshops for cars and lorries, a vehicle washing hall, a filling station, an area for problematic waste materials, open storage space, a lorry parking area and social and office areas. The load-bearing structure is a trussed steel frame with steel columns laid out to a 12 x 10 m grid. The skeleton frame system allows a flexible use of the various sections of this tract.

The refuse collection vehicles are parked on two levels in the 120 x 70 m carport. The lower level is half sunk into the ground; the upper level is protected against the weather by translucent tent-like roof elements supported by a lightweight steel structure set out to a 12 x 10 m grid. The translucent membrane

roofs lend the large-scale garage a quality of diaphanous lightness. The humpback coniform tent roofs are open at the tips and thus ensure a natural ventilation of the parking levels.

In the basement are rooms for mechanical services, a computer centre, a bowling alley and parking spaces for 250 cars.

The consistent material and colour concept imposes a constructional unity on the three different functional areas.

The planting of the roof and the careful landscaping of the areas around the buildings emphasize the friendly and 'green' working environment that has been created here.

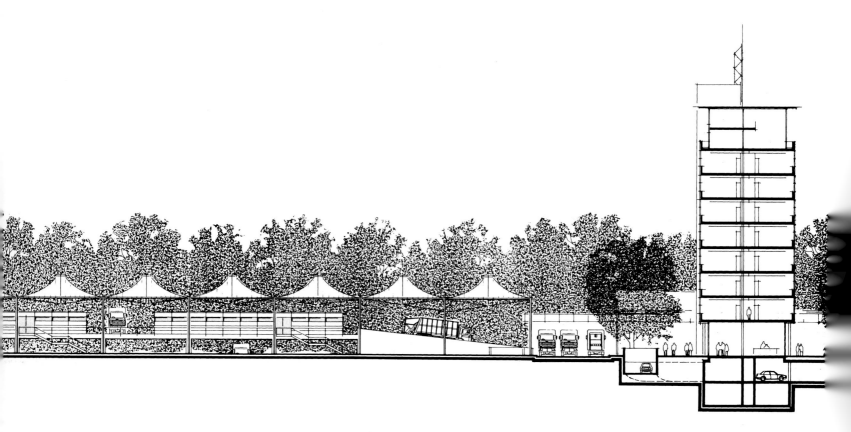

Detailansicht der vorge-
fertigten, geschoßhohen,
7,20 m breiten Element-
fassade, bestehend aus
je drei Achsfeldern von
2,40 m Breite, mit
äußeren Sonnenschutz-
lamellen und inneren
Blendschutzrollos. Die
Brüstungsfelder wurden
mit rückseitig emaillierten
Isolierglasscheiben aus-
gefacht.

Detail of façade with
7.20 m-wide prefabri-
cated, storey-height ele-
ments based on a bay
width of 2.40 m. The
three-bay units have
sunscreen louvres exter-
nally and roller blinds
internally.

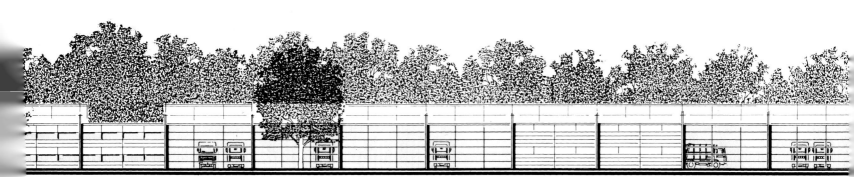

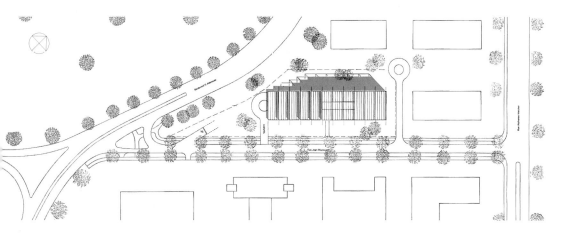

Bayerische Vereins-
bank BVB, Luxem-
bourg

Competition: 1993
Second prize

"The scheme is clear and
straightforward, and that is its
great strength in this location. It
adamantly refuses – much to its
own advantage – to take part in
the competition for individuality
going on among the neighbouring developments.

The stepped-down end of the
building is sufficient to create a
sense of identity without any formal compulsion. As a result, the
position of the entrance at the
end facing Konrad-Adenauer-
Strasse is also resolved unequi-
vocally. Opinions differ as to
whether vehicle access should be
from the tip of the site adjoining
the road, but this is of secondary
importance for an assessment of
the scheme and can always be
corrected. The well-tried concept
for this building, which reveals
the spatial structure externally in
a clear, legible form, is, as one
might expect, equally comprehensible after entering the bright
hall. The simplicity of the design
is in no way boring. Sufficient
spatial tension is generated by

the links between the various
floor levels and the multi-storey
space over the banking hall, or
by the stepped terraces on the
outside, which ensure high-quality workplaces in each storey.

The concept is also sound
enough to accommodate change.
That is good to know, since the
gross floor area is, as in all the
other competition entries, clearly
too large. In terms of banking
practice, the division of the safe-
deposit area into two independent units is not good. Similarly,
the question of security in the
large space over the hall will
have to be examined.

The advantages of the structural system are evident when
one studies the load-bearing system and the technical installation
of the building. The same applies
to the economic viability of the
design. It does not open the
doors to something completely
new, to an innovation in building,
but it is an excellent response to
the conditions of the brief. The
building has no story to tell, but
therein lies its strength. One
expects to find people within it
who will address one with the
same clarity and frankness as the
building itself does."
Excerpt from jury report

Längsansicht von Süd-
osten. Die Terrassierung
dient unter anderem der
Nutzung passiver Solar-
energie und der direkten
Belichtung der Halle.

South-east elevation. The
stepped-down terraces
serve, among other
things, as areas for the
passive exploitation of
solar energy and as a
source of direct daylight
for the hall.

»Die Arbeit ist klar, einfach und gerade deshalb hat sie Kraft an diesem Ort. Sie entzieht sich damit entschieden – und das ist ihr Vorteil – dem individualisieren-den Wettstreit der Nachbarschaft.

Die Abtreppung genügt, um ohne formalen Zwang Identität zu schaffen. Damit ist auch die Lage des Zuganges an der Stirnseite zur Konrad-Adenauer-Straße ein-deutig: Unterschiedlich ist die Meinung, ob die Zufahrt an der Spitze der Straße liegen muß, ein untergeordneter Punkt der Beur-teilung und korrigierbar. Das bewährte Gebäudekonzept, das außen bereits klar ablesbar die räumliche Struktur kundtut, ist denn auch nach dem Betreten der hellen Halle ohne Einschränkung ebenso klar ablesbar, wie man das erwartet. Die Einfachheit ist dabei nicht langweilig, sondern hat genügend räumliche Spannungen durch die Einbeziehung der Kas-senhalle über dem Luftraum in

allen Geschossen oder die vorge-lagerten Terrassen, die eine hohe Arbeitsplatzqualität in der jeweili-gen Etage sicherstellen.

Das Konzept ist genügend sta-bil, um nachträgliche Änderungen zu vertragen. Das ist gut zu wis-sen, denn die BGF ist, wie bei allen anderen Arbeiten, eindeutig zu groß. Banktechnisch gesehen ist die Trennung der Tresorberei-che in zwei eigenständige Einhei-ten nicht gut, wie auch Sicher-heitsfragen im großen Luftraum der Halle zu überprüfen sind.

Die Vorzüge des strukturellen Systems schlagen sich auch in der Bewertung des Tragwerkes und des technischen Ausbaus positiv zu Buche. Dies gilt damit auch für die Wirtschaftlichkeit. Mit dem Entwurf wird die Türe zu etwas Neuem, Innovativen nicht voll auf-geschlagen. Dennoch antwortet die Arbeit sehr gut auf die gestell-te Aufgabe. Das vorgestellte Haus erzählt keine Geschichten und hat gerade darin seinen Vorzug: Man erwartet in ihm Menschen, die einem ebenso klar und mit Offen-heit begegnen, wie es das Gebäu-de selbst tut.«
Aus dem Jury-Protokoll

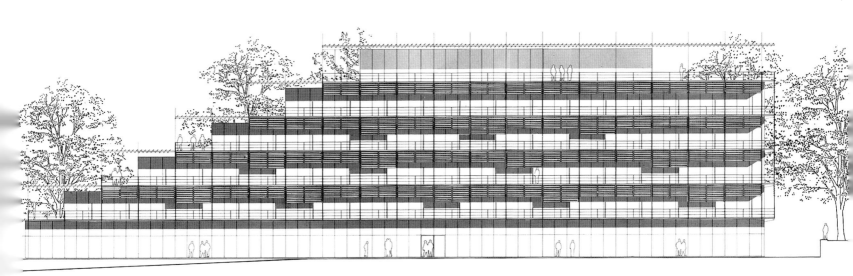

Bayerische Vereinsbank BVB, Luxemburg

Wettbewerb: 1993
2. Preis

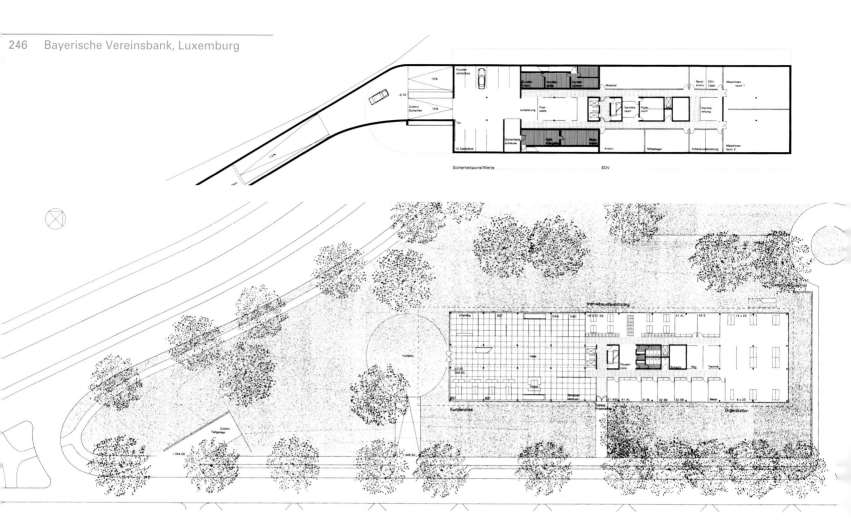

The terraced areas on every floor function as planted open spaces and buffer zones that are oriented to the landscape and the city. The buffer zones serve as extensions to the indoor spaces and are used as conservatories and for the passive exploitation of solar energy. The multi-storey hall space over the banking area is covered with a glass roof spanned between open galleries. The volumetric form of the hall follows the stepped-back outline of the structure itself, an effect that is accentuated by the line of the staircase. The three-bay organization of the building allows a great degree of flexibility. Areas frequented by customers are oriented to the entrance hall. Departments that have less contact with the public are located in the rear part of the building. Linked to the central access core is a zone with WCs, waiting areas and communications facilities.

The plantings in the hall and on the terraces will have a positive influence on the microclimate. The relatively high temperatures of the cooling soffits enable a cooling system to be operated cost-free by an evaporation cooling plant on the roof.

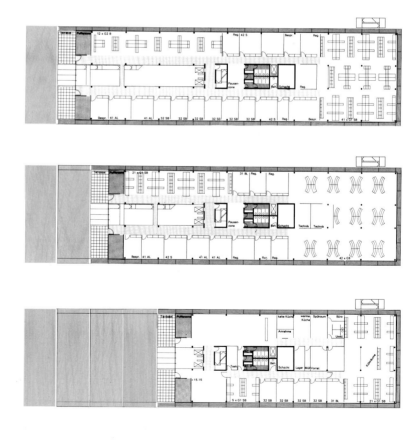

Grundrisse.
Tiefgarage, Erdgeschoß,
erstes Obergeschoß,
zweites Obergeschoß,
viertes Obergeschoß

Plans: basement garage,
ground floor, first floor,
second floor, fourth floor

Jedem Geschoß des Hauses werden durch die Terrassierung Frei-, Grün- und Pufferräume vorgelagert, die sich zum Grün und zur Stadt hin orientieren. Die Pufferräume dienen als Erweiterungsflächen, als Wintergärten und zur Nutzung von passiver Solarenergie. Die mehrgeschossige Halle über dem Kundenbereich ist mit einem Glasdach überdeckt, das sich zwischen offenen Galerien spannt. Das Hallenvolumen folgt der Gebäudestaffelung, deren Wirkung durch eine begleitende Treppe noch unterstützt wird. Durch die dreibündige Organisation kommt es zu einer großen Flexibilität des Gebäudes. Kundenintensive Bereiche orientieren sich zur Eingangshalle, Abteilungen mit wenig Publikumsverkehr sind im rückwärtigen Gebäudeteil angesiedelt. Eine Zone mit WCs, Warte- und Kommunikationsbereich ist dem zentralen Erschließungskern zugeordnet.

Durch die Bepflanzung der Halle und der Terrassen wird das Kleinklima positiv beeinflußt. Das relativ hohe Temperaturniveau der Kühldecke ermöglicht freie Kühlung durch einen Verdunstungskühler auf dem Dach.

Die Modellaufnahme macht die Einfügung in die Umgebung deutlich. Mitte: Längsschnitt mit Eingangshalle. Unten: Querschnitt durch den Hallenbereich

Photo of model, showing the integration of the development in the surrounding urban fabric. Middle: longitudinal section through entrance hall. Bottom: cross-section through hall

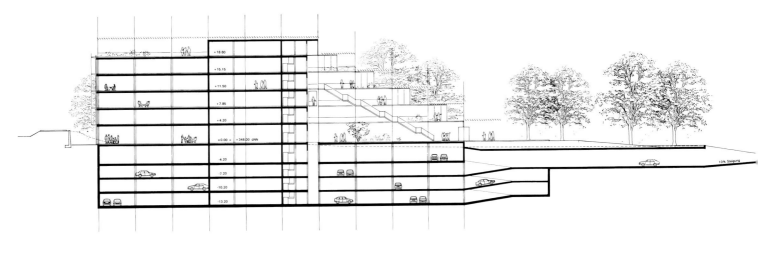

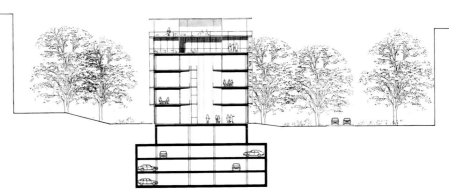

Third Bridge over the
Danube in Ingolstadt

Competition: 1993
First prize
Commencement of
planning: 1994
Construction period:
1996–98

To reduce the traffic load in the old town centre and on the two existing bridges over the Danube, the city of Ingolstadt held a competition for the design of a third road bridge for cars, cycles and pedestrians. The terms of the brief were more a hindrance than a help, however. The fixed points in the planning were the northern exit from the old city ring road near the glacis, and the narrow corridor between the private plots of land leading onto the bridge on the south bank of the river. The municipal authorities had proposed a curving S-shape approach to the bridge.

To make the oblique crossing of the Danube more acceptable and to simplify the bridge construction, the routing was straightened. The changes to the intersection near the glacis that this necessitated were worked out in conjunction with the Institute for Highway Engineering of the University of Stuttgart.

The road through Luitpold-park was designed as an elevated piece of landscape architecture with a solid stone wall. The choice of this material makes reference to its use in the old city fortifications by the architect

Leo von Klenze. The embankment was to be opened up at those points where existing roads, footpaths and cycle paths intersected it, allowing the plane of the park to continue and its unity to be retained. Proposals were also made for the creation of spaces in the wall for cultural, gastronomic and youth purposes as well as for gallery use.

The line of the 162-metre-long bridge reflects the load-bearing behaviour of the cable-supported T-beam structure, with sheaves of cables spanned over two raking reinforced concrete piers and anchored on both banks of the river in concrete abutments.

The horizontal reinforced concrete carriageway slab is raised on cruciform steel columns on top of the cables. The pedestrian and cycle paths on both sides follow the curving line of the cables, to which they are fixed. This separation of uses enhances the experience of crossing the river for pedestrians and cyclists and obviates any unpleasant sense of breadth or tunnel-like

Wettbewerbszeichnung.
Die auf Seilen aufgeständerte Fahrbahn macht
die hybride Brücken-
konstruktion filigran und
transparent.

Competition drawing:
the carriageway, raised
on steel columns on top
of the cables, lends this
hybrid bridge construc-
tion a slender, transpar-
ent character.

Um die Verkehrsbelastung der
Altstadt und der beiden bestehenden Donaubrücken zu reduzieren,
hatte der Stadtrat der Stadt Ingolstadt einen Wettbewerb für eine
dritte Brücke für den Kfz-Verkehr,
Radler und Fußgänger ausgelobt.
Die planerischen Vorgaben waren
sehr eng gefaßt, eher ein Hinder-
nis. Zwangspunkte waren die
nördliche Abzweigung der Alt-
stadtringstraße am Glacis und die
schmale Korridorzone zwischen
Privatgrundstücken als Ankunfts-
punkt der Brücke am Südufer. Die
Stadtplanung hatte eine S-förmig
geschwungene Trassenführung
im Brückenbereich vorgegeben.
    Um die schiefe Querung der
Donau erträglich zu machen und
die Brückenkonstruktion zu verein-
fachen, wurde die Linienführung
der Brücke begradigt. Die dadurch
notwendige Änderung des Ver-
kehrsknotens am Glacis wurde in
Zusammenarbeit mit dem Institut
für Straßenbau der Universität
Stuttgart geplant.

Dritte Donaubrücke, Ingolstadt

Wettbewerb 1993
1. Preis

Planungsbeginn: 1994
Bauzeit: 1996–1998

Wettbewerbsmodell.
Die auf beiden Seiten
angeordneten Fußgänger-
und Radlerstege sind
direkt auf den durchhän-
genden Seilen aufgelegt
und betonen die elegante
Form der Seiltragkonstruk-
tion.

Competition model. The
pedestrian and cycle
paths laid on the curved
suspension cables on
both sides of the road
bridge accentuate the
elegant form of the cable-
supported structure.

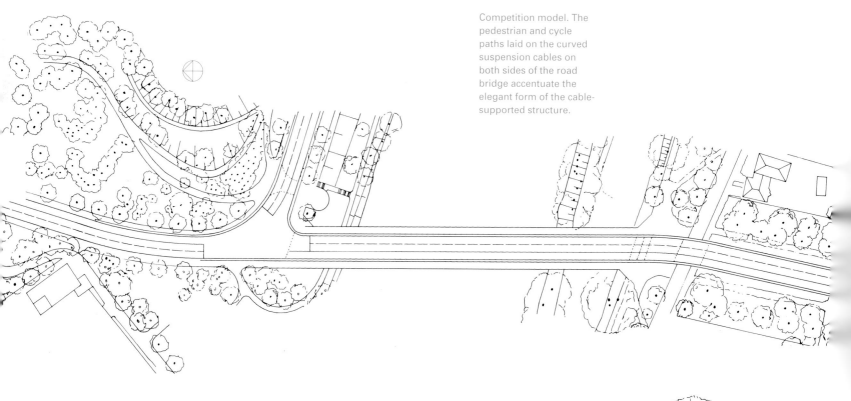

Bauphasen: Zuerst werden die beiden Widerlager und die Seilumlenksättel betoniert, danach die Seilscharen montiert und vorgespannt, dann die Stahlpylone auf die Seile aufgeständert und die Fahrbahnplatte betoniert.

Die Straße durch den Luitpoldpark wurde als Stück einer künstlich gebauten Landschaft in Hochlage geführt mit einer Vormauerung mit massiven Natursteinen. Das Leitbild für dieses Material waren die vorhandenen Festungsbauten des Baumeisters Leo von Klenze. Der Wall sollte dort, wo ihn bestehende Straßen, Fußwege und Radwege kreuzen, durchlässig sein, die Ebene des Parkes als funktionierende Einheit erhalten bleiben. Zusätzlich sollten Räume im Wall für kulturelle oder gastronomische Aktivitäten auch für die Jugend und für Galerien geschaffen werden.

Die Linienführung der auf Seilen gelagerten, 162,0 m langen Plattenbalkenbrücke ergibt sich aus dem Tragverhalten: Die Seilscharen werden an beiden Uferwiderlagern rückverankert und über zwei als Umlenksättel ausgebildete Schrägpylone aus Stahlbeton geführt.

Die Stahlbetonplatte ist mit kreuzförmigen Stahlstützen auf die Tragseile aufgeständert. Die Fuß- und Radwege sind auf beiden Seiten direkt auf die Tragseile aufgelagert. Durch die Trennung der Nutzungen wird der Erlebniswert für Fußgänger und Radfahrer erhöht und eine störende Breiten- und Tunnelwirkung vermieden. Durch ihr Konstruktionsprinzip wirkt die Brücke in ihrem Erscheinungsbild filigran und transparent. Trotz ihrer neuartigen Tragwerkskonzeption von den Ingenieuren Jörg und Mike Schlaich kommt sie mit bewährten Bauelementen aus. Es wurde Wert darauf gelegt, daß die Tragseile auf der ganzen Brückenlänge freiliegen, um sie jederzeit vom Gehweg aus inspi-

zieren zu können. Das freigespannte Tragwerk aus Seilen wurde als Dreierbündel ausgebildet, damit im kritischen Fall auch Seile einzeln, unter Verkehr, ausgewechselt werden können.

Aus landschaftlich-stadträumlicher Sicht fügt sich die Brücke in ihre Umgebung, den Naturraum der Donau mit dichter Uferbepflanzung, den Parkanlagen von Glacis und dem Luitpoldpark mit dem wertvollen Baumbestand ein.

Die Idee des Walles als gebaute Landschaftsarchitektur fand keine Zustimmung beim Stadtrat und bei den Anliegern. Anstelle des Walls wird nun eine Tunnelabfahrt realisiert, die den Luitpoldpark im Bereich des Südufers leider teilt.

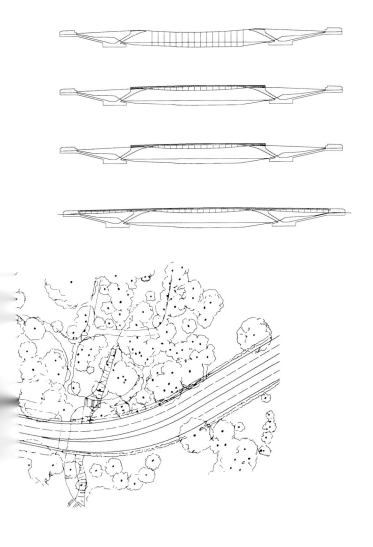

confinement. The finely articulated, transparent appearance of the bridge is the outcome of the structural principles on which the design is based.

In spite of its innovative load-bearing concept, devised by the engineers Jörg and Mike Schlaich, the bridge is constructed with traditional building elements. An important aspect of the design was that the suspension cables – in groups of three – should be exposed over their entire length, so that they can be inspected at any time from the footpath and, in a critical situation, be individually replaced without interrupting the traffic.

The bridge is integrated into the urban surroundings and the landscape. The latter includes stretches of dense natural vegetation along the banks of the Danube, the park-like areas of the glacis, and Luitpoldpark with its valuable stock of old trees.

The idea of the embankment as a section of built landscape architecture was not supported by the city council or the neighbouring residents. In its place, a tunnel exit will be constructed that will unfortunately intersect the Luitpoldpark near the south bank of the river.

Ansicht der Brückenbau-stelle mit aufgeständerter Fahrbahnplatte aus Stahl-beton

View of bridge construction with raised reinforced concrete carriageway

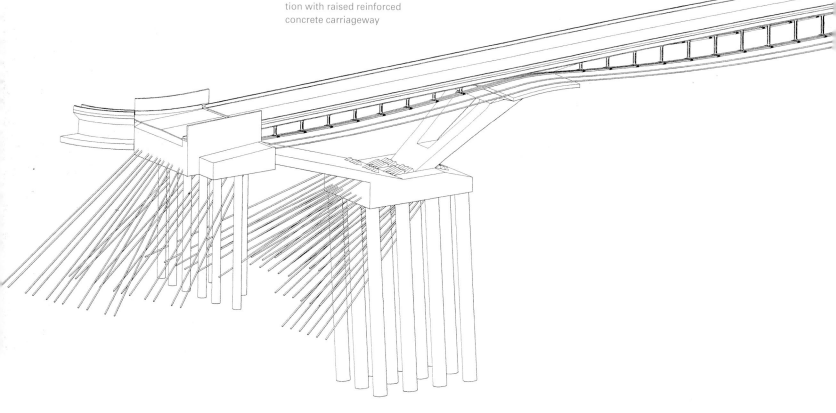

Konstruktion, Charakteristika der Materialien und die Form der Bauteile werden zu einer ganzheitlichen Gestalt zusammengeführt.

The aim of the design was to fuse the structure, the characteristics of the materials and the form of the elements into a single unified whole.

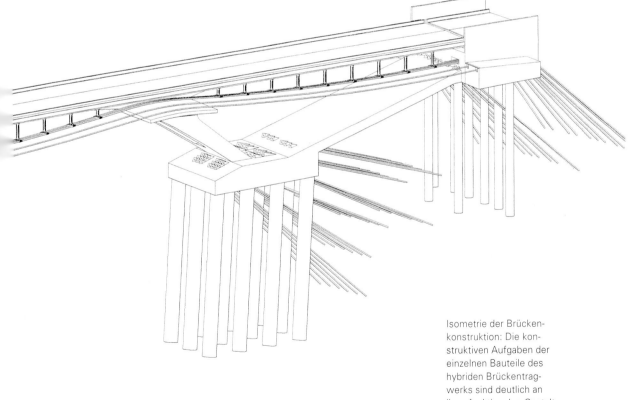

Isometrie der Brückenkonstruktion: Die konstruktiven Aufgaben der einzelnen Bauteile des hybriden Brückentragwerks sind deutlich an ihrer funktionalen Gestalt abzulesen.

Isometric view of bridge: the structural purpose of the individual elements of this hybrid bridge structure are clearly legible in their functional form.

Environmental
Technology Centre,
UTZ, Adlershof,
Berlin

Competition: 1995
Second prize

The development observes the scale and the eaves heights laid down in the outline planning legislation for this area. The articulation of the complex was based on a concept of making the individual functions legible in the design.

The compact, linear layout of the development along Volmerstrasse allowed a continuous, generously proportioned planted area to be created that makes an important ecological contribution to the surrounding residential neighbourhood. The landscaped inner areas of the site also help to improve the micro-climate. A network of attractive routes across the park-like public green connects the buildings with the local transport system.

The research centre is not merely an administrative complex. It forms an integral part of the urban fabric. The individual floors were laid out according to functional needs. At the same time, every effort was made to ensure workplaces of equal quality in all positions. The central hall, about which the various functional realms are grouped

and to which they are visually linked, forms a communicative focus. The offices and the areas open to the public are directly accessible from the hall. Laboratories, workshops and technical areas are grouped together in functional units at the ends of the buildings.

The clear structural principle on which the complex is based allows a high degree of flexibility in the office areas. In the laboratory tracts, vertical shafts facilitate the installation of mechanical services and other runs and allow for subsequent modifications and additions.

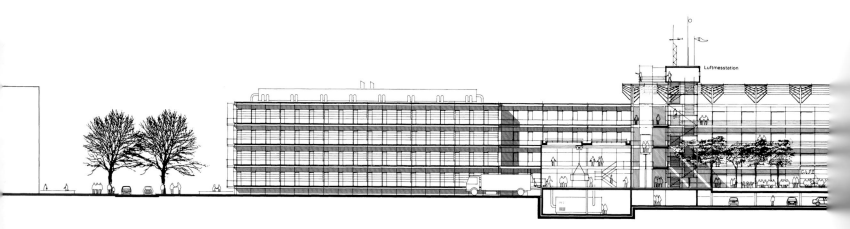

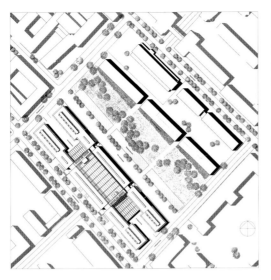

Das Gebäude nimmt den Maßstab und die Traufhöhen der städtebaulichen Rahmenplanung auf. Durch die Ablesbarkeit der Funktionen erhalten die Baukörper ihre Gliederung.

Durch die kompakte, lineare Gebäudeanlage entlang der Volmerstraße verbleibt eine zusammenhängende, großzügige Grünfläche, die einen wichtigen ökologischen Beitrag für die angrenzenden Wohngebiete leistet. Begrünte Innenbereiche sorgen für eine Verbesserung des Klimas, attraktive Wegeverbindungen durch den öffentlichen, parkartigen Anger vernetzen den Bau mit den Stationen des Nahverkehrs.

Das Forschungszentrum ist kein Verwaltungsbau. Die Grundrisse sind nach funktionalen Gesichtspunkten entwickelt; sie bedeuten gleichwertige Raumqualitäten für alle Arbeitsplätze. Alle Funktionsbereiche sind um eine zentrale Halle gruppiert und optisch zu einem kommunikativen Zentrum verknüpft. Die publikumsorientierten Bereiche und die Büros sind direkt von der Halle aus zugänglich. Labors, Werkstätten und Technikräume sind an den Enden der Baukörper zu funktionalen Einheiten zusammengefaßt.

Längsschnitt durch den zentralen Hallenbereich mit den daran angegliederten Hallen des Technikum-Bereichs

Longitudinal section through the central hall with the adjoining research and testing halls

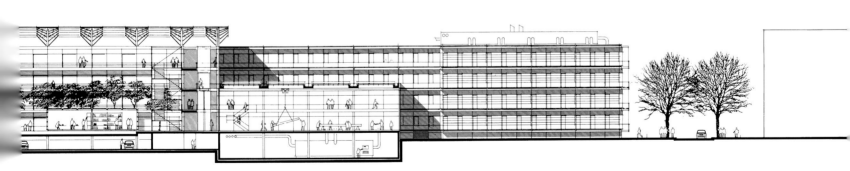

Umwelt-Technik-Zentrum, UTZ
Berlin-Adlershof

Wettbewerb: 1995
2. Preis

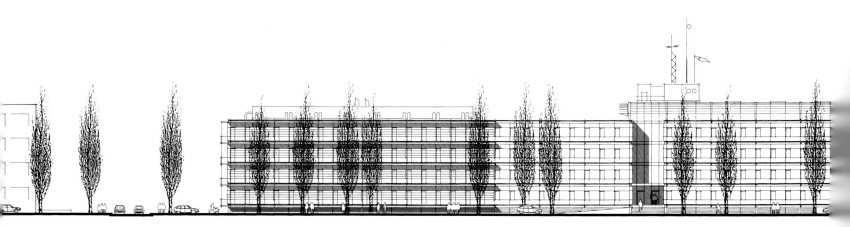

"The design is distinguished by
its balanced ecological concept.
The atrium hall in particular also
helped to integrate energy tar-
gets with architectural and communications goals. All in all,
this is a well-considered and
thoroughly worked out concept
of great architectural quality."
Excerpt from jury report

Das klare Konstruktionsprinzip
ermöglicht maximale Flexibilität
in den Bürobereichen. In den
Labors gewährleisten die Vertikal-
schächte eine optimale Installa-
tionsführung. Notwendige Nachrüstungen sind möglich.

»Der Entwurf zeichnet sich
durch ein abgestimmtes ökologi-
sches Konzept aus und ist auch
fähig, insbesondere über die
Atriumhalle, energetische Ziel-
setzungen mit architektonischen
und kommunikativen Funktionen
zu verknüpfen. Insgesamt handelt
es sich um ein reifes, gut durch-
gearbeitetes Konzept von hoher
architektonischer Qualität.«
Aus dem Jury-Protokoll

Linke Seite: Grundriß
von Erdgeschoß und
einem Regelobergeschoß.
Rechte Seite oben:
Schnitt durch die zentrale
Halle mit der darunter-
liegenden, natürlich zu
belüftenden Tiefgarage.
Mitte: Ansicht von der
Straßenseite. Unten:
Schnitt durch die Hallen
des Technikums und die
Bürobereiche

Opposite page: ground
floor and standard upper
floor plans. This page,
top: section through cen-
tral hall with naturally
ventilated garage area
beneath. Middle: street
elevation. Bottom: sec-
tion through the research
and testing halls and the
office areas

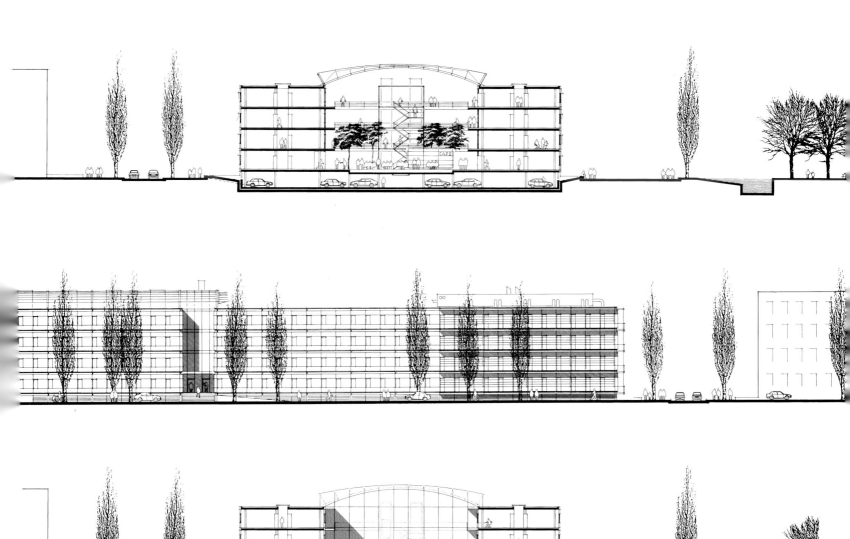

St Nicholas's
Nursery School,
Rosenheim
Student Centre of
the Archbishopric
of Munich-Freising

Commencement of
planning: 1993
Construction period:
1996 – 97

A nursery school for the parish of
St Nicholas and a student centre
for the archbishopric of Munich-
Freising were to be erected in
Rosenheim. The shared site lies
on the outskirts of the town in
an area of heterogeneous urban
development. Nondescript
though the existing urban context may be, the two new buildings are situated in an attractive
landscape. Set at right angles to
each other, they visually define
the common open spaces. The
indoor spaces for general activities, such as group rooms, the
hall, recreation and sitting areas,
open to the south and west on to
quiet landscaped garden areas.

The nursery school and the
dwellings belonging to the student centre can be reached on
foot from a route lined with old
trees along the Lederer stream.
The car ramp to the basement
garage is at the north-east corner
of the site, while access to the
student centre is from the south.

St Nicholas's Nursery School:
The entrance forecourt to the
north of the 31 x 12 m nursery
extends into the building in the
form of a large, two-storey hall.
Laid out on both sides of this hall
are the three group rooms and
the multi-purpose space, which is
directly linked to the garden and
the outdoor play areas. External
staircases at the ends of the
building link the upper floor with
the garden. The kitchen, the children's dormitory and the rooms
for parents and staff are located
on the quiet north side. Services
and stores, as well as a music
room, a romping room, a children's workshop and a pottery
studio are accommodated in the
basement.

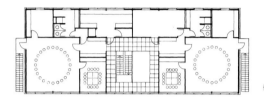

Kindergarten. Grundriß
Obergeschoß

Nursery School. Upper
floor plan

Der dreischiffige Grundriß wird in den Giebelfassaden des Studentenzentrums deutlich ablesbar.

The three-bay layout of the student centre is clearly legible in the end façades.

Kindergarten St. Nikolaus, Rosenheim
Studentenzentrum der Erzdiözese München-Freising

Planungsbeginn: 1993
Bauzeit: 1996 – 1997

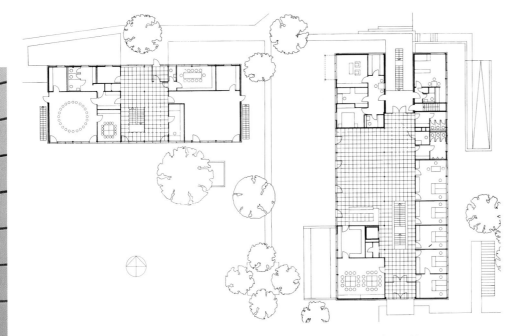

Erdgeschoßgrundrisse:
links der Kindergarten,
rechts das Studentenzen-
trum, die mit der winkel-
förmigen Situierung der
Baukörper den Gartenhof
definieren.

Ground floor plans. Left:
the nursery school; right:
the student centre. The
angular layout defines
the garden courtyard.

Für die Kirchengemeinde St. Nikolaus war ein Kindergarten und für
die Erzdiözese München-Freising
ein Studentenzentrum auf einem
gemeinsamen Grundstück in
Rosenheim zu realisieren. Das
Grundstück liegt am Rande der
Innenstadt in einem städtebaulich
heterogenen Gebiet. In dieser
städtebaulich indifferenten, aber
landschaftlich reizvollen Situation
sind die beiden Baukörper im
rechten Winkel zueinander gestellt und definieren optisch den
gemeinsamen Freibereich. Räume
allgemeiner Aktivitäten wie Gruppenräume, Saal und Aufenthaltsräume sind zu dem sich nach
Süden und Westen öffnenden,
landschaftsgärtnerisch gestalteten
ruhigen Gartenbereich orientiert.

Der Kindergarten und die Wohnungen des Studentenzentrums
wurden fußläufig von dem mit
alten Bäumen gesäumten
Ledererbach erschlossen. Die
Anbindung für den Pkw-Verkehr
erfolgt an der nordöstlichen

Student Centre:
The student centre was designed with a three-bay layout. The 5-metre-wide two-storey open central hall is covered with transparent safety glass at the top. It forms a brightly lit spatial link between the two floors and provides generous zones for communication.

Oriented to the garden on the western side of the centre is a hall and – forming an extension of the foyer – a lounge area for students. Holger Bollinger was responsible for the artistic design of the room for meditation, Tobias Kammerer for that of the hall.

Künstlerische Gestaltung des Glassatteldaches mit der dunkelroten Schleife, die sich je nach Sonnenstand im Innenraum abzeichnet; von Tobias Kammerer

Artistic treatment of the pitched glass roof by Tobias Kammerer: depending on the position of the sun, a sinuous dark-red band is visible internally

Oben: Gemeinschafts-raum im Erdgeschoß, der die offene, lichtdurch-flutete Treppenhalle einbezieht.

Above: the open, light-filled staircase hall is integrated into the common room on the ground floor.

The consistent material and colour concept ensures a formal unity between the different parts of the complex. The load-bearing structure is in a steel composite form of construction with reinforced concrete floors. The façades consist of glazed aluminium window elements with sunscreen blinds. The closed areas of the façades are clad with silver-colour aluminium panels with a rear ventilated cavity.

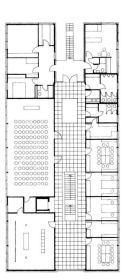

Obergeschoßgrundriß des Studentenzentrums

Upper floor plan of student centre

Grundstücksgrenze zur Tiefgarage, der Zugang zum Studentenzentrum von der Südseite.

Kindergarten St. Nikolaus:
Der nördliche Eingangsbereich des 31,0 x 12,0 m großen Kindergartens weitet sich auf der Südseite zu einer großen, zweigeschossigen Halle. Auf beiden Seiten dieser Halle liegen die drei Gruppenräume und der Mehrzweckraum mit direkter Verbindung zum Garten- und zu den Freispielbereichen. Vom Obergeschoß führen an den Giebelseiten gelegene Freitreppen in den Garten. Küche, Kinderschlafraum, Eltern- und Personalräume sind auf der ruhigen Nordseite untergebracht. Im Untergeschoß gibt es neben den Technik- und Lagerräumen auch Musikzimmer, Tollraum, Kinderwerkstatt und eine Töpferei.

Studentenzentrum:
Das Studentenzentrum ist als dreischiffige Anlage konzipiert. Die 5,0 m breite, zweigeschossige offene Mittelhalle verknüpft räumlich und optisch die Geschosse und schafft großzügige Kommunikationszonen. Die lichte Halle ist in transparentem Sicherheitsglas gedeckt.

Im westlichen, zum Garten hin orientierten Bereich liegen ein Saal und ein sich aus dem Foyer heraus erweiternder Aufenthaltsraum. Der Meditationsraum wurde von Holger Bollinger und die Halle von Tobias Kammerer künstlerisch gestaltet.

Durch das einheitliche Material- und Farbkonzept bilden beide Bauten eine formale Einheit. Das Tragwerk ist eine Stahlverbundkonstruktion mit Stahlbetondecken. Die Fassaden bestehen aus verglasten Aluminiumfensterelementen mit Markisen als Sonnenschutz. Die geschlossenen Fassaden sind mit silberfarbenen Aluminiumpaneelen verkleidet und hinterlüftet.

Künstlerische Ausgestaltung des Meditationsraumes und der Gemeinschaftshalle von Holger Bollinger

Artistic design of the room for meditation and the hall by Holger Bollinger

Pedestrian Bridges, Nittenau, Upper Palatinate

Competition: 1996
First prize
Commencement of planning: 1997
Construction date: 1998–99

Two bridges offset to each other on plan connect the Anger Island with the centre of Nittenau and its suburbs and have made the island a new cultural focus of the town. The route from the open-air swimming baths and camping site across the bridge over the Grosser Regen leads directly towards the church tower, affording a view of the most striking point in the urban skyline. The bridge over the Kleiner Regen links the cultural and recreational area on Anger Island with the church square and thus restores part of the old townscape familiar since the 17th-century Merian engravings. The marketplace is a space for urban activity; the church square, on the other hand, forms a viewing platform to Anger Island and its bridge-

head bastions, to the restaurant terrace and the landing stage for boats.

The fan-shaped layout of the existing buildings on the island is being restored and carefully complemented with clear, simple volumes that conform in area and height to the scale of the existing fabric of Nittenau. The open spaces between the fingers of the fan open on to the Grosser Regen and to the river meadows of the Schiessanger.

The two footbridges, which link the town with Anger Island and the open countryside, are consciously restrained in their formal design. This enabled them to be embedded in the context of the river meadows without marring the skyline of the town or the pedestrian scale of the urban environment. The structure is based on the principle of a suspension bridge with diagonal cables, which are here deflected horizontally at handrail level and fixed to the pylons at the same height. The scheme seeks to combine technical aesthetics with an intelligent structure – designed by Jörg Schlaich – to give the bridges their own distinctive appearance. The piers

Das Städtebaumodell macht die Vernetzung der vier unterschiedlich ausgeprägten Uferbereiche mit den neuen Stegen deutlich.

The urban planning model reveals how the four different riverbank areas are linked together by the new bridges.

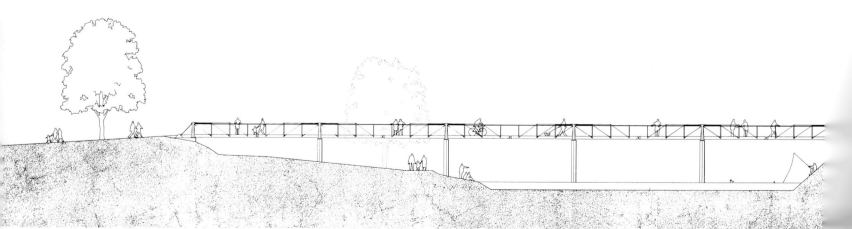

Die Angerinsel wird durch die Anbindung mit zwei zueinander versetzten Stegen an die Stadt und Vorstadt zum kulturellen Mittelpunkt der Stadt Nittenau. Der Weg vom Freibad und Campingplatz mit dem Steg über den Großen Regen ist auf den Kirchturm und damit auf den markantesten Punkt der Stadtsilhouette ausgerichtet. Der Steg über den Kleinen Regen verbindet den Kirchplatz mit dem Kultur- und Freizeitbereich der Angerinsel. Durch die Verknüpfung mit dem neuen Kirchplatz erhält Nittenau einen Teil seines alten Merian-Stadtbildes zurück. Der Marktplatz ist Raum für städtisches Leben, der Kirchplatz die Aussichtsplatt-

form zur Angerinsel und den darauf liegenden Bastionen des Brückenkopfes, der Restaurantterrasse und der Bootsanlegestelle. Der fächerförmige Baubestand auf der Angerinsel wird restauriert und behutsam mit klaren, einfachen Baukörpern, die sich in Grundfläche und Höhenentwicklung an den Maßstab Nittenaus halten, ergänzt. Die entstehenden Höfe öffnen sich zum Großen Regen und zum Auenbereich des Schießangers.

Die beiden Stege verbinden Stadt, Angerinsel und Landschaft. Die formale Ausbildung ist bewußt einfach, eingefügt in die Flußauenlandschaft, zurückhaltend zur Stadtsilhouette, im Maßstab dem Fußgänger angemessen. Das statische Prinzip einer Schrägseilbrücke mit umgelenkten Tragseilen, eine intelligente Konstruktion von Jörg Schlaich, verbunden mit technischer Ästhetik, soll den Fußgängerstegen ein charakteristisches Erscheinungsbild geben. Für die Pfeiler wurde Beton verwendet, Stahl für das Tragwerk der Stege und Holzbohlen als Bodenbelag.

Die Vegetation unterstreicht das Typische des Ortes. Kleine Bäume säumen den Kirchplatz, große Kastanien spenden im Bier-

garten Schatten, Obstbaumhaine in den Höfen der Randbebauung leiten den Blick auf die Flußauenlandschaft, lineare Vegetationsstrukturen auf dem Schießanger führen die städtebauliche Struktur fort, eine Silberweidenallee begleitet den Weg von der Vorstadt zum Regen, Auenwälder gliedern den Überschwemmungsbereich des Schießangers.

»Die Arbeit überzeugt durch Ausgewogenheit der vorgeschlagenen Gliederung der Insel in unterschiedliche Nutzungsbereiche. Die vorgeschlagene Brückenkonstruktion stellt eine glaubwürdige, konstruktiv saubere und der Aufgabe ›Steg‹ angemessene Lösung dar. Die Ausbildung verbindet Detailqualität mit hohem und wohl bewußt nicht überzogenem Gestaltungsanspruch.«
Aus dem Jury-Protokoll

Fußgängerstege, Nittenau/Oberpfalz

Wettbewerb 1996
1. Preis

Planungsbeginn: 1997
Bauzeit: 1998–1999

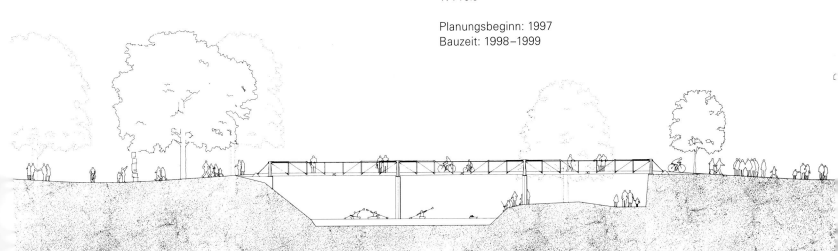

are in concrete; the walkway is in steel with a timber boarded surface.

The vegetation accentuates the characteristics of the location. The church square is lined with small trees. The beer garden is shaded by large horse chestnuts.

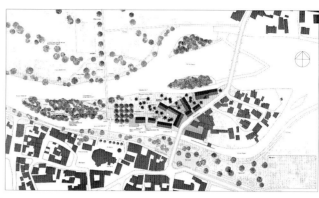

Rechts: Lageplan aus dem Wettbewerb. Unten: die gegenüber dem Wettbewerb veränderte, endgültige und bessere Lage der beiden Stege

Right: competition site plan. Below: the final and better position of the two bridges, changed from the original competition scheme

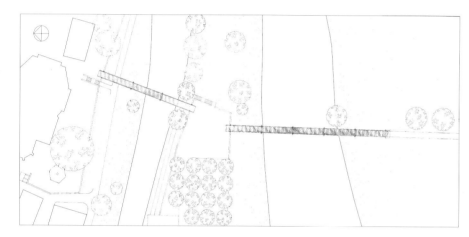

In the gardens of the peripheral developments are fruit trees that lead the eye to the river meadows. Linear planting structures on the Schiessanger provide a visual continuation of the urban texture. The route from the outskirts of the town to the River Regen is flanked by a row of white willows; and the flood meadows of the Schiessanger are articulated by areas of woodland.

"The scheme is convincing for the balanced way in which the island is to be articulated into areas for different uses. The proposed bridge construction represents a credible, structurally clean solution that meets the requirements of the 'footbridge' brief in an appropriate form. The design combines qualitative details with fastidious, though not exaggerated, formal criteria." Excerpt from jury report

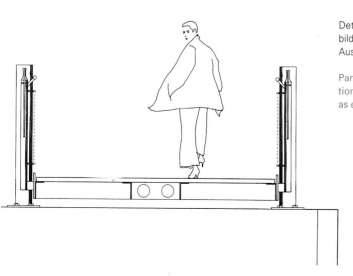

Detailansicht und Schnitt bilden die Grundlage der Ausführung.

Part elevation and section: the basis of the work as executed

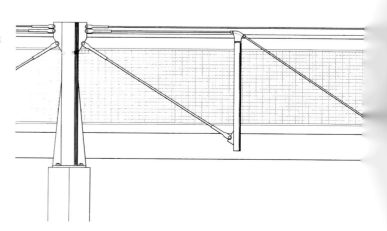

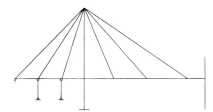

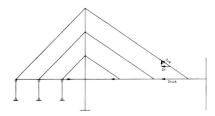

Für die Fußgängerstege wurde vom statischen System einer Schrägseil- brücke das Tragprinzip abgeleitet, die einzelnen Tragwerksteile nach konstruktiven Gesichts- punkten und dem Trag- verhalten aufeinander abgestimmt, das adäquate Material gewählt, mit einer funktionalen Gestalt versehen und zu einem optimalen Tragwerk zu- sammengefaßt.

The structural system of the pedestrian bridges is based on the principle of a suspension bridge with diagonal cables. The indi- vidual load-bearing ele- ments were co-ordinated with each other in com- pliance with structural constraints and their load-bearing behaviour. The appropriate material was chosen for the vari- ous components. They were given a functional form and assembled to create an optimal load- bearing structure.

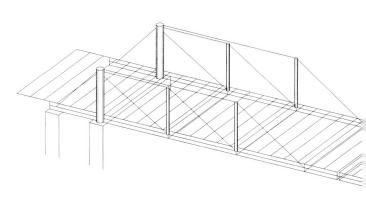

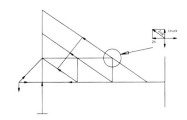

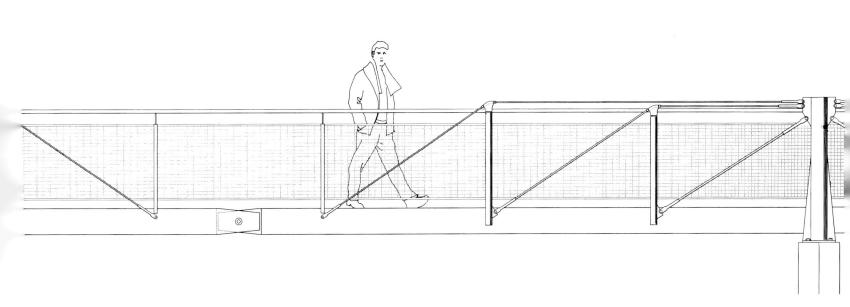

Südwestansicht der Halle
13. Der Eingang West
der Expo 2000, vom ICE-
Bahnhof Laatzen direkt
erreichbar, liegt an der
Westseite der Halle.

South-west view of Hall
13. The west entrance to
the Expo 2000, directly
accessible from the ICE
train station Laatzen, is
located on the west side
of the Hall.

»Die städtebauliche Antwort auf die Aufgabenstellung ist deshalb optimal gelöst, weil Eingangsbereich und Halle eine ausgewogene und gesamthafte Lösung darstellen. Die Ankunftsebene + 1 auf die O-Ebene bietet einen interessanten Wechsel von Räumen verschiedener Identitäten zu der Halle und Allee. Die Halle selbst fügt sich gut in das Gesamtbild der Messe ein. Die Fassade der Halle ermöglicht einen intensiven Wechsel zwischen dem Innen- und Außenraum. Die Bezüge zu der bestehenden Halle 14 sind eng und gut gelöst. Durch die 6 Techniksäulen erhält die Halle eine hohe Funktionalität und klare räumliche Qualität. Diese räumliche Qualität wird durch das Tageslichtkonzept von Fassade und Dach deutlich verstärkt. Die durchgängig unterhalb des Trägerrostes angebotene, minimal geforderte Höhe von 12,5 m ist in bezug auf die Proportionen bei einer so weit gespannten Halle zu überprüfen.«
Aus dem Juryprotokoll

Halle 13 und Eingang West der Deutschen Messe AG und Expo 2000
Hannover

Wettbewerb 1995
1. Preis

Planungsbeginn: 1996
Bauzeit: 1996–1997

Hall 13 and West
Entrance to Deutsche
Messe AG and Expo
2000, Hanover

Competition: 1995
First prize
Commencement of
planning: 1996
Construction period:
1996 – 97

"The urban response to the brief
represents an ideal solution: the
entrance area and the hall form a
balanced, unified whole. The
arrivals level – +1 above 0 level –
affords an interesting sequence
of spaces that are contrasted in
character to the hall and the
avenue of trees. The hall itself
fits in well with the overall picture of the trade fair complex.
The hall façades allow an intense
exchange between indoors
and outdoors. A tight and well
resolved set of relations has been
established to the existing Hall
14. The six technical cores in the
hall give it a high degree of functional efficiency and a clear spatial quality. This spatial quality
is further accentuated by the
daylight concept incorporated in
the façade and roof. The minimum clear height of 12.5 m pro-

vided beneath the grid of girders
should be reconsidered in relation to the proportions of a hall
with such large spans."
Excerpt from jury report

The Deutsche Messe AG Hannover and the Expo 2000 Hannover required a new hall for the
trade fair site. Hall 13 was to have
an area of roughly 27,400 m²
and was designed primarily as
an exhibition space for permanent use. The necessary ancillary
spaces are accommodated at the
edges of the hall in six 15 x 15 m
cores. Two restaurants with
seating for approximately 500
persons are situated in the north-
west and north-east cores immediately next to the main avenue
of 333 trees.

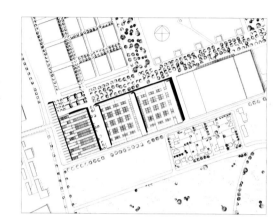

Lageplan des Wettbe-
werbs mit dem großen
Dach des Eingangs West,
das jedoch in dieser Form
nicht ausgeführt wurde.
Rechts: Luftaufnahme von
Südwesten

Competition site plan
showing the large
roof over the western
entrance area. The
roof was not executed
in this form.
Right: aerial view
from south-west

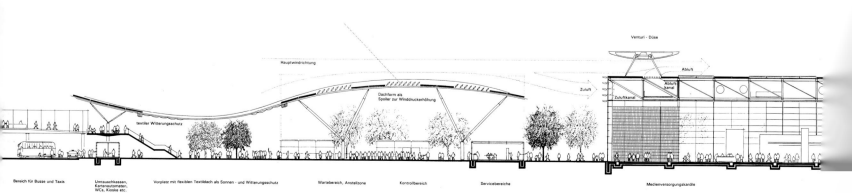

Die Deutsche Messe AG Hannover und die Expo 2000 Hannover benötigen eine neue Messehalle 13 in einer Größe von ca. 27400 qm. Sie soll vorrangig in der Nachnutzung als Ausstellungsfläche bei Messen dienen, die erforderlichen Nebenräume sind in den Randbereichen der Halle in sechs Kernen von je 15 m x 15 m untergebracht. Zwei Restaurants mit ca. 500 Sitzplätzen liegen an den Nordwest- und Nordostkernen der Halle, direkt an der Hauptallee der 333 Bäume.

Der Eingang West und die Halle 13 übernehmen die Konzeption und die maßstäbliche Höhenentwicklung der städtebaulichen Rahmenplanung. Die klare Anordnung und die einprägsame Gestalt des Eingangsbauwerkes und der streng geometrischen Halle betonen die Funktionsbereiche und stützen das städtebauliche Konzept. Die Überdachung und Halle bilden den Auftakt und den Abschluß der ›Südschiene‹ des Messegeländes. Die Haupterschließung erfolgt vom Vorplatz des Eingangs West.

Als Orientierungspunkt für das Messe- und Expogelände wird eine filigrane transparente Dachstruktur vorgeschlagen. Über

einen Verteilungssteg werden ankommende und abfahrende Besucher dezentral verteilt. Ein reibungsloser, kontrollierbarer Ablauf in den Ein- und Ausgangsbereichen ist gewährleistet. Das variable Dach bildet einen perfekten Wetterschutz und ist Forum für multifunktionale und kommunikative Aktivitäten. Seine aerodynamische Form wirkt als Windspoiler und erhöht den Winddruck für das natürliche Belüftungskonzept der Halle 13.

Oben: Ansicht von der Allee der vereinten 333 Bäume. Unten: Wettbewerbs-Schnitt mit dem als Windspoiler gedachten Vordach für den Eingang West und die Halle 13

Top: view from avenue of 333 trees from all parts of the world. Bottom: section through competition area, showing the windspoiler roof for the west entrance and Hall 13

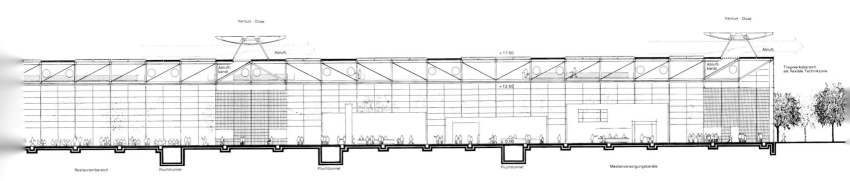

The western entrance to the site and Hall 13 adopt the concept and heights laid down in the urban planning legislation. The clear arrangement and striking design of the entrance structure and the strict geometric form of the hall emphasize the functional nature of these areas and also reinforce the urban planning concept. The entrance roof and the hall are the first impressions one gains of the complex. At the same time, they also form the conclusion to the "southern axis" of the trade fair site. The main line of access starts in the forecourt to the western entrance.

A slenderly dimensioned, transparent roof structure was proposed as a landmark and reference point for the trade fair and Expo 2000 site. The streams of arriving and departing visitors will be dispersed over the broad forecourt. In this way, a smooth, controlled movement of crowds is ensured in the entrance and exit zones. The variable roof structure provides ideal protection against the elements and also allows the area beneath to be used as a forum for multifunctional and communicative activities. The aerodynamic form of the roof acts as a wind spoiler that increases the wind pressure at certain points and serves the needs of the natural ventilation concept for Hall 13.

The hall itself is distinguished by its clear form and restrained appearance. It can be used flexibly in a variety of ways and can be adapted to meet different requirements.

The primary structure of the 120 x 225 m hall consists of a steel girder grid with a system depth of 4.5 metres. The girders are supported by the six tower-like concrete cores, which accommodate mechanical services and other installations. The cores also provide horizontal and vertical

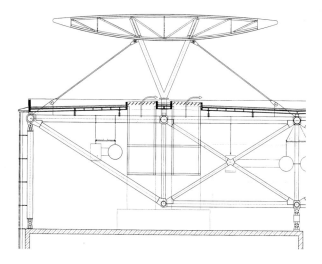

Links: Schnitt durch die Venturi-Flügel. Unten: Grundriß Erdgeschoß der Halle mit den notwendigen Fluchtwegentfernungen

Left: section through Venturi element
Below: ground floor plan of hall with escape routes

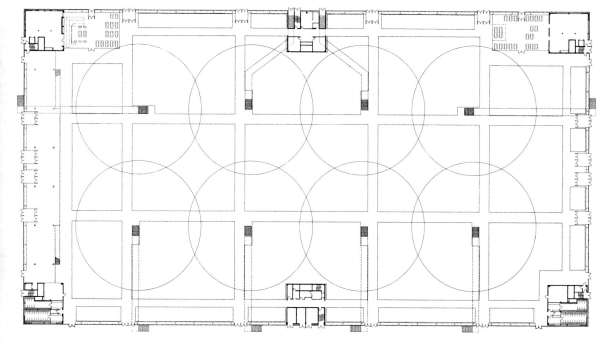

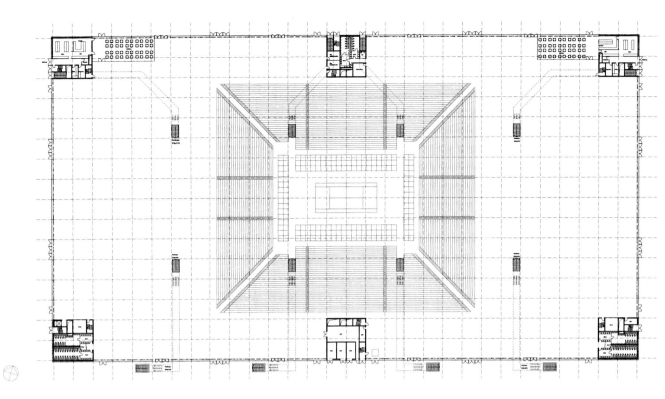

Grundriß Erdgeschoß der
Halle mit eingestellter
Tribüne für die ATP Tennis
Weltmeisterschaft 1997

Ground floor plan of hall
with temporary tiers of
seating for the ATP world
tennis championships,
1997

Unterschiedliche Veran-
staltungen in der Halle.
Oben: Konzert. Unten: die
ATP Tennis Weltmeister-
schaft, 1997

Different events staged in
the hall. Above: concert;
right: ATP world tennis
championships, 1997

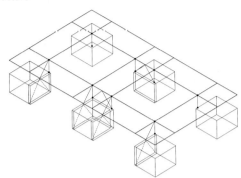

bracing. The 7.5 x 7.5 m grid on
which the hall is based is the outcome of a process of structural
and economic optimization of the
use of materials. The secondary
structure consists of prefabricated timber coffers 2.50 x 7.50 m.
Depending on the required use,
the bays of the grid can be
employed as technical elements
for the mechanical services of
the building – ventilation, daylighting, artificial lighting, light
deflection, etc.

By applying aerodynamic and
thermodynamic techniques to
regulate the indoor climate, only
the air intake system had to be
mechanically operated. The
extract ventilation of the hall is
a natural system that exploits
the almost constant westerly air-
stream in Hanover. Six Venturi
elements on the roof of the hall
directly above the cores, induce
low-pressure conditions that
result in the vitiated air being
sucked, via the escape tunnels
and ventilation ducts along the
façades, up to roof level and
extracted there. On days when
there is little wind, the system is
supported by an axial fan. Further savings are achieved by
the non-glare roof lights, which
ensure a maximum exploitation
of daylight.

Randbereich des Dach-
tragwerks mit den Haupt-
lüftungskanälen der
Zuluft

Edge of roof structure
with main air-supply
ducts

Oben: Detail aus dem
Dachtragwerk

Above: detail of roof
structure

Die Halle 13 ist von klarer Form
und zurückhaltendem Erscheinungsbild. Sie ist variabel nutzbar
und flexibel unterschiedlichen
Bedürfnissen anpaßbar. Die
Primärstruktur der 120 x 225 m
messenden Halle besteht aus
einem Stahlträgerrost mit einer
Systemhöhe von 4,5 m. Dieser
liegt auf sechs turmartigen Instal-
lationskernen aus Beton, die auch
die Aussteifung in horizontaler
und vertikaler Richtung übernehmen. Das Quadratraster von
7,5 auf 7,5 m resultiert aus der
konstruktiven und wirtschaftlichen
Optimierung des eingesetzten
Materials. Die Sekundärstruktur
besteht aus vorgefertigten Holz-
kassetten im Abstand von 3,75 m.
Die Rasterfelder werden je nach
Nutzung und Bedürfnissen als
technische Elemente für die
Gebäudeausrüstung – Lüftung,
Belichtung, Beleuchtung, Ein-
blendung, Ausblendung usw. –
eingesetzt.
    Durch aerodynamische sowie
thermodynamische Maßnahmen
in der Raumlufttechnik wird lediglich die Zuluft mechanisch zugeführt. Die Entlüftung der Halle

Sprengisometrie der
Anschlüsse an einen
Gußknoten

Exploded isometric
diagram of cast node
junction

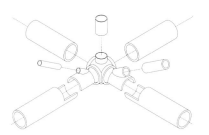

Oben: In den ›Vogelne-
stern‹ sind die Schweiß-
kabinen provisorisch auf-
gehängt.

Above: the welding
cabins temporarily sus-
pended in the "birds'
nests".

Isometrie des Dach-
aufbaus. Auf ein
7,50 x 7,50 m großes
Feld wurden drei Holz-
paneele 7,50 x 2,50 m,
jeweils pro Feld aus
statisch-konstruktiven
Gründen um 90 Grad
verdreht, verlegt.

Isometric of roof con-
struction. For structural
reasons, three 7.50 x
2.50 m timber panels are
laid in each 7.50 x 7.50 m
bay. The panels are set
at right angles to each
other from bay to bay.

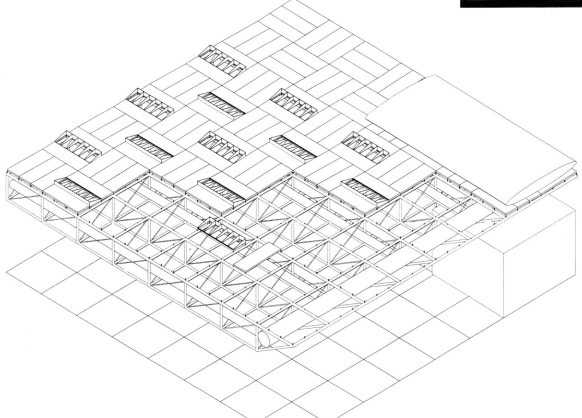

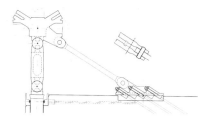

Auflagerpunkt und Rück-
spannung des Tragwerks
auf dem Kern. Rechts
unten: Ansicht des Auf-
lagerknotens mit Pendel-
stütze auf Edelstahlkugeln

Detail of support and
anchoring of roof struc-
ture on core. Bottom
right: structural node with
hinged column on stain-
less-steel ball-bearings

As an ecologically sustainable,
regenerable raw material, wood
was used in the floor and façade
construction and for the finish-
ings and light-deflecting coffers.

"The design for Hall 13 is an
architectural project that demonstrates the quality of normal
things in a most impressive way.
Everything seems to fit together
effortlessly and without any
pomp. In this respect, Hall 13 is
a built symbol of simplicity that
exhibits all the qualities of something special."
Theodor Diener, former
spokesman for Expo 2000,
on 20.10.1996

Galerie im Westteil der
Halle mit Managerbüros für
die Großveranstaltungen

Gallery level in western
section of hall with
administrative offices
for major events

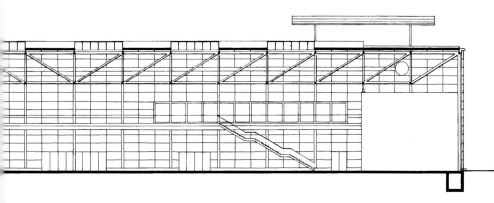

blendfreie Oberlichtsystem führt
zu weiteren Einsparungen im
Betrieb.

Aus ökologischen Gründen
wurde Holz als nachwachsender
Baustoff im Bereich der Decken-
konstruktion sowie der Ausbau-
und Ausblendraster als Baustoff
gewählt.

»Der Entwurf der Halle 13 ist ein
architektonisches Projekt, das
die Qualität des Normalen in
beeindruckender Weise veran-
schaulicht – alles scheint sich
ohne Anstrengung und ohne
Leistungsgehabe zu fügen. So

Südfassade mit dem
außenliegenden Son-
nenschutz, von innen
gesehen

Internal view of south
face with external sun-
screen

gesehen ist die Halle 13 ein bau-
liches Symbol des Einfachen mit
der Qualität des Besonderen.«
Theodor Diener, vormaliger
Sprecher der Expo 2000, am
20.10.1996

erfolgt natürlich und nutzt den in
Hannover fast ständig wehenden
Westwind. Über sechs Venturi-
Flügel auf dem Hallendach direkt
über den Kernen wird Unterdruck
erzeugt, der die verbrauchte Luft
über die Fluchttunnels und Ab-
luftkanäle entlang der Fassaden
absaugt und über Dach bringt.
An windarmen Tagen wird dieses
System von einem Axialventilator
unterstützt. Die optimale Ausnut-
zung von Tageslicht durch das

Schnitt durch den
Fassadenbereich

Section through
façade

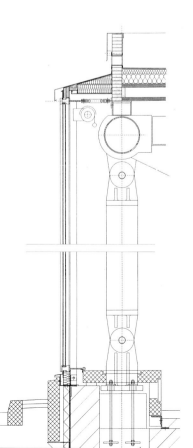

Unten: Gläserner Verbin-
dungsbau zwischen Halle
12 und Halle 13

Below: glazed linking
structure between Halls
12 and 13

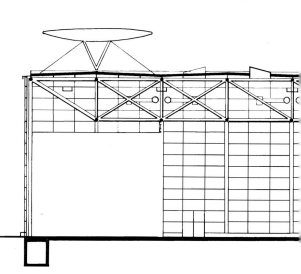

Messenutzung der
Halle 13 während der
Cebit 1998

Hall 13 in use during
Cebit trade fair, 1998

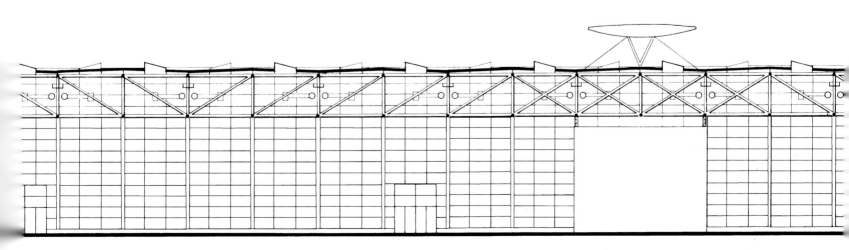

Anhang
Appendix

1953	Wohnhaus Schottenhamel Wessling Projekt
1953	Geschäftshaus Gabler München Projekt
1954–55	Wohnhaus Ebnet München-Pasing
1954–57	Modehaus Kraus München
1955–57	Erweiterungsbau der Volksschule Insingen Insingen über Rothenburg ob der Tauber
1955	Wohn- und Gästehaus Josef Gartner Gundelfingen/Donau Projekt
1956–57	Wohnhaus Holzbauer Gauting
1956–58	Wohnhaus Viktor Gartner Gundelfingen/Donau
1958–59	Wohnhaus Rickert Steinwiesen/Oberfranken
1957–58	Wohnhaus Geisler Gauting
1957–58	Wohnhaus Dr. Peters Sibichhausen bei Starnberg
1958	Wohnhaus Lang Garmisch-Partenkirchen
1958–59	Haus des Hopfens Wolnzach
1958–59	Wohnhaus Eugen Höfter Neuhausen bei Mainburg
1959–60	Wohnhaus Bruno Höfter Mainburg
1957–58	Hopfenhalle HVG Mainburg
1958–59	Märker Zementwerk Titanbrecher Harburg/Schwaben
1958–59	Hopfenhalle Klotz Wolnzach
1959–60	Kreiskrankenhaus Mainburg Erweiterung Mainburg
1960	Hopfenhalle der Stadt Pfaffenhofen Projekt

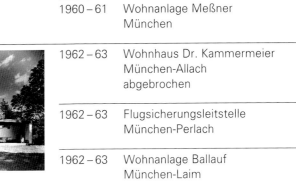

1960 – 61	Wohnhaus Kurt Ackermann Herrsching/Ammersee
1960 – 61	Wohnanlage Meßner München
1962 – 63	Wohnhaus Dr. Kammermeier München-Allach abgebrochen
1962 – 63	Flugsicherungsleitstelle München-Perlach
1962 – 63	Wohnanlage Ballauf München-Laim

1961 – 66	Bayerische Hypotheken- und Wechselbank München-Schwabing
1962 – 63	Fertigungshalle BMW München-Milbertshofen
1962 – 63	Wohnanlage Höfter, 1. BA. München-Freimann
1962	Heizhaus der Bundesmonopol- verwaltung für Branntwein München-Berg am Laim
1963 – 64	Märker Zementwerk Homogenisierungssilos Harburg/Schwaben
1963 – 64	Haus Graf von Norman Icking-Isartal

1963 – 64	Wohnhaus Dr. Fischer München-Großhadern
1964 – 65	Ponystall Graf von Norman Icking-Isartal
1964	Halle 2 Götz Metallbau Deggendorf
1965 – 66	Zentralgarage Korn Rothenburg ob der Tauber

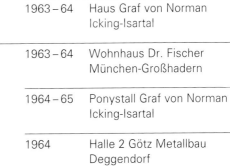

1960 – 67	Lehrwerkhallen Flughafen Neubiberg Neubiberg bei München
1964 – 70	Feuerwache 4 München-Schwabing
1964 – 65	Landwirtschaftliche Berufsschule Mainburg
1965	Umkleidekabinen für das Schwimmbad Mainburg Projekt
1966 – 67	Haus Meisel Feldafing

1960–67	Ausbildungshalle Flughafen Neubiberg Neubiberg bei München
1960–67	Zentralwerkstätte Flughafen Neubiberg Neubiberg bei München
1967	Lagerhalle Cramer München-Obermenzing

1965–68	Halle 3 Götz Metallbau Deggendorf
1966–67	Bürohaus Weißenberger München-Westend
1966–70	Wohnanlage Hermann Moll München-Westend

1969–74	Universität Regensburg Rektorat Regensburg
1969–74	Universität Regensburg Studentenhaus, Studententheater Regensburg
1967–68	Haus Gerhard Moll Pullach
1970–72	Wohnanlage Höfter, 2. BA. München-Freimann

1969–70	Lager- und Verwaltungs- gebäude Schneider + Söhne Unterhaching bei München
1968–71	Wohnanlage Am Biederstein München-Schwabing

1968–69	Friedenskirche Gundelfingen/Donau
1969–70	Verwaltungsgebäude Weishaupt München-Ramersdorf
1969–70	Wohnhaus Schow München-Obermenzing

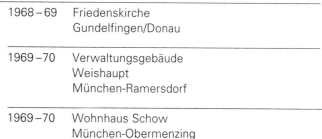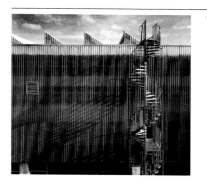

1969–70	Werkhalle IWIS Winklhofer + Söhne München-Sendling

1968–72	Christuskirche Bad Füssing
1967–68	Märker Zementwerk Lehrwerkstätte Harburg/Schwaben

1967–68	Märker Zementwerk Mischbett Harburg/Schwaben
1969–72	Bürozentrum Schulz München-Moosach
1969–70	Wohnhaus Ernst Götz Deggendorf
1969–70	Märker Zementwerk Klinkersilos Harburg/Schwaben
1963–72	Märker Zementwerk Kalkwerk und Kalkpackerei Harburg/Schwaben
1970–72	Wohnhaus Dr. Josef Gartner Gundelfingen/Donau

1971–72	Werkhalle Wanderer Haar bei München
1970–71	Verlagsgebäude Langenscheidt München-Schwabing
1970–72	Hardtschule Weilheim/Oberbayern
1970	Rechenzentrum Hypobank München Projekt

1970–76	Bundesverwaltungsgericht BVG München
1970	Halle 4 Götz Metallbau Deggendorf
1972	Klinik St. Bonifaz München Projekt

1972–74	Märker Zementwerk Wärmetauscherturm Harburg/Schwaben
1972	Wohnanlage Fritz Winterling München-Obermenzing Projekt
1973–75	Struktur- und Entwurfsplanung Sportgastein Projekt

1973–75	Verwaltungsgebäude Wüstenrot München
1974–76	EDV-Verwaltungsgebäude der Landeshauptstadt München
1974–77	Offiziersschule der Luftwaffe Hörsaalgebäude OSLW Fürstenfeldbruck

1974–77	Heizzentrale der OSLW und des Flughafens Fürstenfeldbruck
1974–77	Offiziersschule der Luftwaffe Hörsaalgebäude OSLW Fürstenfeldbruck
1974–77	Offiziersschule der Luftwaffe Unterkünfte OSLW Fürstenfeldbruck

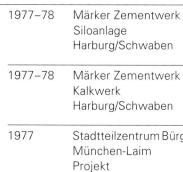

1972–77	Verwaltungsgebäude Verband der Bayerischen Bauinnung München
1977–78	Märker Zementwerk Siloanlage Harburg/Schwaben
1977–78	Märker Zementwerk Kalkwerk Harburg/Schwaben
1977	Stadtteilzentrum Bürgerhaus, Stadtteilbibliothek München-Laim Projekt
1975–88	Klärwerk Gut Marienhof der LH München Dietersheim bei München
1978–79	Wohnanlage Streubert München-Nymphenburg
1979–93	Generaldirektion 2 des Europäischen Patentamtes EPA »Pschorrhöfe« München

1980/84	Pumpwerk am Main-Donau-Kanal Kelheim
1980	Fußgängerbrücke Innsbrucker Ring München, Projekt
1980	Verband der Bauinnung München Verwaltungsgebäude München
1980	Wohnhaus Langguth München-Laim Projekt
1980–83	Eislaufzelt im Olympiapark München

1980–88	Uferanlage mit Fußgänger- und Straßenbrücke Schiffsanlegestelle Main-Donau-Kanal Kelheim
1981–86	Wohnen am Kulturforum Berlin-Tiergarten
1981–88	Wohnanlage BHB am Gottfried-Böhm-Ring München-Sendling
1981–87	Evangelisches Gemeindezentrum Bad Füssing
1982–88	Studentenwohnheim Georg-Lanzenstiel-Haus München-Freimann
1983	Tennishalle München-Obermenzing Projekt
1983	Betonwerk Märker Parsdorf bei München
1983–85	Redaktionsgebäude Langenscheidt Verlag München-Schwabing
1983–91	Postamt I Regensburg
1983–84	Wohnanlage Fritz Winterling München-Obermenzing
1984–87	Stadtteilzentrum, Bibliothek der LH München München-Laim
1984–85	Krauss-Maffei Struktur-/Städtebauliche Rahmenplanung München-Allach
1985	Wohnbebauung BHB Hallschlag Stuttgart Projekt
1986–91	Fußgängerbrücke über den Main-Donau-Kanal Berching/Oberpfalz
1985–95	Technik III und Wissenschaftliches Zentrum GhK-Universität Kassel Kassel
1986	Druckereigebäude Technoprint München Projekt
1986	Postplatz Schweinfurt
1986–93	Forschungszentrum für Bioverfahrenstechnik der Universität Stuttgart Stuttgart-Vaihingen

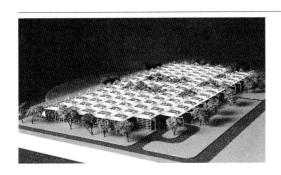

1988	Neubau Brauerei der Löwenbräu AG München und Neubiberg Projekt
1988–91	Konstruktionsbüro Gartner Gundelfingen/Donau
1989–91	Leistungszentrum für Eiskunstlauf im Olympiapark München

1989–98	Ortsumgehung und Lahnbrücke Weilburg/Lahn
1989–93	Kloster Andechs Gesamtplanung und Pfortenhof Andechs
1990	Fernmeldeamt Landshut Projekt
1989	Wohn- und Bürogebäude des Münchener Domkapitels München Projekt

1990–92	Büro- und Technologie- gebäude Hönninger München-Sendling Projekt
1990–91	Atelier Helmut Sturm Pullach
1990–92	Wohnheimanlage und Werkstätten Eglharting bei München

1990–94	Katholisches Kirchenzentrum St. Valentin Unterföhring bei München Projekt
1991–94	Wohnhaus Ulrich Hönninger Grünwald
1991–95	Feuerwache 8 der LH München Unterföhring bei München
1991	Atelier Lothar Fischer Baierbrunn, Projekt

1991–98	Arbeitsamt Suhl/Thüringen
1991–92	Praxis Katrin Ackermann München-Neuhausen
1991–98	Hauptpumpwerk Wilmersdorf Berlin
1991–99	Sozialgebäude für die Berliner Wasser-Betriebe Berlin-Wilmersdorf
1993–98	Dritte Donaubrücke Ingolstadt/Donau

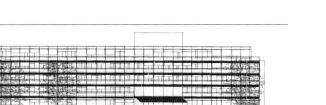

1992–93	Rückbau und Renovierung der Hypobank München-Schwabing
1993–99	Amt für Abfallwirtschaft AFA der LH München München-Moosach
1993–97	Kindergarten St. Nikolaus Rosenheim
1993–97	Studentenzentrum Rosenheim
1994	Molkerei Weihenstephan Freising Projekt
1994	Bürozentrum Dr. Hanns Maier Luxemburg Bebauungsplan
1994	Märker Zementwerk Förderanlage Bräunlesberg Harburg/Schwaben

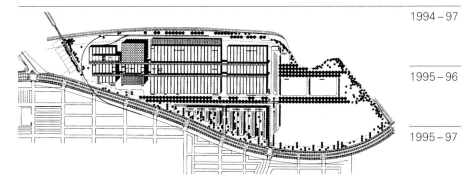

1994–97	Neubau Brauerei der Paulaner AG München-Riem Projekt
1995–96	Produktions- und Verwaltungsgebäude Valeo Erdweg Projekt
1995–97	Halle 13 der Expo 2000 und der Deutschen Messe AG Hannover Hannover
1996–98	Bräustüberlterrasse des Klosters Andechs Andechs
1996–99	Fußgängerstege und Angerinsel Nittenau

1995–99	Eingang West der Expo 2000 und der Deutschen Messe AG Hannover
1997–99	Wohnanlage BHB an der Friedenspromenade München-Trudering
1997	Verbindungsbauwerk der Hallen 12–13 der Deutschen Messe AG Hannover
1997–99	Wohnanlage für die Gewofag München-Allach Projekt
1997–99	Erweiterung der Generaldirektion 2 des Europäischen Patentamtes EPA München
1998–01	Wiedererrichtung der Schrannenhalle München

1953	TH München in Weihenstephan
1955	Wohn- und Gästehaus Josef Gartner, Gundelfingen/Donau 1. Rang
1957	Volksschule in Schäftlarn
	Studentenwohnheim in Erlangen Engste Wahl
	Volksschule in Ingolstadt
	Hopfenhalle Mainburg 1. Preis
1958	Volksschule in Holzkirchen
1959	Siedlung Bürgerstiftung Alte Heimat München
1962	Gymnasium in Haßfurt
	Fabrikgebäude Wolfra in München 2. Preis
1963	Oskar-von-Miller-Polytechnikum, München 4. Preis
	Verwaltungsgebäude Paulaner-Salvator-Thomasbräu München 2. Preis
1964	Kreiskrankenhaus Rain am Lech 2. Preis
	Volksschule in Enzelhausen/Ndb 2. Preis
1965	Landratsamtsgebäude Aichach
	Sparkasse Mainburg Sonderankauf
	Evangelische Kirche und Gemeindezentrum Nürnberg-Gostenhof Engere Wahl
1966	Forum und Mensa, Universität Regensburg 3. Preis
	Neue Pinakothek, München
	Siedlung der Südhausbau, Ingolstadt 2. Preis
	Kreiskrankenhaus Mallersdorf 1. Ankauf
1967	XX. Olympiade München mit den Büros Hans Busso von Busse, Franz Kießling, von Werz-Ottow
1968	Evangelische Kirche, Bad Füssing 1. Preis

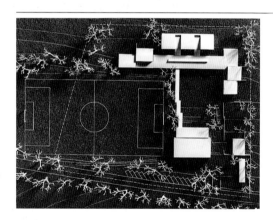

Münchner Freiheit – Städtebau

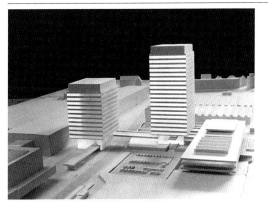

Hauptverwaltung der BMW, München
3. Preis

1969 Verwaltungsgebäude der OPD
Freiburg/Breisgau
7. Rang

Konzertsaal »Richard-Strauss-Halle«
im Arabella-Park, München

Hauptverwaltung und Rechenzentrum
Hypobank im Arabella-Park, München
2. Preis

1970 Verwaltungsgebäude
Bayerische Rückversicherung
Tivoli-Park, München
4. Rang

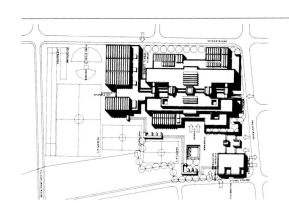

Gesamtschule München-Nord
2. Preis

1972 Grundschule Perlach

Verwaltungsgebäude Verband
baugewerblicher Unternehmer Bayerns,
München
1. Preis

Grundschule Wörthsee/Steinebach

Gymnasium München-Unterhaching
4. Preis

1973 Katholische Kirche Ismaning

Schulzentrum Ingolstadt
4. Preis

1974 Elisenhof, MEPC, München
3. Rang

Fachakademie für Optik, München
3. Preis

Hauptschule Herrsching/Ammersee
2. Preis

Hauptschule Hebertshausen

Flughafen München II
5. Rang

Kaufhof Rotkreuzplatz, München
2. Preis

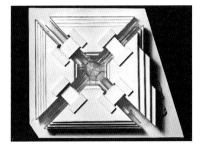

1976 Realschule Unterschleißheim

Realschule Ismaning

Berufsschule Weilheim

1977 Zentralstelle für Ernährung und
Landwirtschaft Feldafing

Berufsbildungszentrum Ingolstadt
3. Preis

Esso-Tankstelle
1. Preis

Arbeitsamt München

BMW Verwaltungsgebäude, Dingolfing

1978   Schulzentrum Perlach-Süd, München

Zoologische Staatssammlung München

Landwirtschaftsministerium des Landes
Baden-Württemberg
Stuttgart

1979   Evangelische Kirche Unterhaching/Grünau

Einweisungs- und Transportanstalt
Heimsheim/Pforzheim
2. Preis

Kassenhalle der Hypo-Bank
Hauptzentrale München

Verwaltungsgebäude der Bavaria-Filmkunst
München-Geiselgasteig

1980   Verwaltung und Werkstätten
der Stadtwerke der LH
München
Ankauf

Fußgängerbrücke über Main-Donau-Kanal
in Kelheim mit Jörg Schlaich
1. Preis

Abfertigungsgebäude des Flughafens Stuttgart
7. Rang

1981   Ostbahnhofbebauung München

Erweiterung der Neuen Nationalgalerie, Berlin,
und Wohnen am Kulturforum
2. Preis,
ein erster Preis wurde nicht vergeben

1982   Wohnbauten am Kolumbusplatz,
München

Studentenwohnheim Georg-Lanzenstiel-Haus
München-Freimann
1. Preis

1983   Postsparkasse Bayerstraße, München
2. Preis

Verwaltungszentrum der Sparkasse der LH
München

Postamt Regensburg 1
2. Preis,
ein erster Preis wurde nicht vergeben

Rieger-Block am Isartorplatz,
München

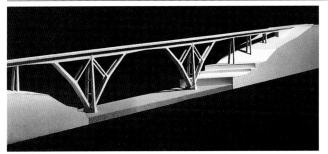

1984	Eisenbahnbrücke Porto, Portugal mit Herbert Schambeck
	Postamt Regensburg 1, Überarbeitung 1. Preis
	Autobahnbrücke Argen mit Herbert Schambeck
	Fußgängerbrücke Landshut mit Jörg Schlaich 5. Preis

	Oberfinanzdirektion OFD München alle 2. Ränge wurden angekauft
	GhK Gesamthochschule Universität Kassel Technik III und Wissenschaftliches Zentrum 1. Preis
1986	Sporthallenanlage Unterföhring
	RMD-Kanal Berching, Fußgängerbrücke mit Jörg Schlaich 1. Preis
	RMD-Kanal Berching, Städtebau mit Peter Kluska 1. Preis
	Postplatz in Schweinfurt mit Karl Kagerer 1. Preis

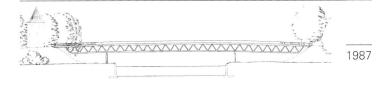

	Straßenbrücken Berching mit Schlaich, Bergermann + Partner
1987	Landesgartenschau 1992, Ingolstadt mit Peter Kluska und Jörg Schlaich 2. Preis
	Zentrum für Informationstechnik der Industrie- und Handelskammer Augsburg 2. Preis

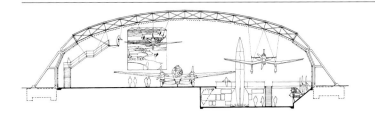

1988	Deutsches Museum für Luft- und Raumfahrt in Oberschleißheim
	Williamsburgbrücke, New York, mit Schlaich, Bergermann + Partner, René Walther, Myron Goldsmith 1. Preis
1989	Ingenieurbauwerke und Straßenbrücke Weilburg/Lahn mit Bernhard Behringer 1. Rang
	Flugabfertigung der Bundesregierung Flughafen Köln-Wahn 2. Preis

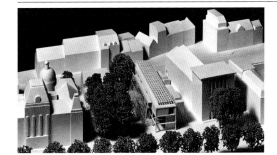

1990	Vorarlberger Landesgalerie Bregenz
	Landeszentralbank BLZ Leopoldstraße, München
	Deutscher Pavillon Expo '92 – Weltausstellung Sevilla
	Bayern-Lux, Luxemburg 2. Preis

Teerhofbrücke Bremen
mit Schlaich, Bergermann + Partner
2. Preis

Kammerspiele München
6. Rang

Hypopassage-Geschäftszentrum
Kaufingerstraße, München
2. Preis

1991 Richti-Areal, Zürich-Wallisellen
Schweizer Kreditbank
4. Rang

Hauptpumpwerk der BWB
Berlin-Wilmersdorf mit Sir Ted Happold
1. Preis

Wohnbebauung Rupprechtstraße, Landshut
2. Rang

Verwaltungsgebäude der
Schörghuber-Holding
Daphnestraße,
München
2. Rang

Deutsche Doka, Maisach
2. Rang

1992 Gutachten Dienstleistungszentrum
für Siemens/Nixdorf
Leopoldstraße,
München

Hauptverwaltung Datev,
Nürnberg
2. Preis

Erweiterung des Maximilianeums,
München
Bayerischer Landtag
3. Preis

1993 Städtebau und Industrie Clemensänger,
Freising
mit Sir Ted Happold

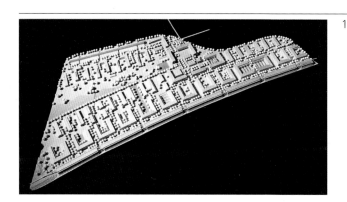

Realisierungswettbewerb
Baureferat München
5. Preis

Bayerische Vereinsbank BVB, Luxemburg
2. Preis

Akademie der Künste, Pariser Platz, Berlin
erste Runde zur Weiterbearbeitung empfohlen

Halle 4 der Deutschen Messe AG, Hannover
mit Sir Ted Happold

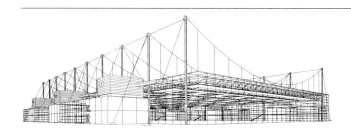

Dritte Donaubrücke Ingolstadt
mit Schlaich, Bergermann + Partner
und Peter Kluska
1. Preis

Amt für Abfallwirtschaft, München
1. Preis

Bebauung Viehhofgelände, München
Gutachten

1994 Landeszentralbank LZB, Regensburg
3. Preis

1995 Umwelt-Technik-Zentrum UTZ,
Berlin-Adlershof
2. Preis

Neubau Schäfflerblock, Bayerische
Vereinsbank BVB München
3. Rang

Messe- und Veranstaltungszentrum Bremen
mit Schlaich, Bergermann + Partner
Ankauf

Brücke über die Oberhavel, Berlin, mit
Schlaich, Bergermann + Partner

St. Josef-Krankenhaus, Berlin-Weißensee

Feuerwache 10, Messestadt München-Riem
4. Preis

Halle 13 und Eingang West für die Expo 2000
Messe Hannover mit
Christoph Ackermann und Bernhard Behringer
1. Preis

1996 Bundesministerium für Verkehr,
Berlin

Städtebau auf der Angerinsel und
Fußgängerstege, Nittenau, mit
Schlaich, Bergermann + Partner und
Neumann und Auch
1. Preis

Ludwig-Maximilians-Universität
München-Planegg
Städtebau und Fakultät Biologie

1997 Halle 8/9 für die Expo 2000 Messe Hannover
mit Dietger Weischede

Stadt am Fluß, Brücke und Brückenköpfe,
Kassel
mit Bernhard Behringer

Bundespresseamt Berlin

1998 Novea 2004, Messe Düsseldorf

Technische Universität
Garching bei München
Neubau Fakultäten Mathematik und Informatik

Neues Bauzentrum der Messe München
in Poing
2. Preis

Biographie
Kurt Ackermann
Biography
Kurt Ackermann

1928	geboren am 2. März in Insingen über Rothenburg ob der Tauber	Born on 2 March in Insingen near Rothenburg ob der Tauber, Bavaria, Germany
	1958 Heirat mit Lorle Höfter 1960 Katrin Ackermann 1963 Peter Ackermann 1967 Christoph Ackermann	1958 Marries Lorle Höfter 1960 Katrin Ackermann 1963 Peter Ackermann 1967 Christoph Ackermann
1946–1948	Praktikant Gesellenprüfung als Maurer und als Zimmermann	Practical training; passes apprenticeship exams to qualify as journeyman bricklayer and carpenter
1949–1954	Studium der Architektur am Oskar-von-Miller-Polytechnikum München und an der Technischen Hochschule München	Studies architecture at Oskar von Miller Polytechnic, Munich, and at University of Technology, Munich
1949–1953	Werkstudent bei der Obersten Baubehörde und am Universitätsbauamt München	Working student with Chief Construction Authority *Oberste Baubehörde* and University Construction Office, Munich
1953	Freier Architekt in München	Own practice in Munich
1962	Mitglied im Bund Deutscher Architekten BDA	Member of Federation of German Architects, BDA
1965–1967	Mitglied im Landesvorstand des BDA Bayern	Member of regional committee of BDA Bavaria
1966	Mitglied im Deutschen Werkbund	Member of German Werkbund
1967	Preis für die Förderung der Architektur der Landeshauptstadt München	Prize of the City of Munich for the Advancement of Architecture
1969	Partnerschaft mit Jürgen Feit bis 1990, Peter Jaeger, Richard Martin bis 1997	Partnerships with Jürgen Feit until 1990, with Peter Jaeger, and with Richard Martin until 1997
1970–1980	Mitglied im Patronatskomitee von ›Bauen + Wohnen‹	Member of patronage committee of the journal *Bauen + Wohnen*
1971	Gastprofessur an der Technischen Hochschule Wien	Visiting professor at University of Technology in Vienna
1971–1983	Mitglied in der Vertreterversammlung der Bayerischen Architektenkammer	Member of representative assembly of Bavarian Chamber of Architects
1972–1975	Mitglied im Präsidium des Bundes Deutscher Architekten BDA	Member of executive committee of Federation of German Architects, BDA
1973–1978	Mitglied im Redaktionsausschuß ›Der Architekt‹	Member of editorial committee of *Der Architekt*
1973–1979	Mitglied der Stadtgestaltungskommission der Landeshauptstadt München	Member of city of Munich town planning commission
1974	Ruf an die Technische Hochschule Darmstadt	Offered professorship at University of Technology, Darmstadt
1974	Berufung zum ordentlichen Professor an die Universität Stuttgart Direktor des Instituts für Entwerfen und Konstruieren	Appointed full professor of University of Stuttgart Director of Institute for Design and Construction

1976–1984	Fachgutachter für Architektur in der Deutschen Forschungsgemeinschaft DFG	Specialist consultant for architecture to German Society for the Advancement of Scientific Research, DFG
1977–1980	Mitglied im Verwaltungsrat der Forschungsgemeinschaft Bauen und Wohnen des Landes Baden-Württemberg	Member of administrative council of the State of Baden-Württemberg Research Society for Building and Housing
1980–1981	Gastprofessor für Entwerfen an der Technischen Universität Wien	Visiting professor at University of Technology, Vienna
1980–1994	Korrespondent von ›Werk, Bauen + Wohnen‹	Correspondent for *Werk, Bauen + Wohnen*
1981	Ruf an die Universität Dortmund	Offered professorship at University of Dortmund
1984	Mitglied der Akademie der Künste, Berlin	Member of the Academy of Arts, Berlin
1984–1991	Wanderausstellung ›Industriebau‹ mit Otl Aicher	Touring exhibition on industrial building, together with Otl Aicher
1985–1991	Erstprüfer im Prüfungsausschuß Architektur für die Große Staatsprüfung – Regierungsbaumeister – im Land Baden-Württemberg	Head of examining board for architecture for Higher State Examinations for government architects of the State of Baden-Württemberg
1986	Architekturpreis der Landeshauptstadt München	Architectural Prize of the City of Munich
1987	Mitglied der International Academy of Architecture, IAA, Sofia	Member of International Academy of Architecture, IAA, Sofia
1987	Ernennung zum Professor h.c. der International Academy of Architecture IAA, Sofia	Appointed honorary professor of International Academy of Architecture, IAA, Sofia
1989	Ehrenpromotion zum Doktor der Technischen Wissenschaften – Dr. techn. h.c. – der Technischen Universität Wien	Honorary doctor of technical sciences – Dr. techn. h. c. – of University of Technology, Vienna
1993	Partnerschaft mit Peter Ackermann	Partnership with Peter Ackermann
1993	Emeritierung	Retirement from academic offices, emeritus professor
1994	Heinrich-Tessenow-Medaille in Gold der Fritz-Schumacher-Stiftung, verliehen von der Universität Hannover	Heinrich Tessenow Medal in Gold of Fritz Schumacher Foundation, awarded by University of Hanover
1994	Ehrenmitglied der Heinrich-Tessenow-Gesellschaft	Honorary member of Heinrich Tessenow Society
1995	Gastprofessor an der Technischen Universität München	Visiting professor at University of Technology, Munich
1996	Honorary Fellow of the American Institute of Architects AIA – Hon. FAIA	Honorary fellow of the American Institute of Architects, AIA – Hon. FAIA
1996	Leo-von-Klenze-Medaille des Freistaates Bayern	Leo von Klenze Medal of the Free State of Bavaria
1998	Ruf als Gründungsdirektor an das Bauhaus-Kolleg, Dessau Nicht angenommen	Called as Founding Director to the Bauhaus-Kolleg, Dessau Not taken up

Peter Jaeger
Peter Ackermann

Peter Jaeger
Peter Ackermann
Kurt Ackermann

Peter Ackermann	1963	geboren in München	Born in Munich
	1983	Architekturstudium an der Technischen Universität München	Studies architecture at University of Technology, Munich
	1985–1988	Architekturstudium an der Akademie der bildenden Künste Wien Meisterschüler von Professor Gustav Peichl	Studies architecture at Academy of Visual Arts, Vienna In master class of Professor Gustav Peichl
	1989	Studium an der Universität Stuttgart	Studies at University of Stuttgart
	1991	Diplom an der Technischen Universität München	Diploma of the University of Technology, Munich
	1991–1992	Mitarbeiter von Renzo Piano Building Workshop Genua	Assistant in Renzo Piano's office Building Workshop Genoa
	1992–1993	Mitarbeiter von Richard Meier + Partner New York	Assistant in office of Richard Meier + Partners, New York
	Seit 1993	Partner von Professor Dr. Kurt Ackermann Mitglied im Deutschen Werkbund	Partner of Professor Dr Kurt Ackermann Member of German Werkbund
Jürgen Feit	1928	geboren in Mannheim	Born in Mannheim
	1948–1953	Architekturstudium an der TH Karlsruhe	Studies architecture at University of Technology, Karlsruhe
	1953	Diplom	Diploma
	1953–1956	im Büro Professor Peter Poelzig	Works in office of Professor Peter Poelzig
	1957–1958	Arbeit in England und Finnland bei Aarne Ervi	Works in England and in Finland with Aarne Ervi
	1960–1969	Mitarbeiter im Architekturbüro Kurt Ackermann	Assistant in Kurt Ackermann's office
	1969–1990	Partner von Professor Dr. Kurt Ackermann	Partner of Professor Dr Kurt Ackermann
	1982–1983	Lehrauftrag an der Universität Stuttgart WS 82/83	Lectureship at University of Stuttgart winter term 1982/83
	1992–1995	Lehrauftrag an der FH München	Lectureship at Technical College FH, Munich

Peter Jaeger	1935	geboren in Lüdenscheid	Born in Lüdenscheid
	1953–1959	Architekturstudium an der TH München	Studies architecture at University of Technology, Munich
	1959	Diplom	Diploma
	1956–1957	Studium der Graphik und Malerei an der Kunstakademie München, Professor Richard Seewald	Studies graphic design and painting at Academy of Art in Munich under Professor Richard Seewald
	1959–1960	Mitarbeit im väterlichen Architekturbüro in Heidelberg	Assistant in father's architectural practice in Heidelberg
	1960–1969	Mitarbeiter im Architekturbüro Kurt Ackermann	Assistant in Kurt Ackermann's office
	Seit 1969	Partner von Professor Dr. Kurt Ackermann	Partner of Professor Dr Kurt Ackermann
Richard Martin	1934	geboren in Haslau, Kreis Asch	Born in Haslau, Asch
	1948–1951	Lehre und Gesellenprüfung als Maurer	Apprenticeship and exams to qualify as journeyman bricklayer
	1952–1956	Studium am Oskar-von-Miller-Polytechnikum, München Abschluß Ing.-grad.	Studies at Oskar von Miller Polytechnic, Munich Ing.-grad. engineering qualification
	1956–1969	Mitarbeiter im Architekturbüro Kurt Ackermann	Assistant in Kurt Ackermann's office
	1969–1997	Partner von Professor Dr. Kurt Ackermann	Partner of Professor Dr Kurt Ackermann

Richard Martin

Jürgen Feit

Richard Martin
Jürgen Feit
Kurt Ackermann

Christoph Ackermann
Florian Aicher
Pierre de Almeida
Ludwig Angerer
Siegfried Arnstadt

Steffen Bathke
Karl Baumung
Stefan Behnisch
Gabor Benedek
Felix Beyreuther
Sieglinde Binnermann
Stefan Blume
Christian Bodensteiner
Ulrich Böhm
Eoin Bowler
Manfred Breiteneder
Uwe Breukel
Günter Burkhardt
Gerhard Busch

Francesco Caravelli

Peter Debold
Patrik Deby

Dieter Eberle
Adolf Ehrlich
Bodo Elleke
Walther Emminger

Peter Fink
Manfred Fischer
Richard Fischer
Richard Forward
George Frazzica

Johannes Geiling
Johannes Gleißner
Zdenek Glöckle
Franz Göger
Marco Götz
Rudolph Graf
Rainer Gulde

Gerold Haas
Marianne Habermann
Brigitte Häring
Friedrich Haindl
Georg Hajek

Bettina Hamann
Christian von
Hasselbach
Thomas Hauck
Moritz Hauschild
Stephanie Heese
Eberhard Heilmann
Robert Heinrich
Gerhard Hemmerlein
Hermann Herz
Jörg Hieber
Dagmar Hingerl
Heinz Hirschhäuser
Claudia Hinterwalder
Frank Höreth
Rainer Hoffmann
Sylvia Hoffmann
Rudolf Hoppe
Miriam Horn
Klaus Huber
Hannelore Huber

Wilfried Jauer
Florentine Jessen
Michael Jockers

Werner Kaag
Barbara Karl
Ursula Kasper
Helmut Katzl
Angelika Kern
Wolfgang Keuthage
Dieter Kiermaier
Ulrich Knoch
Marie Sophie Knopp
Norbert Koch
Josef Köppl
Rainer Koller
Andreas Kopp
Jürgen Krauss
Angelika Kroeker
Helmut Kroner
Beate Kuntz
Stefania Kuszlik

Werner Lang
Klemens Lenz
Helmut Link
Ralf Tristan Linsi
Andreas Luz
Marc Lyon

Peter Mack
Herbert Markert
Katja Moradi

Reiner Nagel
Susanne Nobis

Miriam Oldenbourg

Peter Panitz
Hans Pfaff
Roland Pfauntsch
Heinz-Werner Pieh
Dagmar Plankemann
Jan Podgorski
Ute Poerschke
Vait Pranter
Peter Pugler
Josef Putzer

Dieter Raab
Horst Raab
Martin Reinfelder
Caspar Richter
Klaus Richter
Heinz Riegel
Roland Rieger
Susanne Ruile
Adolf Rulofs
Klaus Ruß

Peter Schaad
Jutta Scheld
Christine Scheiblauer
Franz Schiermeier
Barbara Schmeller
Beate Schmidt
Carlotta Schmidt-Chiara
Eduard Schmutz
Harry Schöpke
Kurt Schöpperl
Marc Schulitz
Heinrich Schuschnigg
Hans Georg Schürmeyer
Richard Schröppel
Gabriele Selgrath
Barbara Sieghart
Matthias Sieveke
Christof Simon
Thaddäus Solonar
Christian Spahn
Monika Stegmann
Fritz Steigenberger
Johannes Striffler
Günter Stückle
Valentin Stürzl

Charlotte von Tettenborn
Roswitha Then Bergh
Wolfgang Thumann
Bernd Tränkner
Klaus Treder
Wolfgang Tröger

Jens Viehweg

Richard Wallner
Georg Wieland
Thomas Wilnhammer
Uwe Willsdorf
Walther Witte
Rainer Wohlmann
Arthur Wolfrum
Roland Woltmann

Friedrich Zandt
Dorothea Zech
Michael Zenkoff
Johannes Zeininger
Barbara Zettel
Ying Zhang
Martin Zoll

Sekretariat   Katrin Ackermann
              Brigitte Breitkopf
              Erika Bültermann
              Edeltraud Eisenschenk
              Brigitte Geilfus
              Christa Graf
              Christa Horneff
              Brigitte Kiermaier
              Margot Lades
              Sabine Maile
              Karin Max
              Brigitte Renner
              Gisela Röglin
              Margarete Savarino
              Gertrud Weiß
              Elvira Zeh

Küche   Alena Gomoll
              Afra Greger
              Erna Gerwenat
              Elisabeth König
              Josephine Wanjek-Schuck
              Ingrid de Werth
              Ulrike Zunner

Preise und Auszeichnungen
Prizes and Awards

1967	Preis für die Förderung der Architektur der Landeshauptstadt München	Prize of the City of Munich for the Advancement of Architecture
1967	BDA-Preis Bayern für die Hypo-Bank Schwabing, München	BDA (Federation of German Architects) Prize of Bavaria for Hypo Bank, Schwabing, Munich
1971	BDA-Preis Bayern für die Wohnanlage Moll, München	BDA Prize of Bavaria for Moll housing development, Munich
1971	Ehrenpreis für guten Wohnungsbau für die Wohnanlage Moll von der Landeshauptstadt München	Honorary prize of the City of Munich for good housing construction for Moll housing development
1971	BDA-Preis Bayern für das Märker Zementwerk, Harburg/Schwaben	BDA Prize of Bavaria for Märker Cement Works, Harburg, Swabia
1971	Förderpreis der Ziegelindustrie für die Wohnanlage Moll, München	Promotional Prize of the Brick Industry for the Moll housing development
1973	BDA-Preis Bayern – Anerkennung für die Christuskirche, Bad Füssing	BDA Prize of Bavaria – recognition of Church of Christ, Bad Füssing
1973	BDA-Preis Bayern – Anerkennung für die Hardtschule, Weilheim	BDA Prize of Bavaria – recognition of Hardt School, Weilheim
1975	BDA-Preis Bayern für Rektoramt und Studentenhaus der Universität Regensburg	BDA Prize of Bavaria for Rector's Office and Student Administration Building, University of Regensburg
1975	BDA-Preis Bayern – Anerkennung für das Verwaltungsgebäude der Wüstenrot, München	BDA Prize of Bavaria – recognition of Wüstenrot administration building, Munich
1976	Preis des deutschen Stahlbaues – Auszeichnung für die Heizzentrale, Offiziersschule der Luftwaffe OSLW, Fürstenfeldbruck	German Steel Construction Industry Prize for heating plant of School for Air Force Officers, Fürstenfeldbruck
1977	Architekturpreis Beton – lobende Erwähnung für Rektoramt und Studentenhaus der Universität Regensburg	Architectural Prize of the Concrete Industry – commendation for Rector's Office and Student Building, University of Regensburg
1977	Fritz Schumacher Preis – Anerkennung für Rektoramt und Studentenhaus der Universität Regensburg	Fritz Schumacher Prize – recognition of Rector's Office and Student Building, University of Regensburg
1977	BDA-Preis Bayern – Anerkennung für die Kommunale Datenzentrale EDV, München	BDA Prize of Bavaria – recognition of Municipal Computer Centre EDP, Munich
1978	›Kurt Ackermann und Partner. Bauten und Projekte‹ als eines der 50 schönsten Bücher durch die Stiftung Buchkunst des Börsenvereins des deutschen Buchhandels prämiert; mit Otl Aicher	*Kurt Ackermann und Partner: Bauten und Projekte*, with Otl Aicher; voted one of the 50 finest books by the Stiftung Buchkunst des Börsenvereins des deutschen Buchhandels – Association of the German Book Trade
1979	BDA-Preis Bayern – Anerkennung für den Kalkschachtofen der Märkerwerke, Harburg/Schwaben	BDA Prize of Bavaria – recognition of vertical limekiln for Märker Cement Works, Harburg, Swabia
1979	Preis für Stadtbildpflege der Landeshauptstadt München für die Kommunale Datenzentrale EDV, München	Prize of the City of Munich for the Cultivation of Urban Form for Municipal Computer Centre EDP, Munich
1979	Preis für Stadtbildpflege der Landeshauptstadt München – lobende Erwähnung für das VBB-Gebäude, München	Prize of the City of Munich for the Cultivation of Urban Form – commendation for the VBB-Building, Munich
1981	BDA-Preis Bayern – Anerkennung für die Offiziersschule der Luftwaffe OSLW, Fürstenfeldbruck	BDA Prize of Bavaria – recognition of School for Air Force Officers, Fürstenfeldbruck

1983	BDA-Preis Bayern für das Eislaufzelt im Olympiapark, München	BDA Prize of Bavaria for tent roof over ice-skating rink in Olympiapark, Munich
1983	Deutscher Architekturpreis – Auszeichnung für das Eislaufzelt im Olympiapark, München	German Architecture Prize for tent roof over ice-skating rink in Olympiapark, Munich
1984	Mies-van-der-Rohe-Preis für das Eislaufzelt im Olympiapark, München	Mies van der Rohe Prize for tent roof over ice-skating rink in Olympiapark, Munich
1984	Preis des deutschen Stahlbaues – Auszeichnung für das Eislaufzelt im Olympiapark, München	German Steel Construction Industry Prize for tent roof over ice-skating rink in Olympiapark, Munich
1986	Architekturpreis der Landeshauptstadt München	Architecture Prize of the City of Munich
1988	Ingenieurbaupreis für die Fußgängerbrücke in Kelheim, mit Jörg Schlaich	Engineering Construction Prize for pedestrian bridge in Kelheim, together with Jörg Schlaich
1989	BDA-Preis Bayern für das Klärwerk Gut Marienhof bei München	BDA Prize of Bavaria for Marienhof Estate Sewage Treatment Plant, near Munich
1989	Deutscher Architekturpreis – Auszeichnung für das Klärwerk Gut Marienhof bei München	German Architecture Prize for Marienhof Estate Sewage Treatment Plant, near Munich
1989	BDA-Preis Bayern – Anerkennung für die Fußgängerbrücke in Kelheim	BDA Prize of Bavaria – recognition of pedestrian bridge in Kelheim
1990	Preis des deutschen Stahlbaues – Auszeichnung für das Klärwerk Gut Marienhof bei München	German Steel Construction Industry Prize for Marienhof Estate Sewage Treatment Plant, near Munich
1990	Constructa-Preis '90, Europäischer Preis für Industriearchitektur für das Klärwerk Gut Marienhof bei München	Constructa Prize '90, European prize for industrial architecture, for Marienhof Estate Sewage Treatment Plant, near Munich
1990	Award for outstanding structures für die Fußgängerbrücke in Kelheim, mit Jörg Schlaich	Award for outstanding structures for pedestrian bridge in Kelheim, together with Jörg Schlaich
1992	Preis des deutschen Stahlbaues – Auszeichnung für die Fußgängerbrücke in Berching	German Steel Construction Industry Prize for pedestrian bridge in Berching
1992	Preis des deutschen Stahlbaues – Auszeichnung für das Leistungszentrum im Olympiapark, München	German Steel Construction Industry Prize for Ice-Skating Training Centre in Olympiapark, Munich
1993	Deutscher Architekturpreis – Anerkennung für Konstruktionsbüro Gartner, Gundelfingen/Donau	German Architecture Prize – recognition of Gartner Construction Office, Gundelfingen/Danube
1993	Auszeichnung Guter Bauten durch den BDA Baden-Württemberg für das Forschungszentrum für Bioverfahrenstechnik der Universität Stuttgart	Good Building Award of BDA Baden-Württemberg for Research Centre for Biological Process Engineering, University of Stuttgart
1994	Preis des Deutschen Stahlbaues – Auszeichnung für Konstruktionsbüro Gartner, Gundelfingen/Donau	German Steel Construction Industry Prize for Gartner Construction Office, Gundelfingen/Danube
1994	Balthasar-Neumann-Preis – Anerkennung für Konstruktionsbüro Gartner, Gundelfingen/Donau	Balthasar Neumann Prize – recognition of Gartner Construction Office, Gundelfingen/Danube
1994	Auszeichnung im Constructec-Preis '94 Europäischer Preis für Industriearchitektur für das Konstruktionsbüro Gartner, Gundelfingen/Donau	Award as part of Constructec Prize '94, European prize for industrial architecture, for Gartner Construction Office, Gundelfingen/Danube
1994	Heinrich-Tessenow-Medaille in Gold der Fritz-Schumacher-Stiftung, verliehen von der Universität Hannover	Heinrich Tessenow Medal in Gold of the Fritz Schumacher Foundation, awarded by the University of Hanover
1995	IAKS-Award in Silver, International Association for Sports, für das Leistungszentrum im Olympiapark, München	International Association for Sports IAKS Award in Silver for Ice-Skating Training Centre in Olympiapark, Munich
1996	Leo-von-Klenze-Medaille des Freistaates Bayern	Leo von Klenze Medal of the Free State of Bavaria

Hopfenrundschau 2/1959 Neuzeitliche Hopfenaufbereitungsanlagen, S. 1/2

Baumeister 10/1962 Der Architekt und das landwirtschaftliche Bauen, S. 1013/1018 · *Bauwelt 40/1965* Möbel kaufen in München, S. 1094/1095

BDA-Informationen 3/1971 Gesamtschule aus anderer Sicht, S. 4/6 · *Baumeister 2/1973* Hardt-Schule in Weilheim, S. 164/168 · *Der Architekt 9/1973* Honorarreform – ein Trauerspiel mit Ignoranz und Unvermögen, S. 209 · *Ein Manifest, November 1973* Manifest für Architektur: mit Max Bächer, Walter Belz, Alexander von Branca, Hans Busso von Busse, Harald Deilmann, Walter M. Förderer, Rolf Gutbrod, Hans Kammerer, Horst Linde, Carlfried Mutschler, Roland Ostertag · *Der Architekt 1/1974* Dieses Heft sieht anders aus, S. 1 · *Architekturwettbewerbe aw 77/1974* Zum Entwerfen von Banken, S. II/XII · *Der Architekt 1/1975* Der Architekt mit einem abermals anderen Gesicht, S. 7 · *Der Architekt 10/1975* Nachruf Karl Schwanzer, S. 414/415 · *Planungsbericht des FBA II München 1975* Offiziersschule der Luftwaffe OSLW in Fürstenfeldbruck, S. 14/93 · *Bauen + Wohnen 12/1975* Nostalgie – Laune oder Herausforderung, S. 486/487 · *Der Architekt 12/1975* Stellungnahme zur Gesamthochschulentwicklung, S. 499/503 · *Baumeister 4/1976* Das Institut für Grundlagen des Entwerfens und Konstruierens, S. 275/277 · *Der Architekt 6/1976* Offene Umgänge an Verwaltungsbauten, S. 247/240 · *Der Architekt 2/1977* Planungs- und Bauablauf eines staatlichen Bauvorhabens, S. 69/73 · *Architekturwettbewerbe aw 90/1977* Vorläufig nichts Neues unter der Sonne, mit Paulhans Peters, S. XIVI/XVI · *db Deutsche Bauzeitung 5/1978* Bauten für die Bundeswehr, S. 5 und S. 39/49 · *Glasforum 3/1979* Architekt und Bauingenieur, S. 3/4 · *Deutsches Architektenblatt 8/1979* Sportbauten – Synthese von Nutzung, Konstruktion und Form, S. 911/913

Deutsches Architektenblatt 5/1980 Bauten für die Olympischen Spiele I, S. 683/684 · *Deutsches Architektenblatt 6/1980* Bauten für die Olympischen Spiele II, S. 847/848 · *Contemporary Architects 1980* Zu meiner Arbeit, S. 12/13 · *Contemporary Architects 1980* Der Ingenieur Fritz Leonhardt, S. 465 · *db Deutsche Bauzeitung 3/1981* Architekt und Ingenieur, S. 10/12 · *Deutsches Architektenblatt 6/1981* Weltausstellungen – vom Kristallpalast bis zum Fuji-Pavillon, S. 899/902 · *Sport und Design,* Ausstellungskatalog des Nationalen Olympischen Komitees für Deutschland 1981, Baden-Baden, Das neue Bauen - Impulse der Olympischen Bauten, S. 64/81 · *Architekturwettbewerbe aw 110/1982* Sportbauten – Synthese von Nutzung, Konstruktion und Form, S. 6/8 · *db Deutsche Bauzeitung 1/1983* Bauen mit Stahl, S. 12/21 · *db Deutsche Bauzeitung 12/1983* Architektur und Industriebau, S. 8/9 · *DBZ Deutsche Bauzeitschrift 1/1985* Industriebau - ein wichtiges Thema, S. 14/15 · *db Deutsche Bauzeitung 8/1986* Brücken ohne Baukunst, S. 48/51 · *archpaper 1985* Architektur USA, Brief an Harald Deilmann, S. 12/17 · *Jahrbuch der Freunde der Universität Stuttgart, 1985* Architektur an dieser Schule, S. 17/33 · *Der Architekt 12/1986* Konstruktive Intelligenz, S. 527/530 · *Rieser Kulturtage Dokumentation 1986* Die technische Ästhetik im Industriebau, Band VI/2, S. 534/539 · *Der Architekt 11/1987* Architektur und Tragwerk, S. 526/528 · *Contemporary Architects 1987* Aus der eigenen Werkstatt, S. 7/9 · *Baumeister 12/1987* Antworten auf ein Pamphlet, S. 17 · *ARCUS 3/1988* ›Architektur und Wissenschaft‹ Das Tragwerk und das konstruktive Detail, Verlagsgesellschaft Rudolf Müller Köln, S. 16/23 · *Der Architekt 10/1988* Corporate Identity - Kontrovers, S. 537 · *archpaper 1988* Architektur Canada, Vier Weltausstellungen: Brüssel – Montreal – Osaka – Vancouver, S. 54/63 · *Bauen mit Aluminium 23. Jahrgang 1988/89* Industriebau und Architektur, S. 6/7 · *Hundert Jahre Märker 1889/1989* Bauen im Märkerwerk seit 1958, Märker Zementwerk, Harburg 1989, S. 18/23 · *Baumeister 1/1989* Kontinuität der Moderne. Bauen und Lehren, S. 31/33 · *db Deutsche Bauzeitung 10/1989* Rund und klar. Klärwerk Gut Marienhof, S. 10/15 · *Deutsches Architektenblatt 12/1989* Architekturpreis München für Werner Wirsing, S. 1777/1778

Deutsches Architektenblatt 3/1990 Kein Vorurteil gegen Industriebau, S. 360/361 · *Der Architekt 10/1991* Unsere Arbeit wird sich immer ändern, S. 493/496 · *BDA-Information Landesverband Bayern 1/1992* Zum Tod von Otl Aicher, S. 5/6 · *Stuttgarter Architektur Schule* Lehre am Institut für Entwerfen und Konstruieren, Universität Stuttgart 1992, S. 102/103 · *Konstruktionsbüro Gartner. Architektur und angewandte Technologie* von Paulhans Peters und Kurt Ackermann, Bauen, ein Bekenntnis zum Machen, Karl Krämer Verlag, Stuttgart 1993, S. 92/93 · *Architektur der Gegenwart* Hrsg. Peter Schweger, Wilhelm Meyer, Intelligente Konstruktionen, Konzepte, Projekte, Bauten, Kohlhammer Verlag, Stuttgart 1993, S. 10/13 · *Architekturschule München, Technische Universität München 1868/1993* Hrsg. Winfried Nerdinger, Über Studienzeiten an der Technischen Hochschule München, Verlag Klinkhardt + Biermann, München 1993, S. 140/141 · *Stiftung F.V.S zu Hamburg, Fritz Schumacher Stiftung 1994* Dank für Tessenow-Medaille, S. 17/20 · *AIT 4/1994 Architektur, Innenarchitektur Technischer Ausbau* Konstruktiv – über intelligente Architektur, S. 16/19 · *JA The Japan Architekt 1994-4* Fumihiko Maki – Place, Scale and Transparency, S. 122/123 · *Der Architekt 11/1994* Machen setzt praktische Kenntnisse voraus, S. 634/635 · *Das Bauzentrum 1/1995* Konstruktionsbüro Gartner, Angewandte Stahlbau-Technologie, S. 1/44–51 · *Entwerfen und Denkmalpflege 1976/1995* Otto Meitinger, Über unsere Arbeit, Technische Universität München, 1995, S. 94/95 · *Jahrbuch für Licht und Architektur 1995* Christian Bartenbach. Ingenieur, Forscher und Erfinder in Sachen Licht, S. 41/45 · *BDA-Informationen 2/1996* Von Klenze lernen, S. 8/11 · *bauintern, Zeitschrift Bayerische Staatsbauverwaltung 7/1996* Leo-von-Klenze-Medaille des Freistaates Bayern, S. 11/12 · *Der Architekt 11/1996* Finden statt Erfinden, S. 704/706 · *Ingenieure und Architekten – eine Entwicklung* Josef Hegger, Winfried Führer, Höher, leichter, weiter? RWTH Aachen 1997, S. 7/14 · *Architekten: Apocalypse now?* Hrsg. Ursula Baus, Brief an Wilfried Dechau, DVA, Stuttgart 1997, S. 72 · *Freundschaft und Begegnung, Erinnerungen an Otl Aicher* Hrsg. Stiftung Hochschule für Gestaltung Ulm, 1997, Brotzeit oder Picknick – auf die Qualität kam's an, S. 44/47

**Buchveröffentlichungen
von Kurt Ackermann**
Books
by Kurt Ackermann

Kurt Ackermann und Partner
Bauten und Projekte
Karl Krämer Verlag, Stuttgart 1978

Grundlagen für das Entwerfen und Konstruieren
Karl Krämer Verlag, Stuttgart 1983

Industriebau
5 Auflagen
DVA, Stuttgart 1984

Tragwerke in der konstruktiven Architektur
DVA, Stuttgart 1988

Building for Industry
Watermark Publications, London, Hongkong 1991

Geschoßbauten für Gewerbe und Industrie
DVA, Stuttgart 1993

Architekt-Ingenieur
Karl Krämer Verlag, Stuttgart 1997

Neue deutsche Architektur 3, Wolfgang Pehnt, Verlag Gerd Hatje, Stuttgart 1965, S. 28/29 · *Bauen und Wohnen 2/1969* Portrait Kurt Ackermann, Ernst Appel, S. 112/114

Journal Retour I 1972 TH München, Hans Doellgast, Eigenverlag, S. 15 · *Baumeister 2/1973* Der Schulbau – das wahre Gesicht einer Gesellschaft, Felix von Cube, S. 160/163 · *Der Architekt 3/1975* Die Universitäten Konstanz und Regensburg, Hans Kammerer, S. 137/142 · *Baumeister 12/1978* skin and skeleton, Paulhans Peters, S. 1044 · *Baumeister 12/1978* Die letzten zwanzig Jahre in der Architektur, Paulhans Peters, S. 1122/1169 · *Das Kunstwerk April/Mai 1979* Architektur in Deutschland, Helge Bofinger, S. 16/17

Contemporary Architects 1980 Über Kurt Ackermann, Jürgen Joedicke, S. 13/14 · *Ein Architekt sieht München* Die Straßenkreuzung am Stiglmaier-platz, von Christoph Hackelsberger, Heinrich Hugendubel Verlag 1981, S. 27/31 · *Baumeister 1/1982* Architekturbüros in sechs Ländern, Paulhans Peters, S. 28/29 · *Vergangenheit–Gegenwart–Zukunft* Gegenwarts-Architek-tur, Frank Werner, Häuser + Architektur, Frank Werner, 1982, S. 174/212 · *Lufthansa's Germany 6/1983* German Architecture Revitalized, Manfred Sack, S. 26/35 · *Stadt 3/1983* Münchens Architekten sind plötzlich wer …, Gottfried Knapp, S. 32/39 · *Baumeister 1/1984* Industriebau – drei Konzeptionen, Paul-hans Peters, S. 8/9 · *Der Architekt 1/1984* Leitartikel 1974/1984, Ingeborg Flagge, S. 3 · *Baumeister in einer umwälzenden Zeit* Leichte Flächentrag-werke, von Fritz Leonhardt, DVA, Stuttgart 1984, S. 232 · *Architekturführer Bayern* Architektur in München, Gottfried Knapp, Hrsg. BDA 1985, S. 13/16 · *db Deutsche Bauzeitung 10/1986* Industriebau, Bernhard Tokarz, S. 17/19 · *Domus 7/8 1987* Portrait Kurt Ackermann, S. IV · *Contemporary Architects 1987* Über Kurt Ackermann, Jürgen Joedicke, S. 9 · *IBA-Berlin 87* Beispiele einer neuen Architektur, Heinrich Klotz, Deutsches Architektur-Museum Frankfurt/Main, S. 107 · *Der Architekt 2/1988* BDA-Rückblick, Ingeborg Flagge, S. 111 · *Der Architekt 3/1988* Kurt Ackermann 60 Jahre, Werner Kaag, S. 174 · *Rückblicke – Ausblicke* Beiträge für Kurt Ackermann zum 2.3.1988, Jürgen Joedicke, Hans Kammerer, Gustl Lachenmann, Werner Kaag u.a., Hrsg. Institut für Entwerfen und Konstruieren, Universität Stuttgart 1988 · *News Internationale Academy of Architecture 4/1989* Portrait Kurt Acker-mann, Pierre Vago, S. 3 · *Art 8/1989* Ein Klärwerk wurde zur Landmarke, Peter M. Bode, S. 19 · *Stadtbauwelt 36/1989* Kai reit panta, Gert Kähler, S. 1687/1693

Baumeister 4/1990 Expo '92 Sevilla, Paulhans Peters, S. 11/12 · *Architektur im Wandel* Hrsg. Friedbert Kind-Barkauskas Entwicklungen der modernen Architektur, Friedbert Kind-Barkauskas, Beton Verlag 1990, S. 9/10 · *Industrie-architektur in Europa '90* Hrsg. Helmut C. Schulitz, Corporate Identity-Indu-striekultur?, Helmut C. Schulitz, Messe Hannover 1990, S. 8/33 · *Deutsches Architektenblatt 8/1991* Zur Planungssituation im Industriebau, Michael Jockers, S. 1193/96 · *Deutsches Architektenblatt 10/1991* Kann Industriebau an einer Hochschule gelehrt werden, Helmut C. Schulitz, S. 1593/1598 · *Deutsches Architektenblatt 12/1991* Die industrielle Arbeitswelt muß nicht schäbig sein, Ingeborg Flagge, S. 1966/68 · *Rund um den Ammersee* Hrsg. Manfred Hummel, Das Wunder von Andechs – über die transparente und funktionelle Architektur des Kurt Ackermann, Wolfgang Prochaska, München 1992 und 1994, S. 26/29 · *Baumeister 12/1992* Über Münchens neue Büro-zentrale, Gerhard Matzig, S. 36/39 · *db Deutsche Bauzeitung 6/1992* Fußball-stadion Stuttgart – Studentenarbeiten bei Kurt Ackermann, S. 176/180 · *Design Journal, Seoul 45/1992* Portrait Kurt Ackermann, S. 18/19 · *Der Archi-tekt 1/1993* Ein anderer Architekt, Ingeborg Flagge, S. 1 · *Deutsches Architek-tenblatt 3/1993* Kurt Ackermann 65, S. 373 · *Andechs* von Josef Othmar Zöller, Marion Kloss, Pfortenhof-Überdachung, Josef Othmar Zöller, Pannonia, Freilassing 1993, S. 44 · *Arch+ 9/1993 Nr. 118* Junge Architekten in Süd-deutschland – Das Stuttgarter Beispiel –, Kaye Geipel, S. 42/48 · *Die neue deutsche Architektur* von G. Feldmeyer, Das Klärwerk Gut Marienhof, Man-fred Sack, Kohlhammer Verlag, Stuttgart 1993, S. 27/31 · *Alfred Toepfer Stiftung F.V.S., Hannover 1994* Verleihung der Heinrich-Tessenow-Medaille in Gold 1994, Laudatio, Klaus Stiglat, S. 11/13 · *Art-EP 9/1994* EPA München. rhythmus im raum, Max Bill, S. 1/2 Titelblatt · *Industriearchitektur in Europa '94* Hrsg. Helmut C. Schulitz, Messe Hannover 1994, Licht und Industrie-architektur, Helmut C. Schulitz, S. 10/37 · *Werk, Bauen + Wohnen 3/1995* Pariserplatz 4, Dieter Hoffmann-Axthelm, S. 49/64 · *Arbeitsplatz Deutschland*

Werkbericht des BM für Raumordnung, Bauwesen und Städtebau Industrie-
bau, Helmut C. Schulitz, Bonn 1995, S. 96/97 · *AIA-Architect 10/1996* Interna-
tional Markets and Practice, S. 8 · *Profil 8/1996* Expo 2000 – Halle 13 und
Eingang West, Hubertus von Bothmer, S. 3 · *Euro-Bau 8/9/1996* Qualität des
Normalen, Günther Ludvik, S. 17 · *Der Architekt 5/1996* Blick zurück, Ingeborg
Flagge, S. 277 · *bau-Intern 7/1996* Leo-von-Klenze-Medaille, Laudatio, Alfred
Sauter, S. 8/10 · *Baumeister 7/1997* Die endlose Stadtbildpflege. Planen und
Bauen seit 1945, Winfried Nerdinger, S. 18/25 · *Baumeister 7/1997* München
bleibt München, vom schweren Stand zeitgemäßer Architektur, Gottfried
Knapp, S. 49 · *Bauwelt 33/1997* Hannover – die Expo – die Stadt, Dietmar
Brandenburger, S. 1788/1797 · *Baumeister 12/1997* Architektur konstruieren,
Ulrich Knaack, S. 50/53 · *Otl Aicher zum 75. Geburtstag* Beiträge zu einer
modernen Zivilisation, Eva von Seckendorff, Ulmer Museum, Archiv 1997,
S. 48/51 · *BDA-Informationen 1/1998* Kurt Ackermann 70, Wolfgang Jean
Stock, S. 22/23 · *Baumeister 2/1998* Campus, Studieren in Stuttgart,
C. Joseph Stein, S. 62/63 · *Baumeister 3/1998* Die ungeliebten Orte –
Zweckbauten für Stadthygiene und Sicherheit, Wolfgang Jean Stock, S. 17 ·
Baumeister 3/1998 Orte der Verdrängung – was nicht geliebt wird, muß
auch nicht schön sein, Gottfried Knapp, S. 38/41 · *Baumeister 3/1998* Wech-
sel im Bauhaus Dessau, S. 12 · *Der Architekt 4/1998* Kurt Ackermann wurde
70 Jahre alt, Walter Belz, S. 191

Publikationen
der Bauten und Projekte
Publications
on the Buildings and Projects

1956 *Bauen + Wohnen 9/1956* Gästehaus Josef Gartner, Gundelfingen/
Donau, S. 308/310; *12/1956* Haus Viktor Gartner, Gundelfingen/Donau,
S. 421/422

1957 *m + d Möbel + Dekoration 6/1957* Haus Erl, Grünwald, S. 302/304.
Blumenfenster von Paulhans Peters, Callwey-Verlag, München 1957, Haus
Erl, München, S. 80; Haus Endter, München, S. 81

1958 *Baumeister 1/1958* Haus Endter, München, S. 36/37; *12/1958* Haus
Holzbauer, Gauting, S. 872/875, Titelblatt · *Das Haus, Mai 1958* Haus Bau-
mann, München, S. 7/8; Haus Erl, Grünwald, S. 8/9 · *m + d Möbel + Dekoration 10/1958* Wohnung Ackermann, München, S. 516/517 · *Wasserbecken im
Garten* von Paulhans Peters, Callwey-Verlag, München 1958, Haus Endter,
München, S. 87 · *Innenausbau im Wohnhaus* von Haberer-Eichhorn, Kohlhammer-Verlag, Stuttgart 1958, Haus Erl, München, S. 173, 176

1959 *Baumeister 1/1959* Modehaus Kraus, München, S. 20/21; *10/1959*
Hopfenhalle Mainburg, S. 624/627, 2 Detailtafeln S. 60/61, Titelblatt · *Die
Kunst, Aug. 1959* Haus Holzbauer, Gauting, S. 427/429 · *Das kleine Haus*
von Rainer Wolf, Callwey-Verlag, München 1959, Haus Lang, Garmisch-
Partenkirchen, S. 44/45

1960 *Baumeister 10/1960* Verwaltungsgebäude Hopfenpflanzerverband,
Wolnzach, S. 714/717 · *Die Bauverwaltung 10/1960* Bundesbediensteten
Wohnungen in Neuburg/Donau, S. 423 · *Die Kunst, Dez. 1960* Haus Peters,
Sibichhausen, S. 112/115 · *Schöner Wohnen, Apr. 1960* Schwimmbecken
Endter, München · *Raumausstatter 12/1960* Wohnung Ackermann, München,
S. 661/662 · *Das Ideale Heim 12/1960* Haus Holzbauer, Gauting, S. 489/493 ·
Zentralblatt für Industriebau 8/1960 Hopfenhalle Mainburg, S. 385/391 · *Ziegel-
arbeitsblätter 8/1960* Haus Holzbauer, Gauting, S. 567 · *Neue Ferienhäuse*r
von Paulhans Peters, Callwey-Verlag, München 1960, Dachdetail, S. 23

1961 *Baumeister 9/1961* Haus Peters, Sibichhausen, S. 622/625; *10/1961* Hopfenhalle Klotz, Wolnzach, S. 980/981 · *ac Internationale Asbestzement Revue 21/1961* Hopfenhalle Klotz, Wolnzach, S. 14/15, 50 · *Deutscher Werkbund 2/1961* Wohnraum Peters, Sibichhausen, S. 47 · *Die Kunst, Juli 1961* Haus Geisler, Gauting, S. 392/395; *Nov. 1961* Haus Eugen Höfter, Neuhausen bei Mainburg, S. 67/72; *Dez. 1961* Haus Bruno Höfter, Mainburg, S. 115/119 · *Zentralblatt für Industriebau 12/1961* Hopfenhalle Klotz, Wolnzach, S. 628/632

1962 *Bauen + Wohnen 1/1962* Hypobank München-Schwabing, S. I1/I2; *4/1962* Haus Ackermann, Herrsching, S. 164/166, 2 Detailblätter · *Baumeister 9/1962* Haus Ackermann, Herrsching, S. 859/864, Detailtafel S. 63, Titelblatt; *9/1962* Wohnanlage Meßner, München, S. 882/884, Detailtafel 64 · *DBZ Deutsche Bauzeitschrift 2/1962* Haus Lang, Garmisch-Partenkirchen, S. 194; *8/1962* Haus Geisler, Gauting, S. 1201/1202; *12/1962* Hopfenhalle Klotz, Wolnzach, S. 1901 · *Detail 1/1962* Hopfenhalle Mainburg, S. 36; *3/1962* Hopfenhalle Klotz, Wolnzach, S. 245, Titelblatt · *Die Kunst, April 1962* Haus Viktor Gartner, Gundelfingen, S. 307/312 · *The Architect + Building News, März 1962* Hopfenhalle Klotz, Wolnzach, S. 447/449, Titelblatt · *Zentralblatt für Industriebau 2/1962* Titanbrecher Märker Zementwerk, Harburg/Schwaben S. 68/71 · *Industriebau, Internationale Beispiele* von Walter Henn, Callwey-Verlag, München 1962, Hopfenhalle Mainburg, S. 54/55 · *Der offene Kamin* von Fritz R. Barran, J. Hoffmann-Verlag, Stuttgart 1962; Haus Geisler, Gauting, S. 176

1963 *Bauen + Wohnen 9/1963* Fertigungshalle BMW, München, S. 392/395, Detailblatt; *11/1963* Wettbewerb Oskar-von-Miller-Polytechnikum, München, S. XI 10/XI 12 · *Baumeister 12/1963* Haus Kammermeier, München, S. 1388/1391, Detailtafeln S. 82/83 · *DBZ Deutsche Bauzeitschrift 1/1963* Wohnanlage Meßner, München, S. 31/32; *7/1963* Haus Ackermann, Herrsching, S. 999/1000 · *db Deutsche Bauzeitung 1/1963* Haus Viktor Gartner, Gundelfingen, S. 44/45 · *Detail 4/1963* Haus Ackermann, Herrsching, S. 430 · *Informationsdienst Holz 4/5/1963* Haus Ackermann, Herrsching, S. 6 · *Ziegelarbeitsblätter 5/1963* Haus Eugen Höfter, Neuhausen, S. 17 · *33 Architekten – 33 Einfamilienhäuser* von Pfau/Zietzschmann, *Bauen + Wohnen*, Otto Maier Verlag, Ravensburg 1963, Haus Kammermeier, München, S. 2/3 · *150 Einfamilienhäuser* von L. Koller, Bruckmann-Verlag, München 1963, Haus Holzbauer, Gauting, S. 64/65 · *Unser Haus* von S. Nagel – K. Frank, Bertelsmann-Verlag1963, Haus Peters, Sibichhausen, S. 61

1964 *Bauen + Wohnen 12/1964* Haus Dr. Fischer, München, S. 486/489, Detailblatt · *Baumeister 1/1964* Fertigungshalle BMW, München, S. 3/7; *3/1964* Offene Kamine, Haus Ackermann, Herrsching, S. EB 22; *8/1964* Märker Zementwerk, Harburg/Schwaben, S. 860/863, Detailblatt 59/60, Titelblatt; *9/1964* Haus Viktor Gartner, Gundelfingen, S. EB 66 · *Bauwelt SH 1964* Eßplatz Haus Peters, Sibichhausen, S. 13; *SH 1964* Eßplatz Haus Ackermann, Herrsching, S. 14 · *DBZ Deutsche Bauzeitschrift 3/1964* Haus Ackermann, Herrsching, S. 313/314; *3/1964* Wettbewerb Oskar-von-Miller-Polytechnikum, München, S. 358/360 · *Die Kunst, Febr. 1964* Haus Ackermann, Herrsching, S. 212; *Sept. 1964* Haus Kammermeier, München, S. 522/526, Titelblatt · *Das Ideale Heim 7/1964* Haus Lang, Garmisch-Partenkirchen, S. 277/280 · *Zentralblatt für Industriebau 8/1964* Fertigungshalle BMW, München, S. 360/365, Titelblatt; *11/1964* Märker Zementwerk, Harburg/Schwaben, S. 510/517, Titelblatt · *Mehrfamilienhäuser* von Gerhard Schwab, DVA, Stuttgart 1964, Haus Holzbauer, Gauting, S. 30/35 · *Kamine* von Ernst Danz, Hatje-Verlag, Stuttgart 1964, Haus Ackermann, Herrsching, S. 13, 124 · *Ziegeltaschenbuch* von O. Banditt, Krausskopf-Verlag, 1964, Haus E. Höfter, Neuhausen, S. 110 · *Treppen* von Franz Schuster, J. Hoffmann-Verlag, Stuttgart 1964, Hopfenhalle Mainburg, S. 112 · *Fenster, Fensterwände aus Holz*, Callwey-Verlag, München 1964, Hopfenhalle Klotz, Wolnzach, S. 12 · *Architektur-Fotografie* von Joachim Giebelhausen, Verlag Großbild-Technik 1964, Haus Viktor Gartner, Gundelfingen, S. 62/63

1965 *Baumeister 4/1965* Gästehaus Graf von Norman, Icking, S. 373/376; *6/1965* Mehrfamilienhaus Höfter, München, S. 629/632, Detailtafel · *db Deutsche Bauzeitung 2/1965* Mehrfamilienhaus Höfter, München, S. 97/99, Detail S. 138 · *Detail 2/1965* Haus Kammermeier, München, S. 176; *3/1965* Mehrfamilienhaus Höfter, München, S. 406 · *ac Internationale Asbestzement Revue 40/1965* Märker Zementwerk, Harburg/Schwaben, S. 34 und 36 · *Deutscher Werkbund 2/1965* Wohnraum Kammermeier, München, S. 22; *2/1965* Wohnraum Peters, Sibichhausen, S. 47 · *Die Kunst, Sept. 1965* Haus Dr. Fischer, München, S. 534/538 · *Geformter Stein* von Hans F. Erb 1965, Flugsicherungs-Leitstelle, München, S. 65 · *Lager und Speicher* von W. Schramm, Bauverlag, Wiesbaden 1965, Hopfenhalle Klotz, Wolnzach, S. 237 · *Wände, Treppen, Außendetails in Beton*, Callwey-Verlag, München 1965, Wohnanlage Höfter, München, S. 54/55; Hopfenhalle, Mainburg, S. 96/97 · *ac agr* von O. Riege, Verlag Girsberger, Zürich 1965, Hopfenhalle Klotz, Wolnzach, S. 159/160

1966 *Bauen + Wohnen 4/1966* Wettbewerb Universität Regensburg, S. IV/12 · *Baumeister 2/1966* Heizhaus der Bundesmonopolverwaltung, München, S. 140/141; *5/1966* Wettbewerb Universität Regensburg, S. EB 37; *9/1966* Städtebau-Wettbewerb Ingolstadt, S. 1058; *11/1966* Wettbewerb Krankenhaus Mallersdorf, S. EB 83; *Bauwelt 25/1966* Wettbewerb Kreissparkasse, Mainburg, S. 730/731; *DBZ Deutsche Bauzeitschrift 4/1966* Haus Dr. Fischer, München, S. 603/606; *4/1966* Märker Zementwerk, Harburg/Schwaben, S. 593/594; *5/1966* Wettbewerb Universität Regensburg, S. 904; *db Deutsche Bauzeitung 9/1966* Landwirtschaftliche Berufsschule Mainburg, S. 745 · *Glasforum 2/1966* Haus Dr. Kammermeier, München, S. 16/18, Detail S. 40; *2/1966* Haus Dr. Fischer, München, S. 19/21 · *Die Kunst, Febr. 1966* Gästehaus Graf von Norman, Icking, S. 218/222; *Zentralblatt für Industriebau 4/1966* Heizhaus der Bundesmonopolverwaltung München, S. 162/165 · *Bauen mit Holz* von Hoffmann/Griese, J. Hoffmann-Verlag, Stuttgart 1966, Haus Graf von Norman, Icking, S. 71; Haus Kammermeier, München, S. 152 · *Bauen in Sichtbeton* von Bächer/Heinle, J. Hoffmann-Verlag, Stuttgart 1966, Wohnanlage Höfter, München, S. 111 · *Einfamilienhäuser 51–100* von Gerhard Schwab, DVA, Stuttgart 1966, Haus Viktor Gartner, Gundelfingen, S. 6, 42, 43 · *Die Geschichte der deutschen Treppe* von Mielke, Verlag Wilhelm Ernst + Sohn, München-Berlin 1966, Hopfenhalle, Mainburg, S. 338 · *Stahlkonstruktionen im Hochbau* von Gatz/Hart, Callwey-Verlag, München 1966, Haus Ackermann, Herrsching, S. 50 · *Farbe am Bau* von Gatz/Achterberg, Callwey-Verlag, München 1966, Haus Ackermann, Herrsching, S. 27

1967 *Bauen + Wohnen 1/1967* Hypobank München-Schwabing, S. 8/13, Detailblätter · *db Deutsche Bauzeitung 6/1967* Wettbewerb Neue Pinakothek, München, S. 439; *10/1967* Zentralgarage Korn, Rothenburg ob der Tauber, S. 800/801 · *Detail 4/1967* Landwirtschaftliche Berufsschule Mainburg, S. 655/656 · *i.e.t.c.c informe de la construción 187/1967* Märker Zementwerk, Harburg/Schwaben, S. 45/51 · *L'Architecture d'aujourd'hui 9/1967* Märker Zementwerk, Harburg/Schwaben, S. XLIX · *Terra 2/1967* Landwirtschaftliche Berufsschule, Mainburg, S. 4/7, Titelblatt · *Bouw, Nov. 1967* Wohnanlage Höfter, München, S. 1638/1639 · *Informationsdienst Holz 446/1967* Haus Kammermeier, München, S. 6 · *Zentralblatt für Industriebau 11/1967* Flugsicherungs-Leitstelle München, S. 470/471 · *Zuhause 10/1967* Haus Dr. Kammermeier, München, S. 10/12 · *Kamine + Kachelöfen*, Callwey-Verlag, München 1967, Haus Graf von Norman, Icking; Haus Ackermann, Herrsching, S. 14 · *Die schöne Wohnung* von L. Koller, Bruckmann-Verlag, München 1967, Haus Ackermann, Herrsching, S. 44, 86, 149; Haus Gartner, Gundelfingen, S. 100, 101; Haus B. Höfter, Mainburg, S. 11, 18, 35; Haus Peters, Sibichhausen, S. 63, 145

1968 *Baumeister 2/1968* Wettbewerb XX. Olympiade Schwimmhalle, München, S. 32/133/151 · *DBZ Deutsche Bauzeitschrift 5/1968* Landwirtschaftliche Berufsschule Mainburg, S. 723/724; *9/1968* Hypobank München-Schwabing, S. 1405/1410; *9/1968* Werkhalle 2 Götz, Deggendorf, S. 1411/1412 · *db Deutsche Bauzeitung 9/1968* Städtebauwettbewerb Münchener Freiheit, S. 687/694 · *I – Punkt Farbe 1/1968* Haus Ackermann, Herrsching, S. 2 · *Zentralblatt für Industriebau 2/1968* Werkhalle 2 Götz, Deggendorf, S. 80; *8/1968* Werkhalle 2 Götz, Deggendorf, S. 336/337 · *Einfamilienhäuser, Bungalows, Ferienhäuser* von Nagel/Linke, Bertelsmann Verlag, 1968, Haus Ackermann, Herrsching, S. 82/83 · *Reiseführer zur modernen Architektur* von Grete Hoffmann, J. Hoffmann-Verlag, Stuttgart 1968, Hypobank, München, S. 129; Haus Dr. Kammermeier, München, S. 127 · *Internationale Architektur Dokumentation 2* von D. v. Kellen, Verlag Ten Hagen NV, 1968, Märker Zementwerk, Harburg/Schwaben; Heizhaus Monopolverwaltung München; Haus Dr. Fischer, München, S. 83/89

1969 *Bauen + Wohnen 2/1969* Porträt Kurt Ackermann; Hopfenhalle, Mainburg, Märker Zementwerk, Harburg/Schwaben; Haus Ackermann, Herrsching; Fertigungshalle BMW, München; Höfter I, Heizhaus Fürstenfeldbruck; Kammermeier, Fischer, Hypo, Oly. Dorf, Neubiberg, Meisel, G. Moll, Wohnanlage Moll, Schulz, Bauwettbewerb, Friedenskirche, Christuskirche, S. II/2, II/4; *10/1969* Wettbewerb Konzertsaal Arabella-Park, München · *Baumeister 1/1969* Wettbewerb Verwaltungsgebäude der BMW, München, S. 16/17; *4/1969* Lehrwerkhalle, Ausbildungshalle, Zentralwerkstatt Flughafen Neubiberg, S. 412/413; *8/1969* Wettbewerb Konzertsaal Arabella-Park, München, S. 970/971 · *DBZ Deutsche Bauzeitschrift 6/1969* Lehrwerkhalle, Ausbildungshalle, Zentralwerkstatt Flughafen Neubiberg, Titelblatt, S. 1079/1082 · *Glasforum 1/1969* Hypo-Bank, München-Schwabing, S. 24/26/42/43 · *Detail 5/1969* Halle II, Götz Metallbau, Deggendorf, S. 32/33/39 · *Zentralblatt für Industriebau 9/1969* Lehrwerkhalle, Ausbildungshalle, Zentralwerkstatt Flughafen Neubiberg, S. 350/353, Titelblatt · *Bauen in Deutschland* von Alfred Simon, Bacht Verlag, Essen 1969, Märker Zementwerk, Harburg/Schwaben, S. 10 · *Der Ein- und Zweifamilienhauskatalog München*, Fachzeitschriften-Verlag Schmiden, 1969, Haus Dr. Kammermeier, S. 170 · *Ziegelkonstruktionen im Hochbau* von Göbel/Gatz, Callwey-Verlag, München 1969, Berufsschule Mainburg, S. 141 · *Verwaltungsbauten* von Nagel/Linke, Bertelsmann-Verlag, 1969, Hypobank, München, S. 182/185, 188 · *Industriebauten* von Nagel/Linke, Bertelsmann-Verlag, 1969, Götz Metallbau, Deggendorf, S. 64/65; Märker Zementwerk, Harburg/Schwaben, S. 8/79 · *Stahltreppen* von Hoffmann/Grieße, J. Hoffmann-Verlag, Stuttgart 1969, Haus Graf von Norman, Icking, S. 19; Hypobank, München, S. 104/105; Haus Dr. Fischer, München, S. 105 · *Internationale Architektur Dokumentation 3* von D. v. Kellen, Verlag Ten Hagen, 1969, Hypobank, München S. 72, Märker Zementwerk, Harburg/ Schwaben, S. 132; Zentralgarage Korn, Rothenburg, S. 140; Hopfenhalle, Mainburg, S. 332

1970 *Bauen + Wohnen 5/1970* Wettbewerb Verwaltungsgebäude Bayerische Rückversicherung, München, S. V/1 bis C/3 · *Baumeister 5/1970* Wettbewerb Hauptverwaltung der Hypo-Bank, Arabella-Park, München, S. 552/553 · *DBZ Deutsche Bauzeitschrift 10/1970* Haus Meisel, Feldafing, S. 1943/1944; *12/1970* Schwimmbad Dr. Märker, Harburg/Schwaben, S. 2405/2406 · *db Deutsche Bauzeitung 7/1970* Mehrfamilienhaus Höfter, München, S. 517 · *Die Bauverwaltung 2/1970* Wettbewerb Oberpostdirektion, Freiburg/Breisgau, S. 82/87; *8/1970* Universität Regensburg, S. 465/471 · *Zement – Kalk – Gips 8/1970* Verladeanlage Märker Zementwerk, Harburg/Schwaben, Titelblatt · *Neue Wohn-Formen* von Walter Meyer-Bohe, Verlag Wasmuth, Tübingen 1970, Haus Dr. Kammermeier, München, S. 115/118 · *Neue deutsche Architektur* von Wolfgang Pehnt, Verlag Gerd Hatje, Stuttgart 1970, Architekturtheorie-Zitat, S. 28/29 · *Güterumschlaglager + Verteiler* von Peters/Wild, Callwey-Verlag 1970, Lager und Verwaltung, Schneider + Söhne, München, S. 48/49 · *Mehrzweckgebäude für gesellschaftliche Funktionen* von Peters/Wild, Callwey-Verlag, München 1970, Konzertsaal Arabella, München, S. 104/107 · *Bauten für Berufsausbildung* von Peter/Wild, Callwey-Verlag, München 1970, Schulungszentrum BMW, München, S. 122/127

1971 *Baumeister 1/1971* Projekt Hypo-Bank, München, Isartorplatz, S. 46/47; *2/1971* Wettbewerb Gesamtschule München-Nord, S. 143; *8/1971* Wohnanlage Moll, München, S. 909/914; *8/1971* Universität Regensburg Zentrumbauten, S. 953/954; *12/1971* Lager und Verwaltung Schneider + Söhne, München, S. 1528/1529 · *Bauwelt 17/1971* Feuerwache 4 – Kinderspieldachgarten, München, S. 711; *18/1971* Planungsbericht Universität Regensburg, S. 749; *33/1971* Wohnanlage Moll, München, S. 1341/1344 Titelblatt · *aw – Architekturwettbewerbe, 67/1971* Wettbewerb Gesamtschule München-Nord, S. 69 · *Schöner Wohnen, Jan. 1971* Feuerwache 4, München, S. 30 · *Z-Ziegel 1/1971* Wohnanlage Moll, München, S. 15/16; *2/1971* Wohnanlage Moll, München, Förderpreis, S. 2/11 · *Landwirtschaftliche Schulbauten* von Harald Deilmann, Bertelsmann-Verlag, 1971, Berufsschule Mainburg, S. 174/175 · *ac – Industrie* von O. Riege, Verlag Girsberg, 1971, Märker Zementwerk, Harburg/Schwaben, S. 91/93

1972 *Bauen + Wohnen 1/1972* Bürohaus Weißenberger, München, S. 16/17; *1/1972* Wohn- und Geschäftshaus Weishaupt, München, S. 32/34 · *Bauwelt 8/1972* Wohnanlage Moll, München, S. 321; *8/1972* Märker Zementwerk, Harburg/Schwaben, S. 321; *48/1972* Christuskirche, Bad Füssing, S. 1829/1831, Titelblatt; *48/1972* Friedenskirche, Gundelfingen, S. 1832/34 · *db Deutsche Bauzeitung 11/1972* Feuerwache 4, München, S. 1196/1201, Titelblatt · *Detail 1/1972* Wohnanlage Moll, München, S. 23/28 · *Deutsches Architektenblatt 4/1972* Märker Zementwerk, Harburg/Schwaben, S. 205; *4/1972* Wohnanlage Moll, München, S. 206 · *Beton 5/1972* Märker Zementwerk, Harburg/Schwaben, S. 12, Titelblatt · *Beton Prisma 23/1972* Wohn- und Geschäftshaus Weishaupt, München, S. 14/15 · *DLW – Nachrichten 53/1972* Universität Regensburg, S. 33 · *Werk 6/1972* Märker Zementwerk, Harburg/Schwaben, S. 318/319 · *Zement 71/1972* Märker Zementwerk, Harburg/Schwaben, S. 11 · *Bauten und Plätze in München*, Callwey-Verlag, München 1972 Wohnanlage Moll, München, S. 158; Hypobank, München-Schwabing, S. 106 · Feuerwache 4, München, S. 133

1973 *Bauen + Wohnen 2/1973* Bürozentrum Schulz, München, S. 72/74; *7/1973* Fertigungshalle Wanderer-Werke, München-Haar, S. 282/284, Titelblatt; *9/1973* Projekt Wohnanlage Winterling, München-Obermenzing, S. 366/367; *12/1973* Haus Dr. Josef Gartner, Gundelfingen, S. 502/503 · *Baumeister 2/1973* Hardtschule, Weilheim, S. 159/170, Titelblatt; *5/1973* IWIS-Kettenfabrik Winklhofer, München, S. 615/617; *7/1973* Haus Gerhard Moll, Pullach, S. 918/919 · *DBZ – Deutsche Bauzeitschrift 10/1973* Hardtschule, Weilheim, S. 1981/1982 · *10/1973* Schulsporthalle, Weilheim, S. 1985/1986 · *db Deutsche Bauzeitung 10/1973* Fertigungshalle III – Götz Metallbau, Deggendorf, S. 1106/1107, Titelblatt; *11/1973* Bürozentrum Schulz München, S. 1256/1258 · *Die Mappe 9/1973* Feuerwache 4, München · *Beton Prisma 25/1973* Märker Zementwerk, Harburg/Schwaben, S. 1/5 · *Zentralblatt für Industriebau 2/1973* Lagerhalle und Verwaltung Schneider + Söhne, München, S. 73/74 · *Stadt für Menschen* von Paulhans Peters, Callwey-Verlag, München 1973; Wohnanlage Moll, München, S. 140, 173; Spielplatz Feuerwache 4, München, S. 177 · *Kirchenbau in der Diskussion*, Deutsche Gesellschaft für christliche Kunst, Kunst-Katalog 1973, Friedenskirche, Gundelfingen, S. 22/23; Christuskirche, Bad Füssing, S. 24/25 · *Fassaden* von Hoffmann/Friese/ Meyer-Bohe, J. Hoffmann-Verlag, Stuttgart 1973, Hopfenhalle Klotz, Wolnzach, S. 125 · *Rechenzentren* von Rohrer/Wild, Callwey-Verlag, München 1973, Hypobank, Isartorplatz, München, S. 20/23, Hypobank, Arabellapark, München, Verwaltungsgebäude BMW, München, S. 62/73

1974 *Baumeister 4/1974* Mischbett Märker Zementwerk, Harburg/Schwaben, S. 387/388; *6/1974* Strukturplanung Sportgastein, S. 623/630; *11/1974* Wüstenrot, München, S. 1198/1200 · *Bauwelt 11/1974* Mischbettanlage Märker Zementwerk, Harburg/Schwaben, S. 438/440 · *DBZ Deutsche Bauzeitschrift 3/1974* Schulzentrum Weilheim, S. 395/398, Titelblatt; *4/1974* Bürohaus Weißenberger, München, S. 643/644; Fertigungshalle Wanderer-Werke, München-Haar, S. 661/664; *7/1974* Friedenskirche Gundelfingen, S. 1247; *9/1974* Wohn- und Geschäftshaus Weishaupt, München, S. 1541/1544; *10/1974* Feuerwache 4, München, S. 1709/1710 · *Detail 3/1974* Haus Götz, Deggendorf,

S. 439/442 · *aw – Architekturwettbewerbe 77/1974* Wettbewerb Hypobank, Arabellapark, München, S. 74/82 · *Beton 12/1974* Christuskirche, Bad Füssing, S. 450 · *DLW-Nachrichten 57/1974* Wohnanlage am Biederstein, München, S. 13; Wohnanlage Moll, München, S. 52/53 · *L'Architecture d'aujourd'hui 9/10/1974* Mischbettanlage, Zementwerk Märker, Harburg/Schwaben, S. XXII · *Zentralblatt für Industriebau 1/1974* Mischbettanlage, Märker Zementwerk, Harburg/Schwaben, S. 16/19, Titelblatt; *4/1974* IWIS-Kettenfabrik, München, S. 120/125 Titelblatt; *5/1974* Götz Metallbau, Deggendorf, S. 165/167; *11/1974* Wandererwerke, München-Haar, S. 421/424 · *Kirchliche Zentren* von Rainer Disse, Callwey-Verlag, München 1974, Christuskirche, Bad Füssing, S. 48, Friedenskirche, Gundelfingen, S. 49 · *Treppen in Stahl* von Hans Gladischefski u. Klaus Halmburger, Bauverlag, Wiesbaden/Berlin 1974, Haus Meisel, München, S. 86 · *Welt des Betons* Deutscher Beton-Verein, Märker Zementwerk, Harburg/Schwaben, S. 88 · *Schulbaubuch* von Karl-Hermann Koch, Bertelsmann-Fachverlag, 1974, Hardtschule, Weilheim, S. 114/117 · *Gewerbebetriebe* von F. Wild, Callwey-Verlag, München 1974, IWIS-Werk Winkelhofer, München, S. 79

1975 *Bauen + Wohnen 4/1975* Mischbettanlage Märker Zementwerk, Harburg/Schwaben, S. 148/149 · *Baumeister 12/1975* Wettbewerb Flughafen München II, S. 1083/1088 · *DBZ Deutsche Bauzeitschrift 9/1975* Wohn- und Geschäftshaus Weishaupt, München, S. 973/974 · *db Deutsche Bauzeitung 6/1975* Wohnanlage Biederstein, München, S. 37/39 · *Detail 2/1975* Wohnhaus Gerhard Moll, Pullach, S. 150/152 · *Binario 10/1975* Wohnanlage Moll, München, S. 411/412 · *Bauforum 46/1975* Sportgastein, S. 42; *48/1975* Nachtrag zu Sportgastein, S. 11 · *Differenzierte Wohnanlagen* von Gerhard Schwab, Karl Krämer Verlag, Stuttgart 1975, Wohnanlage Moll, München, S. 66/69 · *Freistehende Einfamilienhäuser in Stadt, Vorstadt und Dorf* von F. Wild, Callwey-Verlag, München 1975, Haus Gartner, Gundelfingen, S. 124 · *Planungsbericht Offiziersschule der Luftwaffe, Finanzbauamt München II, Mai 1975*, Offiziersschule der Luftwaffe, Heizhaus und Sportanlagen, Fürstenfeldbruck

1976 *Architecture April/1976* Märker Zementwerk, Harburg/Schwaben, S. 49, 122/126 · *Bauen + Wohnen 2/3/1976* Wettbewerb Flughafen München II, S. 112 · *Baumeister 4/1976* Wärmetauscherturm, Märker Zementwerk, Haburg/Schwaben, S. 284/285; *4/1976* Das Institut für Grundlagen des Entwerfens und Konstruierens, Universität Stuttgart, S. 275/277; *5/1976* Universität Regensburg, S. 364/371, Titelblatt · *Bauwelt 34/1976* Wärmetauscherturm, Märker Zementwerk, Harburg/Schwaben, S. 1035/1037 · *DBZ Deutsche Bauzeitschrift 1/1976* Wohnanlage Moll, München, S. 7/8; *6/1976* Wohnhaus Dr. Josef Gartner, Gundelfingen, S. 741/742; *11/1976* Mischbettanlage Märker Zementwerk, Harburg/Schwaben, S. 1425/1426 · *db Deutsche Bauzeitung 12/1976* Wohnanlage Höfter II, München, S. 43/45; *10/1976* Heizzentrale Offiziersschule der Luftwaffe, Fürstenfeldbruck, S. 20 · *Detail 2/1976* Christuskirche Bad Füssing, S. 183/186; *4/1976* Offiziersschule der Luftwaffe, Fürstenfeldbruck, S. 462/463 · *Glasforum 4/1976* Rektorat und Studentenhaus Universität Regensburg, S. 2/16/21 · *a – c Internationale Asbestzement Revue 81/1976* Wohnanlage Biederstein, München, S. 17/19 · *Die Kunst, Nov. 1976* Haus Dr. Josef Gartner, Gundelfingen, S. 691/693 · *L'Architecture d'aujourd'hui 4/1976* Märker Zementwerk, Harburg/Schwaben, S. 122/127 · *Leonberger 4/1976* Haus Götz, Deggendorf, S. 156/157 · *SBL – Schulbauinstitut der Länder 7/1976* Schulzentrum Weilheim, S. 70/77 · *Zement – Kalk – Gips 5/1976* Wärmetauscherturm Märker Zementwerk, Harburg/Schwaben, Titelblatt; *12/1976* Wärmetauscherturm Märker Zementwerk, Harburg/Schwaben · *Zentralblatt für Industriebau 5/1976* Wärmetauscherturm Märker Zementwerk, Harburg/Schwaben, S. 170/173 · *OFD-Nachrichten 4/1976* Heizzentrale, Offiziersschule der Luftwaffe, Fürstenfeldbruck, S. 39 · *4/1976* Bundesverwaltungsgericht BVG, München, S. 44/45 · *Offene Wohnformen*

von S. Nagel/S. Linke, Bertelsmann Fachverlag, 1976, Haus Ackermann, Herrsching, S. 76/77; Haus Meisel, Feldafing, S. 114/115 · *Ohne Vergangenheit keine Zukunft* von Hans Wichmann, Ludwig Auer Verlag, Donauwörth 1976, Wohnanlage Moll, München, S. 118/132 · *Spielraum für Kinder* von Marguerite Rouard/Jacques Simon, Hatje Verlag, Stuttgart 1976, Feuerwache 4, München, S. 51; Wohnanlage Moll, München, S. 59 · *Deutsche Kunst seit 1960 – Architektur* von Paolo Nestler/Peter M. Bode, Bruckmann-Verlag, München 1976, Tafel 32 Wohnanlage Moll, München; Tafel 116 Märker Zementwerk, Harburg/Schwaben; Tafel 126 Mischbett Märker, Harburg/Schwaben; Tafel 225 Christuskirche, Gundelfingen

1977 *Bauen + Wohnen 2/3/1977* Verwaltungsgebäude Wüstenrot, München, S. 59/63; *11/1977* Wettbewerb Berufsschulzentrum Ingolstadt, S. 441/443 · *Baumeister 1/1977* Wohnanlage Moll, München, S. 45/46; *10/1977* Verwaltungsgebäude der EDV, München, S. 909/912, Titelblatt; *10/1977* Wettbewerb BMW, Dingolfing, S. 928/935 · *Bauwelt 26/1977* Bundesverwaltungsgericht BVG, München, S. 894/897; *40/1977* Wettbewerb BMW, Dingolfing, S. 1380/1381 · *DBZ Deutsche Bauzeitschrift 7/1977* Wärmetauscherturm Märker Zementwerk, Harburg/Schwaben, S. 877/878; *9/1977* Haus Gerhard Moll, Pullach, S. 1141/1142; *12/1977* Rektorat und Studentenhaus der Universität Regensburg, S. 1623/1626 · *db Deutsche Bauzeitung 2/1977* Haus Dr. Josef Gartner, Gundelfingen, S. 36/37 · *aw – Architekturwettbewerbe 90/1977* Institut für Entwerfen und Konstruieren, Studienarbeiten, S. 77/80 · *a – c Internationale Asbestzement Revue 87/1977* Lagerhalle in München-Obermenzing, S. 34 · *Die Bauverwaltung 9/1977* Bundesverwaltungsgericht BVG, München, S. 348/349 · *Beton 6/1977* Universität Regensburg, S. 230 · *Beton Prisma 35/1977* Universität Regensburg, S. 8 · *Kenchiku Bunka 6/1977* Haus Dr. Josef Gartner, Gundelfingen, S. 129 · *Stein auf Stein 1977* Offiziersschule der Luftwaffe, Fürstenfeldbruck · *OFD-Nachrichten 4/1977* Offiziersschule der Luftwaffe, Fürstenfeldbruck, S. 25/26 · *Bayerische Staatszeitung 1977* Offiziersschule der Luftwaffe, Fürstenfeldbruck · *Dekorative Türen* von Gretl Hoffmann, J. Hoffmann-Verlag, Stuttgart 1977, Turnhalle Hardtschule Weilheim, S. 111 · *Geplant – gebaut*, Eigenverlag, Universitätsbauamt, 1977, Universität Regensburg, S. 156/159

1978 *Bauen + Wohnen 6/1978* Offiziersschule der Luftwaffe, Fürstenfeldbruck, S. 250/256, Titelbild · *Baumeister 4/1978* Wettbewerb ESSO-Tankstelle, S. 328/330; *5/1978* Offiziersschule der Luftwaffe, Fürstenfeldbruck, S. 395/408; *12/1978* Verwaltungsgebäude Wüstenrot, München, S. 1044; Universität Regensburg, S. 1122/1169 · *DBZ Deutsche Bauzeitschrift 9/1978* Universität Regensburg, S. 1195/1202 · *db Deutsche Bauzeitung 5/1978* Offiziersschule der Luftwaffe, Fürstenfeldbruck, S. 5, 39/49; *5/1978* Heizzentrale Offiziersschule der Luftwaffe, Fürstenfeldbruck, S. 50/54 · *Detail 1/1978* Heizzentrale Offiziersschule der Luftwaffe, Fürstenfeldbruck, S. 1/4; *3/1978* Bundesverwaltungsgericht BVG, München, S. 317/323, Titelblatt · *Der Architekt 1/1978* Redaktionsausschuß – Abschied, S. 9; *7/8/1978* Mischbett Märker Zementwerk, Harburg/Schwaben, S. 385 · *Glasforum 2/1978* Verwaltungsgebäude Wüstenrot, München, S. 2, 21/24 · *a – c Internationale Asbestzement Revue 90/1978* Christuskirche, Bad Füssing, S. 5/7, 57 · *Werkbund-Dokumentation, Auswahl 1978* Siloanlage Märker Zementwerk, Harburg/Schwaben, S. 1963/1964; Mischbettanlage Märker Zementwerk, Harburg/Schwaben, S. 1967/1968 · *Gemeinde-Kurier April 1978* EDV-Verwaltungsgebäude der Stadt München, S. 12 · *DLW – Nachrichten 62/1978* Offiziersschule der Luftwaffe, Fürstenfeldbruck, S. 84/87 · *L'Industria Italiana del Cemento 9/1978* Studentenhaus und Rektorat, Universität Regensburg, S. 649/652 · *Umbau alter Bauernhäuser* von Paulhans Peters, Callwey-Verlag, München 1978, Hirzinger Mühle, Tirol, S. 146/149 · *Geschichte der Architektur des 19. und 20. Jahrhunderts*, Band 2, von Leonardo Benevolo/Paulhans Peters, dtv/Callwey-Verlag, München 1978, Universität Regensburg, S. 568/569

1979 *Baumeister 11/1979* Bürohaus Verband baugewerblicher Unternehmer Bayern, VBB, München, S. 1123/1125 · *Bauwelt 19/1979* Wettbewerb Ernährungs- und Sozialministerium, Stuttgart, S. 788/791 · *DBZ Deutsche Bauzeitschrift 9/1979* EDV Verwaltungsgebäude der Stadt München, S. 1295/96 · *db Deutsche Bauzeitung 12/1979* Wohnhaus Schow, München,

S. 33/34, 98 · *Der Architekt 4/1979* Bürohaus Wüstenrot, München, S. 183 ·
DAB Deutsches Architektenblatt 8/1979 Sportbauten Tragsystem, Form,
Material, S. 911/913 · *aw – Architektenwettbewerbe 98/1979* Arbeiten aus
den Hochschulen S. 104/106 · *Glasforum 3/1979* Architekt und Bauingenieur,
S. 3/4; *3/1979* Heizzentrale der Offiziersschule der Luftwaffe, Fürstenfeldbruck, S. 17/19, 43 · *a + u Architecture and Urbanism Aug. 1979* Offiziersschule der Luftwaffe, Fürstenfeldbruck, S. 70, 79/82, Titelblatt · *Architectura
4/1979* Märker Zementwerk, Harburg/Schwaben, S. 73 · *Das Kunstwerk
April/Mai 1979*, ›Architektur in Deutschland‹, Märker, Harburg/Schwaben, Märker Zementwerk, Harburg/Schwaben, EDV Verwaltungsgebäude der Stadt
München, Bundesverwaltungsgericht München, Offiziersschule der Luftwaffe, Fürstenfeldbruck, Heizhaus, S. 16/17 · *bouwbestek, Dez. 1979* Heizzentra
le der Offiziersschule der Luftwaffe, Fürstenfeldbruck, S. 6/10 · *Zentralblatt für
Industriebau, 2/1979* Heizzentrale der Offiziersschule der Luftwaffe, Fürsten-
feldbruck, S. 84/89, Titelblatt · *Mehrgeschossige Wohnbauten* von Paulhans
Peters, Callwey-Verlag, München, 1979 Wohnanlage Moll, München, S. 18 ·
Bauten und Plätze in München von Haderer/Peters, Callwey-Verlag, München
1979, EDV-Verwaltungsgebäude der Stadt München S. 75; Hypobank Mün-
chen-Schwabing S. 177; Wüstenrot-Verwaltungsgebäude, München S. 224;
BVG S. 238; Wohnanlage Moll, München, S. 272; VBB, München, S. 282 ·
Gebäude für die öffentliche Verwaltung von Harald und Andreas Deilmann,
Verlagsanstalt A. Koch, Leinfelden 1979, Bundesverwaltungsgericht, Mün-
chen, S. 200, 202 · *Die fünfzig schönsten Bücher der Bundesrepublik
Deutschland 1978*, Kommissionsverlag 1979, Kurt Ackermann und Partner,
Bauten, Projekte, S. 21 · *Bauentwurfslehre* von Ernst Neufert, Verlag Friedrich
Vieweg + Sohn, Braunschweig, Feuerwache 4, München, S. 371

1980   *Baumeister 6/1980* Märker Zementwerk, Harburg/Schwaben,
S. 581/584, Titelblatt; *9/1980* Fußgängerbrücke Kelheim, S. 859/862 · *DBZ
Deutsche Bauzeitschrift 2/1980* Bürohaus Wüstenrot, München, S. 181/184;
10/1980 Bundesverwaltungsgericht BVG, München, S. 1475/1478 · *Detail
3/1980* Bürohaus Verband baugewerblicher Unternehmer Bayern, München,
S. 355/357 · *Der Architekt 12/1980* EDV-Verwaltungsgebäude der Stadt Mün-
chen, S. 602 · *DAB Deutsches Architektenblatt 5/1980* Bauten für Olympische
Spiele von 1896 bis 1980 (I), S. 683/684; *6/1980* Bauten für Olympische Spiele
von 1896 bis 1980 (II), S. 847/848; *12/1980* Wettbewerb Fußgängerbrücke
Kelheim, S. 1639 · *aw – Architekturwettbewerbe 104/1980* Wettbewerb
Flughafen Stuttgart, S. 26/33 · *Glasforum 1/1980* EDV-Verwaltungsgebäude
der Stadt München, S. 17/19, 43 · *Beton Prisma 5/1980* Märker Zementwerk,
Harburg/Schwaben, S. 21/22 · *Zentralblatt für Industriebau 5/1980* Kalkwerk
Märker, Harburg/Schwaben, S. 296/297; *5/1980* Industriebau 1955/1980,
Mischbett Märker Zementwerk, Harburg/Schwaben, S. 271 · *Vorhangfassaden*
von Walter Meyer-Bohe, Alexander Koch-Verlag, Stuttgart 1980, Verwaltungs-
gebäude Wüstenrot, München, S. 162/163 · *Contemporary Architects* von
Muriel Emanuel, The Macmillan Press Ltd., London 1980, Offiziersschule der
Luftwaffe, Fürstenfeldbruck, S. 12/14 · *Bauten des Bundes 1965–1980* von
Wolfgang Leuschner, Verlag C.F. Müller, Karlsruhe 1980, Flugsicherungsleit-
stelle München, S. 88; Bundesverwaltungsgericht München, S. 84; Offiziersschule der Luftwaffe, Fürstenfeldbruck, S. 130/132, S. 234/238

1981   *DBZ Deutsche Bauzeitschrift 5/1981* Heizzentrale der Offiziersschule
der Luftwaffe, Fürstenfeldbruck, S. 677/678; *9/1981* Offiziersschule der
Luftwaffe, Fürstenfeldbruck, S. 1299/1302 · *db Deutsche Bauzeitung 3/1981*
Fußgängerbrücke Kelheim, S. 22/24 · *Deutsches Architektenblatt 6/1981*
›Weltausstellungen – vom Kristallpalast zum Fuji-Pavillon‹, S. 899/902 ·
aw – Architekturwettbewerbe 109/1981 Fußgängerbrücke Kelheim, S. 62/73;
110/1981 ›Sportbauten-Synthese von Nutzung, Konstruktion und Form‹,
S. 6/8; *110/1981* ›Arbeiten aus Hochschulen, Innerstädtisches Sportzentrum
in Stuttgart‹, S. 79/81 · *Zentralblatt für Industriebau 2/1981* Esso-Tankstelle,
S. 78/79 · *Ein Architekt sieht München* von Christoph Hackelsberger, Heinrich
Hugendubel Verlag, München 1981, Verwaltungsgebäude Wüstenrot, Mün-

chen, Die Straßenkreuzung am Stiglmaierplatz, München, S. 27/31 · *Chronik und Bauten 1981*, Herausgeber Finanzbauamt München II, Offiziersschule der Luftwaffe, Fürstenfeldbruck, S. 29/33; Heizhaus, Fürstenfeldbruck, S. 29 · *Architektur in Deutschland* von Bofinger/Paul/Klotz, Kohlhammer-Verlag, Stuttgart 1979/1981, Märker Zementwerk, Offiziersschule der Luftwaffe, EDV-Verwaltungsgebäude, München, Bundesverwaltungsgericht München, Heizhaus Fürstenfeldbruck, S. 32/33 · *Fußgängerbrücken*, Dortmunder Werkheft Nr. 3 der Universität Dortmund, 1981, Fußgängerbrücke, Kelheim, S. 78/79

1982 *Werk Bauen + Wohnen 11/1982* Eislaufzelt Olympiapark München, S. 33/36 · *Baumeister 1/1982* ›Architekturbüros in sechs Ländern‹, S. 28/29; *7/1982* Eislaufzelt Olympiapark, München, S. 671/674, Titelblatt; *7/1982* Wettbewerb Neue Nationalgalerie und Wohnen am Kulturforum, Berlin, S. 659/670 · *Bauwelt 1/2/1982* Wettbewerb Neue Nationalgalerie und Wohnen am Kulturforum, Berlin, S. 4 · *DBZ Deutsche Bauzeitschrift 2/1982* Bürohaus Verein baugewerblicher Unternehmer Bayern, VBB, München, S. 197/198 · *db Deutsche Bauzeitung 12/1982* Wohnanlage Streubert, München, S. 24/25 · *DOMUS 2/1982* Neue Nationalgalerie Berlin und Wohnen am Kulturforum, Berlin, S. 31 · *Baukultur 5/6/1982* Fußgängerbrücke Kelheim, S. 19/21 · *DLW – Nachrichten 63/1982* Universität Regensburg, S. 38 · *L'Architecture d'aujourd'hui 2/1982* Wettbewerb Neue Nationalgalerie im Rahmen der IBA, S. XXIII/XXIX · *Stahlbau Nachrichten 5/1982* Eislaufzelt Olympiapark München, S. 14/15 · *Zentralblatt für Industriebau 6/1982* Deutscher Stahlbautag, S. 343/346 · *Element + Fertigbau 5/1982* Eislaufzelt Olympiapark München, S. 31 · *Bauen mit Stahl 34/1982* ›Architekten bauen mit Stahl‹, S. 2/11/31 · *Die Bayerische Finanzverwaltung*, Länderdienst-Verlag, München 1982, Bundesverwaltungsgericht, München, S. 27; Offiziersschule der Luftwaffe, Fürstenfeldbruck, S. 44/45; Offiziersschule der Luftwaffe, Heizhaus, Fürstenfeldbruck, S. 78 · *Verantwortung des Architekten* von Meinhard von Gerkan, DVA, Stuttgart 1982, EDV-Verwaltung München, S. 107 · *Vergangenheit – Gegenwart – Zukunft*, Ausstellungskatalog über Häuser + Architektur 1982, S. 205, ›Gegenwarts- Architektur‹ von Frank Werner, 1982, S. 174/212

1983 *db Deutsche Bauzeitung 1/1983* ›Bauen mit Stahl‹, Wärmetauscher Märker Zementwerk, Harburg/Schwaben; Heizzentrale Offiziersschule der Luftwaffe, Fürstenfeldbruck; Eislaufzelt Olympiapark, München; *12/1983* ›Architektur und Industriebau‹, S. 8/7 · *DAB Deutsches Architektenblatt 7/1983* Eislaufzelt Olympiapark, München, S. 721/724; *12/1983* Eislaufzelt Olympiapark, München, ›Aufzüge und Fahrtreppen. Grundlagen und Vorschriften‹, S. 445/446 · *Argus 2/1983* Eislaufzelt Olympiapark, München, S. 69 · *dm – Der Dachdeckermeister 6/1983* Eislaufzelt Olympiapark, München, S. 46/50 · *IABSE STRUCTURES 4/1983* Eislaufzelt Olympiapark, München, S. 78/79; *11/93* ›Ice Skating Hall at Munich with Jürgen Seidel‹, S. 27/28 · *Lufthansas Germany 6/1983* ›German Architecture Revitalized‹ von Manfred Sack, Eislaufzelt Olympiapark, München, S. 26/35 · *Mannesmann Illustrierte 5/1983* Eislaufzelt Olympiapark, München, S. 10/12 · *Bauen mit Stahl 129/1983* Heizzentrale Offiziersschule der Luftwaffe, Fürstenfeldbruck, S. 19/22 · *Stahlbau Nachrichten 4/1983* Eislaufzelt Olympiapark, München, S. 12/16 · *Stadt 3/1983* Bundesverwaltungsgericht BVG, München, S. 39 · *Zelte, Planen, Markisen 4/1983* Eislaufzelt Olympiapark, München, S. 9/13 · *Wettbewerb aktuell 3/1983* Wettbewerb Verwaltungszentrum der Stadtsparkasse München, S. 188 · *Bauen mit Stahl 39/1983* Sportbauten, S. 2/5/7/8 · *Zeit im Aufriß, Architektur in Bayern nach 1945*, Ausstellungskatalog der Bayer. Architektenkammer, Residenz Verlag, Salzburg, 1983, Offiziersschule der Luftwaffe, Fürstenfeldbruck, S. 34; Märker Zementwerk, Harburg/Schwaben, S. 39; Bundesverwaltungsgericht München, S. 41; Eislaufzelt Olympiapark, München, S. 46; Wohnanlage Moll, München, S. 67; Eislaufzelt Olympiapark, München, S. 74; Universität Regensburg, S. 90; Offiziersschule der Luftwaffe, Heizzentrale, Fürstenfeldbruck, S. 110 · *Flachdach, Architektur, Konstruktion* von Gerd Heene, Bertelsmann-Verlag, 1983, Offiziersschule der Luftwaffe, Fürstenfeldbruck, S. 90

1984 *Baumeister 1/1984* ›Industriebau – drei Konzeptionen‹, S. 8/7; *1/1984* Klärwerk Gut Marienhof, Dietersheim bei München, S. 25/31 · *db Deutsche Bauzeitung 10/1984* Ausstellung ›Industriebau‹ · *Der Architekt 1/1984* Leitartikel, 1974/1984, S. 3 · *Deutsches Architektenblatt 11/1984* Industriebau, S. 1465/1466 · *aw – Architekturwettbewerbe 120/1984* Studentenwohnheim,

München, S. 58/61 · *Glasforum 3/1984* Eislaufzelt Olympiapark, München, S. 4 · *Bouwtechniek 12/1984* Eislaufzelt Olympiapark, München, S. 16 · *Architektur und Technik 2/1984* Eislaufzelt Olympiapark München, S. 28 · *Baukultur 4/1984* Eislaufzelt Olympiapark, München, S. 37 · *Beton 12/1984* Wettbewerb Eisenbahnbrücke, Porto/Portugal, S. 490 · *Bauforum 104/1984* Wohnen am Kulturforum, Berlin, S. 32 · *Wettbewerb aktuell 3/1984* Wettbewerb Postsparkassenamt, München, S. 173/184 · *Werk und Zeit 4/1984* Wohnen am Kulturforum, Berlin, S. 35 · *IBA 84/87*, Projektbericht Wohnen am Kulturforum, Stand Okt. 82, S. 130/131 · *IBA 84/87*, Projektübersicht Wohnen am Kulturforum, Stand Sept. 84, S. 40/41 · *IBA 87*, ›Eine Stadt stellt aus‹, Wohnen am Kulturforum, S. 21 · *IBA 87*, ›Leitfaden‹ Projekte Daten Geschichte 1984, Wohnen am Kulturforum, S. 52 · *IBA-Berlin 87*, ›Beispiele einer neuen Architektur‹, Wohnen am Kulturforum, Deutsches Architektur-Museum, Frankfurt/Main 1986 · *Architektur in Deutschland '83*, Karl Krämer Verlag, Stuttgart 1984, Eislaufzelt Olympiapark, München, S. 33/39 · *München und seine Bauten nach 1912*, Herausgeber: Bayerischer Architekten- und Ing.-Verband, Verlag F. Bruckmann, München 1984, Wohnanlage Moll, München, S. 309; Wohnhaus Kammermeier, München, S. 328; Hypobank, München-Schwabing, S. 378; Verwaltungsgebäude Wüstenrot, München, S. 389; EDV-Verwaltung, München, S. 438; Bundesverwaltungsgericht, München, S. 466; Eislaufzelt Olympiapark, München, S. 583 · *IBA-1984/87 Projektübersicht Stadtneubau und Stadterneuerung 1984* Wohnen am Kulturforum, Berlin, S. 40/41 · *Bauen gestaltet die Zukunft* von Heribert Thul, Beton Verlag, Düsseldorf 1984, Eisenbahnbrücke über den Douro in Porto/Portugal, S. 134 · *Baumeister in einer umwälzenden Zeit*, Fritz Leonhardt Erinnerungen DVA, Stuttgart 1984, Kurt Ackermann, S. 232 · *Stahl und Form* von Christoph Hackelsberger/Manfred Sack, Düsseldorf 1984, Eislaufzelt Olympiapark, München

1985 *Detail 3/4/1985* Eislaufzelt Olympiapark, München, S. 133/138 · *Der Architekt 5/1985* Walter Belz über Wohnanlage Moll, München, S. 217 · *Bauingenieur 8/1985* Eislaufzelt Olympiapark, München, S. 291/296 · *Feuer-Verzinken 6/1985* Eislaufzelt Olympiapark, München, S. 22/26, Titelbild · *Wettbewerbe aktuell 7/1985* Wettbewerb Steg über die Große Isar in Landshut, S. 423; *11/1985* Wettbewerb Erweiterung der OFD München, S. 666/667 · *Neue Gußkonstruktionen in der Architektur* von Anton Peter Betschart, Entwicklungsinstitut für Gießerei- und Bautechnik, Stuttgart 1985, Eislaufzelt München, S. 56/58 · *Zum Wohnen* von Peter M. Bode, Süddeutscher Verlag, München 1985, Haus Josef Gartner, Gundelfingen, S. 142/143 · *Bauen in Deutschland* von Falk Jaeger, Gerd Hatje Verlag, Stuttgart 1985, Offiziersschule der Luftwaffe Fürstenfeldbruck, S. 134; Märker Zementwerk Harburg/Schwaben, S. 181; Bundesverwaltungsgericht München, S. 240; Eislaufzelt Olympiapark, München, S. 242; Universität Regensburg, S. 266 · *Bauten und Plätze in München*, Callwey-Verlag, München 1985, EDV-Verwaltung, München, S. 75; Hypobank, München-Schwabing, S. 177; Verwaltungsgebäude Wüstenrot, München S. 224; Bundesverwaltungsgericht München, S. 238; Wohnanlage Moll, München, S. 272; Verwaltungsgebäude VBB, München, S. 282; Wohnforum Gottfried-Böhm-Ring, München, S. 347; Eislaufzelt Olympiapark, München, S. 358; Klärwerk Gut Marienhof, Dietersheim bei München, S. 360 · *Architekturführer Bayern*, Herausgeber: BDA, Süddeutscher Verlag, München 1985, 1.002 Verwaltungsgebäude Wüstenrot, München, S. 18; 1.030 EDV-Verwaltung, München, S. 46; 1.046 Bundesverwaltungsgericht, München, S. 62; 1.064 Hypobank, München-Schwabing, S. 80; 1.108 Wohnanlage Moll, München, S. 124; 1.113 VBB, München, S. 129; 1.129 Heizzentrale der Offiziersschule der Luftwaffe, Fürstenfeldbruck, S. 145, 1.130 Offiziersschule der Luftwaffe, Fürstenfeldbruck, S. 146; 2.053 Friedenskirche, Gundelfingen, S. 329; 2.054 Wohnhaus Gartner, Gundelfingen, S. 330; 2.058 Märker Zementwerk, Harburg/Schwaben, S. 334; 5.005 Uni Regensburg, S. 539; 5.068 Christuskirche, Bad Füssing, S. 602 · *Landshut an der Isar – Ein Steg*, Baureferat Landshut 1985, Fußgängerbrücke, S. 40/43

1986 *Werk Bauen + Wohnen 6/1986* Eislaufzelt Olympiapark, München, S. 12/01 · *Baumeister 6/1986* Wettbewerb GhK-Universität Kassel, S. 10/12 · *Bauwelt 19/20/1986* Wettbewerb GhK-Universität Kassel, S. 730/732 · *DBZ Deutsche Bauzeitschrift 7/1986* Wettbewerb GhK-Universität Kassel, S. 921 · *db Deutsche Bauzeitung 6/1986* Wettbewerb GhK-Universität Kassel, S. 5 · *Baukultur 4/1986* ›Die Industrie baut – Industriebau‹, S. 1/3 · *Glas am Bau* von Dieter Balkow/Klaus von Bock/Heinz Krehwinkel/R. Rinkens, DVA, Stuttgart 1986, Eislaufzelt Olympiapark, München, S. 130/131 · *Die andere Tradition* von Wend Fischer, Callwey-Verlag, München, 1986, Eislaufzelt Olympiapark, München S. 135 · *Internationale Bauausstellung IBA Berlin 1987*, Beispiele einer neuen Architektur, Deutsches Architektur-Museum Frankfurt/Main, Ernst Klett Verlag, Stuttgart 1986, Wohnen am Kulturforum, Berlin, S. 106

1987 *Baumeister 1/1987* Studienarbeiten – Förderpreis des Deutschen Stahlbaus 86, S. 10; *5/1987* Wohnen am Kulturforum, Berlin, S. 45; *12/1987* Antworten auf ein Pamphlet, S. 17 · *Der Architekt 1/1987* Eislaufzelt Olympiapark, München, S. 27; *11/1987* ›Architektur und Tragwerk‹, S. 526/528 · *DOMUS 7/8/1987* Wohnen am Kulturforum, Berlin, S. 72/73; *7/8/1987* IBA Berlin Itinerario N 26, Portrait, S. IV · *a + u Architecture and Urbanism 5/1987* IBA – Wohnen am Kulturforum, Berlin, S. 108 · *The Architectural Review 4/1987* Wettbewerb Erweiterung der Neuen Nationalgalerie Berlin, S. 47, *4/1987* Wohnen am Kulturforum, Berlin, S. 76 · *Element + Fertigbau 9/1987* Fußgängerbrücke Kelheim, S. 48/49 · *Internationale Bauausstellung IBA Berlin 1987* ›Projektübersicht‹, Wohnen am Kulturforum, Berlin, S. 42/43 · *International Building Exhibition Berlin 1987* von Lore Ditzen/Josef Paul Kleihues · *a + u Publisher* Tokyo 1987, Wohnen am Kulturforum, Berlin, S. 108 · *Contemporary Architects* von Ann Lee Morgan/Colin Naylor, St. James Press, Chicago 1987, Eislaufzelt Olympiapark, München, S. 7/9

1988 *Baumeister 8/1988* Wettbewerb Williamsburgbrücke New York, S. 14; *12/1988* Klärwerk Gut Marienhof, Dietersheim bei München, S. 5; Europäisches Patentamt, München, S. 10 · *Bauwelt 28/29/1988* Wettbewerb Williamsburgbrücke New York, S. 1178/1181 · *Bauingenieur 4/1988* Fußgängerbrücke, Kelheim, S. 143/149 · *Wasserwirtschaft 12/1988* ›Brücken am Main-Donau-Kanal‹, Westtangente und Fußgängerbrücke, Kelheim, S. 550/553 · *Stahlbau 12/1988* Wettbewerb Williamsburgbrücke in New York, S. 373/377, Titelbild · *Silo – Revue D'Architecture 2/3/1988* Wohnen am Kulturforum, Berlin, S. 53/55 · *Wooden Architecture Today*, SC Verlag, Tokio 1988, Eislaufzelt Olympiapark, München, Titelbild, S. 48/53 · *Vom Sinn des Details*, Arcus-Verlag Rudolf Müller, 1988, Heizhaus Offiziersschule der Luftwaffe, Fürstenfeldbruck, S. 16/23 · *Bauen für den Bürger*, Baureferat der Landeshauptstadt München 1988; Klärwerk Gut Marienhof, Dietersheim bei München; EDV-Verwaltungsgebäude der LH München · *Architectures Publiques*, Dépôt Légal: 1er trimestre, Paris 1988, GhK-Universität Kassel, S. 118/119

1989 *Baumeister 1/1989* ›Kontinuität der Moderne‹, Museum für Raumfahrt, Unterschleißheim; Hopfenhalle, Mainburg; Wärmetauscher Märker Zementwerk, Harburg/Schwaben; Universität Regensburg; Offiziersschule der Luftwaffe, Fürstenfeldbruck; Eislaufzelt Olympiapark, München; Postamt, Regensburg; GhK-Universität Kassel; Klärwerk Gut Marienhof, Dietersheim bei München; Fußgängersteg, Berching; Fußgängerbrücke, Kelheim; Westtangente, Kelheim; Brücke bei Berching; Studentenwohnheim, München-Freimann; Stadtteilzentrum, München-Laim; Wohnanlage Gottfried-Böhm-Ring, München; Titelbild, S. 31/55 · *db Deutsche Bauzeitung 7/1989* Wettbewerb Williamsburgbrücke New York, S. 45/47; *10/1989* Klärwerk Gut Marienhof, Dietersheim bei München, S. 10/15 · *Detail 6/1989* Klärwerk Gut Marienhof, Dietersheim bei München, S. 562 · *DOMUS 12/1989* Klärwerk Gut Marienhof, Dietersheim bei München, S. 33/41 · *Stadtbauwelt 36/1989* Klärwerk Gut Marienhof, Dietersheim bei München, Titelblatt, S. 1713/1717 · *Bautechnik 1/1989* Wettbewerb Williamsburgbrücke New York, S. 33 · *Beratende Ingenieure 10/1989* Wettbewerb Williamsburgbrücke New York, S. 38 · *bau intern 10/1989* Studentenwohnheim, München-Freimann, S. 184/185 · *Baukultur 6/1989* Studienarbeiten des Instituts für Entwerfen und Konstruieren der Universität Stuttgart, S. 34/43 · *le mur vivant 8/1989* Fußgängerbrücke, Kelheim, S. 98/100 · *News 4/1989, International Academy of Architecture* Portrait Kurt Ackermann, S. 3 · *Zentralblatt für Industriebau 6/1989* Klärwerk Gut Marien-

hof, Dietersheim bei München, S. 410/415, Titelblatt · *Postbauten*, Karl Krämer Verlag, Stuttgart 1989, Postamt, Regensburg, S. 208/209 · *Tragwerke – Gestalt durch Konstruktion* von Meinhard von Gerkan, Verlag Rudolf Müller, Köln 1989, Eislaufzelt Olympiapark, München, S. 63/66

1990 *Werk Bauen + Wohnen 3/1990* Klärwerk Gut Marienhof, Dietersheim bei München, S. 62/63 · *Baumeister 1/1990* Leistungszentrum für Eiskunstlauf Olympiapark, München, S. 11; *4/1990* Wettbewerb Expo '92 Sevilla, S. 11/12; *6/1990* Wettbewerb Expo '92 Sevilla, S. 15/29 · *DBZ Deutsche Bauzeitschrift 5/1990* Klärwerk Gut Marienhof, Dietersheim bei München, S. 776; *6/1990* Klärwerk Gut Marienhof, Dietersheim bei München, S. 805/810 · *Detail 9/1990* Gemeindezentrum Bad Füssing, S. 288/290; *6/1990* Klärwerk Gut Marienhof, Dietersheim bei München, S. I/IV · *Arch + 4/1990* Klärwerk Gut Marienhof, Dietersheim bei München, S. 28/29 · *Allgemeine Bauzeitung ABZ 3/1990* Klärwerk Gut Marienhof, Dietersheim bei München, S. 11 · *Baukultur 5/1990* Heizzentrale Offiziersschule der Luftwaffe, Fürstenfeldbruck, S. 15/16; Eislaufzelt Olympiapark, München, S. 18/28; Klärwerk Gut Marienhof, Dietersheim bei München, S. 38/40, Titelblatt · *BDB-Nachrichten 1/1990*, Klärwerk Gut Marienhof, Dietersheim bei München, S. 11/19 · *L'Industria delle Costruzioni 11/1990* Klärwerk Gut Marienhof, Dietersheim bei München, S. 28/37, Titelblatt · *Wettbewerbe aktuell 6/1990* Wettbewerb Expo '92 Sevilla, S. 349/366 · *Wettbewerbe 2/1990* Wettbewerb Vorarlberger Landesgalerie, Bregenz, S. 61 · *Architektur in München seit 1900 – ein Wegweiser* von Gerd Fischer, Vieweg + Sohn, Braunschweig 1990, Eislaufzelt Olympiapark, S. 111/126 · *Constructa-Preis '90 – Industriearchitektur in Europa* von H. C. Schulitz, Vincenz-Verlag, Hannover 1990, Klärwerk Gut Marienhof, Dietersheim bei München · *Leicht und Weit – Zur Konstruktion weitgespannter Flächentragwerke*, Herausgeber Günther Brinkmann, DFG-SFB 74, Bericht 1990, Brücke Kelheim, S. 155; Eislaufzelt Olympiapark, München, S. 155/229 · *Gestaltung von Ingenieurbauwerken an Straßen* Kund/Barmauska/Hoffmann/Hügel/Fly, Beton-Verlag, Düsseldorf 1990, Entwerfen und Konstruieren, S. 10; Fußgängerbrücke Kelheim, S. 116/118 und Titelblatt · *Ideen – Orte – Entwürfe*, Architektur und Städtebau in der Bundesrepublik Deutschland, Ernst + Sohn Verlag, Berlin 1990, Studentenwohnheim München, S. 70 · *Architektur, Natur und Technik*, Ausstellungskatalog, Sexten Kultur 1990, Klärwerk Gut Marienhof, Dietersheim bei München, S. 58/61, Titelbild · *Architektur in Deutschland '89*, Karl Krämer Verlag, Stuttgart 1990, Klärwerk Gut Marienhof, Dietersheim bei München, S. 40/45 · *Deutsche Kirchenbaukunst des 20. Jahrhunderts* von Barbara Kahle, Wissenschaftliche Buchgesellschaft, Darmstadt 1990, Christuskirche, Bad Füssing, S. 164

1991 *Werk Bauen + Wohnen 4/1991* Stadtteilzentrum München-Laim, S. 152 · *Baumeister 3/1991* Wettbewerb Hypo-Passage, Kaufinger Straße, München, S. 13; *10/1991* Leistungszentrum für Eiskunstlauf Olympiapark, München, S. 18/23 · *Cement 6/1991* Fußgängerbrücke in Kelheim, S. XL III · *DBZ Deutsche Bauzeitschrift 3/1991* Studentenwohnheim München-Freimann, S. 365/368 · *Der Architekt 7/8/1991* Klärwerk Gut Marienhof, Dietersheim bei München, S. 385/400; *10/1991* Leistungszentrum für Eiskunstlauf Olympiapark, München; Institut für Bioverfahrenstechnik, Stuttgart; Postamt, Regensburg; Konstruktionsbüro Gartner, Gundelfingen/Donau, S. 493/496 · *Deutsches Architektenblatt 7/8/1991* Klärwerk Gut Marienhof, Dietersheim bei München, S. 1193/1196; *11/1991* Studentenwohnheim, München-Freimann, S. 1775/1777; *12/1991* Klärwerk Gut Marienhof, Dietersheim bei München, S. 1966/1968 · *Beton Prisma 5/1991* Studentenwohnheim, München-Freimann, S. 7/8 · *SIA – Schweizer Ingenieur und Architekt 6/1991* Wettbewerb Richtiareal, Zürich, S. 580/589 · *Dach-Atlas, Geneigte Dächer* von Schunck/Finke/Jenisch/Oster, Institut für internationale Architektur-Dokumentation, München 1991, Eislaufzelt Olympiapark, München, S. 368/369 · *Gewerbebau, Industriebau* von Peter Lorenz, Verlagsanstalt Alexander Koch, Leinfelden 1991, Märker Zementwerk, Harburg/Schwaben, S. 218/225 · ›*Spannweiten*‹ *Bayerische Bauindustrie 1991*, Klärwerk Gut Marienhof, Dietersheim bei München, S. 42/43; Fußgängerbrücke, Berching, S. 62/63 · *Usines*, Band 2, von Jacques Ferrier, Editions du Moniteur, Paris 1991, Klärwerk Gut Marienhof, Dietersheim bei München, S. 46/53

1992 *Baumeister 12/1992* Europäisches Patentamt, S. 36/39 · *db Deutsche Bauzeitung 6/1992* Preis des Deutschen Stahlbaus '92, Fußgängerbrücke, Berching, Leistungszentrum für Eiskunstlauf Olympiapark, München, S. 142/151; Studentenarbeiten, S. 176/180; Fußballstadion Stuttgart-Wald, Maik Buttler, Michael Vitzthum · *Detail 6/1992* Leistungszentrum für Eiskunstlauf Olympiapark, München, S. 441/445 · *Der Architekt 5/1992* Konstruktionsbüro Gartner, Gundelfingen/Donau, S. 283 · *Deutsches Architektenblatt 8/1992* Leistungszentrum für Eiskunstlauf Olympiapark, München, S. 1181 · *Bautechnik 8/1992* Leistungszentrum für Eiskunstlauf Olympiapark, München, S. 441/445 · *Design Journal, Seoul 45/1992* Eislaufzelt Olympiapark, München; Klärwerk Gut Marienhof, Dietersheim bei München, Portrait Kurt Ackermann, S. 18/19 · *Poros 24/1992* Wettbewerb Deutscher Pavillon Expo '92 in Sevilla, S. 42/43 · *Wasser + Boden 5/1992* Klärwerk Gut Marienhof, Dietersheim bei München, Titelblatt · *Zentralblatt für Industriebau 1/1992*, Heizzentrale der Offiziersschule der Luftwaffe, Fürstenfeldbruck, S. 17 · *Die Main-Donau-Wasserstraße* von Hannes Burger/Heinz Kapfinger, Neue Presse Verlag, Passau 1992, Fußgängerbrücke Kelheim, S. 251 · *Dachatlas, Flache Dächer* von Busse/Waubke/Grimme/Mertius, Institut für internationale Architektur-Dokumentation, München 1992, Stadtteilzentrum München-Laim, S. 194/197; Eislaufzelt Olympiapark, München, S. 234/237 · *Eric Space: toward the roots of Western Architecture*, Verlag Nostrand Reinhold, New York 1992, Eislaufzelt Olympiapark, München, S. 187 · *Glasarchitektur 1992*, Flachglas AF, Redaktion Lothar Juckel, Postamt, Regensburg, S. 56/61 · *Hallen mit großen Spannweiten*, Senatsbauverwaltung, Berlin 14/92, Eislaufzelt Olympiapark, München, S. 62/63

1993 *Werk Bauen + Wohnen 1/2/1993* Postamt Regensburg, S. 54/57 · *Baumeister 3/1993* Wettbewerb Bayerischer Landtag, Maximilianeum, München, S. 6 · *Deutsches Architektenblatt 5/1993* Postamt, Regensburg, S. 845/846 · *Glasforum 2/1993* Postamt, Regensburg, S. 13/20; Leistungszentrum für Eiskunstlauf Olympiapark, München, S. 43/49 · *AIT Architektur, Innenarchitektur, Technischer Ausbau 12/1993* Postamt, Regensburg S. 40/43 · *Fassade 5/1993* Europäisches Patentamt, München, S. 17/21 · *infobau 2/1993* Zentrum für Bioverfahrenstechnik der Universität Stuttgart, S. 29/31 · *md moebel, interior, design 5/1993* Konstruktionsbüro Gartner, Gundelfingen/Donau, S. 64/69 · *Sb Sportstättenbau und Bäderanlagen 3/1993* Leistungszentrum für Eiskunstlauf Olympiapark, München, S. 528/532 · *Prosekt Revus Slovenskes Architektury 3/1993* Wohnanlage am Gottfried-Böhm-Ring, München, S. 41/51 · *Produktion 14/1993* Konstruktionsbüro Gartner, Gundelfingen/Donau, S. 3 · *Wettbewerbe aktuell 3/1993* Wettbewerb Bayerischer Landtag, Maximilianeum, München, S. 25; *12/1993* Wettbewerb Verwaltungsgebäude Baureferat München, S. 76/77 · *Centrum – Jahrbuch für Architektur und Stadt 1993*, Herausgeber: Peter Neitzke/Carl Steckeweh, Verlag Vieweg, Braunschweig 1993, Konstruktionsbüro Gartner, S. 150/153 · *Die neue deutsche Architektur* von Gerhard G. Feldmeyer, Kohlhammer Verlag, Stuttgart 1993, Klärwerk Gut Marienhof, Dietersheim bei München, S. 27/31 · *Internationale Bauausstellung IBA Berlin 1984/87 Neubaugebiet*, Verlag Gerd Hatje, Stuttgart 1993, Wohnen am Kulturforum Berlin, S. 178/179 · *Architekturschule München 1868 – 1993* von Winfried Nerdinger, Klinkhardt & Biermann, München 1993, Klärwerk Gut Marienhof, Dietersheim bei München, S. 140/141 · *Architektur in Deutschland '93*, Karl Krämer Verlag, Stuttgart 1993, Konstruktionsbüro Gartner, S. 114/119 · *Architektur der Gegenwart* von Peter Schweger/ Wilhelm Meyer, Kohlhammer Verlag, Stuttgart 1993, Klärwerk Gut Marienhof, Dietersheim bei München; Stadtteilzentrum München-Laim; Fußgängerbrücke, Kelheim, Williamsburgbrücke, New York, S. 10/13

1994   *Bauwelt 9/1994* Wettbewerb Amt für Abfallwirtschaft, München, S. 390 · *DBZ Deutsche Bauzeitschrift 10/1994* Konstruktionsbüro Gartner, Gundelfingen/Donau, S. 63/70 · *db Deutsche Bauzeitung 3/1994* Wettbewerb Donaubrücke, Ingolstadt, S. 37; *5/1994* Konstruktionsbüro Gartner, Gundelfingen/Donau, S. 50/55; Postamt, Regensburg, S. 92/95 · *DAB Deutsches Architektenblatt 5/1994* Wettbewerb Amt für Abfallwirtschaft, München, S. 724 · *Glasforum 1/1994* Konstruktionsbüro Gartner, Gundelfingen/Donau; Pfortenhof Kloster Andechs, S. 33/40 · *Fassade 4/1994* Konstruktionsbüro Gartner, Gundelfingen/Donau, S. 7/17 · *Jahrbuch für Licht und Architektur 1993* von Ingeborg Flagge, Verlag Ernst + Sohn, Berlin 1994, Konstruktionsbüro Gartner, S. 26/29 · *Bauen mit Aluminium '94/95*, Alu-Verlag, Düsseldorf 1994, Konstruktionsbüro Gartner, S. 78/80 · *Sports Facilities*, Herausgeber: Francisco Asensio Cerver, Atrium-Verlag, Barcelona 1994, Eislaufzelt Olympiapark, München, S. 120/129 · *Konstruktion und Gestalt* von Karlheinz Schmiedel, Verlag Ernst & Sohn, Berlin 1994, Eislaufzelt Olympiapark, München, S. 72/73; Leistungszentrum für Eiskunstlauf Olympiapark, München, S. 74; Heizhaus der Offiziersschule der Luftwaffe, Fürstenfeldbruck, S. 187; Klärwerk Gut Marienhof, Dietersheim bei München, S. 188/189; Fußgängerbrücke, Berching, S. 214/216; Konstruktionsbüro Gartner, Gundelfingen/Donau, S. 228/229 · *Zeitzeichen – Lebensreisen* von Hannsjörg Voth, Prestel-Verlag, München/ New York 1994, Klärwerk Gut Marienhof, Dietersheim bei München – Lebensbogen, S. 92/97; Europäisches Patentamt, München – Sonnentor und Mondplatz, S. 106/113 · *Industriearchitektur in Europa, Constructec-Preis '94* von H. C. Schulitz, Verlag Ernst + Sohn, Berlin 1994, Konstruktionsbüro Gartner, Gundelfingen/Donau, S. 68/75 · *Batteriefreie Erschließungssysteme von Wohngebäuden*, IBB-Verlag, Stuttgart 1994, Wohnen am Kulturforum, Berlin, S. 35/39 · *Architekturführer Berlin* von Wolfgang Schäcke, Dietrich Reimer Verlag, Berlin 1994, Pumpwerk, Museum im Wasserwerk, S. 258 · *Architektur 1990–1993 in Baden-Württemberg* von K. W. Schmitt/H. W. Krewinkel, IBDA Baden-Württemberg 1994, Zentrum für Bioverfahrenstechnik, Stuttgart, S. 12/13 · *Integrierte Fassade – System Gartner 1994* Konstruktionsbüro Gartner, Gundelfingen/Donau, S. 15, 44/45 · *Architekturlehre in Stuttgart* von Jürgen Joedicke, Universität Stuttgart 1994, Zentrum für Bioverfahrenstechnik, Stuttgart, S. 48/55 · *Fritz-Schumacher-Stiftung 1994*, Universität Hannover 1994, Heinrich-Tessenow-Medaille in Gold, Laudatio, Dankrede, Pfortenhof, Kloster Andechs; Eislaufzelt Olympiapark, München, S. 12 und S. 19

1995   *Baumeister 4/1995* Technik III der GhK-Universität Kassel, Exkursion; *7/1995* Postamt, Regensburg, und Universität Regensburg, Exkursion · *Deutsches Architektenblatt 3/1995* Konstruktionsbüro Gartner, Gundelfingen/ Donau, S. 462 · *AIT Architektur, Innenarchitektur, Technischer Ausbau 10/1995* Zentrum für Bioverfahrenstechnik der Universität Stuttgart, S. 72/75 · *IAKS 43/1995* ›Awards 1995‹ – Leistungszentrum für Eiskunstlauf, Olympiapark, München, S. 26/28; *Wettbewerbe aktuell 9/1995* Wettbewerb Umwelt-Technik-Zentrum, Berlin-Adlerhorst, S. 35/36; Wettbewerb Messe- und Veranstaltungszentrum, Bremen, S. 55/63; Wettbewerb Feuerwache 10, München-Riem, S. 67/78 · *Architektura & Biznes 3/1995* Konstruktionsbüro Gartner, Gundelfingen/Donau, Medalú Tessenowa, S. 24 · *Architectural Record 10/1995* Konstruktionsbüro Gartner, Gundelfingen/Donau, S. 74/77 · *Die Akademie der Künste*, Achtzehn Entwürfe, von Kristin Feiseiss, Verlag Ernst + Sohn, Berlin 1995, Akademie Berlin, Pariser Platz, S. 120/121 · *Arbeitsplatz Deutschland*, Werkbericht des BM für Raumordnung, Bauwesen und Städtebau, Klärwerk Gut Marienhof, Dietersheim bei München · *Solares Bauen. Architekturen für natürliche Lebensräume*, Senat für Bau-Wohnungswesen, Berlin 1995, Konstruktionsbüro Gartner, Gundelfingen/Donau; Hauptpumpwerk, Berlin-Wilmersdorf, S. 24/26 · *Entwerfen und Denkmalpflege 1976–1995*, Katalog und Ausstellung der TU München, S. 94/95, S. 132/133 · *Licht + Reading*, Dietmar Tanderl/Peter Zinganel, Goethe House New York/ German Cultural Center 1995, Fire Department 8, Munich · *Kunst an staatlichen Bauten in Baden-Württemberg 1980–1995*, Cantz Verlag, Stuttgart 1995, Forschungszentrum für Bioverfahrenstechnik, S. 20/22, 218/219

1996 *Baumeister 7/1996* Halle 13 und Eingang West, Expo 2000, Hannover, S. 58/61; *11/1996* Technikgebäude III/2 GhK-Universität Kassel, S. 3, 42/47 · *Bauwelt 18/19/1996* Hauptpumpwerk, Berlin-Wilmersdorf, S. 1097 · *DAB Deutsches Architektenblatt 3/1996* Halle 13 und Eingang West, Expo 2000, Hannover, SBN 55 · *AIA-Architect 10/1996,* International Markets and Practice, S. 8 · *AIT Architektur, Innenarchitektur, Technischer Ausbau 7/8/1996,* Feuerwache 8, München-Unterföhring, S. 16 · *AIT – Intelligente Architektur 4/1996* Halle 13, Eingang West, Expo 2000, Hannover, S. 23, 36/39; *6/1996* Technikgebäude III/2, GhK-Universität Kassel, S. 32/35; *das bauzentrum 6/1996* Wettbewerb Halle 13, Eingang West, Expo 2000, Hannover, S. 72/74 · *Wettbewerbe aktuell 3/1996* Wettbewerb Halle 13, Eingang West, Expo 2000, Hannover, S. 19/20 · *Bauen in Bayerns Städten,* Bayerischer Bauindustrieverband 1996, Universität Regensburg, Postamt, Regensburg · *Jahrbuch für Licht und Architektur 1995,* Herausgeberin: Ingeborg Flagge, Verlag Ernst + Sohn, Berlin 1996, Wettbewerb Luftfahrtmuseum, München-Unterschleißheim, Expo '92 in Sevilla, Fußgängerbrücke, Kelheim; Pfortenhof, Kloster Andechs, S. 41–45 · *Im Gespräch – Bauen in Bayern* von Florian Aicher u. a., Callwey-Verlag, München 1996, Klärwerk Gut Marienhof, Dietersheim bei München, S. 83 · *Kuppeln – aller Zeiten, aller Kulturen* von Erwin Heinle/Jörg Schlaich, DVA, Stuttgart 1996, Eislaufzelt Olympiapark, München, S. 194 · *Guida all'architettura del Novecento: Germania* von Winfried Nerdinger, Verlag Electa, Mailand 1996, Klärwerk Gut Marienhof, Dietersheim bei München; Konstruktionsbüro Gartner, Gundelfingen/Donau; Eislaufzelt Olympiapark, München · *Architekturführer Deutschland – 20. Jahrhundert* von Winfried Nerdinger/Cornelius Tafel, Verlag Birkhäuser, Basel 1996, Klärwerk Gut Marienhof, Dietersheim bei München, S. 471; Konstruktionsbüro Gartner, Gundelfingen/Donau, S. 447; Eislaufzelt Olympiapark, München, S. 475

1997 *Baumeister 7/1997* Feuerwache 8, München-Unterföhring, Baumeister Exkursion; *12/1997* Halle 13, Deutsche Messe AG/Expo 2000, Hannover, Titelblatt, S. 26/33, 85/88 und Detailblätter, Kindergarten St. Nikolaus, Studentenzentrum, Rosenheim, Baumeister Exkursion · *Bauwelt 33/1997* Halle 13, Deutsche Messe AG/Expo 2000, Hannover, S. 1790 · *Architektur-Magazin 6/1997* Halle 13, Deutsche Messe AG/Expo 2000, Hannover, S. 5/7 · *Partner Berlin, Juni – August '97* Hauptpumpwerk Wilmersdorf, Berlin, S. 52I55 · *TSPORT, 10/12)1997* Leistungszentrum für Eiskunstlauf, München, S. 16/20 · *Architecture for Industry* von Carlos Broto, Links International, Barcelona 1997, Klärwerk Gut Marienhof, Dietersheim bei München, Konstruktionsbüro Gartner, Gundelfingen/Donau, S. 128/141 · *Wegweiser Kunst für München* von Helmut Friedel, Heinrich Hugendubel Verlag, München 1998, Europäisches Patentamt, Max Bill, S. 58/59; Bürgerhaus Laim, Lothar Fischer, S. 68/69; Europäisches Patentamt, München, Nikolaus Gerhardt, S. 90/91; Hypobank, München-Schwabing, Asta Gröting, S. 92/93; Feuerwache 8, München-Unterföhring, Dietmar Tanterl, S. 172/173; Klärwerk Gut Marienhof, Dietersheim bei München, Hannsjörg Voth, S. 178/179; Europäisches Patentamt, München, Hannsjörg Voth, S. 180/181 · *The Art of Structural Engineering – The Work of Jörg Schlaich and his Team* von Alan Holgate, Edition Axel Menges, Stuttgart/London 1997, Klärwerk Gut Marienhof, Dietersheim bei München, S. 57; Eislaufzelt im Olympiapark, München, S. 80, Titelblatt; Westtangente, Kelheim, S. 180; Williamsburgbrücke New York, S. 182/183; Dritte Donaubrücke, Ingolstadt, S. 189; Fußgängerbrücke, Kelheim, S. 214/216; Institut für Bioverfahrenstechnik, Stuttgart, S. 287 · *25 Jahre Deutscher Architekturpreis* von Jürgen Joedicke/Heinz Windfeder, Karl Krämer Verlag, Stuttgart, Zürich 1997, Eislaufzelt Olympiapark, München, S. 66/67; Klärwerk Gut Marienhof, Dietersheim bei München, S. 90; Konstruktionsbüro Gartner, Gundelfingen/Donau, S. 113 · *Neue Architektur – New Architecture Berlin 1990 – 2000* von Martin Kieren, Herausgeber: Deutsches Architekturzentrum Berlin, Jowis Verlagsbüro, Berlin 1997, Hauptpumpwerk Wilmersdorf, Berlin, S. 164 · *Grundrisse öffentlicher Gebäude, synoptische Gebäudetypologie* von Walter Meyer-Bohl, Verlag Ernst + Sohn, Berlin 1997, Institut für Bioverfahrenstechnik, Stuttgart, S. 114/115 · *Kunst im Europäischen Patentamt* von Monica Poalas, EP-ART, München 1997, Max Bill, S. 18/19, Nikolaus Gerhardt, S. 34/35, Christian Hinz, S. 45/46, Hannsjörg Voth, S. 112/113

1998 *Baumeister 3/1998* Pumpwerk Berlin-Wilmersdorf, S. 17, Klärwerk Gut Marienhof, Dietersheim bei München, S. 38/41

Landschaftsarchitekten

Prof. Günther Grzimek, München
Gerhard Härlin, München
Gottfried Hansjakob, München
Winfried Jerney, München
Prof. Karl Kagerer, Ismaning
Prof. Dr. Dieter Kienast, Zürich
Peter Kluska, München
Eberhard Krauss, Freising
Peter Leitzmann, München
Prof. Luz und Partner, Stuttgart
Prof. Gunnar Martinsson, Karlsruhe
Prof. Günther Nagel, Hannover
Prof. Klaus-Dieter Neumann und
Wolf Auch, München
Georg Penker, Neuss
Paul Schraudenbach, München
Stefan Tischer, München

Bauingenieure

Dipl.-Ing. Christoph Ackermann, München
Prof. Dr. Rainer Barthel und
Dr.-Ing. Helmut Maus, München
Dr.-Ing. Bernhard Behringer, München
Dipl.-Ing. Friedrich Brosch, München
Dipl.-Ing. A.C. Cronauer, München
Dipl.-Ing. Michael Dickson, London
Dipl.-Ing. Winfried Gehm, München
Dipl.-Ing. Gerhart und Fuchs, München
Prof. Dr. Rudolf Grimme, München
Prof. Sir Ted Happold, Bath/London
Prof. Gustl Lachenmann, Stuttgart
Dipl.-Ing. Gottfried Raffelt, München
Prof. Drs. Gallus Rehm, München
Dipl.-Ing. Sailer, Stepan, Bloos, München
Prof. Drs. Jörg Schlaich und
Dipl.-Ing. Rudolf Bergermann, Stuttgart
Dr.-Ing. Ulrich Scholz, München
Prof. Dr. Dietger Weischede, Stuttgart

Visuelle Kommunikation

Otl Aicher, Rotis
Sepp Landsbeck, Rotis
Rolf Müller, München
Hans Neudecker, Rotis
Walter Schwaiger, München
Stankowski und Duschek, Stuttgart
Eberhard Stauß, München
Sabine Wirsing, München

Sonderfachleute

Assmann Planen und Beraten, Hannover
Prof. Christian Bartenbach, Innsbruck
Climaplan, München
Prof. Dr. Drees, Prof. Sommer, Stuttgart
Fischer Haustechnik Consult, Frankfurt
Prof. Dr. Rudolf Floos, München
Prof. Drs. Gertis, Stuttgart
Ing.-Büro Happold, Bath/London
HL-Technik Prof. Daniels, München
Dipl.-Ing. Franz Hölzl, Steinebach
Ing.-Büro Konrad Huber, München
Ing.-Büro Krebs, Stuttgart
Ing.-Büro Linsmaier, München
Ing.-Büro Müller BBM, München
Dipl.-Ing. Peter Mutard, München
Ing.-Büro Obermeyer, München
Ing.-Büro Pitscheider, München
Ing.-Büro Rentschel und Riedesser, Stuttgart
Dipl.-Ing. Paul Riemhofer, München
Ing.-Büro Schlegel, München

Künstler

Prof. Max Bill, Zürich
Heiner Blum, Frankfurt/M
Dieter Bohnet, Stuttgart
Holger Bollinger, Bergfeld
Ugo Dossi, München
Prof. Lothar Fischer, Baierbrunn/Berlin
Prof. Rupprecht Geiger, München
Blasius Gerg, Glonn
Nikolaus Gerhardt, München
Karl Gerstner, Basel
Christian Hintz, München
Tobias Kammerer, Rottweil
Friedrich Koller, Laufen
Dr. Adolf Luther, Krefeld
Francois Morellet, New York
Tomitaro Nachi, Ulm
Herbert Oehm, Düsseldorf
Panamarenko, Antwerpen
Karl Prantl, Wien
Heimrad Prem, München
Alex Rademacher, München
Helmut Rieger, Steinebach
Gerhard Rothmann, Widdersberg
Chihero Shimotani, Sakurai/München
Markus Stangl, Dachau
Prof. Helmut Sturm, München
Dietmar Tanterl, München
Richard Vogl, Bernhardswald
Hannsjörg Voth, München

Bauleitungen

Harms und Partner, Hannover
Schüle und Renner, Stuttgart
Staatl. Hochbauamt Kassel, Kassel
Krauss und Ortner, München

© Prestel-Verlag, Munich · New York,
and Ackermann und Partner, Munich 1998

Photo credits: see page 319

The project descriptions have been provided by
Ackermann und Partner.

Translation: Peter Green, Munich

Front cover: Tent Roof over Ice-Skating Rink in Olympia
Park, Munich (Photo: Sigrid Neubert, Munich)
Photos on pages 4, 16, 280: Marienhof Estate Sewage
Treatment Plant, Hall 13, Hanover

Prestel books are available worldwide.
Please contact your nearest bookseller or write to either
of the following addresses for information concerning
your local distributor:

Prestel Verlag · Mandlstrasse 26 · D-80802 Munich,
Germany
Phone (89) 38 17 09-0, Fax (89) 38 17 09-35
Prestel Verlag, 16 West 22nd Street New York,
N.Y. 10010, USA
Phone (212) 627 81 99, Fax (212) 627 98 66

Library of Congress Cataloging-in-Publication Data
is available.

Design: Hans Neudecker, Rotis
Production: Konturwerk, Munich

Editorial assistance: Horst Raab, Munich
Editing: Katharina Wurm, Munich

Offset lithography: Repro Ludwig, Zell am See
Typesetting: Setzerei Vornehm, Munich
Printing and binding: Hofmann Druck, Augsburg

Printed on acid-free paper

© Prestel-Verlag, München · New York,
und Ackermann und Partner, München 1998

Fotonachweis: siehe Seite 319

Die Baubeschreibungen wurden von
Ackermann und Partner verfaßt.

Übersetzung: Peter Green, München

Auf dem Umschlag: Fislaufzelt im Olympiapark, München
(Foto: Sigrid Neubert, München)
Abbildungen auf Seiten 4, 16, 280: Klärwerk Gut Marienhof,
Halle 13, Hannover

Die Deutsche Bibliothek – CIP-Einheitsaufnahme
Ackermann und Partner : buildings and projects ;
1978–1998 Hrsg. Ingeborg Flagge. Einf. Wolfgang
Jean Stock. – München ; New York : Prestel, 1998
ISBN 3-7913-1935-3

Prestel-Verlag · Mandlstraße 26 · D-80802 München
Telefon 089/38 17 09-0 · Telefax 089/38 17 09-35

Gestaltung: Hans Neudecker, Rotis
Herstellung: Konturwerk, München

Redaktionelle Mitarbeit: Horst Raab, München
Lektorat: Katharina Wurm, München

Reproduktionen: Repro Ludwig, Zell am See
Satz: Setzerei Vornehm, München
Druck und Bindung: Hofmann Druck, Augsburg

Gedruckt auf chlorfrei gebleichtem Papier

Printed in Germany
ISBN 3-7913-1935-3